Sport and Society in
Victorian Ireland

Sport and Society in Victorian Ireland

The Case of Westmeath

Tom Hunt

CORK UNIVERSITY PRESS

First published in 2007 by
Cork University Press
Youngline Industrial Estate
Pouladuff Road, Togher
Cork, Ireland

British Library Cataloguing in Publication Data.
A CIP catalogue record for this book is available from the British Library

ISBN–13: 978–1–85918–415–8

The author has asserted his moral rights in this work.

This publication has received support from the Heritage Council under the
2007 Publications Grant Scheme.

Typeset by Tower Books, Ballincollig, Co. Cork
Printed by ColourBooks Ltd, Baldoyle, Co. Dublin

www.corkuniversitypress.com

For my two Marys

Contents

List of figures		viii
List of tables		ix
Acknowledgements		xi
A note on sources and methodology		xiii
List of abbreviations		xvi
	Introduction	1
1	The community of the hunt, 1850–1905	10
2	Horseracing development, 1850–1905	39
3	Commercial sports, 1880–1905: new opportunities	75
4	Cricket, 1850–1905	113
5	The embryonic GAA in Westmeath, 1884–1895	141
6	The development of soccer and rugby, 1875–1905	170
7	Cultural ferment and the re-emergence of the GAA, 1900–1905	190
8	Spectator sport, 1850–1905	216
	Epilogue	248
Notes and references		257
Appendices		299
Bibliography		321
Index		339

Figures

1 Westmeath and its principal towns, 1901   7
2 The Mullingar Army Barracks as a venue for Westmeath
   Hunt Club entertainment   17
3 Location of residences of subscribers to Westmeath Hunt
   Club, 1854   20
4 Place of residence of members of Westmeath Hunt Club in 1900   21
5 Knockdrin Castle, County Westmeath, seat of Sir Richard
   Levinge and venue for several hunt balls   30
6 Frequency of race meetings organised in County Westmeath,
   1850–1904   40
7 Venues of Westmeath race meetings, 1850–1905   41
8 Places of residence of owners who raced horses in Mullingar
   at June meetings, 1890–1905   65
9 Venues and dates where Bass, the property of James Yourell,
   raced in 1894   69
10 Five-yearly aggregate of tennis clubs established in Ireland,
   1875–1905   76
11 Early form of nets used in lawn tennis   77
12 Formation of Irish golf clubs, 1888–1905   87
13 Advertisement of William Trimble, cycle agent, Mullingar   96
14 Cricket matches played in Westmeath, 1860–1879   116
15 Number of cricket combinations active and matches played
   in County Westmeath, 1880–1905   119
16 Cricket playing districts in Westmeath, 1880–1905   121
17 Advertisement placed by W. D. Cleary in *Westmeath Examiner*,
   October 1888   145
18 Location of main football-playing districts in Westmeath in the
   1890s   146
19 Number of inter-club football games played in Westmeath,
   1888–1899   151
20 Number of football matches played in Westmeath on a
   monthly basis, 1890–1893   155
21 Lampooning of West Britonism by means of cartoon   196
22 Hurling- and football-playing districts in Westmeath, 1900–1905   200
23 Number of games played in cricket, football, hurling and
   soccer in County Westmeath, 1880–1905   208
24 Monthly variation in number of football games, 1904 and 1905   209
25 Summary justice is dispensed to the three-card-trick man
   at the Mullingar races   234
26 Trouble for a welching bookmaker   241

Tables

1 Average age and conjugal status of subscribers to Westmeath Hunt Club, 1854, 1875 and 1900   19
2 Estate valuation of Westmeath Hunt Club members, 1875   21
3 Type of race organised in Mullingar, Athlone and Kilbeggan, 1890–1905   43
4 Source of prize-money, Thomastown and Garrycastle races, 1857–1868   46
5 Extent and value of holdings, frequency of participation, of the four most active Westmeath resident owners at Mullingar June races,1890–1905   68
6 Social characteristics of members of Westmeath Golf Club and Athlone Golf Club, 1904   91
7 Occupations and professions of officers and committee of Westmeath Bicycle Club, 1882   94
8 Range of membership fees available in Athlone Garrison Golf Club, 1900   105
9 Playing record of Westmeath County Cricket Club, 1865–1873   117
10 Officers, local administration posts held and size of family estate of committee of Westmeath Cricket Club in 1887   123
11 Frequency of army combinations opposition to civilian combinations, 1850–1905   130
12 Social classes of participants of selected cricket clubs in Westmeath, 1900–1902   136
13 Occupations of officers and committee of Mullingar Commercial Football Club, 1890   161
14 Social classes of footballers in Westmeath, 1892   167
15 Record of Athlone Association Football Club, 1887–89   173
16 Names, businesses and places of residence of those attending AGM of Athlone AFC, October 1894   179
17 Social classes of Athlone and Mullingar soccer players, 1900–1904   187
18 Social class of county Westmeath hurlers, 1903–1905   212
19 Social class of footballers in Westmeath, 1898–1905   214
20 Social classes of individual participants of main sports   248

Acknowledgements

This book began life as a PhD thesis and as such the finished product has benefited from the discussions, the insights and the advice of a number of supportive individuals from their own specialist fields. In particular, I would like to acknowledge the input of Dr Paul Rouse, Dr Neal Garnham, Professor Tony Mason, Fr Paul O'Connell, Dr Ian Clarke and Patrick Bracken, Littleton, County Tipperary. Dr Raymond Gillespie and his colleagues provided the initial teaching and inspiration in the Master of Arts in Local History course at NUI Maynooth. Dr Gillespie constantly spoke of the need for historians to ask new questions of old sources and hopefully this study provides a worthwhile example of this process. Dr Jacinta Prunty supervised an initial local history MA thesis in Maynooth and knocked several corners off this rather immature, mature student.

My research was facilitated greatly by the staff in a number of archival institutions and libraries. The bulk of the research was conducted in the local history archive at the headquarters of the Westmeath County Library and I am particularly grateful to County Librarian, Mary Farrell and all the staff there, for facilitating my research and fulfilling my numerous requests in a courteous and efficient manner. Rohit Tailor at the Kimberly Library, De Montfort University, Leicester always managed to deal with a multiplicity of requests on my infrequent visits to that particular institution. For their helpful assistance I would also like to express my thanks and appreciation to the staffs of the National Library of Ireland; the National Archives of Ireland; the Library, NUI Maynooth; the Library, TCD; the library of the Freemasons, 17 Molesworth Street, Dublin; the Representative Church Body Library, Rathgar, Dublin and the Valuation Office, Dublin. In England, the staffs of the British Library at Kings Cross, London and the British Newspaper Library at Colindale were equally supportive.

Teaching colleagues, Ms Margaret Evans and Ms Fidelma Foy-Keane, provided specialist assistance. A number of individuals kept a vigilant eye for appropriate source material and in particular Martin Morris joint archivist with the Westmeath and Longford county libraries, Gearóid O'Brien, senior executive librarian at the Aidan Heavey Public Library, Athlone and former Westmeath County Librarian Ms Marian Keaney are worthy of special mention. Rosaleen Fallon of Athlone; Joe Healy and Michael Bennett of Mullingar; Gerard Quirke of Carrick-on-Suir,

County Tipperary; the Gibson-Brabazon family of Mullingar; Mark Duncan, and Tom Higgins of Sligo provided access to important source material. Peter Wallace from Multyfarnham and Micháel Ó Conláin from Castlepollard answered questions as requested. Ms Joan Keary from Street, County Westmeath; drew my attention to the existence of the William Edward Wilson diary. In 2000, the then Fine Gael TD Paul McGrath, conscious of the importance of heritage issues, believed that a book that commemorated Mullingar's history was necessary as a Millennium project. This author contributed an article on the history of sport in Mullingar in the 1890s and in return was allowed to make copies of relevant microfilm newspaper material held at the local history branch of the Westmeath County Library. This concession was rather liberally interpreted and the material thus accumulated provided an important contribution to the finished product that is this book.

The help, advice and enthusiastic support of my thesis supervisors, Professor Jeffrey Hill and Professor Mike Cronin of the International Centre for Sports History and Research at De Montfort University, Leicester was essential to the successful completion of the initial PhD odyssey. The encouragement, calm reassurance and intellectual stimulation of my chief supervisor, Professor Cronin, was particularly important. The supervision was peripatetic in nature and was carried out at a diverse set of locations and was all the better for that. These ranged from a miserable Cusack Park, Mullingar when Westmeath played football to match the weather, to the Gresham Hotel prior to Waterford's All-Ireland Hurling semi-final of 2004 where we discussed the niceties of Westmeath cricket in the Victorian era (surely the most incongruous discussion ever held in that particular hotel), to the departure lounge of Dublin Airport.

I would like to thank Professor Tom Dunne of Cork University Press for his support of the project and editor Sophie Watson and other members of the staff for their professionalism, help and guidance at various stages.

My final and greatest debt is to my wife, Mary, who tolerated my fascination with the world of Westmeath and its Victorian sport and recreational activities and was supportive and patient throughout the period of research and writing.

Tom Hunt,
November, 2007

A note on sources and methodology

An eclectic range of source material has been used in the research of this book. This includes newspapers, parliamentary papers, private papers, material produced by government agencies and a variety of contemporary printed accounts. Two groups of sources in particular were important. Newspapers, as valuable repositories of historical information and accurate barometers of social activity, formed the chief source for the study.[1] The research was based on an examination of four Westmeath weekly newspapers. These newspapers covered all spectrums of political opinion within the county and provided a comprehensive coverage of the geographic totality of the area. The *Westmeath Independent* concentrated on happenings in the southern part of the county and especially in Athlone.[2] The *Westmeath Guardian* was the newspaper of the unionist and conservative community and its coverage was more focused on Mullingar. In 1882, a nationalist newspaper, the *Westmeath Examiner*, was first published and in 1891 the *Westmeath Nationalist* added to the comprehensiveness of local news coverage. As the century progressed, the amount of international news decreased, as local news coverage improved. Sports coverage became more comprehensive and in the examination of four newspapers the picture that emerges in this work is as detailed as possible, given the nature of source material available. Newspapers carried advertisements for sports events and equipment, reports on events and club meetings, letters on controversies arising from sporting occasions, match reports and news of Westmeath athletic and equine performances in events outside the county. Reportage on individuals who migrated, marriage reports and obituaries were also useful as a source of establishing social and community networks. The absence of contemporary club minute books is compensated for by the frequency with which club meetings featured in newspaper reports. Minute books quite often only record decisions made with no note of the issues debated. In contrast, newspapers contain more in-depth coverage.

A difficulty associated with reliance on newspapers, as a source, is the problem presented by under-reporting of events and the consequent impact this has on quantification. Despite the use of a large sample of papers, this was a problem, especially in a situation where clubs were transitory and where newspaper reportage ranked low in the priorities of club administrators. Reliance on newspaper reports may also

overstate the ephemeral nature of clubs. Under-reporting is easily established but any attempt to establish its extent is fraught with difficulties.
This can be illustrated using cricket as an example. There is evidence
that some clubs did not forward any reports of their activities to the local
press. The Delvin Cricket Club in 1886, for example, organised an athletic sports in which one event was confined to athletes who had played
against the host club during the cricket season. Five members of different cricket clubs competed in this event including representatives of
two clubs, Rosmead and Sheepstown, that never featured in newspaper
reports.[3] In the same season the Delvin club's playing activities went
unreported. The Westmeath County Cricket Club, in an end of season
report, claimed to have won all five games contested in 1887 but newspapers only carried accounts of two of these games.[4] In September 1893,
Cloughan CC had contested seven games but only four of these were
reported.[5] The Ranelagh School cricket team played seven cricket games
in 1897 according to the headmaster in his end of year address. None of
these games merited newspaper reportage.[6] Big House games also went
unreported. Based on the above, an estimate of under-reporting of at
least 20 per cent of cricket matches played may be conservative. Football
games and hurling matches experienced the same phenomenon. Despite
the possibility of under-reporting of games, this survey is as comprehensive as possible given the singular nature of available source material on
sports coverage.

The second major source used was the manuscript census enumer-
ator returns of 1901. Bureaucrats and revolutionaries have destroyed the
earlier returns and so this study was limited to the use of the 1901
forms. These returns give information at the level of the individual
household and their importance as a historical source, rather than as a
resource for genealogists, has received greater appreciation in recent
years.[7] Form A provides the core information used in this study to establish the socio-occupational backgrounds of the men and women active
in organised club and competitive sport in Victorian and early Edwardian Westmeath.[8]

A complete weekly survey was done of the four newspapers the
Westmeath Guardian, the *Westmeath Nationalist*, the *Westmeath Examiner*
and the *Westmeath Independent* over the period of their publication. The
popularity of the various sporting disciplines was established by con-
ducting this fine-grained analysis. Annual aggregates of events held and
of combinations active in team sports and matches played were compiled. The methodology used was similar to that used by Neil Tranter in
his examination of organized sport in central Scotland.[9] Names of individuals active in the various sporting disciplines were extracted from
the newspapers and databases were then constructed containing the
personal details of the individuals. Information extracted from the 1901
census enumerators' forms provided the main source of information for
this process but information on individuals active earlier in the period

was compiled from a range of directories, aristocratic and gentry guidebooks and Church of Ireland parish registers. The *Racing Calendar* was a useful source for the chapter on horseracing in the county. This source was especially valuable as each year a list of the names and addresses of subscribers to the annual was included. The majority of the addresses for owners were extracted from this source. The journal *Sport* also published an annual list of horses in training in Ireland and this included the names and addresses of trainers as well the age and identity of horses based at the stables, the jockeys attached and the names of the owners with horses at the stables.[10]

In order to establish the social class of individual participants a classification system similar to that used by Tranter in his Scottish study was used.[11] This classification was in turn based, with minor amendments, on the system of classification devised by W. A. Armstrong.[12] In this book individual participants identified from census records were divided into one of four classes. Social class A incorporates the gentry and aristocracy, men with private income, army officers, the more substantial employers of labour and the members of the high-status professions. Class B comprises middle-class white-collar employees, farmers of at least five acres and employers of labour. Classes B and C were further subdivided in the original thesis on which this book is based.[13] Skilled workers are represented in class C and include tradesmen, shop assistants and clerks. For the purpose of this book the semi-skilled of class D including farm labourers and the un-skilled of class E, as used by Armstrong and Tranter, are amalgamated. The compilers of the census of 1901 considered that the majority of general labourers could 'be assumed to be agricultural labourers although not having returned themselves as such'.[14] The information on social class is presented in tabular form throughout the book, with the letter U used to denote unidentified personnel.

Abbreviations

AAA	Amateur Athletic Association
AGM	Annual General Meeting
CBS	Crime Branch Special
CWGC	County Westmeath Golf Club
FL	Freemasons' Library
GAA	Gaelic Athletic Association
GGC	Garrison Golf Club
HML	Her Majesty's Lieutenant
ICA	Irish Cycling Association
INF	Irish National Federation
INHSC	Irish National Hunt Steeplechase Committee
INL	Irish National League
IRB	Irish Republican Brotherhood
MFH	Master of the Foxhounds
MGWR	Midlands Great Western Railway
MR	*Midland Reporter*
NA	National Archives
NLI	National Library of Ireland
RCB	Representative Church Body
RIC	Royal Irish Constabulary
RIF	Royal Irish Fusiliers
UIL	United Irish League
VO	Valuation Office
WCL	Westmeath County Library
WE	*Westmeath Examiner*
WG	*Westmeath Guardian*
WHCFR	Westmeath Hunt Club Financial Records
WHCMB	Westmeath Hunt Club Minute Books
WI	*Westmeath Independent*
WN	*Westmeath Nationalist*

Introduction

Modern sport was moulded during the Victorian period. The changes that took place in games playing and organisation at this time have been described by one historian as 'one of Victorian England's most enduring legacies'.[1] This process of change had several dimensions. Levels of player and spectator participation rose dramatically. The sexual and social composition of those involved widened. New sports were introduced that provided opportunities for people who were excluded from participation in sports and games prior to this time. Most importantly, rules of play were codified and management structures were established. Clubs proliferated and sport became increasingly commercialised. By 1900, the size and character of the world of sport had been transformed.[2] Some statistics illustrate the extent of this transformation in Ireland. The GAA was founded in 1884 and by 1890 had 875 clubs attached to the parent body. The Irish Football Association was founded in 1880 and in 1890 had 124 affiliated clubs. This number had increased to 278 by 1905.[3] Rugby's club growth was less spectacular. The Irish Union was established in 1874 with a membership of thirteen clubs and numbers were less than 100 six years later.[4] Non-football code clubs also proliferated. The 1890s was the great decade of golf club formation in Ireland when 97 clubs were started between 1892 and 1900.[5] In 1908, over 100 clubs had affiliated to the Irish Hockey Union (IHU).[6] This book provides an in-depth examination of the implications of these developments for the county of Westmeath.

This growth in leisure activity and participation in sport at both a competitive and spectator level was the product of fundamental social changes that took place in the later decades of the nineteenth century.[7] Rising incomes and greater availability of leisure time for some made participation in sport and leisure activities possible. Improved literacy levels and the growth of a popular press heightened awareness and contributed to a growing interest in sporting events. The proportion of the Westmeath population who claimed the ability to read and write had increased from 46 per cent in 1871 to 74 per cent in 1901 and to 89 per cent by 1911.[8] A specialist sporting press also developed to cater for the growing interest in matters sporting. During the 1890s at least a dozen newspapers that were concerned chiefly with sports reporting were published in Ireland. The availability of a cheap and rapid railway system also facilitated sporting involvement in a variety of ways as will be shown throughout this book.[9]

Despite the significance of these changes, the history of sport has been marginalised as a topic worthy of exploration in Irish academic institutions. The peripheral status of Irish sports history was clearly illustrated recently when the latest edition in the new history of Ireland series was published.[10] This examines the period between 1921and 1984 and ignores the impact of sports on Irish society at this time. Studies on the Gaelic Athletic Association (GAA) dominate the sports history genre. These works, with some pioneering exceptions, are concerned with evaluating the association from a political perspective.[11] This approach is best exhibited in the four major works on the history of the GAA completed by the Australian historian W. F. Mandle.[12] In his initial exploration of the GAA, Mandle based the success of the organisation on the support of the Catholic Church and its 'avowedly nationalist, ostentatiously Irish' stance.[13] Later, he adopted a more inclusive approach to explain the success of the GAA and placed its development in the broader context of contemporary sporting developments. Although the GAA was 'founded, manipulated and sustained, first by the IRB, later by the nationalist movement as a whole' according to Mandle, it was unable to escape the wider influences that came from its being located within the United Kingdom. He also gave some consideration to its attractions as a purely sporting organisation. From 1905, he suggested that Gaelic games had been sufficiently modified and codified to become 'genuinely popular' and no longer simply 'an adjunct to revolutionary nationalism'.[14] In 1987, Mandle published what one commentator considered to be the most important work ever produced on the history of the GAA. However, this work was a very narrowly focused history in that it aimed to examine the connections between the GAA and the evolution of nationalist politics in the period 1884–1924.[15] Only passing reference is made to its wider relationship to sporting development within the United Kingdom.[16] The work is a 'history of the radical IRB as much as it is a history of the GAA', and one in which the overall importance of the IRB to the development of the GAA is overstated.[17] Mandle's emphasis on the contribution of the IRB to the GAA was taken to extreme lengths in an earlier work when he claimed 'there was not a man who meant anything in the organisation of the GAA who was not of the Brotherhood'.[18]

Academic studies of the GAA have contributed to our understanding of Irish political history; the perspective adopted is that of the political historian and as a result our understanding of the development of Irish nationalism has been enhanced whilst our understanding of the history of Irish sport remains relatively uninformed. The social and economic significance of the GAA, the origin and growth of clubs, the diffusion of the rules, the regional demarcations of hurling and football are topics of importance to the history of the GAA that have remained unexplored. In this context, the words of Conor Cruise O'Brien, written in 1960, are still valid. He believed that the GAA's 'importance has perhaps not even yet been fully recognised . . . the tribute which it has not received is the more serious one of sustained critical attention . . . intelligent and, as far as possible, disinterested and dispassionate'.[19]

Other sports have also received academic analysis because of their political dimensions. Hunting qualified in an essay that 'explores a neglected aspect of the Land War, namely the campaign to stop land-lords and magistrates from hunting across tenanted land . . .'. The essay locates the protest within 'the larger context of the Land League's ideology and strategy during the last months of its legal existence'.[20] Hunting in Queen's county was examined in a similar context.[21] Irish cricket received its initial academic probe when its connection to Irish nationalism was explored and the game was chosen as a vehicle 'to demonstrate a sporting–nationalist dichotomy'.[22] Whilst the GAA, hunting and cricket may be examined by historians from a limited polit-ical perspective, other sports have been totally excluded from the arenas of academia, although the balance has been somewhat redressed with the recent publication of a history of association football in pre-partition Ireland and a volume of essays that provide a useful synthesis of current research by historians and sociologists on the history and significance of sport in Irish society.[23] The result of this negligence is that our under-standing of sport in its social and economic context is diminished. A recent comment on the state of our understanding of GAA affairs could be applied equally to any sporting discipline in Ireland. Mike Cronin in an article in *High Ball*, in what might be considered a charter on the future direction of Irish sports history, asked

> Well what do we know about Gaelic games? Not too much really. We have an awareness of men like Cusack or Davin, but we know little about the men who devoted their lives to the Association. We don't really know how the games spread in the late nineteenth or early twentieth century or why some counties are traditionally stronger in football than they are in hurling. We have little or no information on the men who have played Gaelic games, their social background, occupations, family ties and so on. Unlike most other countries we have no awareness of how the games were taken into the schools . . . And then there's the grounds themselves: how and why were they built, why were they named as they are, and how have they changed? . . . we have little or no information about the use of rail travel to games, the links between the Association and the railway companies, the regular coach trips . . . And what about before and after the game, the social scene that has so fruitfully attached itself to matches? . . . How central have pubs been in underpinning the success of Gaelic spectacle?[24]

The lack of a general survey on the development of popular sport 'in the crucial Victorian era' and the political partiality of the research has

allowed, as Paul Rouse has pointed out, 'a series of stereotypes and cari-
catures to prosper, while distortions of history have blossomed as
inherited truths', a development compounded by the 'fact that
respected historians have adopted these distortions into the mainstream
of historical discourse'.[25]

The aim of this book is to examine how the 'revolution in sport'
impacted at the micro-level by investigating the development of sport
in County Westmeath in the period between 1850 and 1905. Because of
the political dimension of previous sports studies the focus of this book
is firmly on the development and management of sport in its own
right. This is achieved by examining a number of common themes.
Quantification is a key feature of each chapter where the frequency
with which events were organised and the development of clubs to
cater for the individual needs of the participants is measured. The club
formed the institutional basis around which sport was organised and
therefore an in-depth profile of a number of clubs forms a key feature
of individual chapters. Clubs are composed of individual members and
each chapter will also contain a social profile of club membership and
participants in the individual sports. Financial viability and access to
an appropriate playing arena were crucial to individual club and sports
survival. Although availability of financial information and account
material is limited, when possible the financial management of selected
clubs is evaluated.

Westmeath was chosen because of the range of sports that developed
in the county over the period. This range of sports means that the
county provides the evidence to conduct a valuable case study of the
evolution of Irish sport during the crucial Victorian period. Events of
significance in the political and social history of the county determined
the timescale of the study. The cataclysmic events of the Great Famine
had concluded by 1850 and the year marks an appropriate starting
point. The extension of the study to 1905 was influenced by important
events in the socio-cultural history of the county. The last years of the
century saw a revival of political nationalism that was accompanied by
a growth in cultural nationalism that continued into the new century.
This period witnessed the re-emergence of the Gaelic Athletic Association (GAA) as a viable organisation; this provided an alternative
sporting outlet for certain classes, which in the process led to a decline
of popular cricket. The period between 1900 and 1905 also saw important developments at the Mullingar racecourse, which was enclosed and
became a gate-money meet. This meant that horseracing at Mullingar
became commercialised and commodified, a development of significance
in the evolution of modern sport. Any study of nineteenth-century
sport that purports to be comprehensive could not exclude these
developments.

This book is organised thematically with each chapter dealing with
the development of an individual sport or sports. The opening two

chapters examine the role of the horse in hunting and racing for recreational purposes, initially by the landed gentry and as the century progressed, by the more prosperous, adventurous and status-conscious of the Westmeath farming community. A chapter that examines the development of the new commercially driven sports of golf, tennis and cycling follows this. This chapter in some respects continues the investigation of elite culture of the earlier chapters. However, these sports also provided an outlet for social groups who were recreationally disenfranchised in earlier decades. Golf and tennis provided opportunities for women, and cycling for the middle classes to partake in the recreational experience. In Chapter Four cricket is examined. Cricket was the most popular sport in the county in the 1880s and for some time after. It enabled cross-class participation and at the end of the century had developed as a recreational outlet dominated by the farm-labouring class.

Chapter Five deals with the introduction of the GAA to the county and suggests that in its initial manifestation in the county, it was essentially seen as a recreational activity, rather than as a means of establishing a nationalist identity. The initial decline of the organisation in the county came about through the failure of the internal management structure, the lack of clearly codified and understood rules and the unwillingness of individual clubs to accept the decisions of the regulatory authorities. In Chapter Six the growth of soccer is examined particularly in Athlone where it benefited from the fall-out from the internal GAA disputes and from the popularity of the sport with the military garrisons in the town. The limited development of rugby and its importance to the schools in the county will also be examined in this chapter.

Chapter Seven examines the re-emergence of the GAA in the county in 1903 inspired by a broad national movement of cultural nationalism. This produced a very different GAA product than that which initially developed in the county. This time the movement had a very definite political agenda, namely the establishment of a distinctive Irish identity, through the medium of playing what were considered to be Irish games and the exclusion of those associated with games identified as West British. The implication of this for other sports, particularly cricket, is considered. The majority of people during the Victorian era enjoyed the sporting experience as spectators and the final chapter is devoted to an analysis of spectator sport in the county. In this chapter the function of the sports venue in presenting a multi-faceted entertainment experience is explored.

The study is inclusive in that it examines the importance of sport to all the groups that form Westmeath society and ranges from an investigation of the recreational habits of the aristocrats of the county to the agricultural and general labourer. The importance of sport in the lives of women is also examined. The range of sports examined also contributes to its inclusiveness. A study that concentrated on a single sport would have produced a very different picture of the recreational habits of the various social groups and the associated social networks. In its entirety, the book makes an important contribution to the history of sport and social interaction in Ireland and demonstrates how, in the context of Westmeath, sport developed as a major focus of people's lives. Although the study is particular to Westmeath, and its distinctive commercial agricultural economy, our knowledge and understanding of Victorian society is considerably enhanced. However, until we have more detailed regional studies of this type one should be careful about generalising too freely from the evidence presented here.

II

Westmeath, located in the Irish midlands, was a county of 454,104 statute acres that formed 2.2 per cent of the total area of Ireland in 1901.[26] This included 21,797 statute acres of rivers and lakes, 39,336 acres of turf bog and marshland, as well as 7,758 statute acres of woods and plantations.[27] This diversity produced a natural environment that was somewhat surprisingly considered by Lewis to be 'highly picturesque,' and in his opinion a county that ranked behind only Kerry, Wicklow, Fermanagh and Waterford in order of beauty.[28]

The population of the county declined over the period of this study and is illustrated in Appendix 1. In 1841 it peaked at 141,300 but following the Great Famine years had decreased to 111,407 by 1851.[29] This pattern continued to 1901.The decline was accompanied by some change in its distribution as populations became more concentrated in small towns. Pre-Famine Westmeath was one of ten Irish counties that had between 10 and 15 per cent of its population resident in small towns but in 1851 this had changed and more than 17 per cent of its population was small-town based.[30] In 1901, the percentage of small-town residents had increased to over 26 per cent.[31] The distribution of these small towns is illustrated in Figure 1.[32] While the majority of the population was Roman Catholic (92 per cent), there was a substantial Protestant minority of 8 per cent.[33]

The two principal urban centres were Athlone and Mullingar. They shared some economic and administrative characteristics. Both were important garrison and market towns, with the former function more important in Athlone and the latter dominant in Mullingar. The Victoria Barracks in Athlone was 'adequate for 3,000 men' and the extensive military barracks in Mullingar was capable of holding 1,000 soldiers.[34] Despite the dearth of research the emphasis on the importance of the military in the diffusion and popularising of certain sports in Ireland has been a recurring theme.[35] The recreational habits of the men based in these barracks and their role in supporting and promoting sport is examined throughout the study. The population of both towns fluctuated, although this variation was in part due to changes in the number

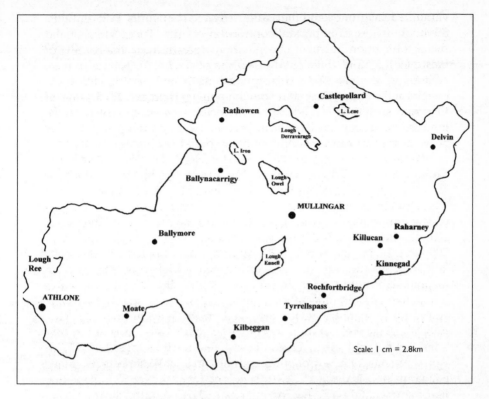

Figure I. Westmeath and its principal towns, 1901

of inhabitants in the institutions of state based in both towns.[36] Athlone, particularly in the later decades of the century, experienced the greater stability of population.[37]

Industrial employment of the type common in Britain at this time was almost unknown in the county. The Athlone Woollen Mills, established in 1859, was the chief provider of factory-based employment. In 1881, the factory employed 200 people and reportedly turned out 600 yards of cloth weekly to meet the demands of English, Scottish, French and American markets. In 1885, 350 were employed in the mill and in 1892, 400 (mostly women), were employed.[38] Athlone Saw Mills, established by Laurence Wilson in the early 1870s, also offered industrial employment until it ceased to be a viable concern in 1894.[39] Locke's distillery in Kilbeggan is also worthy of note in this context.[40]

The Westmeath agricultural economy was a specialist one with a strong commercial emphasis. Only Meath was more important as a grazing county in Ireland, with the larger farms concentrating on the fattening of dry cattle and sheep.[41] This branch of agricultural production expanded dramatically during the period of this study. The number of dry cattle raised in the county increased from 68,588 in 1851 to 92,564 in 1871 and to 101,967 in 1901.[42] Dry cattle aged two years or older amounted to 53 per cent of all cattle raised in the county in 1901, while 30 per cent were aged between one and two years. There was a similar increase in the number of sheep, which rose from 82,000 to 140,000 between 1850 and 1900.[43] Westmeath graziers purchased cattle from farmers in Munster and Connacht and also from farmers within the county, at the end of their store-grazing period. These were fattened and then sold for slaughter. This expansion in animal husbandry was driven by a sustained upward trend in prices. Although the upward price movement was broken intermittently by sharp falls, prices were particularly buoyant from 1869 to 1883 and after 1900.[44] The November fair at Mullingar was the main venue for the sale of Westmeath livestock. At the conclusion of that fair, the railway line to Dublin was packed with trucks full of cattle, horses and sheep bound for Britain.[45]

The importance of grazing is reflected in the number of large farms found in the county. In 1901, the county had 553 farms between 100 and 200 acres in size, 282 between 200 and 500 acres and 47 in excess of 500 acres.[46] It also meant that the county had a high proportion of un-tenanted land at the end of the century.[47] The landlords held some of this in their own hands; others they let to large graziers. In the post-1881 era, such lettings were frequently arranged on the 'eleven-month system', which lettings were exempt from the fair rent fixing terms of the 1881 Land Act.[48] The distinctiveness of Westmeath is illustrated by comparison with some of its surrounding counties. In total Westmeath contained 882 farms over 100 acres in 1901: King's county, a larger county in areas had 861 over 100 acres, Roscommon had 834, Longford 280 and Cavan only 261. Only Longford was smaller in area and the proportion of grassland in Westmeath was greater than any of the others.[49]

The nature of the economy has important implications for this study as it created a number of wealthy farmers and estate proprietors who invested finance in their recreational activities and also provided the patronage to support the recreational activities of others. Captain Butler commented on this prosperity in his monthly reports on the state of Westmeath in December 1882. According to Butler

> Grazing is the industry of this country; every grass farmer and every small farmer whose land will carry grass, lives by cattle . . . Mr. Vize, manager of the National Bank here, told me that in the three months ending 30 November his bank had received deposits amounting to £30,000 and that bills to the amount of £25,000 had been taken up. . . . Such a state of business is hitherto unknown; it is all graziers' money.[50]

Almost a decade later, the continued prosperity of the Mullingar district enabled the shareholding for the Westmeath (Mullingar) Racing Company in 1890 to be over subscribed by 550 £1 shares.[51]

The development of a rail network was the most important infrastructural improvement to take place within the county in the period under review and was important to the development of the grazing economy described in the preceding paragraphs. The Midland Great Western Railway was the third largest in Ireland and linked the county with Galway to the west and Dublin to the east. The connection between Mullingar and Dublin was completed and rail traffic to the capital commenced on 2 October 1848.[52] This offered the prospect of 'civilisation, trade and commerce' to the town according to the *Westmeath Guardian*.[53] The line from Mullingar to Galway was completed on 20 July 1851 and was opened for business on 1 August.[54] Throughout the 1850s Mullingar's railway connections continued to expand. In November 1855, the line from Mullingar to Longford was completed and was followed by the Inny Junction branch line to Cavan. The Mullingar–Longford connection was extended to Sligo by 1862 and a branch line to Clara in Offaly was opened in 1863.[55] The entire MGWR system covered 538 miles when completed in the 1890s with extensions from the Galway line to Clifden and from Westport to Mallaranny on Achill Island.[56] This brought Mullingar into direct communication with every part of Ireland. The Cavan line facilitated connection with the northern parts of Ireland and the Clara junction with the Great South Western (GSW) line enabled southern connection to be made.[57]

Athlone also developed as an important railway centre. Apart from the MGWR line, the opening of the GSW line to Tullamore in 1859 provided links with the south. The nominally independent Great Northern & Western Railway Company opened the Athlone to Roscommon line in December 1859 and this was connected to Castlerea by March 1860. Eventually this route was extended to Claremorris and Castlebar in 1866 and Ballina in 1873.[58] Westmeath residents had nationwide access by rail at the end of the century. In 1897 there were four through trains each day from Dublin to Galway, and Sligo was served by three lines from Dublin as well as an additional train from Mullingar.[59] This network also facilitated internal communications. Despite the county's small size, eleven towns or villages possessed a rail station. The social and economic implications of this freedom of movement were substantial and its significance in the development of sport will be considered throughout the study.

1. The community of the hunt, 1850–1905

The centrality of hunting to gentry lifestyle has been documented with varying degrees of hyperbole in newspapers, memoirs and contemporary articles. Sir John Power claimed that the Kilkenny gentry were saved from careers as murderers, adulterers and thieves when he introduced them to the sport. J. P. Mahaffey claimed that not to hunt was 'the certain sign of a fool or an ass'. In Meath, according to Lady Fingall, summer was spent waiting for winter and 'if you didn't hunt you might as well be dead'. Sam Reynell believed that a county without foxhounds wasn't fit to live in.[1] Some Westmeath devotees more modestly promoted hunting's practical value. At a supper given in his honour in April 1858, the retired Westmeath master, G. A. Boyd informed the guests that 'a man never betook himself to matters of business half so efficiently as after half an hour's burst with hounds the preceding day'.[2] Mr Adamson of the South Westmeath Hunt Club had his ideas influenced by muscular Christianity and suggested in 1895 that hunting 'was a sport and an education; one that tended to make a young man a manly man'.[3] Despite its significance to elite culture, hunting as a recreational activity has received minimal academic consideration. L. P. Curtis has studied Irish hunting in its political context as 'a neglected aspect of the land war' as has J. H. Carter as part of a local study on the land league in Queen's county.[4] This chapter will concentrate on the recreational and social nature of the activity and its importance in the lifestyle of members of the Westmeath landed gentry.

As the powerbrokers in their local districts, members of the hunting community were responsible for the diffusion of several different sporting disciplines at county level. They exercised a central importance in the spread of sport. Cricket, polo and tennis in particular were closely associated with members of the hunting community; the latter two sports remained the preserve of landed society but cricket became increasingly broad-based and democratised in Westmeath as the century concluded. Members of the hunting community provided much of the patronage essential for the survival of a variety of the sporting disciplines examined in this book. This varied from financial support, to facility provision, to the supply of prizes for particular events. This importance was recognised by the athlete Tom Davin, in the course of a meeting of the Carrick-on-Suir branch of the Land League, where a discussion took place on the plan to prevent Lord Waterford from hunting.

Davin unsuccessfully opposed the moves to stop hunting and pointedly argued that 'if you stop fox-hunting you will stop every sort of sport in Ireland'.[5]

The Westmeath Hunt Club provided the structure around which most of the hunting activity of the county was organised during the second half of the nineteenth century. The horse was more important for recreational purposes in Westmeath than in most counties. The annual agricultural statistical returns allow for some comparison of this aspect of horse ownership on a county basis. In 1901, the population of recreational horses in Westmeath was only exceeded in eight counties.[6] However, when their number is expressed as a percentage of the total number of horses in each county then only in Meath, Kildare and Dublin were recreational horses proportionately more numerous than in Westmeath, as can be seen in Appendix 2. In 1901, roughly one out of every twelve horses maintained in Westmeath was for recreational purposes and this represented an advance on the situation in previous decades.[7] This importance was partly a product of the land ownership structure and agricultural economy of the county and of the number of individuals resident in the county who possessed substantial land portfolios. There were 47 units of land of over 500 acres in the county in 1901 but 78 individuals resided in the county who owned over 500 acres of land in total.[8] The contrast with the counties forming the western boundaries of the county illustrates the social and economic differences that existed between Westmeath and its more westerly neighbours. In King's county 4.5 per cent of horses were used for recreation, 2.4 per cent in Longford, 3.8 per cent in Roscommon and only 2.1 per cent in Cavan. Hunting provided the most important outlet for horses maintained for recreation and amusement and was central to the lifestyle of a section of the Westmeath gentry.

II

A recent work on the history of hunting uses printed evidence from medieval and later sources to show that fox hunting in its modern format was carried out at least from the early fourteenth century. This view challenges the conventional view of historians that the sport began in the late eighteenth century.[9] Hunting in Westmeath dated from the end of the seventeenth century when Bishop Dopping of Meath maintained a private pack at Killucan in 1697.[10] Access to hunting for the next century and a half in the county was by means of invitation from wealthy individuals who maintained private packs.[11] The organisation of the sport in Westmeath changed fundamentally in 1854 when Sir Richard Levinge recruited a 'huntsman and thirty-five couple of Fox-hounds selected from the best blood of England'.[12] Within a few weeks forty-two individuals subscribed £600 to maintain the pack and the first subscription pack in the county had been established.[13] The practice whereby those who hunted regularly supported the master by paying him an agreed sum and contributed to the hunting expenses was the most fundamental change that took place in the history of foxhunting. In England, by the 1860s, the subscription pack was the norm; their numbers had increased from twenty-four in 1810 to 100 by 1854.[14] In Westmeath, the establishment of a subscription pack represented the response of an elite community to the changed post-Famine economic circumstances.[15] The newly established pack hunted for the first time on 1 November 1854 at Ballynagall, the then seat of J. W. Middleton Berry, and on 4 November at Rosmead, on the estate of Lord Vaux of Harrowden.[16]

Hunting embraced two separate skills of horsemanship: the ability to hunt and the ability to ride horses and ideally these skills complemented each other in the field. The emphasis was on the chase and hunting memoirs abound with accounts of lengthy chases conducted across hunting country. Hunting notes in the local newspapers and Dease's history of the Westmeath hunt document several of these spectacular chases.[17] On 22 February 1878 one run through north Westmeath hunting country covered an estimated eighteen miles and ranged from Pakenham Hall to Drumcree.[18] Another 'red letter day in the annals of hunting' was Friday, 3 December 1880 when a 'glorious run of two hours and five minutes' took place in south Westmeath country centred on Moate and covered a distance that could not 'be less than eighteen miles'.[19]

The frequency with which a pack hunted was governed by the size of the hunting country, the supply of foxes, the number of coverts in the district, the size of the subscription received by the master and the willingness of the members to pay for their hunting pleasures. Frequent hunting required a more elaborate hunt club infrastructure and this necessitated larger subscriptions to the master or a willingness on his part to invest his own personal resources. Within a season the number of days hunted was governed by weather conditions and in particular, heavy frost prevented hunting as hounds were unable to pick up a scent on such days.

Initially, the Westmeath pack hunted two days a week, but during the master-ship of John Fetherstonhaugh Briscoe (1858–60) hunting was increased to five days a fortnight, which he worked with ten horses.[20] Towards the end of the master-ship of Gerard Dease (1861–68) hunting was extended to three days a week.[21] The 1866–67 season saw seventy-three days hunting with twenty-three foxes killed and only two blank days.[22] A quarter of a century later, in the 1890–91 season, sixty-six days of sport were enjoyed in a season that began on 3 November, with hunting stopped on ten days because of frost, during which thirty-three brace of foxes were killed and forty-five ran to ground.[23] In the 1895–96 season, hunting was extended to the maximum the Westmeath environment was capable of sustaining, when hunting four times weekly began.

This required an additional subscription of £100 to the Pakenham brothers who shared joint master-ship. The season saw the hounds out for 105 days and that included thirty days at the cubs.[24]

It is impossible to quantify the actual number who hunted on a particular day in the county. Contemporary newspapers published lists of names but made no reference to the numbers in the field. Fitzpatrick, who was familiar with the Irish hunting scene, suggested in 1878, that the average size of a Westmeath hunting field was thirty.[25] Newspaper reports of numbers present in the field vary over the period and are not comprehensive. The numbers reported hunting during the second week of February 1897 support Fitzpatrick's estimate. The three meets attracted an average attendance of thirty-five.[26] Large numbers were attracted to special hunting occasions such as the opening meet of the season or by the possibility of a celebrity joining the field. The numbers hunting in early November 1878 were increased by the presence of Lord Randolph Churchill and the Ladies Churchill in the field.[27] In February 1880, 'there could not be less than 300 horsemen of all grades and classes' present, attracted by the rumour that the Empress of Austria would be hunting.[28] In November 1886, seventy-four took part in the opening meet of the season.[29] The meeting place was an important factor in determining the number present on any particular day. Venues that were served by the rail network were particularly attractive. It was estimated that the Westmeath hunt attracted up to 150 participants when hunting near Moate in February 1898.[30] At least eighty-seven turned out for the Mullingar meet of 8 February 1904.[31]

Individual devotees hunted as often as possible in the course of the season. Evidence from hunting diaries, attest to individual obsession with the sport.[32] Analysis of the hunting diary of Mr J. M. Moore, who resided in Rathganny House, Multyfarnham, illustrate his passion for the sport and the extent of his immersion in the leisured lifestyle.[33] In 1879, Moore began his hunting season on 22 September when cub hunting with the Westmeath pack. He went cubbing on five other occasions in October before the hunting season proper began in November. In that month, he hunted on ten occasions, on seven occasions in December, ten in January and March, and twelve occasions in February. The Westmeath pack concluded their season in early April with two meets attended by Moore and with his hunting appetite still unsatiated he joined the Multyfarnham Harriers on one occasion and on three occasions travelled to the western edge of the county to Glasson for a drag hunt. In total, Moore hunted on 59 occasions between September and April during a season in which nine hunting days were lost due to frost.[34] Only on six occasions did Moore not take part in the hunt during the season. In the period between August and January 1879–80 he also went shooting on twenty-seven occasions.[35] Moore was less active the following season. In the period between 21 October and 25 March, he chose not to hunt on eight occasions, but was less fortunate with the weather with fourteen hunting days lost because of frost. Nevertheless he still managed to hunt with the Westmeath pack on fifty occasions.[36] The evidence is quite clear from the involvement of this relatively small landholder. Those who were devotees of the hunt participated on every occasion possible.

Not only did individuals hunt as often as possible they also travelled outside their own hunting country regularly to experience the sport with other packs. Membership of more than one subscription pack was not unusual. Valentine McDonnell was so enamoured of the sport that he rode regularly with five hunt clubs, the Roscommon Staghounds, the Roscommon Harriers, the Athlone and District Harriers, the Rockingham Harriers and the Westmeath Hunt Club and as a committee member of two of these clubs involved himself in their administration.[37] McDonnell was a grazier who resided in County Roscommon and at the end of the century farmed just over 1,250 acres in six different townlands located in the rural districts of Athlone and Roscommon.[38] The *British Hunts and Huntsmen* is a useful survey of individual hunting habits and documents the multi-dimensional nature of the participation by Westmeath huntsmen and women in the early 1900s. A few examples illustrate the obsession. Edmund Dease followed the hounds with the Meath, Kildare, Louth, the UHC in Cork, Old Muskerry, Duhallow and occasionally the Ward Union Staghounds in Ireland and the Worcestershire, Cheshire, Cottesmore and the Old Berkshire in England.[39] Theobald Fetherstonhaugh hunted with the King's county, Kildare, East Galway and the Blazers.[40] Familial contacts, an English public school education and a British-based military career facilitated this aspect of an individual's hunting career. Members of the hunting community belonged to what David Cannadine has termed 'a truly supra-national class' that 'embraced the whole of the British Isles with its patrician tentacles'.[41] This characteristic found expression in the community's hunting habits.

The social structure of a Westmeath hunting field remained relatively consistent during the second half of the nineteenth century. The typical field was dominated by members of the local aristocracy and gentry, supplemented by officers from the Mullingar and Athlone military barracks and a number of women devotees of the sport.[42] Also worthy of note is the presence in the hunting fields, especially when the pack hunted the south Westmeath district, of Canon Kearney 'our honoured and reverend pastor from Moate'.[43] Kearney was one of the most substantial land holders amongst the Catholic clergy of Westmeath and according to Griffith's Valuation of 1854 he was the occupier of 161 acres of land, which had a valuation of £134.[44] Nineteenth-century British army officers were primarily from landed families and it followed that the values and pastimes of that class dominated the British officer corps. The passion for field sports was one of the defining characteristics of the British army officer.[45] According to J.D. Campbell team sports and field sports transcended recreational importance for Army officers. 'They were professionally important as well.' The social dimension associated with field sports and games had an important bearing on a man's career prospects. These occasions were gathering places for upper-class society, and as members of that society the opportunities for officers to mingle and establish networks of influential contacts were crucial. An officer's place in society, his relationship to senior officers, his connections, relatives and friends, all influenced promotion prospects and duty assignments.[46]

In the time between completing their formal education and inheriting the family estate many heirs to Irish estates pursued a military career. At officer level Ireland was proportionally over-represented in the British Army as a whole with Irish officers forming about 17.5 per cent of the officer class throughout the nineteenth century.[47] The Westmeath gentry included many men who had engaged in army service and retained their military titles or were men with military rank. The list of subscribers for the 1895–96 season, for instance, included twenty-eight (27 per cent) members of Westmeath families who held military titles and included a lieutenant colonel, four colonels, twelve majors and eleven captains.[48] Thirty-seven of the 114 subscribers in 1900 were current or retired army officers from Westmeath landed families.[49] Hunting thus enabled Athlone- and Mullingar-based army officers to fraternise with many men who had experience of a similar milieu.

Hunting was central to the lifestyle of many members of the Mullingar-based military regiments. It offered a seamless introduction and a means of integration into local elite society and an opportunity to sample the other sporting and social opportunities of the district. Military personnel are ever present in lists of hunting participants. On 5 March 1867, the officers of the 28th Regiment based in Mullingar, hosted a lavish hunt breakfast in the barrack square. Up to 70 male members participated in a reception that included 'not only the substantials of a hunt repast, but also all the delicacies of the season'. During the meal the regimental band performed 'a variety of popular airs'. Ladies inhabited a large number of carriages drawn up in the square and viewed the events from the periphery.[50] The opening meet of 1877 included Adjutant Maunsell and officers of the 103rd Royal Bombay Fusiliers and officers from Athlone and Longford.[51] In the period while they were based in Mullingar, Colonel Burnett and the officers of the Royal Irish Rifles (RIR) hunted regularly and the military barracks was one of the meeting places for the hunt where 'lavish hospitality' was dispensed before the hunters departed.[52] They showed their appreciation of the skills of the Westmeath huntsman Will Matthews, by presenting him with 'a hunting crop massively mounted in solid silver' in recognition of the efficiency and skill he displayed during their time in Mullingar.[53] This regiment enjoyed a particularly close relationship with the local hunting community and Colonel Burnett and his officers were guests at

the revived hunt ball of 1889.[54] Initially, army officers were non-sub-
scribing members of the hunt but as the century progressed regimental
subscriptions are recorded in the financial records of the Westmeath
Club, as are subscriptions by individual officers. In the period between
1890–1901 officers from the East Lancashire Regiment, the King's Own
Yorkshire Light Infantry, the North Lancashire Regiment and the
Inniskilling Dragoons are featured as group subscribers.[55]

In his autobiography, Lieutenant Alexander Godley of the 1st Battalion Royal Dublin Fusiliers documented the popularity of the
Mullingar district to army personnel and the role hunting played in
establishing networks with influential families. He found Mullingar in
the 1880s, 'a paradise for a young and impecunious subaltern'. Lord
Greville and his family, the Smyths of Gaybrook, the Tottenhams of
Tudenham, the Levinges of Knockdrin and many other families provided 'unbounded hospitality'. Non-hunting days were spent on
shooting expeditions. After morning parade, 'a jaunting car, with a
professional poacher in attendance was invariably to be found waiting
in the barrack square', which would transport the officers to a 'likely
looking bog' where shooting for snipe, partridge, duck, hare and
pheasant would take place until nightfall. Godley's 'delightful life' was
interrupted by orders to transfer to Sligo.[56] An entry in the journal of
the East Lancashire Regiment in August 1890 is equally positive on the
attractions of a Mullingar posting and offers an insight into the pre-
occupations of the officers. Mullingar's amusements were 'an incessant
round of tennis parties, polo, fishing, and later on excellent shooting
and hunting. The polo ground is a very good one, and very prettily
situated . . .'.[57]

Apart from direct participation in the hunt and financial contribution,
members of the military establishment provided additional support to
the hunt club that also promoted the integration of the two communities. The Mullingar army barracks was made available as a venue for
social and fund-raising events promoted by the hunt club and personnel
were provided to participate in dramatic shows (Figure 2). In May 1875,
a literary and musical soirée in aid of the fowl fund was held at the
Lecture Hall, Mullingar. Colonel Addington made available the band
and the Ethiopian serenade troupe of the 100th Regiment for this
event.[58] In January 1893, a theatrical performance in aid of the sub-
sidiary funds of the Westmeath hunt was held in the gymnasium at
which the officers and men of the East Lancashire Regiment were
assembled in great numbers as both dramatic players and spectators.[59]
Profits from the theatricals organised by the officers of the Loyal North
Lancashire Regiment provided £11 to the funds of the hunt committee in
the 1893–94 season.[60] The Yorkshire Light Infantry officers provided the
prizes for the farmers' races of 1897.[61] On such occasions and at the
annual hunt club steeplechase and point-to-point race meets, the presence of the military band was an integral part of the occasion. In 1889,

AN

𝔄𝔪𝔞𝔱𝔢𝔲𝔯

𝔇𝔯𝔞𝔪𝔞𝔱𝔦𝔠 𝔓𝔢𝔯𝔣𝔬𝔯𝔪𝔞𝔫𝔠𝔢

IN AID OF THE

SUBSIDIARY FUNDS OF THE WESTMEATH HUNT

WILL TAKE PLACE IN THE

Gymnasium, Mullingar Barracks

(By kind permission of the Officer commanding).

On FRIDAY, FEBRUARY 5th, at 8 p.m,
(Doors open at 7.30 p.m.),

And on Saturday, February 6th, at 3.30 p.m.
(Doors open at 3 p.m.)

STERLING COYNE'S amusing Comedy in 3 Acts, entitled—

EVERYBODY'S   FRIEND.

ACT I.—Mr. Featherly's House at Clapham.
ACT II.—Mrs Swandown's House at Maida Hill.
(Three days are supposed to have elapsed since the Second Act).
ACT III.—Ante Room in Mr Featherly's House.

CHARACTERS by The Honble. VERONIQUE GREVILLE, Mrs MAYNE, Mrs R. W. IRVINGE, Mrs DALLAS,. Captain P. H. O'HARA, Hon. C. FULKE GREVILLE, Capt. C. G. MORRISON, &c.

The splendid String Band of the 2nd Batt. East Lancashire Regiment (by kind permission of Col. GOODWYN) will perform a Selection of Music on each occasion.

Figure 2. The Mullingar Army Barracks as a venue for Westmeath Hunt Club entertainment (*Westmeath Guardian*, 29 January 1892)

after a lapse of some years the Westmeath hunt ball was revived and was attended by 180 guests at the gymnasium of the Military Barracks. The venue was used throughout the 1890s for the glittering social highlight of the year that was the hunt ball.[62]

Women from a landed background, frequently accompanied by a male family member, hunted in Westmeath almost from the time of the foundation of the subscription pack. Newspaper accounts regularly mention female participants from the 1860s onwards. In March 1864, at a dinner given in honour of the master, Captain Dease, it was claimed that fifteen women had hunted at Clonyn the previous week.[63] Ten women joined the field for the initial meet in 1879.[64] Hunting became more popular with women in the 1880s and at this time, it could claim the seal of royal approval, when the Empress Elizabeth of Austria rented Summerhill house in County Meath in 1879 and 1880 and hunted regularly with the Meath, Kildare and Ward Union packs in which she jumped the 'banks and ditches more recklessly than the most daredevil Irish'. Elizabeth's social standing, and her skill as a horsewoman made hunting a more acceptable pastime for women. The Empress, described as the 'most exalted as well as the most dashing and glamorous huntswoman in Europe', was attracted to Ireland by the hunting reputation the country enjoyed.[65] In 1886, twenty-seven women were present at Clonhugh for the opening meet of the season.[66] At any given time there was a solid if small core of female hunting followers active in the county. The eight married and four single ladies who subscribed to the ladies' damage fund for the 1894–95 season were the central element of this group in the 1890s and these women had also begun to play some role in the administration of the sport.[67] In the concluding year of this study, for the 1905–06 hunting season women formed approximately one-third of the hunting field.[68] A photographic collage of the 1906 members of the Westmeath Hunt Club featured thirty-seven female members out of a total of 102.[69]

Unlike Lady Fingall, who wrote of the fear and trepidation she experienced whilst hunting with the Meath Hounds, many Westmeath women participated fully in the hunting field and received the support and encouragement of their male colleagues for their efforts.[70] In his memoirs Godley identifies Miss Dolly O'Hara and Mrs Jem Locke as women who were 'particularly hard to beat'.[71] The British Hunt and Huntsman claimed that there were few finer riders to hounds in the Westmeath country than Mrs Locke and her daughters Mrs Batten and Miss Flo Locke, not unsurprisingly as all three women had hunted since childhood.[72] A swift gallop across rough country intersected by railway lines, fences topped with wire, ditches and streams was a dangerous and exciting activity and demanded far more sterling qualities than the kindness, courtesy and politeness associated with the stereotypical Victorian female.[73] Stamina, strength, skill and courage were essential in the high-speed chases that were one of the key features of the sport. The requirement that women ride side-saddle increased the demands for dexterity and equestrian skills and added to the hazardous nature of the activity. Westmeath hunting accounts identify several women who were present at the kill or at the conclusion of a chase, one of the real indicators of merit for the hunting community. At a meet in February 1873, the MFH was accompanied by his wife, described as one of the most accomplished and pluckiest riders in the world.[74] On the day, Mrs Greville Nugent gracefully rode over the largest fences 'without effort, at which many a good man and horse came to grief in the vain attempt to follow'. In a two-and-a-quarter-hour chase in November 1882, described as 'as good a run as any man ever saw with foxhounds', Mrs Magill rode the run all through in an 'A1' manner and would have got the brush 'had the brave little owner surrendered it'.[75] At the opening meet in 1886, Miss Hall was presented with the brush.[76] At a 'clipping' run in 1887 Mrs Magill was one of only five of the party present at the finish.[77] In an exceptional run by the South Westmeath Hounds, the stag was chased for an estimated sixteen miles and amongst those up at the finish were

Miss Murtagh and Mrs and Miss Ffrench.[78] In February 1898, it was the preserve of the married ladies Mrs Malone, Mrs Jackson and Mrs Rowland Hudson to accompany Miss Hall at the final event.[79] Miss Hall in particular had become fully immersed in the traditional male world of the hunt and her prowess was eulogised by the Earl of Longford as a lady who was 'so judicious at a double, so audacious at a wall'.[80] The Reynell sisters were also frequently recognised for their ability in the field and were also distinguished by the length of their hunting careers. Evidence from the personal diary of Laeda Reynell establish her presence in the hunting fields in 1862 and at least one of the Reynell sisters was still hunting in February 1906.[81]

The social structure of a typical Westmeath hunting field remained consistent during the period of this study. The published attendance at the opening meet of the 1905 season, 'one of the largest ever seen', is indicative of this consistency. The resident landed gentry and their wives or daughters monopolised the field.[82] Professional representation was confined to three solicitors, two veterinary surgeons, three doctors, a bank manager, and important civil servants such as the county surveyor and the resident magistrate.[83] Also in the field were a few substantial farmers who were accepted as subscribing members of the hunt since 1887.[84]

Middle-aged, mainly married members of social class A dominated the membership of the Westmeath Hunt Club. The forty-two founding subscribers named by the Westmeath Guardian on 18 May 1854 were a group of men with ages that ranged between twenty-three and sixty years with an average age of thirty-eight.[85] Males ranging from eighteen-year-old Cecil Fetherstonhaugh to seventy-seven year old Henry Murray dominated the 1875 list of 105 subscribers. The 1900 list of 114 ranged from the seventy-three year old Captain W. M. Smyth of Drumcree to the twenty-year old Arthur Boyd-Rochfort.[86] The average age and conjugal status of the subscribers for the chosen dates is illustrated in Table 1.

	N	Average Age	% Married	% Single
1854	25	37.8	64	36
1875	46	43	61	39
1900	67	44.67	77	23

(N = Number of identified subscribers)

Table 1. Average age and conjugal status of subscribers to Westmeath Hunt Club, 1854, 1875 and 1900

Geographically, the 1854 members resided in the eastern half of the county (Figure 3), and in particular they occupied picturesque demesnes near the three main lakes of mid-Westmeath, whereas the whole county was represented in 1875 and 1900 (Figure 4). The gentry of the western part of the county subscribed to the county pack from the early 1870s

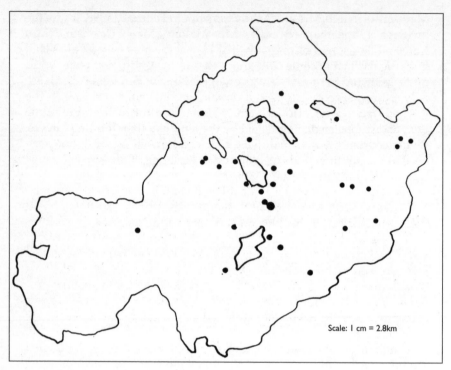

Scale: 1 cm = 2.8km

Figure 3. Location of the residences of subscribers to the Westmeath Hunt Club, 1854

and it was a truly representative one in spatial terms. Athlone-based John Longworth disposed of his pack of forty couples of hounds and his large stable of horses in mid-season 1870 and his hunting country was taken over by the Westmeath Club. According to the *Westmeath Independent* the decision was inspired by the scarcity of foxes in the district that arose from a conflict of recreational interest amongst the landed gentry. The foxes were 'said to be trapped for the purpose of preservation of pheasants', by several of the gentry in the locality.[87]

In 1876 the Government published, on a county basis, lists of all landowners in the country. A comparison of this list with the list of subscribers to the Westmeath Hunt Club in 1875 gives an excellent insight into the landed wealth of the club members. The 1875 identified members were the owners of 369,697 acres of land valued at £222,314. Slightly over half of this, 189,348 acres was Westmeath land valued at £127,392. The members identified owned 44 per cent of the total land of the county.[88] Thirteen subscribers possessed estates larger than 5,000 acres headed by the Earl of Longford with a Westmeath estate of 15,014 acres valued at £9,348. However, the most valuable parts of Longford's assets were located outside Westmeath. His Dublin lands of 420 acres were valued at £31,713 whilst the Longford section of his estate of 4,555 acres was valued at £6,101.[89] A classification of the identified members in terms of land valuation is illustrated in Table 2.

Valuation	% members
£5,000+	25.0
£2,000 <£5,000	15.3
£1,000 <£2,000	15.3
£500 <£1,000	18.0
<£500	26.4

Table 2. Estate valuation of Westmeath Hunt Club members, 1875

Smaller landed proprietors formed the majority of club members but the real men of substance formed the core of the club in 1875. These members of the Pakenham, Nugent, Chapman, Smyth and Fetherston-haugh families owned between them over 76,000 acres of Westmeath land or 17 per cent of the total land of the county. A comparison with a similar profile of the Limerick Hunt Club suggests that the Westmeath Club was a more exclusive one at this time and had a much stronger wealth base. T. K. Hoppen's analysis shows that only 6 per cent of the Limerick Hunt Club members held estates valued in excess of £5,000

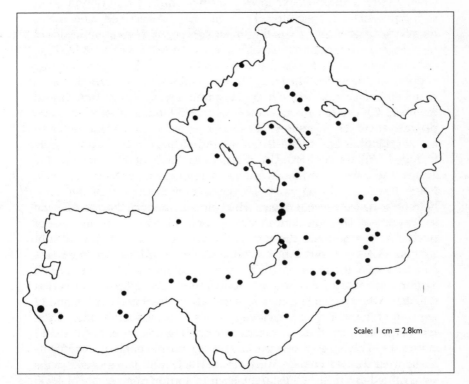

Scale: 1 cm = 2.8km

Figure 4. Place of residence of members of Westmeath Hunt Club in 1900

whilst those holding estates valued at less than £500 formed 53 per cent of the membership.[90]

It is possible to establish the proportion of the landed gentry who actually supported the sport. A comparison of the 1875 list of sub-scribers to the Westmeath hunt with the 1876 return of owners of land for the county illustrates the importance of hunting to the lifestyle of a particular section of the county gentry and major landowners. In 1876, fifty-eight resident owners possessed estates in excess of 1,000 acres and twenty-seven held estates of between 500 acres and 1,000 acres in the county.[91] Thirty-five members of the former group (60 per cent) and seven (26 per cent) of the latter group subscribed to the Westmeath Hunt Club in 1875. It seems the culture of hunting was most important to those who held estates in excess of 1,000 acres and the majority of the members of this group were active supporters. These were the ones who could afford the expense of maintaining a hunting stable and the cost of hunting on a regular basis. Outside this elite group the sport was very much one with a minority appeal. These may have joined the hunt in their areas as non-subscribers, paid their field money and participated on an irregular basis.

All subscribers did not support hunting in equal measures. Unlike other sports where the annual individual subscription was designed to cover seasonal running expenses hunting required a minimum sub-scription for membership. The majority subscribed the basic membership fee whilst a small number subscribed several multiples of the basic. The financial details of individual subscriptions for 1854 are not available but are for 1862 and are used here to measure individual support for the sport.[92] In 1862, fifty-four subscribers contributed £682 to maintain the pack. The bulk of this amount was sourced from fifteen members (28 per cent) who contributed £385 (56 per cent) of the total between them. These main subscribers were some of the leading land-owning families and highest-ranking individuals in the county. They included William Pollard Urquhart, Lord Vaux of Harrowden, the Tuites, the Earl of Granard, Colonel Greville, Sir R. Levinge, Sir P. Nugent and Sir B. Chapman. The gentlemen at the top of the land-holding scale were also the ones who helped to finance the sport for the lesser owners. This imbalance was greater in 1875 when an elite core of twelve members made the heaviest financial contribution and sub-scribed £350 or 30 per cent of the total. An additional ten members subscribed £20 each so that 21 per cent of total membership subscribed 47 per cent of the total amount contributed. The 26 per cent of the members who held land valued less than £500 subscribed £141 or just 12 per cent of the total. In 1900, eleven members subscribed 38 per cent of the total with thirty-four members contributing 63 per cent of the £983 subscribed. Patronage was a crucial factor in the development of Victor-ian sport and as can be seen from this analysis it was as important to the survival of hunting as it was to the farm-labourers' cricket.

Some subscribed to the club but never participated. One of these was William Edward Wilson of the Daramona estate (1,264 acres in 1876) in Street, County Westmeath. Wilson's diaries for the period between January 1889 and January 1908 make frequent reference to his participation in shooting expeditions in the locality.[93] However, more academic pursuits provided Wilson with personal challenges. In 1871, a small observatory with a twelve-inch reflecting telescope was built in the garden of Daramona House by Sir Howard Grubb and in 1881 Wilson built a new and larger observatory attached to his house. In 1889 a photographic dark room for the development of his astronomical plates was constructed and in 1892 a twenty-four inch mirror was remounted and used almost entirely for photographing star clusters and nebulae.[94] Wilson devoted much of his time to the determination of the temperature of the solar atmosphere, the electrical measurement of the brightness of the stars and to the photography of the sun and the stars. On 13 August 1898, for instance, he recorded in his diary that he had taken 'almost 400 photographs of a sunspot from 10.45 to 12.30'.[95]

The period covered by the minute books of the Westmeath Hunt Club from 1877 to 1905 was dominated by financial discussions. Officials and committee members were stretched to the limit trying to persuade members to meet their financial commitments and to subscribe the necessary funds to maintain infrastructure. In the 1877–78 season the energy of the secretary was devoted to encouraging the members to subscribe to the kennel repair fund and to clear the deficit on the fund.[96] Over the period subscriptions were sourced for the retirement of huntsman Will Matthews, for presentations to a retired Master of the Hounds (MFH), for covert maintenance, kennel repair, for steeplechase and point-to-point meets, for the fowl damage fund, for the maintenance and repair of the huntsman's residence, for the erection of a new boiler house, for hunt ball deficits, for wedding presents for Lord Longford and for the purchase of horses and hounds. The list must have seemed endless for the individual subscriber. The Westmeath club's financial difficulties were not unusual for the time. D. C. Itkowitz has shown that many British hunts faced serious financial challenges from the 1870s.[97] The difference in Westmeath was that the landed gentry were dependent on their own resources to finance the sport. The middle-class passion for hunting so common in Britain, and a valuable source of finance for hunting organisations there, did not manifest itself in Westmeath.[98]

It is difficult to estimate the annual expenditure incurred by an individual involved in hunting. A near contemporary English estimate calculated that an initial investment of £140 and annual costs of £40 were required, which 'considering the health and pleasure, that it affords' made hunting good value for money.[99] A Westmeath estimate, in 1897, suggested that the costs were similar, with keep and maintenance of a horse estimated at £35 annually, and when minimum subscription costs and other essential contributions are included, then a sum in excess of £50 annually was required.[100] Those seriously involved in the sport would, of course, have to meet the expense of keeping a number of horses.

These financial demands were made at a time when the landlords faced economic retrenchment. Economic depression, declining rental income and lowered rents under the terms of the 1881 Land Act meant that landlords were unable to meet interest obligations for earlier borrowings. Nationally, renewed agricultural depression from the mid-1880s, which was accompanied by the Land League inspired Plan of Campaign, meant that rental incomes declined still further.[101] The effects of the land war and the accompanying depression did not impact as acutely on Westmeath as in many other counties but the events outlined above did impact on the economic performances of many estates. From 1882 to 1902, 5,183 Westmeath tenants entered the land courts and had their rents reduced by 18 per cent under the fair rent fixing terms of the 1881 Land Act. As a result, Westmeath landlords' rental income declined by more than £32,000.[102] Under the terms of the Arrears of Rent Act of 1882, 199 Westmeath landlords had £17,797 extinguished from their rentals.[103]

The generosity of the Master was important in maintaining the viability of the Westmeath Hunt Club. The Master of the Fox Hounds was the most important individual in Victorian sport. Apart from a range of managerial duties, the master of the Westmeath Hunt in the 1890s dispersed considerable patronage to the organisation. The Pakenham brothers, members of a family with distinguished military careers, succeeded Lord Greville as joint masters in 1893. At the time of their accession both were in the army.[104] The brothers remained in military service and organised alternate leave that allowed one or other of the brothers to be in Westmeath hunt country during the season. The Longfords were particularly generous, with their patronage taking a variety of forms. In January 1890, the Honourable Edward Pakenham agreed to pay the deficit of £23 on the race accounts outstanding from the previous year.[105] In 1893, the brothers donated £55 to help clear the deficit from the 1891–92 season.[106] In December 1898 they agreed to carry out the kennel repairs at their own expense.[107] In addition, the list of subscribers for the three seasons 1890–91 to 1892–93 was headed by the Earl of Longford with donations of £60 each season and topped by a subscription of £100 in the season 1900–01.[108] The influence of the family was also responsible for the return of their neighbour, Major Pollard-Urquhart, as a leading subscriber in the period of their mastership. In five successive seasons between 1893 and 1897 he subscribed £50 each season and £40 in each season 1898–1900.[109]

III

If as Hoppen suggests, Grand Jury membership was important to the maintenance of tribal solidarity, then hunting, where members assembled as often as four times a week, provided an essential component of communal identity. The members of the Westmeath Hunt Club used the club as the main vehicle for the maintenance and development of social networks. In Victorian times, Dublin and London social clubs played an important role in aristocratic and gentry lifestyles. Accommodation at reasonable rates, quality food, reading and writing rooms, billiard rooms, card rooms and smoking rooms were provided in all clubs.[110] The two most important Irish clubs were located in Dublin, the Kildare Street Club on the south side of the river Liffey and the Sackville Street Club located north of the river.[111] Club membership was, however, a relatively unimportant aspect of the lifestyle of the members of the Westmeath Hunt. In 1854, only eight, or 19 per cent, were members of an Irish club while ten subscribers conducted sufficient business in London to make it worthwhile to join one of the many clubs available there. Only eighteen subscribers seem to have joined one of the Dublin clubs and twenty-three subscribed to sixteen different London clubs in 1875.[112] Three members joined the Junior United Services Club, which was confined to those who were princes of the blood royal, officers of the navy and army, persons holding appointment in military departments and lords lieutenants of Great Britain and Ireland.[113] The Earl of Granard, Lieutenant-Colonel John James Nugent and Thomas J. Smith were the members of the Westmeath Hunt Club who reached the exacting standards required for membership of this exclusive club. Those who wished to experience locally based male conviviality, undertake charitable projects, become involved in self-improvement exercises and who were unfulfilled by the rituals of the hunting field found an outlet in the local branches of the Freemasons. Athlone, Mullingar and Castlepollard had Freemason branches in the second half of the nineteenth century. A small number of hunt club subscribers were members of these branches. In 1875, 12 per cent and in 1900, 14 per cent were Freemasons.[114]

Communal identity was also solidified by shared political belief. The ethos of the individual members of the group at this time was distinctly unionist. In April 1893, a major open-air assembly was held in Mullingar 'to protest against the Home Rule Bill and also to show that there were Unionists outside of Ulster'.[115] The published list of those in attendance might in different circumstances be listed as the members of the Westmeath Hunt Club, such were their dominance of the meeting. Sir Montague Richard Chapman, MFH from 1876–1881, chaired the assembly and delivered the introductory address in which Westmeath Unionists affirmed their 'right to live as citizens under the rule of the Queen and the glorious Empire which their forefathers helped to build'.[116] Three other members of great Westmeath hunting families –

the Earl of Longford, who would accept the position of MFH before the year ended, Edward Dames-Longworth and Edmund F. Dease – also addressed the meeting. In July 1893, a formal Westmeath branch of the organisation to oppose Home Rule, the Irish Unionist Alliance, was established with an officer board that were all subscribers to the hunt club. The sixteen-man committee included thirteen members of the Westmeath Hunt Club.

Despite the Unionist majority it would be a mistake to view the membership of the Westmeath County Club as politically or devotionally homogenous. Lord Greville, MFH between 1886–1893, was one of the few peers to support the Home Rule policies of Gladstone. The club was never the type of monolith portrayed by L. P. Curtis. For Curtis the 'core of virtually every hunt consisted of the Anglo–Irish Ascendancy: Church of Ireland as well as landed and wealthy'. Curtis accepts that a small number of 'Catholic farmers of substantial acreage' could be found in most packs but only members of the Protestant Ascendancy could afford the expenses associated with regular hunting.[117] The membership of the Westmeath County Club illustrates the ability of individuals of different religious and political affiliations to co-operate in the management of their recreational affairs. Some of Westmeath's most important hunting families belonged to the Catholic Church.

The Dease family was the most important of the Westmeath Catholic hunting families. Captain Richard Dease held the position of MFH in the period between 1861 and 1868 and Edmund authored a history of the Westmeath hunt in 1898. The family estate was located at Turbotstown, near the village of Coole in the north of the county. The family succeeded in holding on to their estate (2,315 acres in 1876) and in remaining Catholic through all the vicissitudes of the sixteenth, seventeenth and eighteenth centuries. As a family they 'consistently punched above their weight' and intermarried over the centuries with some of the foremost nobles and gentry of the Pale such as Lords Slane, Fingall and Delvin.[118] The different strands of the Nugent family may have varied at times in their devotional allegiance but were generally Catholic. The leading member of the family at the time of the conclusion of this study, Sir Walter, represented South Westmeath as an MP between 1907 and 1918, and consistently advanced the 'most conciliatory and imperialist of views' whilst advancing the full gamut of Redmondite Home Rule ideas.[119] When not engaged in running their Kilbeggan Distillery the Locke brothers spent much of their leisure time riding horses. James Harvey also took care of the family's farming interests at Ardnaglue, a farm that was effectively his countryseat.[120] Peak output from the distillery coincided with the managership of the two brothers from the 1880s onwards. The Lockes managed to combine Catholicism, support for nationalist causes and hunting and racing without any apparent difficulty. However, the relationships of the brothers with doctrinal Catholicism tended towards the à la carte variety. Their high social status enabled them to ignore the Church position on marriage. J. H. Locke never married but maintained a mistress, Florence Savage, for whom he built a small cottage close to Ardnaglue. In 1880, John Edward Locke married Mary Edwards, a marriage that ended in divorce in 1896. Despite these unconventional arrangements there was a very strong relationship between the Lockes and the Sisters of Mercy order in Kilbeggan.[121]

The O'Reilly family from Coolamber was another Catholic family that played a leading role in organising the Westmeath hunt. Percy O'Reilly also defied the orthodoxy of the day, both Catholic and gentry, when he eloped and married Alice Rochfort the Protestant daughter of Mrs and the deceased Major Hamilton Boyd-Rochfort in December 1899.[122] T. M. Reddy was another Catholic member who supported nationalist causes but also immersed himself in the cultural practices of the landed gentry. The involvement of Eddie Shaw and Thomas Maher are detailed later in the chapter. Maher was a cousin of Paul Cullen, Ireland's first Cardinal, and Cullen stayed at the Maher mansion on the night prior to the consecration ceremony of St Patrick's Church, Moate in October 1871.[123] Social status, rather than political or religious affiliation, supported by the necessary wealth was the required ticket of entry to the elite world of landed gentry recreation. The divorce settlement of a payment of £600 annually negotiated between J. E. Locke and Mary Edwards in 1898 implied that J. E.'s income was in the region of £1,200 annually. As manager of the family farm J.H. Locke would have enjoyed a greater income. This would indicate that the income of the Lockes' was much greater than that of the most successful lawyer or other professional at the time.[124]

The community in 1900 was still dominated by members of the aristocracy and the landed gentry. There is very little evidence that the sport became democratised or that members of the more prosperous middle classes became part of the support structure of the sport. The subscribers included the manager of the Mullingar Hibernian Bank (where the hunt club accounts were located), two doctors and five lawyers. Three of the lawyers combined land agency with their legal work. Two of these, Edmund Dease and Theobald Fetherstonhaugh were members of Westmeath hunting and landed families. The county surveyor and the resident magistrate also subscribed. Four females were also listed amongst the subscribers. Three of these were widows with strong family connections to the world of the hunt and the fourth was the divorcee, Mrs Locke. The hunting community, as measured by those who subscribed in 1900, was still essentially a closed community, its membership confined almost exclusively to those of an aristocratic or gentry background and members of the professions of similar social standing.

A notable exception to the above generalisation was Mullingar solicitor Eddie Shaw, who made the transition from his middle-class Catholic background to become fully immersed in the hunting, shooting, fishing and racing world of the landed gentry. The Shaw family were proprietors of one of Mullingar's largest wine and spirit stores, operated a large wholesale and retail grocery trade, and were 'midland agents for the products of Messrs Guinness'.[125] At the end of the century, the legal profession was a popular, laborious and expensive career choice for aspiring Catholic professionals. Progress in the profession was heavily dependent on contacts within the field.[126] Eddie Shaw qualified as a lawyer in 1892 (finishing in seventh place of the thirty-one who completed the final examination), and the profession provided him with access to elite social circles which he exploited to become fully integrated in the exclusive sporting world of the hunt.[127] Shaw used his legal qualifications to enhance his social status and recreational opportunities and any career benefits were incidental. His activities embraced all aspects of equestrian sports and he participated in puppy walking, hunting, and racing and polo both as a participant and as an administrator.[128] He competed successfully in steeplechasing both as an owner and amateur jockey.[129] He combined these activities with the position of secretary of the hunt races and the point-to-point races and acted as clerk of the scales at the annual polo club races.[130] Shaw, however, was an exception; there is little evidence of newly established professionals making the transition from their middle-class background to the landed society of the hunting community.

The most significant change in the membership profile of the group after 1875 was the presence of thirteen 'bona fide' farmers as subscribers, a number that had declined since the 1895–96 season when eighteen farmers subscribed.[131] These were eligible for membership from December 1887 when a motion proposing 'that bona fide working farmers be admitted as members of Westmeath hunt, subject to the approval of hunt committee, on payment of a subscription of two guineas', was accepted.[132] This move was instigated by Lord Greville and was in keeping with the liberal principles of the master who was a strong supporter of tenants' rights and the only peer in the House of Lords to support the 1893 Home Rule Bill.[133] The decision according to Dease 'brought about a material change in the Hunt as a club' and 'the new rule carried so far that one prominent member of the Hunt gave up his place on the committee, and joined as a two guinea member'.[134]

The Westmeath Hunt Club was the first established hunt club to extend its membership eligibility and the decision had a number of practical implications for some wealthy farmers who wanted to extend their participation in racing. Farmers who subscribed had access to a wider range of steeplechase races and were no longer restricted to participation in farmers' races at hunt-club organised meets or point-to-point races. They were also qualified to compete in National Hunt meets as steeplechase riders. The development of a large Westmeath racing community was partly a product of the hunt club membership facility that Westmeath farmers enjoyed.

In practice the term 'bona fide' farmer meant a tenant who earned his living from farming the land as opposed to being a proprietor of a landed estate. These men farmed substantial areas of land as revealed by the information contained in the valuation records, and the size and value of their holdings is reproduced in Appendix 3. These were the men involved in the commercial sector of Westmeath agriculture, the graziers who specialised in the raising of dry cattle and sheep. Profits generated by the grazier provided a means of status enhancement that was manifested particularly in a tendency to adopt many of the norms and habits of the gentry. The landlord provided the model of social worth and imitation of the gentry lifestyle was a central feature of the societal and familial roles performed by the upwardly-mobile rancher.[135] In Westmeath, a small group of commercially successful, upwardly-mobile farmers chose participation in the hunting and allied racing field as a means of proclaiming this success.

Thomas Maher, who farmed at Moyvoughley in Moate, County Westmeath, was an example of this category of farmer. A subscriber in 1875 and 1900 he leased 524 acres from John Ennis and a further 200 acres in nearby Mount Temple. Maher's primary economic activity was cattle fattening. He purchased two-year-old store cattle at fairs throughout Ireland and fattened them for a further two years at Moyvoughley before they were transferred to Maher's County Meath farm where the fattening process was completed before the cattle were sold on the Dublin market. An extensive sheep-farming and horse-breeding enterprise was carried on in association with the primary cattle grazing enterprise. The Maher mansion became a centre of elite entertainment and the demesne was frequently used as a meeting place when south Westmeath was hunted, and was also used for private coursing meets. The centrality of hunting to the status and lifestyle of its followers frequently precluded any economic retrenchment. At Maher's death, in 1903, the estate was valued at £4,243 but his wife Mary inherited debts in excess of £16,000.[136]

IV

Hunting provided the fulcrum around which much of the social life of its participants and supporters revolved. The season extended from the opening of the cubbing season in September to the conclusion of the hunting season in April. Hunt sponsored balls, dinners, puppy shows, breakfasts, fundraising entertainments, steeplechasing and point-to-point racing events contributed to the style of life of a hunting district and were a central part of the social life of the resident landed gentry. The hunt ball was the major social event for the gentry of the region. The first hunt ball advertised for the Westmeath Hunt Club was that of 1865 when Ballinlough Castle, Delvin was the advertised venue.[137] The earliest documented hunt ball in Westmeath was held in 1866 and was

Figure 5. Knockdrin Castle, County Westmeath, seat of Sir Richard Levinge and
venue for several hunt balls

attended by over 260 guests. This was hosted by the founding father of
the Westmeath Hunt Club, Sir Richard Levinge at his Knockdrin Castle
seat (Figure 5). The mansion offered 'ample dimensions, great accommodation,' and proximity to Mullingar, the venue of the 'most
important station on the Midland Railway'.[138] Early hunt balls were
held in the natural environment of the mansions of the leading aristocrats, a feature that added to their exclusivity and attractiveness.
Richard C. Levinge hosted the 1871 ball at his seat at Levington Park.
The host was prepared to remodel some of his rooms to facilitate the
large attendance of guests. The walls between two reception rooms
were removed to create adequate space for dancing while two other
rooms were converted into one to provide a supper room. On the night,
the rooms and corridors were richly ornamented with draperies, ever-
greens and trophies of the chase.[139] Catering was of the highest
professional quality. The main meal was supplied by Mr Ingram
Murphy, recruited from Harcourt Street in Dublin and was of 'the most
recherché description and the wines furnished by Messrs. Heinekey
were equally choice'.[140] Throughout the 1870s the hunt ball took prece-
dence over all other local social events, but lapsed for some years in the
1880s. It was revived in 1889 and attracted 180 guests to the Military
Barracks.[141] It continued throughout the 1890s with the Military gymnasium the usual host venue. One of the most spectacular events was
held in January 1905 promoted by the 'Fox-Hunting Bachelors in Westmeath'. About 300 attended the event, at which the floor was
overcrowded during some of the dances and 'the diversified dresses of
the ladies, the scarlet coats of the huntsmen, and the sombre evening
dress of the remaining gentlemen, intermingled in brilliant contrast'.[142]
   On other occasions, especially in the 1870s, the Courthouse in
Mullingar hosted the ball with the 1872 event a particularly spectacular

one.[143] Here 'two apartments were prepared for dancing'. Mr Liddel's string band was placed in the Grand Jury room and the 'splendid band of the 97th Regiment' was based in the 'spacious hall of the Court'.[144] The three categories of venue used encapsulated the wealth, social standing and power of the participants. The big houses provided the power symbols of the local landscape; the Courthouse was where administrative and judicial power was exercised by many who were members of the Westmeath Hunt Club and the Mullingar military barracks expressed the symbiotic relationship between landed gentry and army officership.

Hunt dinners were normally exclusively male events organised on special occasions such as those held to mark the retirement of important hunt personnel. Towards the end of the century, more paternalist events were organised such as the annual earth-stoppers' dinners, which acknowledged the contribution of those from the lower end of the social spectrum to the season's hunting. Earth-stoppers were a critical element of the infrastructure of hunting and part of its informal economy. They worked during the night prior to the hunt, and their duties were 'to stop every drain, shore or rabbit hole into which a fox could squeeze himself, on the whole of their beats, or farms of which they have charge and to keep the rabbit holes closed during the entire hunting season'.[145] Payment to these individuals was normally the responsibility of the master. In 1882, Captain Macnaghten paid the night stoppers 5s each, the morning stoppers 2s 6d each and those who found foxes were paid 10s inclusive of stops.[146]

Annual hunt club races were an important part of Westmeath racing culture and provided a range of entertainment to all classes (see Chapter 8 below). Held towards the end of the hunting season, the races provided one of the final opportunities for the followers of the hunt to assemble and socialise en masse before dispersing for the summer season. Only a minority of subscribers actually participated or offered financial support to the steeplechase races but the ancillary social events attracted a wide range of support. The social dimension of the hunt was extended considerably during the mastership of Harry Whitworth (1903–09). Joint meetings with neighbouring packs were organised and the sporting dimension was extended to the playing of a soccer match between the footballers of the Westmeath Hunt Club and the Galway 'Blazers', who chartered a special train for the journey to Mullingar.[147]

Informal social activities were also part of the hunting experience. The concept of the hunt breakfast was important at different stages during the second half of the nineteenth century. Captain Charles Coote began his first outing on 30 October 1871 with a champagne breakfast held at his Culleen base. Coote lived a life of some style supported by little substance. His heavily mortgaged Cootehill estate was never allowed to interfere with his heavy gambling. On one occasion betting at a cock fight by the gentry of Cavan and Monaghan was so heavy that the floors of the entrance hall of his Cootehill residence were said to have been paved with gold. A short-head defeat of a horse he had heavily backed in the Derby failed to land a gamble that would have been sufficient to clear his massive estate debts.[148] Coote's financial difficulties, according to one jaundiced commentator, was the inevitable result of a national flaw:

> Where no mental culture has taken place in early youth, the Irish lordling is an imbecile for life; and for want of useful employ betakes himself to the chase and the turf, to gambling and tippling, and all kinds of frivolity and dissipation.[149]

As the size of hunting fields increased, hunt breakfasts and mid-hunt dinners became more difficult to organise, but they were a feature encouraged by Lord Greville during his mastership (1886–93). The consumption of alcohol was a vital ingredient of this socialisation. The hip flask was as much a part of the hunter's equipment as stirrups and acted as a stimulant, protection against the cold and a social lubricant as it was passed around amongst friends.[150] The 'socialisation' of a group known as the 'Longford Slashers', who regularly hunted in Westmeath in the 1850s, is illustrative of the strong drinking culture that surrounded male hunting at the time. The group were noted for their 'hard riding by day and hard drinking by night' and at their regular meeting place at Bunbrosna egg-flip and hot punch consumed out of stable buckets was the favoured refreshment.[151] The 1862 diary of Laeda Reynell illustrates the centrality of hunting to the social life of the male members of the Reynell family. Almost all of the family friends were members of the Westmeath Hunt Club. Many came to dine and stay overnight at the family home at Killynon during 1862 and Reynell family members regularly visited the homes of some of these members. Eliza's brother Dick, during the 1862 season, visited the homes of many of those listed as subscribers of the Westmeath hunt in that year, often staying overnight in preparation for the following day's hunt.[152]

V

Despite the financial challenges faced by the hunting community in the 1890s and later, some members became involved in the expensive and socially exclusive sport of polo. According to one Irish source, 'to play polo regularly and in proper style costs a man as much as to hunt'.[153] A contemporary English estimate put the average cost at £102 for a London polo player with a stable of two ponies and the required outfit, in addition to £58 to cover the season's working expenses.[154] Participation in polo at competitive level added to the expense. Away matches necessitated the transport of ponies to venues and required the availability of more than one mount. In Chapter 4 the association between cricket and the landed gentry will be examined but cricket faced a challenge for gentry loyalty from 1881 onwards when polo was available to cater for the sporting and equestrian summer pleasures of the wealthy landed and professional classes. Those who found the latter activity too expensive also had the option of tennis as a summer activity, a more family oriented sport than any previously available. Polo provided the local gentry with an opportunity to participate in an exclusive and elitist sporting activity that provided an equestrian continuity with winter hunting. The organisation of the game included a sporting and social construct that involved intra-club members' matches, inter-club games, regimental matches and from 1890, a national competition, managed by a national polo association. Annual polo club races as well as a comprehensive range of social activities that culminated on at least three occasions with a polo club ball, were also available to members. The county polo club also provided a recreational curriculum that extended beyond polo as the members participated in the occasional challenge cricket match and organised clay-pigeon shoots confined to members and their friends.[155] Polo, with its social dimension, its equestrian sport and its annual race meet replicated in the summer what hunting offered in winter, in a more reserved and exclusive setting.

The 10th Hussars reputedly introduced polo to Ireland in 1871 and in 1872 the first game was played on Gormanstown Strand between teams representing County Meath, captained by John Watson, and the officers of the 9th Lancers.[156] The establishment of the All-Ireland Polo Club (AIPC) in 1874 was an important milestone, as this club received a free lease of a playing ground in the Phoenix Park with permission to construct a pavilion for the use of its members.[157] In polo's embryonic stage, the majority of the players were either serving soldiers or gentlemen who had returned to Ireland after a period of military service.[158] John Watson (master of the Meath Hunt between 1891–1908) is credited with transforming the game 'from chaos into scientific play'.[159] According to British Hunts and Huntsmen it was his influence that destroyed the 'vulgar brawls from which, in the process of evolution, the game of polo phoenix-like has arisen'.[160] His introduction of the backhanded stroke to England, a revolutionary stroke he practised in India, entirely altered the character of the game.[161]

Three polo clubs were established in Westmeath. The Mullingar based Westmeath County Polo Club was the most important one and was founded on 8 April 1881 at a meeting held at the Greville Arms Hotel. The membership subscription was set at £1 1s. Gentlemen who became members after 15 May, the date set for the commencement of play, were required to pay an additional £1 entrance fee.[162] In 1900, the North Westmeath Club was established in Castlepollard when Lord Longford gave his demesne for 'the use of the gentry' during the season.[163] Four years later this ground had been considerably enlarged and boasted a pavilion of 'generous proportions' described as 'a substantial and well appointed structure built of wood and contains *inter alia*, tea rooms, dressing rooms etc.'.[164] The South Westmeath Club was organised in the Moate district in 1903, due to the influence of Colonel Harrington.[165] As a result of these developments, there were sufficient numbers involved to allow locally organised tournament games to take place in the early 1900s. A week-long handicap tournament organised by the Westmeath Club was held at Ledeston in July 1904 in which each of the three Westmeath clubs entered two teams.[166] The following season six teams competed for Captain Bayley's £50 Challenge Cup.[167]

The most important competitive outlet for the members of the West-meath clubs was the annual All-Ireland County Club polo competition. This was introduced in an attempt to broaden the civilian appeal of the game. With this purpose in mind the Irish County Polo Club Union was established on 10 June 1890 at a meeting held in the Shelbourne Hotel, Dublin. The limited popularity of the game within the landed community at the time is clear; only representatives of five county polo clubs attended the meeting, including John Lyons from Westmeath. The objective of the organisation was to promote the game of county polo and therefore it was decided to organise an annual competition for a polo challenge cup played under Hurlingham Club rules. More wide-spread civilian involvement was encouraged by restricting the eligibility to compete in these competitions. *Bona fide* clubs were required to have a club ground and regular and fixed days of play. Competition rules were designed to limit participation to the resident landed gentry. Eligible players had to reside in the county within twenty miles of the polo ground and to own or hold land in the county. Officers of the army and navy were eligible to play for their native county provided they had played on the county club grounds at least twelve times during the season.[168]

The formal All-Ireland inter-county polo challenge cup competition was established in 1890. The popularity of the game in Westmeath and the quality of player was such that teams from the county were successful on a number of occasions in this competition. The Westmeath County Club were winners in 1896 and 1897 and the North Westmeath Club became All-Ireland champions in 1903, 1904 and 1905.[169] Two members of the North Westmeath Club, Percy O'Reilly and A. M. Rotherham were members of an Irish team that beat England for the first time in an annual contest for the Patriotic Cup in 1905.[170] They achieved their finest moment in sport at the 1908 Olympic Games when they represented an Irish team that were Olympic silver medallists.[171] Rotherham, whose landed interests were in County Meath, was educated at Cheltenham and the Royal Military College, Sandhurst, where presumably he was initiated in the skills of the game. The formation of two new clubs in Westmeath in the early 1900s was a reflection of the growing popularity of the game nationally. Only five clubs contested the 1896 competition; this number had increased to eight in 1903 and

nine in 1904. The columns of the *Irish Field* carried regular advertisements for tournaments organised by clubs.[172] According to this journal
fifteen clubs existed at the beginning of the 1903 playing season.[173]

The Westmeath County Club had its first ground at Belmont, the residence of Rowland Hudson, who was responsible for introducing the
game to the county.[174] Hudson had enjoyed a successful business career
in India where he controlled a substantial indigo plantation. He retired
from his Indian position and took up residence in Belmont, Mullingar.
During his time in India he became an expert polo player and on taking
up residence in Westmeath introduced the game to the local gentry and
under his guidance and supervision the polo grounds were established.[175] In 1882, Ledeston, the demesne of J. C. Lyons, became the polo
headquarters of the county. The switch from the 'rough and ready
ground' at Belmont was accompanied by the decision to affiliate non-
playing members after which the club progressed rapidly with the
erection of a pavilion and a properly prepared ground.[176] In 1885, the
club claimed to be the only *bona fide* county club in Ireland, 'the great
difficulty in obtaining a suitable ground for the game probably being
the chief obstacle'.[177] Apart from the grounds the venue provided stabling for the polo ponies, 'a fixed refreshment bar and dressing room'
and a marquee for the ladies. Tuesday and Friday evenings were polo-
playing days and those who required transport to the venue could
travel by brake from the Market House for the 'reasonable charge of 1s.
6d'.[178] Friday evening sessions were normally accompanied by a musical
recital courtesy of the military band. Socialisation was facilitated by the
sale of excisable liquor at the club's refreshment bar between the hours
of eight in the morning and ten at night.

A rule book from 1905 provides evidence of the nature of the club and
its activities. In 1905 the club had a membership of eighty-four as well as
the officers of the Connaught Rangers.[179] The club was a strong one as at
this time the County Carlow Club had a membership of thirty-five.[180]
Those who found the sport too demanding physically or too expensive
but who wished to participate in the exclusive socialisation offered by
the club had the option of becoming non-playing members of the club.
Playing members paid a subscription of £2 2s and a similar entrance fee.
Non-playing members paid half the standard fees.[181] In 1905, the membership list isn't categorised but in 1911 there were thirty-five playing
and forty-four non-playing members.[182] The social milieu of the club
guaranteed elitism and the rules were designed to maintain its exclusiveness. Membership was achieved by being proposed and seconded
followed by a ballot amongst the members. According to rule nine, one
black ball in eight excluded a potential member.[183] A member who
behaved in an 'obnoxious' manner or whose conduct was 'unbecoming'
of a gentleman was liable to expulsion.[184] As with other clubs catering
for a similar clientele, the Westmeath Club made special efforts to
accommodate the requirements of the military. Officers of the Army,

Navy and Auxiliary forces not having a residence in Westmeath were admitted without having to pay an entrance fee and the committee had the power to offer honorary membership to officers quartered at Mullingar, Athlone and Longford.[185]

The Westmeath County Polo Club was the exclusive preserve of representatives of social class A. The membership list of 1905 contained eighty-four individual males and seventy have been positively identified, all of whom were either members of the Westmeath landed gentry, men with private income, army officers or members of the wealthiest sections of the professional community. The age of the members ranged from twenty-five to seventy-four, with an average age of forty-seven years.[186] The membership of seven titled aristocrats included four peers, (Lords Castlemaine, Greville, Longford and Kilmaine), two baronets (Sir Richard Levinge and Sir Walter Nugent) and the Honourable Edward Pakenham. Twenty held military titles or were current army officers and the list also included four doctors, three lawyers, three bank managers, the assistant county surveyor, the MFH, a racehorse trainer, the resident magistrate, J. H. Locke of the Kilbeggan distillery firm, and the county inspector of the RIC. Forty-eight individuals were members of Westmeath landed families. Those who held military titles included regular officers who lived in the district and held individual membership and members of the county gentry who retained their ranks from army service.

The membership was also closely associated with the hunting community. An examination of the list of subscribers to the hunt in 1900–01 indicates that 54 per cent of the polo-club members of 1905 had subscribed to the hunt in that year.[187] The membership of the polo club included some of the better-known personalities of Westmeath hunting society and the 1905 list includes two previous holders of the position of MFH as well as the incumbent, Harry Whitworth. In 1878, John Lawrence suggested that hunting and cricket were complementary and that cricket 'formed a bond of union between the country gentlemen of the day; and the same sportsmen who met in winter by the covert side, hailed each other again joyfully in summer'.[188] In Westmeath, as the century progressed, this function was increasingly fulfilled by the polo club. This social profile gave the polo club an exclusivity that distinguished it from the Westmeath Hunt Club. The latter club accepted farmers from the late 1880s. The polo club experienced no such cross-fertilisation and its colonial character remained undiluted over the period of this study.

Polo provided a structured and location-specific recreational activity unlike the more peripatetic and ad hoc nature of cricket, which depended on individual invitation, initiative and effort to organise an event. It provided the kind of pastoral setting later associated with golf and was the locus around which the 'pick and fashion' of the surrounding counties could assemble amidst 'the magnificent scenery of Nonsuch

[Castlepollard], with its splendid trees; also the lofty castle which stands in a quaintly terraced hill overlooking many beautiful lakes which appeared so picturesque to the strangers'.[189] Ledeston offered a social world where afternoon tea was served in the large marquee, the pavilion where 'cold tea' and other light refreshments were to be had without stint' and with military bands present to 'play a charming selection of music'.[190]

The annual polo club races constituted an additional layer of recreational activity. They began in 1881 at Belmont where a programme of 'five events, which with a challenge match produced a first class evening's sport'.[191] The races effectively brought the polo season to a close and as one report noted a 'polo race will always partake more of the nature of a social than a great public function', where the rank and fashion were largely in evidence.[192] The emphasis was as much on the entertainment as on the racing and club members and individuals took advantage of the occasion to entertain friends. In this way, the races fulfilled a similar purpose to the annual hunt club steeplechase and point-to-point race meetings. At the 1901 event, for instance, 'hospitality was liberally dispensed by the members of the club in the pavilion and also by Mr. Boyd-Rochfort, J. H. Locke and others'.[193] Musical entertainment, provided by the band of the Mullingar based regiment, was a constant feature of the races.[194]

The introduction of the All-Ireland Challenge Cup added to the social dimension of the game as from 1896 it was decided to play all matches in the competition in Dublin; these were normally held in the month of August either prior to or after Horse Show week. In the 1896 final, won by Westmeath, it was reported that 'the two counties were represented by many of both sexes who came to town purposely to see the match'. There was a very 'smart and fashionable gathering on the Pavilion and in the Inclosure [sic] where the 13th Hussars had a big tea table and dispensed hospitality'.[195] According to the *Irish Field* 'there was a large turn out [sic] of smart vehicles of all kinds and description containing elegantly attired ladies who always make it a point to show up at such functions'.[196]

VI

It is clear that hunting transcended sport in the period analysed. It was the essential compound that bound a particular community together and set them apart from other groups. Some members of this community were active as local administrators, some shared the common bond of a military career, a minority found conviviality in membership of a Dublin or London club, denominational allegiance and political affiliation were also unifying elements, but the community dimension was created by the shared hunting experience. Hunting regenerated and re-energised the community on an annual basis as the members

assembled each September to renew their activities following the diversions and divisions of the summer season. By 1905 it was an ageing
community that found it difficult to meet the financial demands essential to its survival, with members suffering from the trauma associated
with a decline in political, social and economic power, a trauma that
was intensified by the frequent attempts made to interfere with the
activity within the county. However, there is no Westmeath evidence to
support the suggestion of R.V. Comerford that attempts to stop the
hunt were actually welcomed by some landlords who were becoming
increasingly indebted.[197] The opposite was the case in Westmeath in the
early 1900s, where attempts to interfere with the right of the members
to hunt were resisted in the strongest possible manner. The polo
campus provided a haven for those whose proprietorial rights had
been significantly diluted by the various land acts; their incomes were
similarly affected and their political power at local and national level
seriously eroded but perhaps most importantly in a sporting context,
their ability to hunt unhindered across the fields of Westmeath was
strongly challenged on occasion.

2. Horseracing development, 1850–1905

Westmeath horseracing had an established tradition by the mid-nineteenth century. The first recorded meeting was held at Athlone in August 1731.[1] Forty-six years later the earliest recorded meet for Mullingar was held.[2] The first recorded races at Kilbeggan were not held until March 1840 and, despite the impact of the Famine, a meet was held there for each year of the 1840s.[3] These steeplechase meets were strongly linked to hunting but as the nineteenth century progressed this link diminished in importance.

Horseracing, with the notable exception of Fergus A. D'Arcy's excellent monograph, has remained outside the pale of Irish academic inspection.[4] However, a number of excellent narrative studies of racing have been published which were important in identifying personalities and trends and establishing contexts.[5] In the British context serious and extensive scholarly studies of the social and economic importance of flat racing have been undertaken.[6] Questions raised in these works, as well as issues examined in the detailed thematic approach of John Tolson, are explored in the Westmeath context.[7] Iris Maud Middleton has also produced a model local study of horseracing that has influenced some of the approaches to analysis adopted in this chapter.[8]

A surprisingly large number of racing meets were organised in Westmeath from the 1850s to the end of the century. At least one meet was organised in Mullingar or its hinterland annually. Three distinct phases of racing occurred at Kilbeggan: initially between 1840 and 1855; the second phase between 1879 and 1885 and a revived meeting that continues to the present day, began in 1901.[9] Racing was held over two periods in the Athlone district between 1857 and 1868 and between 1893 and 1905.[10] A meet was also staged at Moate beginning in 1889 but this was abandoned by 1899.[11] Only Mullingar managed to hold more than one meeting yearly and by 1903, the Newbrook racecourse was holding three meetings annually. The five-year aggregate totals for Westmeath racing events is illustrated in Figure 6.

The close connections between hunting and steeplechasing meant that many of the race meets were organised by clubs such as the Westmeath Hunt Club, the South Westmeath Hunt Club, or by an individual who possessed a pack of hounds. Members of the landed gentry with strong hunting associations organised small local meets at various venues. In March 1857, for example, on the lands of John Malone, near

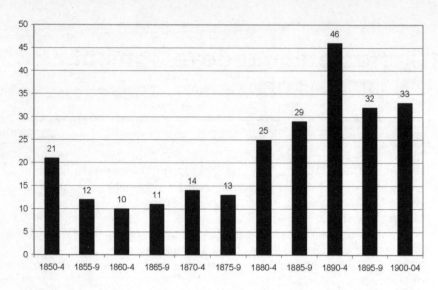

Figure 6. Frequency of race meetings organised in County Westmeath, 1850–1904

Ballymore, a three-event steeplechase meet was organised that featured an open sweepstake, a welter stakes confined to horses regularly hunted with any identifiable pack of foxhounds in Ireland, and a selling stakes.[12] Owners of private harriers also hosted small point-to-point or steeplechase meets. Cecil Fetherstonhaugh organised a two-event meet at Bracklyn in 1890 to entertain his hunting friends and to recognise supportive farmers. The winner of each race was presented with one of 'Whippy's best hunting saddles'.[13] Hunt club meets typically consisted of four events, the most important of which were a welter and a light-weight race confined to *bona fide* hunters (the property of members of the hunt club or family associates). Links between the hunting and the military communities were recognised by including amongst those eligible to compete officers quartered at Mullingar, Athlone or Longford, and Westmeath-based officers of the RIC who had subscribed to the funds of the hunt.[14] The importance of farmers to the hunting community was acknowledged by the inclusion of two farmers' races on a programme. In the 1890s, these races were included in the spring meet held at the Newbrook course in Mullingar.

The Westmeath Hunt Club also organised its own point-to-point meeting beginning in 1877.[15] The South Westmeath Hunt Club also organised an annual point-to-point meet at various venues in its hunting district in the 1890s. The meets, in the words of John Malone, one of Westmeath's leading hunting personalities, were organised where possible 'over a fine natural line of country calculated to test the merits of horse and man', and not over the 'so called steeplechase courses of the present-day . . . where there is not a fence that would test the capabilities of a good hunter or good rider'.[16] They provided the opportunity to

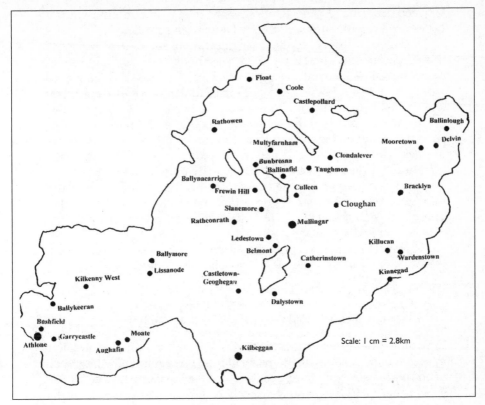

Figure 7. Venues of Westmeath race meetings, 1850–1905

enjoy 'steeplechasing as the sport was known in the early days, divested of much of the modern innovations'.[17] The races were a reaction against the increased professionalism of racing and in a different context, replicated the amateur–professional divisions evident in other sports.

The increased power of the central controlling authority, the Irish National Hunt Steeplechase Committee (INHSC), was such that by 1890 these races were regulated and by 1900 the Irish *Racing Calendar* included six regulatory point-to-point rules. Steeplechase rules, except those relating to illicit practices and disqualification, did not apply to these meets and no other races were allowed to take place in the hunting country on the same day. Organisers were forbidden to charge for entrance to any part of the course and flags were permitted only to identify turning points. The meets were held under the stewardship of the MFH and only one meet was allowed to each hunt club annually.[18] Riders in the hunt races had to be members of the hunt or their sons, or officers of a Westmeath based regiment that subscribed to the hunt.[19] Many of those who took part in these races also competed in the more formal and refined Westmeath Polo Club annual races that were held between 1881 and 1904 in the first year at Belmont and afterwards at Ledeston. The programme normally featured five races.

An important aspect of the racing culture of the county, especially during the late 1880s and early 1890s, was the £4 19s races. These were a reaction against the centralising tendencies of the INHSC. First prize was limited, to avoid the control of the central authorities whose remit was limited to races offering a minimum first prize of £5. Many districts in Westmeath organised these meets as can be seen from Figure 7. They were normally managed by a local committee of gentry, farmers and business people and were easily arranged because of the low value prize-money. Finance was raised by subscription and by imposing a levy on carriages entering the course. The Multyfarnham races of 1893 for instance charged cars 2s 6d on entrance while four wheelers paid 5s. Those who subscribed 10s to the race fund were admitted free. Other venues operated a similar system.[20]

These meetings had a reputation for doubtful practices. According to the *Westmeath Examiner* the Moate races of 1890 were races where

> there are no rules to bind owners and riders of horses at meetings of this description except such as the stewards may frame, and no penal-ties to be inflicted for infringing the rules of justice and fair play.[21]

In such an environment incidents of 'gross injustices and scandalous misbehaviour of some of the participants' were normal.[22] Eventually national problems with these events forced the INHSC to take action and in September 1893 the meets were declared illegal. Horses and riders that took part in these events from 1 January 1894 were suspended.

According to Fergus d'Arcy, a bifurcation trend had emerged in Irish race-meeting organisation by the end of the century. He distinguished between commercial and professional park courses and the semi-pro-fessional local meets. The former were organised and run as limited companies; the latter were organised by alliances of enthusiasts that included tradesmen, solicitors, doctors and gentry, with meets partly financed by subscriptions and door-to-door collections.[23] These trends were evident in Westmeath with the Kilbeggan and Athlone meets pro-moted by committees of enthusiastic locals, while the Mullingar meet from 1890 was promoted by a limited company established specifically for the purpose. The identity of thirty-three individuals who were active at committee level in organising and promoting the Athlone race meet between 1893 and 1900 has been established. The landowning classes were in a minority and were represented by the aristocratic Lord Castle-maine and also included F. T. Longworth-Dames, land agent R. A. Handcock and two 'gentlemen farmers', F. W. Russell and E. Wakefield. The higher status professionals dominated the committees over the period and included five doctors, four lawyers, three vets, a bank manager, a civil engineer and a newspaper editor. Businessmen formed the third category of committee representative and included two hoteliers, four general merchants, a timber merchant, three drapers, two publicans, a commercial traveller and a brewer's agent.[24] The Athlone experience illustrates how race management and organisation was transformed during the second half of the nineteenth century. It changed from an activity organised by landed elites for their own equestrian and social pleasures to one organised by the middle and professional classes, but still frequented by representatives of the landed gentry or those professionally engaged in the sport.

Racing during this period was dominated by steeplechasing and the majority of meets were held in the months of March and April as the hunting season concluded. The number of days over which races were run was initially associated with their status in terms of aristocratic or gentry attendance, number of entries received and the prize money offered.[25] In Westmeath, only Mullingar and Athlone supported two-day meets and these were abandoned in Athlone in 1866 and Mullingar in 1873, with racing thereafter confined to one-day events.[26] Steeplechases dominated a typical meet until the 1890s. Race meets held over the first two decades of this study were in all cases steeplechases and of 220 races held in Athlone and Mullingar between 1857 and 1875, 111 were raced over one- or two-mile heats.

	Steeplechase	Hurdle	Flat
Mullingar (N=231)	177	34	20
Athlone (N=61)	36	5	20
Kilbeggan (N=25)	11	6	8
Percentage of total	70.66	14.20	15.14

(N= total number of races held)

Table 3. Type of race organised in Mullingar, Athlone and Kilbeggan, 1890–1905

The close links between steeplechasing and racing had become considerably diluted by the end of the century as can be seen in Table 3. An analysis of the 231 races held at Newbrook from 1890 to 1905 is indicative of this change. The steeplechase category was still the most popular type of race held at the venue consisting of 77 per cent of all races. Hurdling was growing in popularity accounting for 15 per cent of the races and 8 per cent were flat races. Restrictions operated that confined entries in several races to defined categories of horse and encouraged entries from a wider group than that involved in steeplechasing. Races confined to maidens, to horses owned by farmers and tradesmen, to horses that had not won a minimum or maximum prize, and to hunters regularly hunted with defined packs were part of the programme. These events broadened the participant base but also provided a more varied and interesting programme for spectators. Greater professionalism and the increased importance of the professional trainer were further indicators of this trend. The pool of steeplechasers was no longer hunters schooled over natural fences in the hunting field but consisted of animals more likely to have been prepared by a specialist trainer.[27]

II

The most important race meeting in Westmeath in the late 1850s and 1860s was held between 1857 and 1868. It began when the resident landlord, Thomas Naghten, hosted a meet at his Thomastown Park demesne in March 1857,[28] but was transferred east of the Shannon to Garrycastle in 1858 where it survived until 1868.[29] This was a steeplechase meet featuring two main events, the Garrycastle Handicap and the Glynwood Hunt Challenge Cup. These were steeplechases raced over two circuits of the purpose built one-and-a-half-mile course. The Garrycastle Handicap allocated weights to the horses on the basis of their previous public form or the stewards' awareness of it. Additional penalties were imposed for horses winning a race after the publication of the weights, the scale of the penalty based on the value of the race won.[30] This type of race appealed to the racing fraternity because of the element of betting uncertainty inherent in the category. Owners had the opportunity of landing a gambling coup because a horse carried a lighter weight after its form had been concealed in earlier races, and appealed to bookmakers because they could sometimes profit through their access to betting information about such horses.[31] The Glynwood Hunt Challenge Cup was a weight for age event, with the weight carried allocated on the basis of the horse's age.[32]

Three other categories of races were also held. A race confined to farmers over whose land the Glynwood Hounds had hunted was organised on six occasions. Gentlemen farmers were excluded from these races and the inclusion of this type of race recognised the importance of the co-operation of the local farmer in facilitating the hunting activity of the south Westmeath gentry. Selling stakes were held on five occasions and were attractive to owners. There was the possibility of making money in a variety of ways, including selling the successful horse. An inferior horse in an inferior event could win prize-money and by a careful manipulation of the odds and form a betting profit could be achieved.[33] Three consolation races were held, an event as its title suggests, confined to runners who were unsuccessful at the meet. Organised by means of a sweepstake, with some prize-money added from the racing fund, consolation stakes encouraged owners to enter their horses in Athlone and presented them with an additional opportunity to win prize-money or land a gamble.

Races were normally decided over a number of heats. Only the Glynwood Cup, the Garrycastle Handicap and the 1860 Railway Plate were held as three-mile steeplechase events. On all other occasions events were decided by the first horse to win two heats of a one-and-a-half-mile race. Horses that finished more than a distance behind the winner in a heat were eliminated and up to a half-hour was allowed between heats for recovery. This type of event was attractive to both meet organiser and horse owner. The former was able to present an afternoon's racing using a small pool of horses. The requirement that horses had to race possibly four times before the winner was decided reduced the financial pressures on the meet patron. Owners who raced horses in these events also enjoyed benefits. An owner who had entered for an event decided over a series of heats had more than one opportunity of victory or winning a bet. The opportunity for a coup on one's horse was trebled or quadrupled in some cases.

The Garrycastle meet was primarily the work of one individual. The principal figure associated with the races was John Longworth, who inherited the Glynwood estate of 3,264 acres, 964 of which formed the private demesne, in 1854.[34] Longworth became involved in race promotion because of his hunting profile. As the master of the Glynwood Hounds he was one of the most important hunting personalities in the Irish midlands.[35] The Garrycastle races were, in essence, an event organised by a wealthy benefactor for the entertainment of his hunting colleagues. Longworth provided the venue for the meet and improved the course and facilities. Adjustments were made to the natural terrain of the course to reduce its degree of difficulty and to provide a safer racing environment for horse and rider. In 1863, six stone walls were removed and replaced with sunk and raised fences. Despite the intervention 'severe falls occurred during the running of the event'.[36] Spectating facilities were also improved. A stand house was constructed and later extended, a telegraph room erected and separate refreshment, stewards and jockey rooms provided.[37] Longworth also sponsored the two feature events of the meet, the Glynwood Hunt Challenge Cup valued at 100 sovereigns with fifty sovereigns added in specie and the Garrycastle Handicap with 100 sovereigns added by Mr Longworth.[38] The former event was confined to horses that had hunted with the Glynwood Hounds at least four times over the previous season. In 1865, in an attempt to encourage more owners to send their hunters to Athlone the event was opened to all horses hunted at least six times with any established pack of hounds in Ireland.[39]

The source of the prize-money paid out at the Garrycastle meets was identified using returns from the Irish *Racing Calendar*. The information is presented in Table 4 and it emphasises the importance of sweepstake contributions to the fund. Essentially, the Garrycastle race meeting was one in which wealthy individuals raced for prize-money, the majority of which was self-financed. Owners who competed or intended to compete subscribed a significant portion of the prize-money. Sweepstake contributions formed almost 28 per cent of the total prize-money of £3,563. From its inception in 1857 to the final meet in 1868, sixty-five different races were held at the Thomastown and Garrycastle venues. The majority of these were sweepstakes or combined a sweepstake contribution with some element of private patronage. Even the liberally funded Garrycastle Handicap and the Glynwood Hunt Challenge Cup regularly included a sweepstake of five sovereigns per person. This method was a simple system of ensuring a reasonable prize without each competitor having to subscribe a prohibitively large amount. It also created self-financed races without the patron or meet organisers having to provide the funding.

Not all those who entered horses presented themselves on the day of the event. Forfeits were payable in some cases to prevent this occurrence but did not always act as a deterrent. Handicap races were likely to experience the withdrawal phenomenon more than other events as owners, having examined the allotted weights, decided that the chance of a win was minimal and withdrew. The 1865 version of the Garrycastle Handicap had twelve subscribers but only eight runners; in 1866 nine subscribed but only six ran; twelve subscribed to a race that featured only four runners in 1867 and in the final running of the event fourteen subscribed to boost the prize fund of the five who ran on the day.[40]

	Stewards £	Sweep-stake £	Gentry sub-scription £	Railway con-tribution £	Unspeci-fied £	Athlone traders £
1857	60	28	—	—	10	—
1858	—	49	—	—	60	25
1859	35	86	—	20	115	30
1860	—	119	100	20	120	50
1861	10	85	100	20	155	50
1862	30	90	120	20	75	40
1863	10	140	100	20	75	40
1864	10	51	100	20	110	40
1865	10	126	100	20	75	40
1866	20	56	80	20	40	—
1867	20	86	110	20	40	—
1868	20	72	110	20	40	—
Total	225	988	920	200	915	315

— = zero subscription

Table 4. Source of prize-money, Thomastown and Garrycastle races, 1857–1868 (*Racing Calendar*, 1857–68)

Patronage by members of the landed gentry was the next most important source of prize-money, accounting for 26 per cent of the total. John Longworth subscribed £840 of the £920 total in this category. In 1862, Sir Charles Dunville presented twenty sovereigns for the running of the Moyvannon Stakes.[41] In 1867 and 1868, the Shinglass Stakes were held, financed by John Malone who presented thirty sovereigns to the event.

The final form of gentry patronage identified was the contribution made by the stewards to certain events. The initial Thomastown meet of 1857 featured races with contributions of sixty sovereigns by the stewards.[42] The unspecified category includes money described as 'added' in the race articles without specifying whether it was provided by the stewards or, as was more likely, sourced from the race funds.

Commercial sponsorship by the Athlone town traders (who were likely to benefit from the organisation of the races), and from the directors of the MGWR provided 14.45 per cent of the total. The MGWR first became involved in 1859 and its twenty sovereign sponsorship was conditional on an added contribution of ten sovereigns by the stewards, support that had increased to twenty sovereigns by 1866.[43] The railway company was obviously interested in carrying large numbers of spectators and transporting horses to the event and therefore insisted on the stewards boosting the prize-money for their event by donating to the company race. Ultimately, it was the failure of the commercial sector in Athlone to continue their subscriptions after 1865 that precipitated Longworth's decision to abandon the meet after 1868.

The race fund was created from the subscriptions of owners who raced horses at the meet. The basic subscription was the payment of an entry fee determined by the size of the first prize. The Garrycastle Handicap required a five sovereign entry fee with a three sovereign forfeit at the time of entrance. This event also required each person at the time of naming an entrant to pay two sovereigns to the race fund.[44] The winning owner was also responsible for a contribution to the race fund. The high value races demanded the highest donation. The Garrycastle Handicap winner in 1862 was required to pay eight sovereigns and the Glynwood Hunt Challenge Cup winner paid six sovereigns.[45] At this time there were no second prizes for owners of second-placed horses. The best a second-place owner could hope for was to have his stake fee refunded.[46] Selling races also provided a means of financing the race fund. In these races, the winning horse was auctioned immediately after the race for a predetermined minimum sum. Any price raised above the stipulated minimum was donated to the racing fund. In 1864, for example, Mr G. Coote's Maude was entered for the Railway Plate at a proposed selling price of £30 but having impressively won the race was auctioned for £50. The surplus of £20 was paid to the race fund.[47]

Analysis of the races held between 1857 and 1868 establishes that 118 individuals were responsible for the 275 different entries made over the period. The frequency with which they participated is illustrated in Appendix 6. The place of residence for seventy-five (64 per cent) of these owners has been identified. Owners from fourteen different counties were represented at the meet, with the majority coming from the west and northwest of Ireland. Geographical location was a major factor in determining participation, as owners from Galway, Roscommon and Westmeath were by far the most active at the races.[48] The size of the race purse was also important, as a number of owners who entered horses on a single occasion, did so in one of the two feature events. John Lanigan, an MP for Cashel, County Tipperary, brought his horse National Petition from Templemore, County Tipperary, to win the Garrycastle Handicap on the only occasion he competed at Athlone in 1865. Earlier in the week he had been a winner at Punchestown.[49] In 1860, the Marquis of Drogheda was successful in the same race on his only occasion to enter a horse at the meet, as was (in 1866) Mr Bell from Newbridge, County Kildare, on only his second occasion to race horses at the venue.[50]

The comprehensive railway links to Athlone enabled these owners from outside the immediate district to access the meet. Of these Mr O'Ryan from Cahir, County Tipperary, with six appearances, attended most often. Little Tiney was his favoured horse for the Athlone meet and was entered four times, which included one victory in the Garrycastle Handicap in 1859. The previous year this hunter was raced in Tipperary, Athlone, Carrick-on-Suir, Dungarvan and Armagh winning almost 200 sovereigns in the process.[51] Personal contact was likely to have been a factor in attracting O'Ryan to Garrycastle as Longworth's hunting network extended to Tipperary where he 'paid an annual visit to Roscrea for a week or ten days'.[52]

The confined nature of some of the races ensured that a significant proportion (25 per cent) of the owners were locals. The Glynwood Hunt Challenge Cup was until 1865, confined to members who hunted with the Longworth hounds, for a specified number of occasions, during the hunting season. Twenty members of the Longworth hunt competed in Athlone, as well as nine local farmers over whose lands the hounds were hunted. The majority of the owners with unidentified places of residence entered only one race at Garrycastle, and of these six were army officers (probably members of the Athlone garrison), and six entered the farmers' race. These individuals were unlikely to have been regular racing men and may have entered a race at their local meet for the pleasure and excitement of competing and for the opportunity it gave them to experience a social world from which they were normally excluded.

The two most active owners at Garrycastle possessed demesnes located within ten miles of the venue, and were immersed in the hunting and steeplechasing culture that was central to the lifestyle of some landed gentry.[53] The most important was J. M. Naghten from Thomastown demesne, located to the west of Athlone, where he owned 4,829 acres of land, the income from which provided the capital to support his racing and hunting stable.[54] Naghten was a member of an elite group of the landed gentry, who maintained a stable of quality racehorses and his own pack of hounds. In association with Longworth, he initiated and hosted the meet at his Thomastown demesne in 1857. He was the chief supporter of the meet, entering horses on thirty-five separate occasions. His stable at this time included a number of quality steeplechasers that were regularly raced nationally. In 1857, his horse Kate was raced at Ballymore (County Westmeath), at Thomastown, Elphin, Galway, Turrock and Roscommon, winning 152 sovereigns in total. Mr Naghten also used the horse in two match races with the Tipperary owner Mr O'Ryan.[55] In 1859, two of his horses, Thomastown and Blind Hookey, won 237 and 159 sovereigns respectively at venues such as Tullamore, Punchestown, Skerries, Fairyhouse, Kingstown, Carrickmacross, Ardee and Kilcock.[56] Naghten enjoyed his most successful year in 1860 when Nanny O'Leary won 212 sovereigns in ten appearances and Thomastown scored two significant wins from her eight racing appointments. At the Howth and Baldoyle Great Municipal Steeplechase, Thomastown was a winner of 148 sovereigns and topped this in the Kildare Hunt Steeplechase with a win of 300 sovereigns. In total, Naghten won 686 sovereigns in 1860.[57] Naghten's lack of success in the later 1860s illustrates the difficulty owners faced in attempting to turn out winners on a consistent basis. In the years between 1864 and 1868 his total earnings amounted to 288 sovereigns; he failed to earn any prize-money in 1865 or 1866.

John Malone was one of the leading landowners in County Westmeath, where he possessed 12,554 acres of land in 1875.[58] His sixteen runners made him the second most frequent racer of horses at Athlone. Malone was heavily involved in the world of hunting and was a leading figure in the Westmeath Hunt Club. He was the most successful owner to have competed at Garrycastle, winning on eight occasions including four times in the prestigious Glynwood Hunt Challenge Cup. He also competed nationally, winning 214 sovereigns with Nannie, in 1859, at Mullingar, Athlone, Athenry, Galway and Roscommon.[59] Next in importance was Denis Colohan of Ballinasloe, who raced horses on fifteen occasions. The Colohans were a property-owning Galway family, resident at Ballinasloe, with strong associations with the medical profession.[60] Christopher Ussher sent horses to Athlone on nine occasions between 1858 and 1861 and in that time was twice successful in the major events of the meet, winnng the Glynwood Hunt Challenge Cup and the Garrycastle Handicap. Ussher's land base was at Eastwell, Kinrinckle, County Galway, where he owned 3,666 acres of land with a rateable valuation of £1,781.[61]

Lord De Freyne was the most active aristocrat at the Athlone meet. He raced horses on six occasions and on every occasion except one, concentrated on the major events. De Freyne was one of the largest landowners in the country and possessed an estate of 34,400 acres valued at £13,584, at Frenchpark, County Roscommon. He also had 4,052 acres in Sligo and 328 in Galway.[62] He was a Protestant clergyman who 'kept race-horses from his boyhood', and reportedly attended every important race meeting. He worked to improve the breed of horses in Ireland by importing good sires from England and at his death he owned almost seventy horses and maintained his own pack of hounds.[63]

The Garrycastle meeting was ended in 1868 with the later years characterised by low levels of support. Contemporary newspapers suggested various reasons for this predicament. In 1862, the *Westmeath Independent* reported that 'the number of horses starting was very much below what might be expected'.[64] Four of the six events attracted only three entrants and Thomas Naghten's Nannie O'Leary faced the starter twice on the same day, running five heats over a distance of seven-and-a-half miles. In 1864, the scarcity of horses was attributed to the almost total cessation within 'the last few years' of breeding hunters and the proximity to the Punchestown meet.[65] The 1865 meet clashed with the opening of the Great Exhibition in Dublin.[66] One-day racing was introduced in 1866, but the clash with the Ardee meet impacted 'both as regards the attendance of sporting men and the number of horses starting'. In three of the races only three runners contested each race.[67] The Ardee meet, in contrast, was considered to be 'the most brilliant' meet held at the venue with 'the fields in each race very large', and 'sharp contests were the order of the day'.[68] The 1867 event suffered from a shared date with the Derby, which reduced 'speculation in the different events, the absence of nearly all the professionals in Surrey being a sufficient cause'.[69] Small fields were a characteristic feature of this local meet and in 71 percent of the races five horses or less faced the starter. In twenty of the sixty-five races held between 1857 and 1868, two or three horses competed; twenty-six of the races were contested by either four or five horses and only two races attracted fields of ten or eleven horses.

The Athlone experience was part of a broader trend of decline experienced nationally between 1862 and 1864. However, this was confined to the early 1860s and the situation changed sharply in the later 1860s as the number of races held, horses raced and available prize-money increased. (This is illustrated in Appendix 7.)

It has been suggested that violence at the meet was responsible for bringing the meet to an end.[70] This was not a peculiarly local or indeed Irish phenomenon. Wray Vamplew has pointed out that almost any event in Victorian England where large groups of people gathered could result in crowd disorder and, in particular, spectators frequently got out of control at mid-Victorian race meets.[71] According to the reminiscences of a special contributor, published in the *Westmeath Guardian* in May 1899, violence at the Garrycastle meet in 1868 resulted in Longworth banning racing from his course. According to this account the final meet 'was disgraced by a faction fight of more than ordinary fierceness which is alleged to have resulted in several deaths'. An army officer from Athlone died from injuries received from a riding accident at the water jump, the peasants 'brutally assaulted a jockey who was riding to the winning post' and in one race the 'whole field dashed wildly through the spectators, occasioning a number of accidents'.[72] Spectator control was a problem in all unenclosed courses and the racecourse provided a convenient meeting place for factions to conduct their ritualised violent affrays. These incidents, the contributor incorrectly believed, forced the patron John Longworth to abandon racing at Garrycastle.

Inadequate financial resources were the main factor in the decline of the meet and, in particular, the ending of commercial support after 1866 when the Athlone traders ceased to contribute, convinced John Longworth that the time had arrived to abandon the event. The Ardee meeting of 1866 mentioned above provides a clear illustration of the extent to which the Garrycastle meet was financially challenged. Excluding sweepstake money, this two-day event offered prize-money of 420 sovereigns at a time when Garrycastle offered 160 sovereigns.[73] After the final meet, the *Irish Times* commented on the decline of the races from 'one of our crack meets' to what was 'merely the semblance of one' in 1868. This was due to the 'diminution in the sums added' and the commentator recommended that 'the sooner the gentry of Westmeath put their heads together and exert themselves towards improving matters, the better for the credit of the county'.[74] The Westmeath gentry never put their heads together as their recreational world was focused towards the east of the county.

The Garrycastle meet was a transitional one, positioned between the unregulated pounding cross-country steeplechase matches of the early decades and the commercially-driven, centrally-regulated events of the later decades of the century. As an event, it was closer in spirit to the tenets of modern sports organisation than the early nineteenth-century events. The development of a purpose-built racecourse with consideration for the safety of horse and rider and the construction of accommodation for spectator comfort are indicative of a growing modernisation. The races were part of what was a national circuit for some owners but in which each event operated independently and free of the influence of a controlling authority. They depended on local owners for their main support but they also attracted support from outside the immediate locality. The local stewards independently organised the management of the races. This freedom was about to change and two of the major processes that characterise the development of Victorian sport – codification and the establishment of a national controlling authority – transformed the nature and management of steeplechase racing in the final quarter of the century.

III

Henry Moore, the third Marquis of Drogheda, was the key contributor to the formulation of a code of rules for steeplechase racing, which he 'published as a comprehensive canon' in the Irish *Racing Calendar* in 1866. He was also the central figure in the formation of the INHSC in 1870, the controlling body for that branch of the sport in Ireland.[75] The

Turf Club was established in the 1780s but in the first century of its existence its claim to any kind of authority outside the Curragh district was essentially based on agreement with the local organising committee.[76] Its powers were incrementally increased from the 1830s, and gradually its role was changed from a body that exercised informal influence to one of positive control.[77] According to Fergus D'Arcy 'the decisive occasion when the Turf Club assumed the role of general law-giver' was the first meeting held under the chairmanship of the Marquis of Drogheda in October 1866. On this occasion a major revision of the rules of racing was undertaken. In particular the power of the Turf Club stewards was extended nationally. Rule 42 decreed that a suspension sentence passed upon a jockey could not be remitted by the local stewards without the authority of a steward of the Turf Club. In the following two years this control was extended to include other racing personnel and was solidified with the extension of the licensing system for riders, trainers and officials.[78] In 1891, the 'Turf Club's bid for power' was completed when the rule that required all racecourses to be licensed and all meetings sanctioned by the stewards of the Turf Club, was passed.[79] This legislation brought fixtures and their management under the authority of the Turf Club. In the final quarter of the nineteenth century the organisation's control over racing personnel – trainers, jockeys and its own officials including starters, judges, clerks of the scales, clerks of courses and handicappers – was also extended.[80]

Members of the Irish Turf Club took a close interest in the evolution of rules for steeplechasing in England where a set of steeplechase rules was finally accepted in the early 1860s and a controlling body – the National Hunt Committee – was established in 1866.[81] The Marquis of Drogheda played the leading role in adapting the English regulations to Irish conditions. He inspired the publication of the 'Grand National Steeple-Chase Rules 1864' in the Irish *Racing Calendar*. The rules were identical to the English ones with two exceptions made for local conditions.[82] These were little more than guidelines for local stewards as there was no controlling body to enforce them. Drogheda used his authority to progress matters further and in 1869 he formulated proposals for the setting up of the Irish National Hunt Steeplechasing Committee. Seventeen gentlemen prominently involved in the sport were nominated by him as the first committee and were accepted as such by the Turf Club stewards. The first meeting of the new organisation was held in 1870 and its relationship with the Turf Club was regularised with the appointment of the Keeper of the Match Book, R. J. Hunter, as secretary of the new organisation.[83] The codification of the sport that followed can be measured by examining the rules and regulations governing steeplechasing published in the *Racing Calendar*. In 1866 the canon of regulations included seventy-three rules; by 1877 the number had increased to 160; to 184 by 1894 and this remained constant until 1905.[84] The Turf Club and the INHSC had moved from a permissive to a prohibitive control over Irish racing between the 1860s and 1890s.[85]

IV

As racing became more regularised it also became more commercialised. A limited company was established in Mullingar in 1890 to promote the sport. The role of the limited company as a vehicle for promoting sport has received little attention in Irish historiography. Fergus D'Arcy makes reference to the importance of the limited company in Irish racing towards the end of the 1890s but any attempt to identify or analyse the companies involved was outside his terms of reference.[86] Irish publicly-owned companies were of limited importance in the management of sport. At least three football clubs – Cliftonville in 1889, Belfast Celtic in 1901 and Glentoran in 1902 – were launched as limited liability companies. In Belfast also, the Ulster Cricket Club was floated in 1898 in order to raise money for a new ground. Apart from Neal Garnham's football analysis, the social profile and motivation of individual shareholders who invested in Irish sport has been ignored.[87]

In contrast, the motivation of those who invested in limited companies as a means of promoting British sport, has received considerable scrutiny by economists and social historians. Some analysts have regarded the desire to profit from the growth in spectator interest as the primary motive for investment. James Walvin suggests that those who invested in sports stadia were those who realised that there was 'money to be made by providing the right kind of leisure facilities'.[88] Charles Korr's examination of West Ham football club emphasises the importance of the profit motive behind developments.[89] Other and more empirical analyses suggest that the desire for personal financial gain was not a primary consideration. Wray Vamplew's and Tony Mason's examination of the nature of shareholders and their assessment of the management of football club activities, concludes that personal financial gain was unimportant and that surplus income was channelled into ground improvements and producing successful teams.[90]

The directors and shareholders of the Westmeath (Mullingar) Racing Company Limited replicated the management and investment practices of the football club directors as identified by Vamplew and Mason. The company was launched in early 1890 with a share-capital target of £2,500 to be raised by the issue of £1 shares. The objectives of the company were outlined in the published prospectus. The company aimed to 're-establish the famous old racecourse at Newbrook, near Mullingar', and to promote steeplechasing and flat racing. Promoting activities such as athletic sports, cricket and 'other amusements', as well as 'agricultural, horse and other shows', and the organisation of 'sales for horses and stock in or near the town of Mullingar' were other potential revenue-generating possibilities outlined. Stud and other farming on the lands of

Newbrook were also suggested as commercial possibilities. The proposed new company had obtained the tenant's interest in the land that had formed the chief venue for Mullingar racing since 1852.[91]

The seven-man board of directors, who held shares of a minimum value of £25 each, consisted of significant landed and business interests in the town and its hinterland.[92] Lord Greville, residing at Clonhugh, Mullingar, was company chairman. Greville was the proprietor of the town of Mullingar and held extensive landed interest in the county as well as in Roscommon, Cavan, Cork, Longford and Kent.[93] The board also included three gentlemen who were the proprietors of substantial landed estates in the county: Captain Ralph Smith, Gaybrook, Mullingar, owned 6,287 acres; Colonel J. R. Malone, Rath, Ballynacarrigy*, possessed 12,554 acres and Captain Cecil Fetherstonhaugh, Bracklyn, Killucan, controlled 4,711 acres. Commercial interests on the board were represented by John W. Gordon, proprietor of Mullingar's leading drapery store; Christopher Downes, a Mullingar based lawyer; Joseph P. Dowdall, a Dominick Street leather dealer and seed merchant and Owen O'Sullivan, a publican and proprietor of one of Mullingar's most important horse repositories. The final director was Eugene Salmon, a landowner with a history of involvement in field sports. Salmon farmed three areas of land of 121 acres, 65 acres and 69 acres in extent with a combined valuation of £182 10s.[94] Involvement in hunting and steeplechasing bound these men together. Greville, at the time the company was formed, was MFH in Westmeath. Malone, Fetherstonhaugh and Smith were key figures in the hunting community. Downes, Gordon and Dowdall had significant business dealings with that particular community and O'Sullivan, as a proprietor of a horse repository, conducted substantial business with hunting folk. They may have been inspired by a group of businessmen who set up the Leopardstown Club in 1888 with a capital of £20,000 and launched the Leopardstown race meet as a south Dublin rival to the older established Baldoyle meeting.[95]

The original list of shareholders has not survived but according to the *Westmeath Examiner* it was representative of all classes: 'the principal shareholders belonged to the town' with 'many of the shopkeepers acting most generously in the number of shares subscribed for [sic]', a development that was likely to 'enhance the trade of the town to a considerable extent'.[96] The buoyancy of the Mullingar economy, the status and influence of the board of directors and the desire to have a regular race meeting in the town was such that 350 oversubscribed the share issue.

Directors and shareholders identified from newspaper reports of the company's annual general meeting are listed in Appendix 8 as well as the nature of their business. Unfortunately, the value of shareholding held by each is not identifiable, so that no conclusions can be made on the proportion of shares held by the different social groups. Of the

---

* Ballynacarrigy is the correct spelling although 'Ballynacargy' is in general usage.

forty-one shareholders identified all except one were local residents. Aristocratic and gentry involvement excluding the directors included Sir Walter Nugent, a second member of the Fetherstonhaugh family, Percy O'Reilly (who was also a director of the MGWR in the 1890s) and E. T. F. Briscoe. The remainder of the shareholders were drawn from the business and professional classes of the town. The group included a number of doctors, lawyers, six grocery and spirit dealers (whose business might be expected to benefit from the crowds drawn to the town for the race meets), as well as the proprietors of two of the town's leading drapery supply stores. Several of the identified shareholders were also politically active and held elected office as either town commissioners or district councillors. Their role and self-image as community leaders and promoters of local development would have required that their support be given to the racing company.

The directors operated the principle of profit-maximisation in their management of the company, a profit that was initially re-invested in further development. They were cost conscious and appreciated that profits were a function of both revenue and expenditure.[97] The launch of the company was accompanied by the promise of dividend payments to investors. The prospectus suggested that a net profit of £125 was sufficient to pay a five per cent dividend.[98] Despite these promises, the directors operated a strict policy of re-investing profits in the early years. No dividend was issued to shareholders until 1904. The first annual general meeting established a financial management policy that was continued throughout the period of this study. Profits of £72 9s 10d and £123 were generated in the first two years of trading. These were sufficient to pay close to the suggested dividend but this option was rejected and the profits were transferred to the capital account. This policy reduced the need to make a further call on the shares and allowed a working fund to accumulate.[99] The result was that nearly 7 per cent was added to the value of the subscribed capital. The loss-making autumn meets of 1890 (£7 7s 10d) and 1891 (£53 16s 3d) were promptly dropped from the annual programme.[100]

The executive transformed the Newbrook venue into one of the best in a provincial town and developed the infrastructure over its first fifteen years. The course was re-modelled and weaknesses were eliminated. Their initial task was to prepare the course for the opening major meet of June 1890. The sum of £450 was invested in obtaining title to the lands of the course. The course was enlarged and the finishing straight extended by 'the acquisition of a racetrack from Miss Donlon's' farm for a period of fifty years. Mullingar building contractors G.W. Scott erected the stand and offices, buildings that 'could not be surpassed in this country for both appearances and usefulness', with their solid nature assuring 'perfect safety to visitors'. Extensive track improvements were carried out that required considerable levelling and drainage work. Access from the town to the racecourse was also improved.[101]

Commentators attached to the national press provided positive views of the new developments. In August 1890, the correspondent of *Sport* on a visit to the course 'recognised a fairy palace arisen in the place of the rotten old wooden scaffolding that used to represent the Grand Stand at Newbrook'. The complex now included twelve horseboxes, a jockeys' dressing room with 'a dozen lockers for colours, saddles, cloths etc.', a pressroom, 'a fully appointed telegraph office', a members' stand that resembled 'the Vice-regal box at Leopardstown' and a refreshment bar. Extensive drainage work was undertaken. 'The treacherous old bog' on the approach to the regulation fence was removed. Modern land reclamation techniques were used to renovate this area of ground. Two thousand tons of soft peat were dug up and were replaced by a layer of stones topped by a layer of gravel and this in turn was covered by 'half a foot of best upland clay'.[102] Additional tenurial security was obtained in 1891 when the lands of Clonmore were secured on a long-term lease, which allowed the management to develop a flat course that was used for the first time in October 1891.[103] In June 1896, a three-acre site had been enclosed and converted to show yards suitable for the holding of horse and agricultural shows and athletic events. Five permanent jumps were constructed including a fly jump, a narrow bank, a double, a stonewall and water jump. A stand was erected along one wall of the enclosure and comprehensive stabling of a hundred stalls and fifteen loose boxes was available.[104] The development of the Horse Show Grounds paved the way for the holding of an annual horse show in Mullingar. The first was held in June 1894, in which three jumping competitions were held and a variety of competitions were organised that catered for seventeen different classes of horse.[105] The venue later hosted athletic events as well as hurling, football and soccer matches.

Throughout the early 1900s the directors continued to invest in course improvement. In 1900, for example, a new road was laid down from the entrance gate to the grandstand.[106] The autumn meeting of 1905 featured a seven-furlong flat track, commended for its speed and safety, which was used for the running of the Lough Ennell Plate.[107] A new series of buildings in the enclosure were also in use for the first time at this meet. These included separate dressing room apartments, which separated the professional jockeys and gentlemen riders, opening directly to the weigh rooms, as well as additional press facilities. These enabled 'the exclusion of all who have not business or right to be in these apartments' and 'an amount of annoyance, overcrowding and confusion is avoided'.[108] Work on the construction of a new stand for owners and trainers was also in progress.[109] The revised valuation of the buildings on the course provided a measure of the extent of the improvements carried out. In 1891 the buildings were valued at £1 10s but by 1904 they were assessed at £60.[110] The value of the capital assets of the company had also increased, and at the end of the 1905 season, it was also able to show a balance of over £3,000 in the reserve fund.[111]

The policy of investing profits in course infrastructure required that the company use traditional fundraising methods, similar to those used by the enthusiastic volunteer committees of other venues, to generate prize-money. The Town Plate depended on voluntary subscriptions, initially enthusiastically donated by the traders, but as the decade progressed, subscribed with increased reluctance. The subscription pattern of an initial burst of enthusiasm followed by years of decline repeated the trend of the 1870s and 1880s. At the initial shareholders meeting, Lord Greville was fulsome in his praise of 'the town commissioners and other public-spirited men of Mullingar for their generous subscriptions and the support they have generally given'.[112] This generosity however was temporary; the 1891 accounts reported a shortfall of £11 9s 6d of subscriptions to the town and traders' plate.[113] In 1892 the directors complained that 'small country meetings have received more support in their own localities than [that given by] the inhabitants of this large and prosperous town', despite the fact that 'the races brought a great number of people to the town who had to eat something, get wearing apparel and all these things were to be purchased in Mullingar'.[114] An attempt to revive the autumn meeting in 1893 was abandoned when the town commissioners failed to respond to the communications of the company directors. This prompted Lord Greville to suggest that

> It must really be understood by the wealthy inhabitants of this town that unless they help us, not only shall we more or less come to grief, but I venture to say that it would be desirable from a pecuniary point of view, . . . because if they give us contributions to enable us to have another meeting in the year it will bring a large number of people into the town, and they won't go out of it without spending money and if they spend their money it must be a very good thing for the trades-people, merchants and others in this town.[115]

Those who supported the meet were rewarded by the publication of their names and the amount of their subscription in the local press. These lists provide clear evidence that Lord Greville and his co-directors were justified in their condemnation of the level of support from the commercial elements of the town. Over 230 individuals and business people subscribed to the Town Plate between 1890 and 1896.[116] With sixty-five different drink and food dispensing establishments subscribing, the licensed grocers and vintners was the most supportive grouping. This group subscribed 32 per cent of the total amount of £377 11s collected, and their contributions ranged from 40 per cent of the total subscribed in 1892 to 25 per cent in 1891. A second commercial group with a strong vested interest in the success of the races was that of draper and milliner, and eleven traders provided support to the fund. Two of these, shareholder James Doyne, and director J. W. Gordon, were particularly generous and regularly topped the list of contributors. Doyne contributed

£19 to the fund over the period and Gordon £17. A race meeting had considerable commercial potential for drapers as an advertisement placed by the management of Wallis's drapery store pointed out in 1891: 'at no social gathering is a badly dressed person more noticeable than at a race meeting. A good pipe and a handsome walking stick are necessary requirements to a well-dressed man'.[117] Social etiquette imposed rigorous sartorial standards on those who frequented the grandstand.

The total amount collected annually declined sharply over a six-year period. In 1890, the commercial men of Mullingar contributed £83 4s 6d but the 1891 collection decreased to £58 14s 6d. This pattern continued for the rest of the period. This happened despite the positive impact the hosting of the races had on the local economy. At the June 1890 meet the *Westmeath Examiner* reported 'that the shops of every class, from the hotels down to the humblest eating houses were packed', and 'judging from the numbers of people in the shops around, purchasing and spending, from a financial point of view the Newbrook race meeting must have been as good to the business people of the town as three or four fairs'.[118] The problem faced by the directors was that consistent support was lacking, with a high turnover rate evident among subscribers.

A number of factors may explain reluctant financial support for the race meets as the 1890s progressed. The likelihood was that those who were expected to subscribe had already supported racing by becoming shareholders. Race organisers faced competition from other sports organisers. As can be seen in Chapter 3, members of the bicycle club promoted a major athletics meet in the 1890s and depended on the support of the business classes for its success. The merchant class of the town also organised their own form of conspicuous recreation from 1894 onwards when an annual regatta – traditionally one of the great forms of gentry and aristocratic summer recreation – was promoted at Lough Belvedere [Ennell].[119] The regatta provided a more 'respectable' recreational outlet than the race meet. Here middle-class respectability was the order of the day:

> Town-folk can spend a most enjoyable time, a well-spent time, without being deafened by the eternal shouts and the exhaustless chatter of the ring. At a regatta people are not jostled about by perhaps shady specimens of humanity and are not tempted on 'hearing a straight thing' by putting 'a bit on'.[120]

The organising committee of the regatta was formed from some of the main commercial men of the town, a committee of similar social structure to those active in organising race meets in Athlone and Kilbeggan. The limited company established to promote racing in Mullingar liberated these individuals to organise their own form of recreation and, as a result, a regatta at Lough Belvedere became an almost permanent feature of the Mullingar social calendar.

The uncertainty of commercial support encouraged the directors to convert the Mullingar meet to a gate meet, where spectators would be charged for admission, by erecting an enclosing wall around the course. This was first suggested in 1893 and overdraft facilities of £1,800 were negotiated with the Hibernian Bank.[121] Enclosure would also make it possible to extend the range of events hosted at the course. These included coursing meets 'on which they [the directors] expected to make considerable profit', horse and agricultural shows, football matches and other games.[122] The death of the landlord P. N. Fitzgerald in 1893 halted these plans and negotiations were re-opened with the agent of the estate that ended with the purchase of the landlord's interest in the Newbrook lands.[123] The purchase cost led to the temporary abandonment of the proposed enclosure. A permanent improvement account was then set up and the annual profits were henceforth paid into this account.[124] The plan was revised in 1901 and at a special meeting held on 15 July 1901 the shareholders approved the funding of the development by the issue of 2,000 £1 preference shares, limited to the original shareholders, and the shares bearing a special preference cumulative interest of 5 per cent annually.[125] At the same time negotiations were conducted with the MGWR Company to erect a siding that allowed direct access to the racecourse for visitors and horses travelling by rail. Agreement was reached in early 1902 and the work was completed the following year.[126] The commercialisation and commodification of racing was completed in the early part of 1903 when the surrounding wall was completed and the spring meeting of 1903 became the first gate meeting held in Westmeath.

The conversion allowed the directors to recommend the payment of a 5 per cent share dividend to both categories of shareholders for the first time in 1904. The directors, particularly the managing directors, were also remunerated following some debate on the most appropriate method of reward. The suggestion that a fixed sum of £50 be paid annually to the directors was rejected in favour of a payment of 10 per cent of the net profits with half of this sum being paid to the managing directors. Supporters of the former option favoured providing more resources for prize-money to induce 'the owners of valuable horses to bring them to Mullingar'.[127] However, at the 1905 annual general meeting, the fixed sum option of rewarding directors was adopted. It was felt that the percentage of net profits option was insufficient to recompense the directors for their input to the organising and managing of races, the racecourse and events.[128] The debate was somewhat academic as the Directors' Plate with prize-money of £150 was the feature event of the June meets from 1903 onwards and, in effect, the directors returned their fees.

The conversion of the Mullingar racing meet to a gate one had important implications for the organisation of the races. The era of the free show was ended and extra funds were placed at the disposal of the race company. Those managing the turnstiles did so with exemplary zeal and according to *Sport*, complaints were made that the men employed were not familiar with those entitled to free admission and in 'one instance a steward of the meeting would not be allowed pass'.[129] The additional finance generated allowed the directors to abandon revenue-generating activities that damaged the course. Cattle grazing was ended in 1903 and as a result the course 'enjoyed a large supply of herbage' and the improved safety encouraged owners to race their horses at the 1903 summer meet despite the long spell of dry weather experienced.[130]

By 1905 the nature of the Mullingar races had been transformed. The immediate impact of enclosure was an increase in annual prize-money as the directors attempted to attract large crowds and good quality horses. The amount on offer increased by 73 per cent from £565 to £975 between 1902 and 1905. The spring and autumn meets were regularised and these meets were the major beneficiaries of the additional revenue. The available prize-money at the autumn meet was increased by 59 per cent from £195 to £310 while the spring meet money was almost quadrupled. The impact was perhaps most clearly evident in the transformation of the spring meet from a typical hunt club meet to one that was open and commercially driven. In 1905, fifty horses took part in a meet that offered total prize-money of £265 and also offered the Greville Cup valued at 100 sovereigns and the similarly valued Westmeath Hunt Cup.[131] The Directors' Plate of £150 became the feature event of the June meet from 1903 onwards and replaced the Town Plate and its financial uncertainties. In 1905, the *Westmeath Examiner* claimed that

> From a pleasant and large but entirely provincial meeting in character, the Mullingar races have been raised to a level in which the pleasure is enhanced by increased accommodation and good order, the interest augmented by the attraction of the best class of horses to the contests, and the importance of the fixture brought to a grade where Newbrook ranks practically in all respects, but proximity to the city – as a metropolitan course.[132]

Success was reflected in the growth in the annual profits. The gross profits for 1905 were £1,035 12s and gave a net return of £661 15s.[133]

Mullingar now offered greater prize-money than provincial towns of similar status. In 1904, the Mullingar summer meet offered a prize-fund of £415, far greater than towns such as Claremorris (£137), Ballinasloe (£233), Ballinrobe (£131), Enniscorthy (£152) and Thurles (£205).[134] The Mullingar races had been transformed 'from a mere local event' to 'one of first rate importance' and 'one of the foremost and most popular in Ireland'.[135]

V

In this context, the impact of the railway on the development of racing is worthy of consideration. The contribution of railways to the development of racing has been the subject of some debate among British sports historians. The railways revolutionised racing according to Wray Vamplew and transformed many local meetings into national events that attracted both horses and spectators from all over the country. More horses were raced and the coming of the railway line was responsible for increased prize-money.[136] Fergus D'Arcy has expressed similar opinions in relation to Irish racing.[137] Neil Tranter also believes the sport was transformed, in the third quarter of the nineteenth century, by the effect of rail travel on the interested parties 'from a localised activity of mediocre standard to a thoroughly commercial and professional recreation based around a calendar of major meetings from all parts of the country'. Proximity to a railway station soon became crucial to the success of a course.[138] According to Denis Brailsford the railway was 'a main factor in the success or failure of individual meetings'.[139] More recent and detailed analysis conducted by John Tolson has challenged these conclusions. Tolson concludes that change in flat racing came from within the sport itself and was made possible when the post-1870 Jockey Club 'made its previous tenuous control a reality' and totally reshaped the industry in the final decades of the century. The role of the railway was one that 'facilitated and assisted certain trends and events'.[140]

Evidence from Westmeath would tend to support the Tolson thesis. The development of the Westmeath railway infrastructure has been outlined in the Introduction.[141] Racing in Mullingar experienced difficulties in the 1870s and particularly in the 1880s despite the proximity of the course to the railway station, and it was only when the limited company was established that the races were permanently revived and then transformed. Crucially, this company provided a designated racing venue in Mullingar and this specialised setting ended uncertainty regarding the promotion of races and allowed the development of a summer meet where previous events were generally confined to end of hunting season meets. The development of a national controlling body made this factor more important as courses had to be sourced, inspected and approved, prior to the completion of the national fixture list. When a suitable venue was sourced in Athlone in 1897 and 1904 the most appropriate dates had been allocated. As a result, the organising committee was forced to abandon their intended meets.

An individual, whose primary business depended on railway-generated trade rather than the rail company, initially influenced the development of racing in the town. Patrick Costello was the proprietor of the refreshment saloon at the Mullingar station and was conscious of the commercial potential of race promotion to his primary business.[142] In 1850 and 1851, Costello was involved in the promotion of a race meet at ·

Lynn, located about two miles from the railway terminus. He developed improved spectator facilities and for the 1851 meet he constructed a stand-house to accommodate at least 2,000 people with an interior divided into two saloons supplied 'with all the good things to which field sports are supposed to give a peculiar relish'.[143] The MGWR offered cheap return fares in 1851 and for the 1852 meet the first special train to serve a Westmeath race-meet was dispatched from Dublin with 200 passengers on board.[144] Despite Costello's entrepreneurial zeal and rail company support, both meets failed as spectator events.

Costello believed that this was partly due to the inconvenience of the journey from the station to the racecourse and he developed a new venue for the 1852 meet. He obtained a lease on lands at Newbrook, located much closer to the terminus, and fitted them out with the normal racecourse infrastructure that included a stand house, saloons that stocked 'every description of refreshment' and an enclosure reserved in the stand house specifically for ladies. A new link road to the course was built, and passengers on the trains from Galway and Dublin were able to disembark on a special platform built by the MGWR directors close to the stand house.[145] The new course was considered to be one of the best in Ireland and consisted of a two-mile circuit of fourteen fences that included six water jumps 'of a fair hunting character'.[146] The 1852 two-day meet offered Costello additional commercial opportunities as each night many of the racing gentlemen attended the ordinaries, at Costello's railway saloon.[147] Costello's involvement was unashamedly commercial with his investment designed to exploit the opportunities the new rail system provided to the racing community. He maintained his involvement until the mid-1870s by which time he combined the duties of secretary, treasurer and clerk of the course, and during which time he continued to invest in course and infrastructure improvement.[148]

At this time, the Westmeath Hunt Club began to organise steeplechases and with Costello apparently based in Dublin, the Newbrook annual meet became uncertain. The 1875 and 1876 meets failed to take place. The revived meet of 1877 was helped by the fact that Percy Nugent Fitzgerald was the new tenant of the Newbrook course and he combined the duties of secretary, treasurer and clerk of the course.[149] Fitzgerald was based in Multyfarnham, about six miles from Mullingar, and was involved in racing, breeding and hunting.[150] Criticism of a 7s 6d entry fee to the stand house encouraged Fitzgerald to outline some of the difficulties and expense involved for the racing promoter. A proper stand house had to be provided, loan ground purchased, stake money guaranteed, damage to farm land repaired in addition to the funding of a variety of incidental labour and other expenses.[151] Despite the fact that the 1882 meet was considered to be 'one of the most successful meetings ever held over the celebrated Newbrook course', the committee experienced difficulty in financing the annual Newbrook meet for the remainder of the decade.[152] The 1884 and 1885 events failed to take place and this prompted the town commissioners to organise an event for 1886. The enthusiasm of the commissioners was exhausted and this meeting was the last organised in Mullingar during the 1880s. Despite the proximity to the railway station, difficulties with organising finance, the maintenance of course infrastructure and problems with reaching agreement with the course proprietor proved insurmountable.

The fate of the Newbrook meet during the 1880s supports the summary of Huggins and Tolson that 'closure was usually linked with refusal to renew a lease, the withdrawal of upper-class support, building development, poor entries or the death of a major organiser and supporter rather than with poor attendance'.[153] The demise of the Garrycastle meet analysed earlier in this chapter provides similar supportive evidence. In the nineteenth century, mass spectator attendance wasn't an important factor in racecourse viability, as entrance was free for the majority of those attending. It wasn't until 1903, when the Mullingar meet became fully commercialised, that the role of the railway in transporting large numbers of spectators to the June meet in particular, became important in the promotion of the Mullingar races.

The introduction of commercial sponsorship associated with railway development in Ireland was considered by Fergus D'Arcy to be of 'major benefit' to Irish racing.[154] Rail company support of the Mullingar races was first given in March 1849 when the MGWR directors ordered that '£25 be placed at the disposal of the Revd. Mr. Savage, Mullingar, as its contribution to the Mullingar steeplechase'.[155] This contribution was increased in 1853 when the directors subscribed a sum of £30 to the race fund.[156] The MGWR board, according to D'Arcy, more generously supported Irish racing than other companies, as its directors included many personalities deeply involved in racing.[157] The Westmeath influence on the board of directors included members of the Nugent, Rochfort and O'Reilly families, all strongly associated with the racing business. While D'Arcy produces no supporting statistics to confirm the claim of MGWR benevolence, the overall contribution by rail companies to national racing sponsorship was quite small. In 1876, rail companies contributed £632 10s or just 2 per cent, to the total national race prize-money of £30,502. In 1901, this sponsorship had increased to £903 but proportionally had declined to only 1.76 per cent.[158]

The impact of railway sponsorship on prize-money in Westmeath was more significant. The Mullingar meet was the chief beneficiary. In the period between 1890 and 1905 a total of £10,248 was available in prize-money in the county and of this, £515 or 5.02 per cent was provided by the MGWR company in direct sponsorship of a railway plate. The Garrycastle meet during the period 1857 to 1868 received £200 in direct sponsorship from the MGWR, a sum that amounted to 5.6 per cent of the total prize-money of £3,563. However, MGWR sponsorship was more important than the above quantification. The MGWR offered special deals to owners for the transport of horses to and from the Athlone and Mullingar meets and also subscribed to the fund for the Athlone races in the 1890s. In 1899, for instance, in addition to providing a range of special excursion trains the company offered to subscribe £5 to the race funds or 5 per cent of their total race related receipts whichever was greater.[159]

The rail link was also crucial in extending the hinterland of the Mullingar course. An analysis of the addresses of those who raced horses at Newbrook at the summer meet illustrates the importance of this aspect. Horses owned by 292 different owners competed in Mullingar at this meet. The place of residence of 191 of these has been identified and their level of participation is illustrated in Appendix 9.[160]

The county base of the identified non-residents is illustrated in Figure 8. The well-developed railway network provided access to Mullingar, from all parts of the country. Distance was no longer an obstacle to those who wished to race a horse in the town. Therefore, owners from twenty-six different counties raced horses in Mullingar, some from places as distant as Waterford, Londonderry, Tyrone, Mayo, Antrim and Cork. The main group of identified non-Westmeath owners came from three eastern counties: thirty-four owners were from Dublin and twenty-four each were Kildare or Meath residents.

Racing, with the development of the enclosed course at Mullingar and the establishment of a limited company to promote the sport and develop course infrastructure, became an industry. It was now part of the economic order, rather than part of the landed gentry social scene. Greater specialisation of tasks had emerged. Trainers were now a well-established part of the racing scene and jockeys were licensed professionals. Trainers were the most important part of the group who raced horses at the June meet at Mullingar. Their role had become increasingly important; according to Sargent since the early 1860s when 'men have given up by degrees home-training'.[161] They are also a reflection of the entry of men to the sport who had earned their money in business and industry and had no landed estate connections. These men could send their horses to be trained, secure in the knowledge that it was not the 'pedigree of the owners but that of the horses that counted'.[162] The list of trainers racing in Mullingar included some of the best-known individuals involved in Irish racing at the time.[163]

VI

The examination of those who raced horses at the June meet provides evidence of the extent of Westmeath owner involvement in racing. Sixty-one different Westmeath owners, or 21 per cent of the total number, raced horses at the summer meet. The common denominator between these was land ownership, whether as landed gentry or substantial tenant farmers. A small number of professional men were also

Figure 8. Places of residence of owners who raced horses in Mullingar at June
meetings, 1890–1905

involved. Westmeath farmers who raced horses formed a representative cross section of the county's farming community of the time. Many
shared common membership of the Westmeath Hunt Club; forty-four
of the sixty-one had subscribed to the hunt club at least once between
1890 and 1901.[164]

Members of the Westmeath landed gentry formed less than half of the
owners; twenty-seven of the Westmeath resident owners were landed

estate proprietors. Members of this group tended to be involved in more than one aspect of the business. The Boyd-Rochfort family, of Middleton Park, Castletown-Geoghegan, was the most important of this group. Three members of the family raced horses at Mullingar on fourteen occasions between 1898 and 1904. The Boyd-Rochforts were involved in all aspects of equestrian sport and developed an important stud farming operation at Middleton Park. The *Westmeath Examiner*, in May 1905, reported on a visit made by one of its journalists to the demesne, and while it is essentially a propagands piece, the report gives some idea of the professional nature of the business carried on there. Two thorough-bred stallions with impressive racing and breeding records and six brood mares were at stud. The chief of these was Simony II, a stallion that was purchased as a yearling for 3,200 guineas. Evie, the progeny of Simony II and the Boyd-Rochfort brood mare Liz, was a winner of the Stanley Stakes at Liverpool in 1904 and was later sold for £1,000.[165] Two others with connections to the Boyd-Rochfort estate also raced horses in Mullingar. G.V. Reid contested races on five occasions between 1895 and 1903. Reid gained his experience during the minority of George Rochfort, when for almost a decade he managed the stud farm and racing business of the estate.[166] While based at Middleton Park, he maintained a few horses of his own and 'had more than average success'.[167] On leaving Middleton Park, he purchased a farm at 'Kilgarvan', Bishopstown near Streamstown, and established a small racing stable.[168] James Cheshire, who raced on only one occasion, had acted as a jockey for the Rochfort family and by 1900 had set up his own training establishment in Castletown-Geoghegan and was also a registered professional jockey.

A. J. Pilkington was another with a landed gentry background who raced a number of times at Mullingar. Pilkington was a member of a family that owned an estate of 1,683 acres at Tyrrellspass, according to the returns of 1875.[169] He was educated in England and a graduate of the Oxford Military College where he received a solid training in horsemanship. Pilkington applied these skills by regular participation in the Westmeath Hunt and he was also active in the events organised by the Westmeath Polo Club.[170] He entered horses on five occasions and his wife and brother had one entrant each. Pilkington was a professional trainer and by 1898 was based at Woodlands, Mullingar where he trained a string of thirteen horses for a number of mainly Westmeath-based owners.[171] In 1898, he turned out six winners nationally with total earnings of £642 10s and in 1899, he trained ten winners earning £1,172 in the process. One of those who placed horses in Pilkington's stable was William Thomas Brabazon, a farmer who resided at Johnston House, near Mullingar.[172] Brabazon raced horses on six occasions at the summer meet and enjoyed some success as he finished in the winner's enclosure on two occasions. Thomas Dibbs, a Mullingar farmer, also raced horses on six occasions there. Another local supporter of the meet was James Brabazon of Mount Dalton, Rathconrath, Mullingar. In the seven years prior to his sudden death in 1893 he had been one 'of the leading supporters of the Irish turf', and as an owner and breeder had produced the winner of some of the principal Irish races.[173]

Infrequent participation in the June Mullingar meet did not necessarily mean a low level of involvement in the racing business. In some cases it meant a more serious involvement in steeplechasing; for others it meant that their interests were concentrated on flat racing. This is illustrated by the involvement of T. M. Reddy. Reddy only raced once at Mullingar but was extremely committed to the sport and was involved in hunting, steeplechasing and breeding. Reddy emigrated to Argentina as a seventeen-year-old in 1856 and established himself as a sheep, cattle and goat farmer.[174] He invested in land and on his return to Ireland he purchased two areas of land outside Mullingar at Culleen. He maintained his Argentine properties and in 1905 he was the owner of 45,000 acres of land within 120 miles of Buenos Aires. The *British Hunts and Huntsmen* reported that in 1910 he owned 30,000 sheep, 8,000 horned cattle and 500 horses and mares 'of superior class' in Argentina.[175] The horses were bred from eight Irish mares that he had imported in 1874 and he also purchased well-bred sires in Ireland and had them exported to Argentina. Reddy was a nationalist and supporter of nationalist causes who immersed himself in the culture of the landed gentry in so far as it involved recreation. He became a member of the Westmeath hunt and also enjoyed 'sport' with the Ward Union and Meath hunts.[176] A racecourse was set out on his land and was used as the venue for the Westmeath Hunt Club races and point-to-point meets during the 1880s. He raced his horses extensively, being successful at Westmeath, Roscommon and Athboy hunt and point-to-point meets. However, his racing activities weren't limited to confined hunt events as he also raced horses successfully in the Curragh, Leopardstown and the Phoenix Park.

Cornelius Hannan was the proprietor of a 'well ordered though small home of the thoroughbred', at Riverstown, Killucan who also raced only once. He was the proprietor of one of the most professional and racing oriented stud farms in the county. The thoroughbred, Marmiton, in whose 'ancestry were the winners of classic races' was its prize asset and was standing from 1892 at a 'fee of £10 for matrons of pure descent'.[177] The sire was successful and regularly featured in the annual lists of leading studs, its progeny winning £1,348 19s in 1898.[178] Captain Cecil Fetherstonhaugh, director of the race company, was another once-off competitor at Mullingar who was also heavily committed to breeding. In 1896, he claimed to have been involved in breeding for over twenty years, during which time he had been the owner of several stallions and had acted as judge at several shows nationwide.[179] Others who raced on only one or two occasions included members of the professions such as E. A. Shaw, a solicitor, Michael Cleary, a veterinary surgeon, and Dr Dooley.

Frank Mitchell, James Cole, Christopher Taaffee and James Yourell were the men who raced horses most often in the Mullingar summer meet. The altered nature of the Westmeath racing scene and the changed fortunes of the landed interests involved in the sport are best illustrated by the economic profile of those individuals. These men were at the opposite end of the land ownership hierarchy to those who raced horses most often at Garrycastle in the 1860s. These men were farmers, rather than estate proprietors, and of the four, two subscribed to the hunt. Their frequency of participation and the size and valuation of their holdings is illustrated in Table 5.

Name	Size of holding (acres)	Valuation £	Frequency horses raced in Mullingar
F. W. Mitchell	280	166	19
James Cole	201	120	18
Christopher Taaffee	118	95	13
James Yourell	118	75	10

Note . Numbers for 'acres' and '£ valuation' have been rounded.

Table 5. Extent and value of holdings, frequency of participation, of the four most active Westmeath resident owners at Mullingar June races, 1890–1905

Mitchell maintained a small stable of steeplechase horses that were raced nationwide. He raced his best horse, The Admiral, an incredible 162 times over a ten-year period, in which the horse was a winner fifty-four times.[180] Mitchell's involvement in national racing can be illustrated by looking at the performance of The Admiral in 1892, when he raced twenty times between February and November. This returned eleven wins for prize-money of £275 5s. Mitchell combined the role of trainer and jockey and was able to reduce his racing expenses considerably, so in 1892 his stewardship of The Admiral was likely to show a net profit.[181]

In the same owner-trainer-jockey-farmer tradition as Mitchell was Ballynacarrigy resident James Yourell, who raced horses on ten occasions in Mullingar and was jockey on all but one occasion. Like Mitchell, he was also active on the national scene. The 1894 national odyssey of Yourell with the horse Bass was extraordinary under any circumstances. His season began on 26 March at Fairyhouse where the horse finished third in the Irish Grand National and ended on 3 November at Leopardstown; in the season the horse earned a total of £265 10s from ten race wins.[182] The horse was raced an incredible thirty times at venues as distant from Mullingar as Enniscrone, Cork and Kilkenny (Figure 9). James Yourell farmed approximately ninety-five acres of land at Ballynacarrigy and Sonna and used the income generated from the land to finance his racing activities. According to family tradition, he emigrated to Argentina around 1870 and returned twenty years later with finance, which he may have used to begin his racing career. His interest in racing was solely for the sport and reputedly he had no interest in

Figure 9. Venues and dates where Bass, the property of James Yourell, raced in 1894

the gambling or breeding aspects of the business.[183] Christopher Taaffee contested thirteen races at Mullingar and was also involved in the breeding business and hired a private trainer, Frank Byrne, for his small racing stable at Rathaspic, Rathowen, where he farmed 118 acres of high-quality land valued at £95.[184]

The broad appeal of racing in the county in the 1890s is illustrated by the different family and personal circumstances of the Westmeath owners who raced most often in Mullingar. These men, with the exception of Yourell, farmed extensive and high-value holdings and occupied substantial dwellings. The homes did not match those of the landed gentry, but they stood apart from other houses in their localities with substantial out-offices. All occupied first or second-class houses as defined by the 1901 census criteria. F.W. Mitchell who lived in a second-class house, was a thirty-nine-year-old member of the Church of Ireland in 1901, and was married with a young family of four children, ranging in age between one and six years.[185] Yourell was a forty-year-old bach-elor who lived with his mother in a second-class house (valued at £5 15s) with four stables attached at Piercefield, where they farmed 118 acres of land.[186] James Cole, was a sixty years old, and farmed two holdings of land with a combined area of 201 acres, valued at £120. He shared a first-class house at the Pass of Kilbride with his wife Mary. His two sons also resided in the family home and acted as jockeys on occasion. He also employed one stable boy in 1901.[187]

Five Westmeath women raced horses in Mullingar between 1890 and 1905.[188] All were the wives, widows or daughters of known male owners. The racing world was male dominated and the actual female involvement in preparing and managing the horses is likely to have been minimal. Miss Alice Boyd-Rochfort raced on five occasions between 1897 and 1899; her mother Mrs Boyd-Rochfort on four occa-sions between 1899 and 1901. Mrs Boyd-Rochfort had managed the family estate during the nine years' minority of her eldest son, Arthur, following the death of her husband Major Hamilton Boyd-Rochfort in January 1891.[189]

Evidence from a 1900 court case that involved Alice Boyd-Rochfort and her mother illustrate the complexities of female ownership at this time. Alice Boyd-Rochfort attained her majority in December 1899 and eloped in January 1900 and married P.P. O'Reilly, an important figure in the world of Westmeath sports, from Coolamber, in north Westmeath. As the court evidence suggested 'he was the son of a gentleman of high position in County Westmeath, a Deputy-Lieutenant, a director of a bank'.[190] He was also a member of a Catholic family and the ecumenical tastes of the Protestant, Mrs Boyd-Rochfort, were unable to accommo-date a Catholic son-in-law. Jewellery, some property and horses were confiscated and the younger lady initiated court proceedings for the return of the articles and horses and claimed '£1,000 damages for the detention of the goods and chattels'. Evidence from the case presents an opportunity to examine the complicated business of female horse ownership at the turn of the century. Alice claimed ownership of seven horses 'some of which were well known to racing men in Ireland'. She began her ownership career in 1894, when her mother made her a present of a pony and a chestnut horse. In 1896, these were sold for a sum of £170. Her mother retained the finance raised from the sale and distributed it to her daughter as required. In 1897 the plaintiff owned four horses and in December a fifth horse called Coollatin was sourced for her by the agent and was raced in her name in 1898–99. The steward and agent of the estate had entered these horses under 'Miss Alice's' name. The agent purchased three more horses for her in 1899. These horses were also raced under her name and she accepted the prizes that were won. However, the young lady never paid any money for these horses, her mother paid from the amount that remained from the original 1896 sale. In her evidence to the court she claimed to have always settled with the jockey. At the end of each racing year the racing accounts were settled and her mother always received the monies because the transactions were carried out in her mother's name. Alice never paid for any of the horses of disputed ownership because it was her understanding that the money for them came out of the amount in her mother's keeping. Following this evidence the court was adjourned for a short period during which time a settlement was reached with the senior Boyd-Rochfort agreeing to pay a sum of £275 damages to her daughter while maintaining that 'neither in law nor on the merits had the plaintiff any right to any portion of the property beyond that admitted'.[191]

The case illustrates the somewhat tenuous nature of the ownership title possessed by the females. This case was played out between two women but there is no doubt that in the relationship between male and female family members the hierarchy of authority would be more rigidly demarcated. Miss Mina Reddy was the nineteen-year-old daughter of T. M. Reddy and her name appears three times as the owner of a runner in Mullingar in 1904–05.[192] The participation of women as registered owners in racing at this time was extremely limited. The evidence based on the Westmeath experience suggests their involvement resulted from their domestic circumstances. Of the married ladies, all were married to men with an involvement in racing and the two unmarried ladies also shared unusual domestic situations. A. J. Pilkington's involvement has already been documented while Mrs C.E. Levinge was the daughter of Captain Lewis, one of the chief figures in the hunting community in the 1880s and later. Alice Boyd-Rochfort's situation has already been described and Miss Reddy was an only daughter of an extremely wealthy Mullingar landowner, the real wealth-generating elements of his economic enterprises being in Argentina.

The sixty-one individuals who raced horses at the Mullingar summer meet formed a strong community, bonded by their involvement in racing, and they regularly raced horses outside the county. A distinguishing feature of this community was the number of farmers involved. The most active farmed their land and owned and trained their horses such as F.W. Mitchell and James Yourell, but J. H. Locke and other wealthier owners adopted a more specialist approach and placed horses with professional trainers in the Curragh. Locke typified the man of industry who entered racing without the backing of a landed estate and who obtained the services of a professional Curragh trainer to manage his racing interests. He was an industrialist based in Kilbeggan, who with his brother John managed the family whiskey distilling firm. Andy Bielenberg, in his history of the firm, documents the involvement of Locke in the traditional hunting-steeplechasing pursuits of the country gentleman. He began hunting at the age of seven with the Tullamore Harriers, a pack that frequently stopped for lunch at the family home at Ardnaglue. Locke, when he wasn't managing the distillery business, lived the life of a country gentleman.[193] He was one of the main initiators of the revived Kilbeggan meeting in 1901 but despite his involvement his only runner at the venue did not compete until 1920.[194] His chief summer recreational passion was polo and he regularly participated in Ledeston during the summer months. His polo ponies were also raced at the annual Westmeath Polo Club races. His interest in racing was in the more expensive flat racing sector where he had a number of horses based with professional Curragh trainers. Members of the professions such as Eddie Shaw would have followed a similar practice.

Westmeath owners also raced horses regularly outside the county as we have seen in the case of F. W. Mitchell and James Yourell in particular. The *Westmeath Guardian* reporter on 8 May 1896 boasted 'of the long and practically unbroken succession of victories' achieved by Westmeath owners and suggested that 'Westmeath horses just now seem to be making their own of the Irish racecourse'. At Birr, horses from the county won four of the five races on the card; in the same week Westmeath owners had three victories in Enniskillen and two successes at the Trim meet.[195] In a single week in May 1900 three Westmeath owners (G. V. Reid, R. G. Cleary and P. Casey), had winners at Enniskillen and James Yourell, A. J. Pilkington and J. J. Ham turned out winners in Tullamore.[196] At Carrickmacross, County Monaghan in August 1901 all the races were won by Westmeath-owned horses.[197] Westmeath owners won an average of forty-one races annually and collected between 3 and 6.5 per cent of total national prize-money available (Appendix 10 and 11).

The size of this racing community and the number of farmers involved was influenced by a number of factors. The central location of the county, with its well-developed rail network, provided easy access to race meets nationally. Secondly, as documented earlier, numerous small local meets were an important part of the racing culture of the county and these provided farmers with an opportunity to participate in racing and some progressed from the local to the national scene. The hunt-club-promoted races also presented farmers with an opportunity to become involved. Thirdly, the decision made in 1887, by the MFH Lord Greville to allow bona fide farmers to become members of the Westmeath Hunt Club provided farmers with access to additional steeplechases that were confined to 'horses regularly hunted'. This improved their opportunities to compete nationally. F.W. Mitchell, in particular, would have benefited from this decision. Finally, the specialist agricultural economy of the county also helped to support those interested in racing. The importance of the profitable grazing activity in Westmeath has been outlined in the Introduction. Farmers involved in racing had substantial holdings of high-value land and used grazing generated profit to support their racing activities.

There were many reasons why people became involved in horse racing, both social and economic. Making money from horse racing was a difficult business. The initial cost of animal purchase in addition to what has been termed the running costs of horse ownership created an extremely expensive sport. Ongoing costs included training bills, entry fees and forfeits, bookage fees, feeding stuffs, veterinary accounts, stabling costs at the course and at home, purchase of equipment and as Vamplew suggests 'for some owners the list must have seemed endless'.[198] Owners hoped to recoup some of their investment by collecting prize-money, by gambling or by the sale of a successful or promising horse. The level of prize-money available in Ireland increased by 55 per cent from £39,524 in 1890 to £61,324 in 1902 but declined between 1903 and 1905. The figures are illustrated in Appendix 11 and are accompanied by the calculation of the average prize-money available per horse competing. Vamplew concludes from his study of English racing that it was virtually impossible for owners to earn a regular profit on their activities and even of those owners who won large amounts, few did so consistently.[199] This conclusion is reached for an area where average prize-money was significantly higher than that available to the Irish or Westmeath owner.[200] Harry Sargent, in a contribution to the *Sportsman* reproduced in *Sport* in December 1894, outlined the cost of owning, training and racing in Ireland in 1891.[201] Sargent calculated that to own and maintain a racehorse in Ireland and race him once would cost an owner approximately £96 annually. Based on these calculations the Irish owner who depended solely on prize-money had very little chance of returning a profit in a country where the average prize-money available per horse that raced between 1890 and 1905 amounted to £37 16s.

The Westmeath owner who depended on prize-money to support his racing activities was likely to have been involved in a loss-making enterprise. The annual prize-money won by Westmeath owners for selected years is illustrated in Appendix 10. The average annual winnings by successful owners amounted to £45 15s and falls well short of Sargent's minimum requirement, although the leading money winner for each year would have surpassed the figure. Inconsistency of performance also contributed to the difficulties of earning profits regularly. J. H. Locke was one of only three owners nationally in 1898 to win a four-figure sum when his winnings amounted to £1,084.[202] Locke's Westmeath fellow-owners, who were chiefly involved in steeplechasing, competed far more often to win significantly less prize-money. F. W. Mitchell achieved winnings of £289 in 1892 with thirteen victories; J. Cole's most successful season was in 1896 when he collected £385 for five winning races, while J. Yourell's twelve victories in 1894 earned him £298. The conclusion from this analysis is that Westmeath owners who competed nationally in racing were unlikely to have returned consistent profits. Horse racing was an economically irrational pursuit with ownership positioned towards the consumption rather than the investment sector of the racing spectrum. In many cases this consumption was conspicuous.[203]

People involved themselves in racing for non-monetary motives also. Land-ownership and position in society were closely linked and, for the gentry, ownership of horses and attendance at meetings reinforced their position in the social hierarchy. Some wealthy individuals involved themselves in racehorse ownership and breeding as an expensive hobby. For many landed owners the glory and prestige associated with winning races was always important.[204] For others the appeal lay in betting and according to Huggins, 'unless an owner betted on a grand scale he could scarcely hope to train and run horses without being seriously out of pocket'.[205] Evidence of the gambling habits of Westmeath owners is scarce but there is one example of a member of an aristocratic family rapidly dissipating his fortune by injudicious gambling.[206]

Involvement in racing enhanced social status. For the successful farmer-grazier it was a form of conspicuous consumption that provided the entry into an elite social world and confirmed economic status. 'The excitements and uncertainties of ownership and associations with the famous and infamous had their own rewards.'[207]A love of horses, the excitement of competing and the pride of winning in the rugged sport that was steeplechasing underpinned all these considerations.

3. Commercial sports, 1880–1905: new opportunities

Opportunities for Westmeath people to participate in sporting and recreational activities increased dramatically during the final quarter of the nineteenth century. A number of 'new' sports, in particular cycling, tennis and golf, were developed. Versions of tennis and golf may have been played several centuries earlier but it was only during the last quarter of the nineteenth century that the sports were codified and developed formally organised club and competitive structures. The growth experienced by these sports was underpinned by the commercial imperative. Tennis and golf to a certain extent were complementary sports. The restriction of golf to the winter and spring months at this time facilitated those who desired to transfer from the manicured tennis lawns to the more naturalistic landscapes of the golf course. Social groups, previously unrepresented in recreational terms, availed of the opportunity to enjoy the sporting experience and, in particular, these sports provided the chance for female participation, an opportunity that was availed of by a small group of women drawn from the ranks of elite society, within the county. The enthusiasm that some Westmeath women displayed in sporting involvement can be seen from the achievements of two members of the Athlone Garden Vale Tennis and Croquet Club who held national croquet titles in the early 1900s.

The modern history of lawn tennis can be traced to the patenting by Major Walter Wingfield on 23 February 1874 of a 'New and Improved Court for Playing the Ancient Game of Tennis', and his publication two days later of a set of rules for the game he termed Sphairsitke. A London firm, Messrs French and Co., dispatched large numbers of boxed equipment sets and the newly defined game became popular immediately. A year later, the tennis committee of the Marylebone Cricket Club attempted to formulate a standardised set of rules based on the various forms of lawn tennis. This committee had consulted Wingfield and included his hourglass shaped court in its code of rules.[1] In 1877, the All-England Croquet Club introduced tennis into their Wimbledon programme. There was still considerable variation in the scoring system, the size of the court, the height of the net, the position of the service line and the method of serving. Therefore, the tennis sub-committee of the All-England Club framed what were virtually a new set of rules, one of which introduced a rectangular court that was twenty-six yards long and nine yards wide with the net suspended from posts placed three

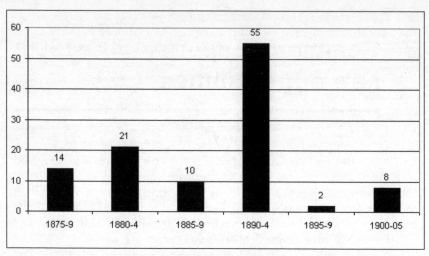

Figure 10. Five-yearly aggregate of tennis clubs established in Ireland, 1875–1905

feet outside the court. The first Wimbledon championships gave the new pastime a style and a status, clarified conflicting codes and lent form and substance to conditions of play.[2] The game became popular in Ireland very quickly with the Lansdowne Lawn Tennis Club being established in 1875, followed by the Dublin University, the Fitzwilliam, Monkstown and County Limerick clubs, all founded in 1877.[3] The five-yearly aggregates for club development are illustrated in Figure 10.

The early popularity of lawn tennis in Ireland was partly related to the simplicity with which the required equipment could be organised; the relatively inexpensive equipment could be purchased and delivered by parcel post. Tennis was the perfect game for the large gardens and lawns that were an integral part of the infrastructure of the landed demesne. A lawn, a racket, a soft ball, a net and a pot of paint were all the materials needed for lawn tennis and most country houses could supply these essentials.[4]

The croquet mania of the earlier decades meant that country houses contained vast areas of trimmed and largely unused croquet lawns. The decline in popularity of croquet was the result of a number of factors. The game had become too complicated for some because of the intro-duction of a set of new complex rules; for others the game suffered from an image problem, it was either too simple or too sissy, considered to be a girls' pastime at best.[5] For a small investment the necessary tennis equipment could be purchased and was much advertised in the Irish sporting press. John Lawrence in his *Handbook of Irish Cricket* first adver-tised tennis sets in 1875 and made available a set of equipment for as little as £2 with the most elaborate sets on offer for £6.[6] The foundation for growth had been laid in the previous two years when a version of outdoor badminton remarkably similar to tennis was advertised in 1874, and in 1873 parlour rackets were promoted, which could be 'played on the lawn in more genial weather'.[7] The announcement by Elvery's, one of the leading sporting goods retailers in the country, of the wholesale purchase of 1,400 tennis rackets in April 1881 is indicative of the popularity of the game in Ireland.[8]

Crucially, tennis provided the ideal opportunity for 'big house' residents to extend their recreational and social activities. Tennis was enjoyed during the hunting closed season, was far less expensive and was much more inclusive in that it catered for female participants in a controlled environment. Initially tennis developed as a strictly private recreation, played in the seclusion of the Victorian demesne and therefore it offered female family members the opportunity to participate in gentle physical recreation and to develop their basic skills free of public gaze. The wings on the early form of nets used on court contributed to the maintenance of privacy (Figure 11). That this exercise might be carried out in the company of invited male guests, in a supervised environment, was an additional attraction.

Tennis facilitated the development of additional tiers of entertainment on the social circuit of the landed wealthy and those considered to be their social equals. These were conducted in the public and private domain. The gaiety of Westmeath country-house life was enhanced considerably by the presence of officers from the depots at Athlone and Mullingar. In 1890, Mullingar, according to the officers of the East Lancashire Regiment, was an area where 'an incessant round of tennis parties were [sic] held'.[9]

A deeply ironic, contemporary description of a tennis party, written by 'one who has had a good deal of expertise in that line', was published by the *Westmeath Guardian* in July 1887 and provides an important insight into the associated posturing. According to the piece,

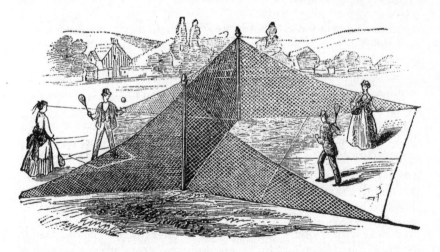

Figure 11. Early form of nets used in lawn tennis

once one was a 'swagger player' it did not matter whether one 'was a lord or threadbare curate' as 'society was above making these differences nowadays'.[10] The importance of the game to the courtship ritual is clear from the exchange that followed as the non-tennis playing guest was approached by a 'swagger player' and invited to participate:

> Why aren't you playing Miss M— really you should; you don't play well enough? What does that matter, nothing is done without a beginning you know. Good players don't like it you think? I, for one should be delighted to play with you. This with a look meant to be trilling, but which had not quite the melting effect, one would have expected from his appearance.[11]

The rebuffed suitor is then heard to remark to his friend in reference to his partner's efforts in an earlier set, that 'girls who can't play should not make fools of them-selves and spoil a good set'. At this particular party, the married women are specifically identified as the non-playing portion of the assembly for whom the party presented an opportunity for disseminating the latest gossip and social chitchat:

> The last runaway match is discussed, the latest divorce case is not forgotten; old china, new dresses, pugs, servants, Ouida's last novel, somebody's character, someone else's personal appearance (whether 'made up' or otherwise), the new shape in bonnets, and the 'state of the country'. So it goes on. How can they talk so much! Do they ever stop to think?[12]

Partaking of tea was an integral element of the tennis party but on this occasion a few indefatigable players 'who were evidently above caring for their complexions' continued to play. This negligence provoked the writer to suggest that for some young ladies tennis had become, in some sense, the new religion:

> Ladies now a days do not mind any amount of sun when lawn tennis is going on (though really the heat in church on Sunday was something dreadful. It prevented many from attending morning service!).[13]

Tennis spectating added a new layer to the public summer social calendar. The games became a focal point of social gatherings, particularly in Mullingar, where the army band entertained on a fortnightly basis; tea was enjoyed in the pavilion adjacent to the courts and guests had an opportunity to mix with their social equals. Unlike attendance at other sporting occasions, where the featured sport event was the central attraction and where the spectators were active participants, spectators at the weekly tennis events were participants in a social occasion, where the musical entertainment rivalled the sporting activity, and where social networking, more important than either, was facilitated in pleasant surroundings. Gossip was exchanged, deals negotiated, potential brides and grooms identified and matches made as the army band provided a background of music. In Mullingar, Thursday afternoons were devoted to public tennis events, and on alternate Thursdays classical music was performed by the regimental bands. On 1 June 1893, for example, the band of the 2nd Loyal North Lancashire Regiment performed a choice selection that included 'the celebrated intermezzo from Rustic Chivalry'.[14] On one notable occasion, it was possible to share with one's social peers the satisfaction of having a composition premiered by the military band. This was a distinction enjoyed by Mrs Loftus Lewis, when her waltz composition *Harmony* was performed by the Loyal North Lancashire Regiment band at the opening meet of the 1894 lawn tennis season, in Mullingar.[15] The Garden Vale club in Athlone provided a similar programme of summer recreation. These occasions provided a comfortable community of like-minded people who shared the same social origins, beliefs, values, customs and lifestyles with an opportunity to engage in conspicuous recreation.

It is possible to trace the origin and development of Westmeath lawn tennis clubs with considerable accuracy, as their activities were covered in detail in the local newspapers. The earliest reference to the playing of tennis in the county dates to 4 June 1879. This is found in the fishing diaries of Dubliner, George L. Adlercorn.[16] He spent a number of days fishing in north Westmeath and then made the journey into Mullingar to spend some time with Thomas Chapman at his residence 'beautifully situated in a park at the edge of Lough Owel'. The men fished the lake unsuccessfully for some hours and then returned home and 'from 5 to 7 played lawn-tennis'.

Tennis quickly made the transition from a private to a public recreation, a development that was facilitated by the formation of 'publicly' accessible clubs. The two main clubs were located in the urban centres of Mullingar and Athlone and catered specifically for those involved in local administration, members of the local landed gentry, the higher status professionals and officers from the local regiments. In Athlone, the Garden Vale club was dominant from the time of its formation in 1884 and achieved some national distinction through the performances of one of its lady members.[17] The club had as its core membership some of the leading establishment figures in the district. F.T. Dames-Longworth, Lord Lieutenant, and one of the leading gentry figures in the county, was President of the club until his death in 1899. Seven military officers and three of the area's senior RIC officers including the district inspector, B.R. Purdon, who was elected secretary-treasurer of the club, attended the AGM in 1889. The O'Donoghue who was one of the county's largest landowners was present as was Orlando Coote, the founding father of Athlone soccer. One member of the medical profession attended as well as a Protestant rector.[18]

Attempts to develop a tennis club in Athlone for the commercial middle classes proved less successful. A cricket club was established in

Athlone in May 1886 which catered mainly for the commercial personnel of the town. Soon after its formation a lawn tennis branch was added. At its first annual general meeting, in April 1887, the club claimed a membership of sixty-four including nineteen females.[19] The summer months saw 'all courts occupied each evening with contestants of both sexes and much pleasure and healthy exercise was enjoyed by the members'.[20] The members were not as fortunate the following year as the ground was under water for up to two months of the summer.[21] The club actively sought to promote tennis and cricket amongst the 'employees in the different businesses established in town', by making available family membership tickets.[22] This club disbanded and was replaced in 1895 by the Athlone Lawn Tennis Club, with a committee dominated by some of the leading commercial men of the town.[23] This club had only 'a brief and uneventful existence', and according to the *Westmeath Guardian*, Athlone's reputation as a tennis district was under 'the shield of the Garden Vale Tennis Club'.[24] The authorities of Ranelagh School in Athlone also encouraged tennis. Newspaper reports make reference to the annual general meetings of the lawn tennis club attached to the school, and the game was regularly featured at the annual school sports.[25] It was sufficiently popular with the boys of the school to attract an entry of thirteen, for the tennis competition of the 1886 school sports.[26] Voluntary associations also promoted lawn tennis. In 1895, the Athlone members of the YMCA held an informal meeting to make arrangements for the establishment of a lawn tennis club in association with the members of the Young Women's Christian Movement.[27]

The first organised club in Mullingar, the Westmeath Lawn Tennis Club, was established in April 1892 by 'a number of influential gentlemen in the county' who secured a field for the purpose at Annebrook, on the edge of the town.[28] At the initial meeting of the club, held in May 1892, at the Bank of Ireland, a membership of 130 was claimed.[29] A committee of twelve, dominated by members of the local landed gentry, was formed to manage club business. Three members of this committee held the position of deputy lieutenant at the time. Colonel Goodwyn of the East Lancashire Regiment was included, as was the resident magistrate and M. F. Barnes, the deputy sheriff. The manager of the Hibernian Bank was also a member. His fellow bank manager, R. Macbeth of the Bank of Ireland was treasurer and H. W. Lloyd was secretary.[30] The grounds of the club were officially opened for play on 16 June 1892, and by early August, the *Westmeath Guardian* reported that on 'every Thursday lively games are to be witnessed on the picturesque ground'.[31] Membership had increased to 150 according to the report of the 1894 annual meeting.[32] At the commencement of the 1894 season the club had developed four tennis courts and a croquet court and in July the game of badminton was introduced 'and afforded additional amusement to both players and onlookers'.[33] However, by 1901 the priority of the members had changed. Three 'good' tennis courts and two large croquet courts and one small croquet court now served the member's needs.[34]

The game was introduced to the town of Moate in March 1893.[35] The club was organised by 'several of the principal families' of the district 'under rules similar to those at Athlone', and a member of one of those families, W. C. Clibborn, placed a 'field' at the disposal of the members. The club claimed an initial membership of sixty and elected a committee of six to manage the affairs of the club and develop its facilities. The social profile of this committee was similar to that found in Mullingar and Athlone. It included representatives of the local gentry (F. W. Russell and W. C. Clibborn), the professional classes (bank manager, Stoppford Halpin and Dr H. Moorehead) and C. H. Winder, the district inspector of the RIC.[36] At the end of the first season, the membership of the club consisted of 'the elite of the town and district, and many of the principal merchants and business people'.[37] In May 1893, the tennis grounds had 'been properly staked off and all the appliances for the game provided'.[38]

The Moate club trumpeted its elite profile and the contributed club notes to the *Westmeath Independent* highlighted the club's exclusiveness. In May 1893, it was reported that the 'club comprises all the aristocracy of the district'.[39] In June 1893, the weekly meeting was attended by 'a large and representative gathering of the elite of Moate and the neighbourhood'. These included the parties of the Maher, Wakefield, Adderley, Clibborn and Russell families, the district inspector of the RIC and the Moate bank manager.[40] In May 1895 'an excellent little pavilion had been permanently erected on the grounds' and by October the club claimed to be one of the best equipped and most popular to be found in any provincial town.[41] According to an article published in the *Westmeath Independent* in October 1895, an image problem associated with the game had been overcome. Women gave the game so much attention that it was perceived as being 'too feminine'. It was seen 'as an agreeable outdoor recreation quite unsuitable to male tastes'. The writer believed that the prejudice that existed against the game was simply the result of ignorance and as the younger element became more familiar with the principles of the game, notions about its 'feminine propensities' would disappear. The author had seen 'sets played that try the endurance and skill of a wielder of the racquet far more than the more brawny champions of the camen [sic]'.[42] A club was also formed in Castlepollard where the tennis courts were located beside the polo grounds and Mrs E. F. Dease acted as secretary and the Church of Ireland rector, Rev. A. Drought, held the post of treasurer.[43]

An analysis of membership of the Garden Vale Club of Athlone and the Westmeath Lawn Tennis Club in Mullingar revealed a similar pattern of social class background.[44] Membership of both clubs was drawn almost totally from social class A, with one bank official member of Garden Vale and two clerks who were members of the Mullingar club responsible for the slight dilution of the social class of

the clubs. Those with a landed-estate background dominated membership of both clubs and formed 30 per cent and 40 per cent of the
Athlone and Mullingar clubs' identified membership. This reflects the
extent to which the tennis club was a public manifestation of a recreational activity that initially flourished in the environment of the
landed demesne. It also illustrates the important role played by tennis
in providing a communal social outlet for landed-estate families during
the summer months. At this time golf was a winter activity which
clashed with the hunting season, and consequently was of little interest
to people of that milieu.

High-ranking office-holders in local administration who were
members of either the Athlone or Mullingar clubs also had strong associations with landed estates. Seven RIC inspectors were members of the
clubs as was the resident magistrate of both regions. The magistrates
were drawn mainly from the ranks of the lesser ranking country gentry,
the professions and substantial businessmen.[45] Army officers formed 23
per cent of the Garden Vale membership and the combined membership of both clubs included nine Protestant clergymen. The Mullingar
club membership included the managers of the four main banks in the
town and both clubs included doctors and lawyers as members. A
profile of the Moate club would produce a similar social construction as
the club boasted of its elite status and the number of local aristocrats
who were members.

Tennis also had a strong denomination bias. It was closely associated
with the Protestant Church. Only landed estate-proprietors The
O'Donoghue and P. P. O'Reilly, bank managers J. J. O'Connell and V.
Lucas as well as Dr Dillon-Kelly were Catholic members of the tennis
clubs examined. The Mullingar club had a 91 per cent Protestant membership and the Garden Vale Club was 89 per cent Protestant. Some of
the key individuals involved in club development were also active at
organisational level in the Protestant Church. This association provided
one of the points of contact for the personnel involved and this was
extended to an involvement in lawn tennis administration. The Protestant community in Mullingar was particularly active at the time and in
1888 had completed the building of an impressive parochial hall that
became a cultural centre for the community; touring opera companies
staged their productions on a stage that was especially built for the
purpose and concerts, plays, whist drives and dances were organised
there.[46] The Mullingar Parochial Club and the Mullingar Young Men's
Parochial Club were the institutions around which much of this entertainment was arranged. In 1901, an attempt was made to encourage
young Protestants to adopt the game. The Mullingar Parochial Association formed a tennis club and a tennis court was laid at the
schoolhouse in Harbour Street, Mullingar.[47]

The 1892 committee of the Westmeath Tennis Club (Mullingar)
included several who were elected select vestrymen for their respective

parishes. Colonel Cooper, chairman of the club and committee member, T.C. Levinge, were appointed select vestrymen for the Mullingar Union of parishes. Club secretary, H. W Lloyd, and treasurer, Robert Macbeth, were elected select vestrymen for the All-Saints Church.[48] The connection had been solidified by 1901 when the Parochial Hall became the venue for tennis club meetings and the committee elected for the season included three Protestant clergymen. These included the parish incumbent Rev. Dr Seymour, DD. He was joined on the committee by fellow clerics Rev. A. E. Crotty and Dr Hill Wilson White, DD.[49] M. F. Barnes, who was secretary of the Westmeath Lawn Tennis Club in 1903, acted for many years as a member of the select vestry. He was also a parochial nominator and diocesan synods-man, the incumbent churchwarden in 1903 and was a leading figure in the organising of concerts in aid of church funds.[50] The connection was similar in Moate with the parochial hall providing the venue for entertainment events organised by the lawn tennis club.[51] Several of the male members associated with the club were also active in the administration of their Church of Ireland parish, fulfilling the roles of select vestrymen.[52]

A competitive structure to cater for those who wished to extend their tennis participation beyond the mere recreational evolved, initially, through the invitational tournaments hosted at the homes of the landed gentry, and eventually to the intra- and inter-club events, as well as the open tournaments promoted by the local clubs that attracted players from all areas. An invitational tournament, which was claimed to be the first tennis tournament played in the county, was hosted by Robert Smyth at his Gaybrook demesne near Mullingar, on 1 August 1888. The three-day event featured a ladies' and gentlemen's doubles, a gentlemen's doubles, a ladies' singles and gentlemen's singles. A handicap system was developed that allowed members to compete on an equal measure and this increased the attractiveness of the events to the individual contestants. The singles competitions for ladies and gentlemen attracted an entry of twelve in each case. The integration of gentry and military society ensured that the band of the Royal Irish Rifles entertained on a number of occasions at the private invitational event.[53] Later in the year, a County Westmeath representative side was defeated by a County Longford team in a game played at Mount Murray, Mullingar, at the time the residence of the County Longford gentry couple Mr and Mrs T. N. Edgeworth.[54]

These events, which were in essence an extension of the tennis garden-party, were followed by the development of inter- and intra-club members' events as more clubs were established on a formal basis. Both the Westmeath Lawn Tennis Club and the Garden Vale Club of Athlone organised an annual tournament programme that included one intra-members' tournament and an open tournament. The Westmeath Lawn Tennis Club hosted its first tournament in 1893, within a year of its formation, an event that featured a gentlemen's singles and doubles and a mixed doubles competition. The report on the event carried by the *West-meath Nationalist* suggested that 'the big and brilliant Fitzwilliam Terrace Tournament' which received 'such a booming in the Metropolitan papers' inspired the local club.[55] Although 'many of the general public were conspicuous by their absence' the social cachet associated with the game ensured that 'a fair muster of aristocracy' attended.[56] The social field of the membership of the Mullingar club had a wide geographic range, judging from the place of origin of some of the contestants. Players from Trinity Hall, Cambridge; New York; Banagher, County Offaly; Roscrea and Shinrone, County Tipperary; Boyle, County Roscommon; Newcastle-on-Tyne and the North of Ireland Club competed.[57] The 1894 event attracted an entry of twenty-two to the gentlemen's singles; twelve pairs contested the gentlemen's doubles and nine pairs the mixed doubles.[58]

The members of the Garden Vale Club preferred to maintain the recreational and social dimension of the sport and were reluctant promoters of the open tournament concept. The club's initial attempt to organise such an event did not take place until 1898. The members shared a number of concerns about the promotion of open tournaments. There was anxiety about attracting the best players and organising credible opposition for outside competitors. Some were unhappy at the idea of 'throwing open the trophies to all comers'. The competitions were not very popular with Athlone spectators owing to the absence of musical entertainment. On the occasion of the first open competition hosted by the Garden Vale Club, it was specifically requested by the serious competitors that musical entertainment be excluded from the event.[59] Like the initial attempt organised by the Mullingar club, this tournament attracted entrants from a wide geographic area. Competitors such as Fry, the northern Scottish champion, Clifford of Trinity, Periott, the champion of the Lansdowne Road Club, were joined by those from Roscrea and Galway.[60] The promotion of an open tournament also involved some financial risk. The 1900 Garden Vale open tournament, for instance, incurred a severe financial loss for the club.[61]

Inter-club games were confined to two or three matches annually against clubs located within the region and were simply a means of expanding the social dimension of the tennis club. The Garden Vale Club played a number of games against the Tullamore Club, beginning in 1888 with an event that involved gentlemen's singles and doubles, mixed doubles and ladies' doubles.[62] This fixture became an annual event, with the elite nature of the club clear from the composition of the team that competed against Tullamore in 1890. The team consisted of members of the Hodson family and Orlando Coote.[63] Games against regimental teams also took place. In 1891, the Garden Vale Club challenged the Mullingar-based East Lancashire Regiment and the local Athlone Garrison players.[64] In 1893, the Westmeath Lawn Tennis Club challenged the army personnel of the 2nd Loyal North Lancashire Regiment.[65]

As the century concluded many tennis devotees increasingly turned their attention to croquet. The sport was undemanding physically, lacked any possibility of serious injury occurring to the participant, could operate at the lowest common denominator in terms of skill levels and catered for mixed gender recreation. The game required a high degree of fine motor skill and hand-eye co-ordination and was one in which women made no concession to male supremacy.[66] It was also an age-appropriate activity. The timing of the growth is also relevant to any explanation of the game's popularity. It happened approximately ten years after the initial tennis boom. The age profile of the tennis player at this stage was one that made croquet a particularly attractive proposition for both genders.

The growth in popularity of croquet that emerged in the late 1890s in Westmeath was typical of developments in Britain. Membership of the All-England Croquet Association increased fifteen-fold between 1896 and 1906. This expansion was associated with a refinement of technique and codification of the rules. By 1904, the Association's code of play was generally accepted and success in the game became dependent on scientific precision and skill.[67] Tennis clubs provided the support structure for croquet and the Westmeath Lawn Tennis Club and the Garden Vale Tennis Club in Athlone both developed their facilities to cater for croquet devotees. The Moate club had similarly extended its range by 1901.[68]

In 1901, the Garden Vale Club included three full-sized croquet grounds in its facilities.[69] Earlier, in June 1898, the Garden Vale Club promoted what was claimed to be the first open croquet tournament in 'this part (or possibly any part) of Ireland' and it attracted entrants from Birr, Banagher and Ballinasloe. Annual club competitions were strongly supported by members of both genders. Ten competitors, including four females, competed for the championship title and sixteen contested the handicap singles in 1898.[70] Despite the absence of 'three crack players', Lord Castlemaine, Captain Dignam and Mrs Preston, ten players contested the confined club championships in September 1898.[71] In 1900, six Garden Vale players were confident enough of their skills to compete in the open singles tournament promoted by the club, nineteen contested the handicap singles and a similar number entered the handicap doubles.[72] The following year twelve contested the open championship singles, eight the open ladies' singles, fifteen contested the handicap singles and nine pairs participated in the handicap doubles.[73] In July 1901, sixteen players competed for the championship of the Mullingar club.[74] Inter-club matches were also occasionally organised with the Dublin Croquet Club providing the opposition in July 1901 for the Garden Vale Club and the social network associated with the game was such that the visitors remained in Athlone to compete in the open tournament.[75]

As the century concluded croquet provided a strong challenge to tennis, a development that was worthy of editorial comment in the *Westmeath Independent* in July 1901:

The older games and pastimes are ever changing to make room for newer innovations, which in turn have to give way to still something more of a novelty. Cricket is not now much seen in many centres and tennis unknown to our fathers in the form we are accustomed to seeing it played is struggling for an existence against croquet, which is the most recent addition to out-door exercise. The uninitiated see nothing in the game but it was the same with golf and others. Croquet has taken a firm hold in Athlone and those acquainted with the detail of its play speak highly of it as a form of exercise and as a game of considerable skill.[76]

The game complemented tennis and its attractions went beyond the realm of exercise and skill. It became a focal point of the elite summer social gatherings, which provided a vehicle for conspicuous display of the latest summer fashion. Wednesday afternoon was croquet time at the Garden Vale Club. On these occasions the 'elite of the entire district' were present as the ground displayed 'a bright and animated scene'. 'Fashion with all its variety' was everywhere in evidence with 'many rich and beautiful costumes forming a pleasant setting to the wealth of feminine beauty'.[77] Afternoon teas were enjoyed amidst the glitz and glamour. Croquet parties hosted in the privacy of the demesne were an important part of elite socialisation at this time. The diary of W. E. Wilson contains several references to the croquet parties he organised when he took a break from photographing and studying astronomical phenomena. On 18 August 1898 he organised a croquet party; on 20 August he hosted a croquet tournament with 'about 90 present' and on 23 August 'the Whitneys came over for croquet'.[78] Croquet allowed women and men to play together and enjoy a modest element of competition in a context that was essentially social and recreational. The sport required only the minimum amount of physical exertion; it placed little or no demands on stamina and as such was suitable for all ages and genders.

II

Bill Gibson, in a 1988 publication, traced the early history of golf in Ireland.[79] He has shown that as early as 1606 the game of 'goff' was mentioned in Ulster and that a golf club was active in Bray, County Wicklow in 1762. In 1852, the first modern version of a golf course was laid out in the Curragh, County Kildare by David Ritchie, who was a member of the Scottish Musselburgh Club. The Curragh, mainly because of its importance as a military headquarters, became the early centre of golf in Ireland but no properly constituted club was established there until 1883. Two years earlier, on 9 November 1881, the Royal Belfast Club was founded, making it the oldest in the country.[80] Five clubs were established in the period between 1881 and 1887 and in the next twenty-five years the game enjoyed a period of extraordinary growth in Ireland. In the 1880s eleven clubs were founded; from 1890 to 1899, 116 clubs were formed and between 1900 and 1905, a further thirty-nine clubs were established. Figure 12 below illustrates the number of clubs founded annually between 1888 and 1905.[81] The game had also spread nationwide. Only County Leitrim was without a golf club, and by 1910 this had been rectified with the opening of the Ardcarne Club.[82] Unlike the many transient clubs that catered for team sports, these clubs proved to be permanent features of the Irish sporting landscape; seventeen of the initial twenty-one clubs founded between 1881 and 1891 were still active organisations in 1991.[83]

The growth of the game required the establishment of a regulatory authority and the Golfing Union of Ireland (GUI), was established on 13 November 1891, at a meeting held at the Royal Hotel, Belfast that was attended by representatives of eight Ulster clubs. The objectives of the union, which were to popularise golf, to arrange championship competitions and to provide a universal handicapping system, were defined. The meeting also adopted a definition of an amateur golfer.[84] The development of a universally acceptable handicap system engaged the organisation in much early discussion. The introduction of a standardised handicap system was complicated by the variable standards of courses in play and the variety of terrain used.[85]

Four golf clubs were established in County Westmeath during the period of this study, with the first club established at Athlone. The introduction of the game to Athlone is directly associated with its status as a military town. The Athlone club was of military origin, established

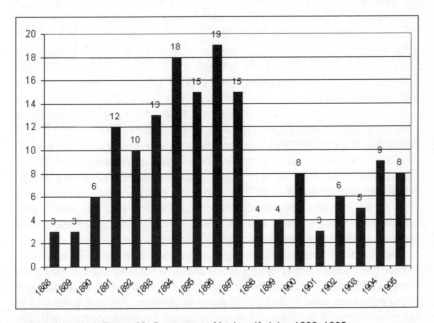

Figure 12. Formation of Irish golf clubs, 1888–1905

in 1892, according to *The Golf Annual*.[86] The game was first mentioned in the press in November 1895 when the *Westmeath Independent* reported that a handicap golf match was played amongst the members of the Athlone Garrison Club.[87] Only military and RIC personnel were involved. These included Majors Gaussens and Harrison, Captain Preston, RM, Lieutenants Hamlin and Shaw and Mr Joy of the RIC. Initially, the game was confined to the army officers based in Athlone, who were joined on occasion by the higher-ranking officers of the RIC.

The folklore associated with the Westmeath County Club of Mullingar is specific on how golf was introduced. The explanation is clichéd and simplistic and was outlined by David Walsh in a recent publication on the history of the club. According to Walsh, the introduction of the game was simple and straightforward. P. J. Nooney visited Scotland in 1890 and returned with the game.[88] Contemporary reportage is at odds with this version of the story. There is no reference to Nooney's presence at the initial meeting when it was decided to establish the club or at the opening ceremony.[89] Neither was he part of the community of the founder members. At the opening ceremony, it was the RIC district inspector, A.E. Triscott, who was identified as 'one of the prime movers in introducing the game into the district'.[90]

The founding members of the Westmeath County Club were important members of county and professional society. The fifteen who attended the initial meeting of the club were drawn from a limited number of socio-economic groups. The aristocracy and landed gentry were represented by Lord Greville, H. A. S. Upton, Colonel Smyth and Mr Delamere; county administrators present included the resident magistrate, Major O'Brien, as well as the county RIC inspector and A.E. Triscott, district inspector of the RIC. Mr M. F. Barnes, the sub-sheriff also attended, as did three members of the medical profession including Surgeon-Major Osbourne of the military. Commercial men present included the managers of the Bank of Ireland and the Ulster Bank, Mr Lyndon and Mr Lucas respectively. Some of these individuals were also associated with the Mullingar tennis club and their presence would suggest that they perceived golf as a means of transferring their recreational social networks to the golf course over the winter months. Commercial considerations may have had some role to play in introducing the game to Mullingar. Lord Greville was the patron of the club but he was also a director and chairman of the Westmeath Racing Company Limited. The introduction of golf may have been seen as an additional means to generate revenue by extending the usage of the racecourse over the winter months.

The club was initially successful and 'advanced with rapid strides in the favour of the people of the town and district and each season had seen an increase in the number of the patrons of the links'.[91] An increase in membership was experienced early in 1896 with the arrival of the regiment of the King's Own Yorkshire Light Infantry to the town; the officer ranks of the regiment included some 'keen and experienced golfers'.[92] Their presence helped in the diffusion of the skills of the game.

After their formation, the fortunes of the two clubs in the main urban centres experienced contrast in the social composition of membership. The Mullingar club evolved from one that was initially civilian dominated to one in which the military were more important, and formed the core of the playing membership at the period of conclusion of this study. In Athlone, military influence declined in importance and by 1904 the club membership was almost entirely civilian. This development was given constitutional recognition in October 1904 when the Athlone Garrison Golf Club was disbanded and Athlone Golf Club established. The change was needed as the club was no longer 'a purely garrison club', but was 'very largely composed of the professional and commercial classes'.[93] This development was reflected in the composition of the Athlone Garrison Club and the Westmeath County Club teams when they opposed each other in 1904. The Mullingar-based team included five army officers in its ten-man team while the Athlone selection was all civilian. The civilian members of the Westmeath team included Dr Gibbon, W. C. McCullough, the Presbyterian Minster, two members of the banking community, J. H. Long and E.C. Fitzpatrick, and W. T. Shaw, a leading member of the Mullingar retail community.[94] The sixteen who competed for the captain's prize at Mullingar, in 1904, included eight military personnel.[95]

A second golf club was established in the Mullingar area in 1902. This was a private club, based at Tudenham, on the demesne of C. L. Tottenham. The club was reported to have twenty-five members. Tottenham also placed a house at the disposal of the members where on Saturdays 'teas were given' by some of the lady members. This was a nine-hole course and the *Westmeath Guardian* reported that it was hoped 'after a little more practice to organise competitions'. Unfortunately, this was the only newspaper report on this particular club.[96]

The third public club formed was that in Moate. The 'links were developed along a line of gravel hills adjacent to the town' and were opened in 1900. Members of the landed gentry dominated the main positions with Charles O'Donoghue, president and H. A. S. Upton, the captain.[97] Upton was a member of all three clubs. He was one of the founding members of the Westmeath Club at Mullingar and was also a member and delegate to the Golfing Union of Ireland for the Athlone Club.[98] Upton's demesne was located at Coolatore, near Moate and this central location made it possible for him to enjoy golf at all three Westmeath clubs. Upton was involved in the early development of the game in Dublin and brought expertise to the embryonic clubs. He had been a member of the Leinster team that participated in the first inter-provincial match organised by the GUI in April 1896.[99] 'Pat' writing in the *Irish Golfer* in November 1899, on the leading players in the province commented that 'for his mechanical precision, consistency and grace, H. A. S. Upton is inimitable'.[100]

Initially Westmeath golf was a winter sport with the playing season extending from 1 September to 30 April. In summer, grass was too long to allow the game to be played and the grazing interest of the farmers with claims to the land used for the golf courses in both Mullingar and Athlone predominated. The first venue used in Mullingar was the New-brook racecourse where the major June race meet precluded the possibility of golf until the summer season had passed. In Athlone, many of the golfers abandoned the game in favour of water-based summer sports. In addition, the army personnel had a full programme of manoeuvres that left them with little time for playing golf.[101] As a winter game it clashed with the hunting season and this meant that the game held little interest for members of the landed gentry. Summer golf was introduced to Athlone in 1899 when eighteen members agreed to subscribe a sum not exceeding 5s each to cover the expense of keeping the 'links open during May, June, July and August', and the cost of employing 'Sam Smyth at 5s a week to keep the greens in order'.[102] The move was a success and in 1900 twenty-six members subscribed the sum of 4s each for summer golf.[103] The following year it was hoped to keep the links open without an additional levy but equipment replacement necessitated the imposition of a levy.[104] Summer golf only became possible in Mullingar when the club moved to a new nine-hole layout designed by W. C. Pickeman of Portmarnock, in November 1909.[105]

Golf offered the combination of modest physical exertion with open-air activity, 'an idealised antidote for office-bound middle-class men'. Medical men championed the therapeutic value of the game. The game, unlike the 'manly games', could be taken up in mid-life and practised as long as the modest physical fitness it was claimed to foster was maintained.[106] These were the values identified by Lord Greville when he addressed the assembled guests at the opening of the newly established course on the Mullingar racecourse, on 3 April 1895. According to Greville, 'golfing was an amusement as healthy as it was innocent'. The game would help to bring the people of the 'county very much together' and had the advantage over other games that 'people of all ages could play it'. 'Cricket, football, and even hockey, debar people from engaging in them after they have passed a certain age; but such was not the case with golf.' The potential of the game to provide employment for young people was also one of the attractions identified by Greville. The game would bring large sums of money into the county, which would be paid to the boys, who would act as 'carriers'. Excellent remuneration would be given to the boys 'for carrying the instruments of which it would be necessary to carry a large number in playing the game'.[107]

Empirical evidence illustrates the extent to which golf club membership was dominated by members of social class A. An analysis of the membership of Westmeath County Club and of Athlone Golf Club for 1904 indicates the extent to which members of the elite group dominated. The social characteristics of the membership of both clubs are illustrated in Table 6. Golf was the sport of the time-rich middle-aged professional. The Mullingar membership was numerically dominated by eight bank officials below the rank of manager who were classified as social class B for the purpose of this analysis and also included four bank managers, six doctors, five solicitors, six clergymen, six landowners and three army officers who had opted for individual membership in addition to the group subscription of the Connaught Rangers. The Athlone membership displayed a similar social construct albeit with a greater variety of professions represented. Based on the average age of participant, Lord Greville's identification of one of the essential virtues of the game as one that 'people of all ages could play' was fulfilled.[108] Professional status, the possession of leisure time and disposable income, were the essential requirements for qualification, factors reflected in the religious mix of the two clubs.

	Westmeath County Club	Athlone Golf Club
Social class A	43.00 (82.69 %)	29.00 (93.54%)
Social class B	8.00 (15.38 %)	2.00 (6.46%)
Social class C	1.00 (1.93 %)	
Average age	40.19	39.16
Average age: male	41.92	39.89
Average age: female	30.8	36.83
Religion: Catholic	21.00 (47.72 %)	8.00 (32 %)
Religion: Protestant	20.00 (45.45 %)	14.00 (56%)
Religion: other	3.00 6.83 %)	3.00 (12 %)
Westmeath native	55.17%	36.36 %
Non-Westmeath native	44.83%	63.64%

Table 6. Social characteristics of members of Westmeath County Club and Athlone Golf Club, 1904.

The idealised image of the golf course as an oasis of tranquillity and sylvan splendour and the clubhouse as a bastion of elite sociability and business networking, was far from the reality in the initial manifestation of the game in Westmeath. The early golf clubs in the county were challenged to maintain and develop the space required to play the game. The Athlone Club enjoyed a stability of base over the period of this study but by contrast the Mullingar club's experience was a peripatetic one. The officers of the Athlone Garrison Club developed their course on an area of ground known as the Batteries. The ground was composed of a number of gun emplacements and magazines, constructed for defensive purposes, on an area of high ground to the west of the town. The Batteries were abandoned in the 1860s when the introduction of long-range rifle guns rendered them obsolete and the land was used by local people, as commonage for the grazing of cattle and sheep.[109] A course was laid out that fully occupied the area of the Batteries and this was later extended into some adjoining fields.[110] It was a nine-hole course and according to the *Golfing Annual* of 1896 it was 'a difficult course being around an old fortification. The hazards are walls, moats, ditches, roads and railways.'[111]

The reduction in the military importance of the Batteries led to problems for the golf club as gradually the lands were leased to private individuals and this meant that by 1900 the committee was paying rent to a number of different landlords. James Kilroy was the main landlord but in 1900 the club also paid rent of £3 to Guinness & Mahon, land agents for Major Lloyd, who at this time was owner of a section of the course. P. Macken joined these landlords in 1901 and was paid £2 in annual rent, a sum that was increased to £5 in 1902.[112] A makeshift clubhouse was created in 1901 by adapting a stone cottage rented from J. Vaughan at a cost of £1 1s annually.[113] The members of the Westmeath Club were more ambitious and had a new clubhouse purpose built on their Mount Prospect grounds in 1904, at a cost of £38 14s 3d. Funding for this was organised by means of members' subscriptions and the proceeds of two musical concerts. Members' subscriptions accounted for 70 per cent of the total. They included a donation of £5 from the officers of the Connaught Rangers.[114]

Competition was an important element in the golf portfolio at this stage. Internal club competitions were numerous and provided the members with an opportunity to test their skills against fellow members. Inter-club games were also organised but were generally confined to games against clubs in the local region. The first contest at Newbrook took place between the Westmeath County Club and the Tullamore Club in April 1896. The novelty of the event inspired one spectator to describe the game 'as billiard playing on the ground'. The game resulted in a fifteen-hole victory for the home club. The mandatory entertainment for the visiting team was organised at the County Club and the spectators were treated to tea at the stand house of the racecourse.[115] An annual home-and-away match between the Athlone clubs and the Mullingar-based Westmeath County Club was part of the competitive curriculum of these clubs. The series began in December 1896 at Athlone when the Garrison Golf Club was the winner by six holes.[116]

III

·The cycling boom in the United Kingdom has been well documented with the peak of the boom years located between 1895 and 1897, when according to one commentator 'almost everyone who could afford a bicycle and who was not physically incapacitated rode avidly'.[117] The early history of Irish cycling still awaits its chronicler. The only historical work that examines the early years of Irish athletics and cycling takes a typically political approach to the subject and avoids any quantification of the growth in popularity of cycling and athletics.[118] The *Irish Cyclist* magazine listed the affiliated clubs on its masthead for some years but this practice was discontinued after November 1893. The magazine documents a club growth that was rapid in the early 1890s. In March 1891 fifty-nine clubs were listed; by the end of May seventy-eight clubs had affiliated and by November 1893, 107 clubs were identified.[119]

Alternative indices provide some measure of the popularity of cycling. Information published in the census reports document the extent of the Irish cycling boom in the 1890s. In 1881, thirty-two people were employed in Dublin in the manufacture of bicycles and tricycles and by 1901 this figure had increased to 213. In Belfast, 103 people followed a similar occupation and the total nationally was 704. In March 1901 it was estimated that 3,000 bicycles were bought annually in Ireland. These were manufactured in England but assembled in Ireland to create a sense of local identity.[120] Despite the popularity of cycling nationally, only one Westmeath individual considered bicycle and tricycle making or dealing to be his main occupation in the returns for the 1901 census.[121] However, there were several agencies and outlets operating within the county where bicycles could be purchased. M.H. Foy's store in Athlone was probably the most progressive and specialised. He claimed to have one of the largest and best-equipped workshops in Ireland capable of carrying out all types of repair. In 1898 he installed an enamelling oven at 'great expense' and could quote for 'enamelling at bottom prices'.[122]

Cycling was sufficiently popular in Ireland and advertising revenue such that two cycling journals remained viable enterprises during the 1890s. The *Irish Cyclist* was first published on 20 May 1885 in Tralee, County Kerry by J. G. Hodgins. Early in 1886 its editor, R. J. Mecredy, an outstanding competitive cyclist, purchased the paper and it relocated to Dublin.[123] Later a rival for the *Irish Cyclist* appeared in the shape of the *Irish Athletic and Cycling News*, which eventually became the *Irish Wheelman* and was amalgamated with the *Irish Cyclist* in 1903.[124]

Cycling's popularity is reflected in the number of cycling events included in the programmes for Westmeath athletic meetings and the increased number of cyclists who contested these events as the 1890s progressed. This can be measured by outlining the experience of the organisers of the small scale Street athletics meeting. The committee acted prematurely when they included a bicycle race in their programme of events for September 1892 as it failed to attract any entrants despite the 10s first-prize on offer.[125] This was to change over the decade as the 1901 programme for the sports meet included five bicycle races. The confined two-mile race attracted four competitors, the boys two-mile race had three competitors and the number of entrants for the three open events ranged from eight to ten cyclists.[126] Cycling had sufficient profile in rural Westmeath in 1891 to merit the inclusion of a bicycle race in the Wardenstown sports meet, an experiment that was repeated in 1892, but its limited appeal is evidenced in only three competitors entering on each occasion.[127] The 1893 event featured a bicycle race attracting an entry of fourteen.[128] In 1895, the Wardenstown Cycle Club had become the promoters of the event and the programme was extended to included three cycling events.[129] The initial Crookedwood sports held in October 1893 include a two-mile bicycle race that attracted only two competitors, one from Mullingar and one from Raharney. Ten years later cycling was popular enough to justify the inclusion of three bicycle races including one confined to those living within three miles of the village.[130] At the 1898 Delvin Athletic and Cycling sports the three- and five-mile bicycle handicap races attracted an entry of ten and eight competitors respectively.[131] In 1903, a bicycle race at the RIC sports confined to boys under seventeen years of age resident in Mullingar attracted an entry of six, while fourteen competed in the two-mile, and sixteen in the five-mile open handicaps at the same event.[132]

The first cycling club established in the county was the Westmeath Bicycle Club founded at a meeting held in the Lecture Hall, Mullingar, on 20 March 1882.[133] The club provided a form of organised recreation for its members, as is clear from the list of its activities for the month of May, published in the *Westmeath Guardian* of 29 April 1882. The programme consisted of nine outings to villages and beauty spots, the longest trip being one of fifteen miles to the village of Kinnegad.[134] The activities of the club for June were also publicised but newspaper reportage of cycling activities then ended for a number of years. At this time the expense of purchasing a bicycle restricted the activity to the upper echelons of the middle classes and in particular to business entrepreneurs and to members of the more exclusive professions. Members of this socio-economic constituency dominated the list of officers and committee elected to manage and organise the affairs of the new club. Their names and occupations are illustrated in Table 7.

Name	Office	Occupation/Profession
Mr Cleary	Captain	Bank official
R. J. Downes	Vice-captain	Solicitor
T. F. Nooney	Secretary	Ironmongers/hardware proprietor
J. P. Dowdall	Treasurer	Leather seller and seed merchant
W.E. Gill	Committee	Bank official
W. C. Corcoran	Committee	Bank official
Dr English	Committee	Doctor
W. D. Cleary	Committee	Publican
E. C. Fitzpatrick	Committee	Bank manager
W. Canton	Committee	Publican
J. P. Vernon	Committee	(Unknown)
E. M. Mahony	Committee	(Unknown)

Table 7. Occupations and professions of officers and committee of Westmeath Bicycle Club, 1882 (*Westmeath Guardian*, 24 March 1882)

Cycling in Westmeath was initially confined to a narrow group of commercial proprietors and landowners. Members of the former group were engaged in a novel but affordable form of conspicuous consumption, one that cost far less than a carriage or a hunting horse to buy and maintain. The ordinary or 'penny-farthing' was the chosen steed of these young male cyclists. For prosperous middle-class individuals cycling was an ideal form of self-expression, especially for those who wished to be the trendsetters of social behaviour, at a time when values were fast changing and active forms of recreation were increasing in popularity.[135] Minor participants were those whose occupation required some use of the bicycle, especially members of the military and the RIC.

The 1890s was the decade of the cycling boom when fundamental technological changes made the bicycle cheap and accessible to the middle classes. Firstly, the penny-farthing was replaced by the safety bicycle, which considerably reduced the degree of skill required for 'piloting' such a machine and dramatically cut the number of accidents. The safety bicycle had a chain-driven rear wheel, which gradually became identical in size to the front wheel, a development made possible by the work of John Starley. Secondly, the development of John Boyd Dunlop's pneumatic tyre of 1888 produced a product that was far superior to the earlier types of solid rubber tyres. Thirdly, the mass production of cycles brought about a considerable reduction in the cost of machines and indirectly established a second-hand market in cycles. Fourthly, the availability of hire-purchase schemes made it possible for the lower middle classes to access the required finances for cycle purchase. As a result, cycling became a method of transport and recreation accessible and suitable to both sexes and most ages and provided an opportunity for improved personal mobility to individuals across the social classes. Mullingar residents had access to these advanced cycles in the early 1890s as can be seen from the advertisement of William Trimble of the Grove Street Stores in Mullingar reproduced in Figure 13. He advertised as the sole agent for J. P. Starley & Co., described as the inventors of the safety bicycle, and he also offered pneumatic and cushioned-tyred safeties for either hire purchase or cash.[136]

The growing popularity of cycling in the county is reflected in the occasional newspaper report. In August 1894, according to the *Westmeath Examiner*, 'lovers of the road are to be found in every direction on Sundays,' in Mullingar. The *Westmeath Nationalist* reported in August 1896 that cycling had become so popular that 'people are beginning to look forward to the day when the possession of a cycle will be as much a necessity of everyday life as a pair of boots or a shirt'. The growth in popularity increased the possibility of accidents, as happened to the unfortunate Mr McFarlan 'who met with such shocking injuries, as he was riding along the road, totally oblivious of the dangers ahead of him until he dashed into a man carrying a scythe on his shoulder, and had his arm almost severed from his body'.[137]

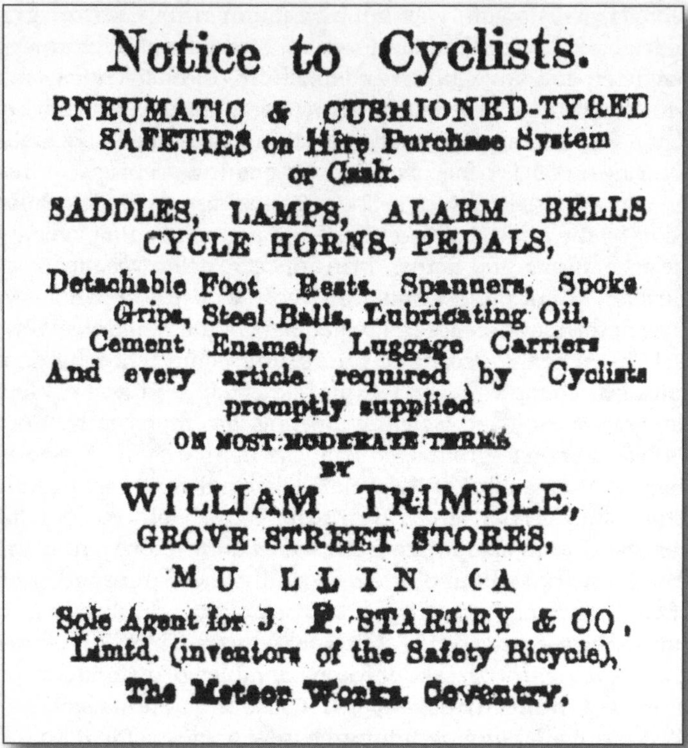

Figure 13. Advertisement of William Trimble, cycle agent, Mullingar (*Westmeath Examiner*, 4 November 1893)

A cycling club was re-established in Mullingar in July 1890, a time when even 'the most unobservant cannot fail to observe the very large numbers of pedal pushers that pass and repass with such startling rapidity in Mullingar and its vicinity'. Almost all of the mounted gentlemen were 'young men doing business in the commercial houses in town' and these were the men who were the founding fathers of the club.[138] The club survived and in April 1891 the *Westmeath Guardian* briefly documented the general meeting of the club and published a list of the appointed officers and committee.[139] According to the *Westmeath Examiner*:

> In the early hours of the morning on the roads adjoining the town may be seen several novices trying to become proficients [sic] and all under the able guidance of one well known in football and cycling circles.[140]

The one who was well known in football circles was James Mulvey, who occupied a variety of administrative positions with the Mullingar Football Club and who was secretary of the county GAA committee.[141] There was some overlapping of membership between the Mullingar Cycling

Club, Mullingar Football Club, Mullingar Cricket Club and the Mullingar Catholic Commercial Club. The phenomenon that Michael Wheatley refers to as 'the intermeshed network of clubs, branches, societies and committees' was as much a reality of the 1890s as it was of Wheatley's period of study between 1910 and 1916.[142] These clubs attracted support from the constituency of the non-property-owning commercial men, especially from shop assistants and clerks. The bicycle had become accessible to this class, who were enthusiastic club supporters and were constantly interested in new challenges and opportunities for self-expression, improvement and advancement. The Sunday outing was the staple diet of the members of this club and twelve members participated in the first seasonal outing to Killucan. J. Henehan's latest model 'safety' attracted most attention on this outing. The club was reported to have a membership of twenty-eight but the weekly outings were supported by less than one-third of the members.[143]

The strength of the club at the time was uncertain and in 1893 the *Westmeath Nationalist* reported that there were about fifty cyclists in Mullingar but the absence of a club was a source of embarrassment for young gentlemen 'when pleasure or business' called them away 'for a time to some other portion of the country'.[144] In July 1893, three of these ardent young cyclists were reported to have cycled from Mullingar to Dublin in 'four hours and a couple of minutes'.[145] In September, the members were experimenting with bicycle polo, an experiment that suggested that 'polo on bicycles had a good future'.[146] The Mullingar club was still active in 1894 but disbanded in 1895.[147] Attempts to revive the club were encouraged in the local press. The *Westmeath Examiner* in July 1896 lamented that 'it was strange that in such a populous and central district as Mullingar, athletic and cycling sports could not be provided'. This apathy was remarkable as a suitable enclosed ground with a purpose built track was available.[148] A similar concern was expressed in March 1897 in the same journal:

> Several towns in the midlands, of not half the importance of Mullingar, have very thriving clubs, and there is no reason why the young men of the capital of Westmeath, who seem to be always behind hand in such matters, would not at least pluck up sufficient spirit now and form an organisation.[149]

A club was eventually re-established in the town in July 1897 and the Horse Show Grounds at the Newbrook enclosure were secured for practices and matches.[150] Shortly afterwards the club organised two five-mile races, confined to its members, on the track.[151] In August, an inter-club match between the cycling clubs of Mullingar and Athlone was held at the same venue.[152]

Developments in Athlone followed a similar pattern. In 1892, the Athlone Bicycle Club claimed to have between fifty and sixty members and engaged in recreational journeys. On Easter Monday, the club organised an outing to Birr, a journey that was completed in three-and-a-half hours. At Birr, noted places of interest including Birr Castle were visited and 'Lord Ross's world famous telescope' was examined.[153] The 1893 season began, on Easter Monday, with a day trip to Longford that included a visit to Auburn 'the natal home' of the writer Oliver Goldsmith and guided tours of the Longford Barracks and Cathedral. Fourteen members took part in this trip that included members of Athlone's commercial classes as well as police and army members.[154] The following season opened on 19 March when thirty cyclists travelled to Moate where refreshments were enjoyed in Mrs Harford's hotel and on Easter Monday ten turned out for the run to Banagher, the highlight of which was a visit to Banagher distillery.[155] In May, fourteen members participated on the outing to Glasson and nine on the mid-week run to Ballinasloe.[156] The next outing to Ballinahown Court saw the members entertained by the estate proprietor Charles O'Donoghue.[157] A similar programme of events was organised for 1896 and included a journey to Mullingar where a social occasion held at Kelly's Hotel, between the members of the Athlone club, the National Club, Dublin, the Tullamore Ramblers club and the Kells cycling club, was a seasonal highlight.[158] The captain of the Athlone Bicycle Club throughout part of this era was Mr John McCue, who was employed in the furniture department of Messrs Burgess.[159] His replacement as captain was Michael H. Foy of the Athlone retail family.[160]

The voluntary societies also organised cycling as an adjunct to their core activities. In early 1894 the Athlone YMCA organised a cycling club.[161] The first outing organised by this club took place to Glasson with cycle-related prizes on offer.[162] Later in the year a ten-mile road race to Glasson and back attracted five entrants, namely N. Lowe, G. V. Telford, S. Lowe, J. S. Vaughan and H. Vaughan.[163] A similar club was established by the Catholic Young Men's Society and had its first outing in May 1896.[164] The cycling club attached to the Mullingar Temperance Club organised cycling events in 1897.[165]

Cycling clubs were also established outside the main urban centres. A club known as the Wardenstown Cycling Club (later the Killucan Ramblers) was formed in March 1893 at a 'very representative' meeting held at the Killucan dispensary. The club was typically middle class and included the local Catholic priest as its president, the dispensary doctor as secretary, and the national school teacher served on the committee with the local post-office clerk. Shortly afterwards, the club organised its first run of the season to Delvin and took responsibility for organising the annual Wardenstown sports meeting.[166] In 1900, the St Michael's Cycling Club was established at Castlepollard with 'all the drapers and publicans of the town sending representatives'.[167]

The analysis of a sample of Athlone and Mullingar cycling clubs illustrates cycling's importance to the lower middle classes in the 1890s. Forty-eight cyclists (67 per cent) from a total list of seventy-two were identified and their social status established. Participants from social class C dominated the group and in particular those clerks and shop assistants who formed 48 per cent of the total. Overall 21 per cent of cyclists were from class A, 15 from class B and 65 from class C. The labourers of class D were unrepresented and the average age of a Westmeath cyclist was 27.72 years.

The occupational group most strongly associated with cycling was the Royal Irish Constabulary and it was members of this body that established the most stable club to develop within the county. The bicycle was promoted by the police authorities at the training depot in the Phoenix Park, both as a labour-saving device that improved police efficiency and as a recreational tool. Members of the RIC were involved in the cycling clubs in Mullingar and Athlone in the 1890s and this involvement was formally recognised by the Athlone Bicycle Club in 1895 when both police and military representatives were appointed to the club's committee.[168] A designated RIC club was founded in Athlone in 1893 and reportedly had a membership of forty.[169] The RIC were active patrons of the sport in both Mullingar and Athlone, providing prizes to the Athlone Bicycle Club and the Mullingar Cycling Club sports. The feature event of the Mullingar cycling and athletic sports, held between 1897 and 1899, was the open three-mile bicycle race for the RIC Challenge Cup.[170] The *Westmeath Examiner* reported in May 1901 that the Mullingar Cycling Club was 'a thing of the past'. However, any vacuum that existed by its demise was partly filled by the establishment of the County Westmeath RIC Cycling Club in May 1901. The club exhibited a strong Mullingar bias in its officer list but some attempt was made to encourage all-county participation by including personnel from Castlepollard, Delvin, Moate and Kilbeggan at committee level.[171] A variety of points of departure for the weekly recreational outings also encouraged geographical inclusiveness. In May 1901, for instance, the outings departed from Stoneyford, Rathowen and Mullingar.[172]

The most important function of a cycling club was that it provided an organised programme of recreation for its members. The recreational outings of the 1890s Athlone Bicycle Club were well established and have been outlined above. These weekly outings attracted an average attendance of about one-third of members. This aspect of cycling was strongly supported by the writings of R. J. Mecredy. The *Irish Cyclist* in an 1892 editorial promoted 'the quiet potter through leafy lanes and shady woods' as an activity that was far superior and enjoyable to the rush of the 'road scorcher'. The latter,

> In his desire to annihilate space and time cannot afford to examine the scenery, or to chat pleasantly with his companions. The potterer jogs on, chatting cheerily to his companions, and enjoying shade and sunshine, wood and water to the full. There is little that escapes

the watchful eye and he reaches his destination cool, fresh and in a
pleasant frame of mind well satisfied with the days outing.[173]

Clubs also organised road races but these were less popular and
usually attracted only a few members. These benefited from the sponsorship of the local cycle agent who used the events as a means of
promoting the latest innovation in cycling product. The Athlone Bicycle
Club organised a ten-mile road race in June 1894 that attracted five
members and was won by Sergeant Bacon of the RIC.[174] The winner of
the first race of the 1896 season was reported to have ridden a 'Griffiths
Corporation' cycle supplied by H. Dagg, who also presented a pair of
Dunlop pneumatic tyres to the winner of the second of the season's
races. On this occasion, the winner rode a 'Swift Popular' supplied,
inevitably, by Dagg.[175] In August 1894, a ten-mile road race confined to
members of the Mullingar Cycling Club attracted an entry of seven who
competed for the prize of 'a splendid field glass'.[176] In the Killucan and
Raharney district the cycling club in the area also promoted road racing.
The Killucan-Wardenstown club organised a ten-mile road race over the
Killucan–Raharney course but only three contested in 1893.[177]

Cycling clubs promoted athletic and cycling sports meets. The three
clubs in the two main urban centres promoted major athletic and
cycling sports annually and it was this role that established a civic
importance for the clubs and impacted on the local communities to a far
greater extent than the golf or tennis clubs. These were important spectator events that transcended the local and attracted some of the major
national athletic and cycling figures to Athlone and Mullingar. The
Athlone Bicycle Club promoted major meets between 1893 and 1896.[178]
The Mullingar Cycling Club successfully promoted three annual events
during its relatively short lifespan.[179] The second such event organised
by the club featured one of the great athletic performances of the
century by Westmeath athlete, Walter Newburn, at the time a teacher at
Claremont College, Dublin. Newburn was essentially world long-jump
champion in 1898 having won the AAA title in June, a title he retained in
1899. Newburn arrived in Mullingar in great jumping form; on the Saturday prior to the meet he became the first athlete in history to
long-jump over twenty-four feet, when he jumped twenty-four feet and
a half-inch in the international match against Scotland at Ballsbridge on
16 July 1898. In Mullingar, he produced an even more spectacular leap,
and cleared twenty-four feet six-and-three-quarter inches. Controversy
surrounded the achievement and the jump was never officially recognised as a record.[180]

The County Westmeath RIC Cycling Club became the promoter of the
major non-equestrian related sports event held in Mullingar in the early
1900s. A number of factors combined to ensure that these sports became
events of national importance. The Horse Show grounds developed by
the directors of the Westmeath Racing Company Limited included a
purpose-built cycle racetrack in its facilities and provided a quality

venue that very few provincial towns could equal. The prizes for the individual events were generous, estimated to be worth in excess of £100 in 1901, and attracted entries from some of the leading athletes in the country. [181] Even the novelty event of the sack race offered a first prize of a suit of Irish tweed, presented by Mullingar draper, Mr Joseph Kirwan. The appearance of quality athletes in Mullingar was encouraged by the centrality of the town and the accessibility facilitated by the rail network. Tom Kiely, who won the Olympic All-Around event at the St Louis Olympic Games of 1904, competed in 1901, 1902 and 1903 and Denis Horgan competed in a number of weight-throwing events at the 1904 meet.[182] He won thirteen AAA shot putt titles between 1893 and 1912 and was a silver medallist at the 1908 Olympic Games in the same event.[183] Walter Newburn made one of his last competitive appearances at the 1902 meet.[184] The association with the RIC and the active involvement of the highest-ranking officers of the force in the organisation of the event brought status to the promotion. The good order and management associated with the sports were such that the organisers were awarded the hosting of championship events, which added to the meet's attractiveness. In 1902, the Leinster long-jump and three-mile cycling championships were hosted.[185] Musical entertainment was an integral part of any sporting promotion of significance and the Dublin RIC band were recruited to provide this essential feature; the Mullingar Brass and Reed Band joined them at the 1903 and 1904 events.[186]

Just as organising tennis tournaments placed pressure on lawn-tennis clubs, the promotion of open sports meetings was also financially demanding. Despite a reported attendance of several thousand at the 1894 meet, the Athlone Bicycle Club made a loss of £20, a loss attributed to the difficulty in collecting gate receipts, as hundreds passed in without paying. The cost of bringing a band from Mullingar, to perform the essential musical accompaniment, was another contributory factor.[187] The difficulties involved in the organisation of a major athletics meet was also demanding on the energy and enthusiasm of the members and may have contributed to the shortened lifespan of the typical cycling club. Despite the problems, the promotion of events such as the above occasionally allowed the relationship between clubs and patrons to become transposed, as clubs became the providers rather than recipients of local patronage. The County Westmeath RIC Club became a donor of finance to local charity in 1901. At the annual meeting of the club in December a sum of £10 was donated to the St Vincent de Paul society from club funds, for 'the relief of the poor of all denominations'.[188]

IV

Although their origins were different and their strength varied over time golf, tennis and cycling clubs were essentially managed and organised in a similar manner. Members elected principal officers and a committee who were responsible for managing the clubs' affairs between periods of election, in a manner that paralleled the management of the Westmeath Hunt Club. Tennis and golf required considerable investment in infrastructure with the sourcing of specifically designated playing arenas and the development of appropriate pavilions essentials of the sports. Financial viability and the access to a playing field were crucial factors in determining the survival rates of sports clubs. Sports clubs in the Victorian era tended to be ephemeral organisations with an unpredictable lifespan. As was seen earlier even the club at the apex of the pyramid, the Westmeath Hunt Club, faced constant challenges to maintain financial viability. The three gentry-associated tennis clubs in the county were financially secure with well-developed playing facilities and basic pavilions, factors that ensured their stability.

The development and maintenance of these facilities provided the main drain on the finances and resources of the clubs. The main source of finance for clubs was the individual subscriptions calculated to cover the running expenses for the year. Fragmented newspaper evidence provides some insights into the financial demands on members and the investments made by the tennis clubs within the county. In 1887, male members of the Athlone Cricket and Lawn Tennis clubs paid 10s annual membership and ladies paid 5s. Combinations of three ladies were entitled to a discounted family membership of 12s 6d.[189] The club, including its cricket branch, had an income of £25 16s in 1886 and an expenditure of £24 8s 4d.[190] The principal item of expenditure for the season was the payment of rent to Mr Curley for the use of his field. This was renegotiated down to £10 for the 1887 season.[191] The following season it was necessary to increase membership fees by 50 per cent to 15s and 7s 6d respectively, because of the additional expense incurred the previous season in the erection of the pavilion. At the AGM, it was decided to purchase new nets, roof the pavilion, mark out some new courts and 'employ a man as a court keeper'.[192] The club was rather unfortunate in making this investment, as the club ground was flooded for over two months during 1888.[193] Its successor, the Athlone Lawn Tennis club was able to report to the AGM of 1896 that the club had no balance, no debt and a considerable amount of lawn tennis equipment purchased.[194] This communal ownership of playing equipment was a common feature of some early sports clubs and helped to reduce the cost of individual participation.[195]

In contrast, the more up-market Garden Vale club reported a credit balance of £20 at its 1888 AGM.[196] At the 1901 AGM, the treasurer reported to the members that the club was financially flourishing despite the severe losses incurred in running the open tournament.[197] In Mullingar, a similar pattern emerged. Following the opening season of 1892, the committee of the County Westmeath Lawn Tennis club invested considerable finance in installing a drainage system and levelling the courts. A sum of £75 was paid to the labourers of Mullingar who were involved in this work.[198] One of the club's courts was completely re-structured during the closed season of 1897–98 at a cost of £34 19s 7d but the club was still able to report a credit balance of £10 18s 10d at the 1898 annual meeting.[199] The Moate Lawn Tennis Club also invested in their facilities and for the 1900 season had moved venue to 'a very nice walled in premises' on which was developed two tennis courts and two croquet courts.[200]

The organisation of an annual tournament presented financial risks to the clubs. Tournaments did not always return a profit. The first such tournament was organised by the Athlone Lawn Tennis and Cricket Club in 1886. It was a week-long event for which a large tent was erected, refreshments served to visitors and the band of the Berkshire Regiment supplied the music, free of charge.[201] Financial donations made by supportive patrons provided the main finance for the event. At the time it was impossible to promote a sports event of any significance without such patronage. Committees responsible for the promotion of regattas, race meetings, athletic sports and yachting festivals inevitably began their work with the opening of subscription lists for sponsorship. On this occasion, the tennis club attracted donations from thirty-nine patrons, many of them also members of the club.[202] The levying of entry fees also provided finance. Ladies paid 2s and males 3s to enter the open events.[203] This initial venture into the world of tennis tournaments proved a profitable one for the club as a total of £22 5s 6d was received in subscriptions and entry fees and the sum of £20 2s 2d was invested in prizes, leaving a balance of £2 3s 4d to the credit of the club.[204]

Inter-club games were also a source of expense for clubs. Entertain-ment had to be provided and while tennis matches were organised in an alcohol free environment, teas were an essential part of the day's business. The Garrison Golf Club provided entertainment outside of the military environment. Included in their accounts for May 1899 was the cost of £1 3s 1d for 'lunch etc.', at the Shannon café for the Tullamore team and transport costs of 10s.[205]

The organisation of fund-raising events added to the social dimension of the clubs. Golf and tennis clubs organised concerts and musical enter-tainments that normally featured a combination of local and outside entertainers. The Westmeath Golf Club organised a 'successful and inter-esting' concert at the Parochial Hall, Mullingar, for 'the purpose of paying off such debt as yet remains in connection with the erection of the New Pavillion [sic] at the Golf Club links'.[206] The event offered an addi-tional illustration of the integration of military personnel into elite society as the event was organised by Lieutenant-Colonel Carpendale.[207] The concert raised the sum of £9 11s and a similar event organised by Mrs Murray contributed £2 19s 2d. The combined amounts provided almost 28 per cent of the building costs of the clubhouse.[208] Concerts pro-moted by the golf and tennis clubs provided some of the highlights of the social scene in the Moate district. The lawn tennis club promoted a concert in 1894 that featured vocalists, instrumentalists and recitation.[209]

Golf clubs recruited professionals to improve the skills of the members. This also added to the expenditure incurred by these clubs. This willingness to invest in expertise and engage personnel to carry out the more menial duties was a characteristic that distinguished the clubs of the wealthier members of society. The Athlone Garrison Golf Club made such an investment in October 1898 when the committee sanctioned the hire of George Ferrie, 'the professional to the Irish Golfing Union', for two weeks at £1 per week.[210] He was eventually paid £4 for his efforts in Athlone and travelling expenses of 13s 6d.[211] The Athlone Golf Club hired Sam Smith as a professional and green-keeper in 1904 at a weekly rate of 10s.[212] In January 1903, the committee of the Westmeath County Club announced that a professional had been hired from the St Andrews Club, on the recommendation of Mr Auchterlonie, the Open champion of 1893.[213] The professional, A. Gourlay, arrived as scheduled and his earnings were partly governed by the number of lessons he delivered. He was available on the course each day between 10.00 a.m. and 6.00 p.m. Lady members were requested to take their lessons as far as possible in the morning. Each lesson cost 1s for a round of nine holes or an hourly rate of 1s.[214]

The most important person hired by a golf club was the groundsman. He was responsible for the maintenance and management of the course as well as a range of additional, fundamentally menial, duties. The basic duty of the groundsman at the Westmeath County Golf Club was 'to keep the links in proper order to the satisfaction of the green committee', a duty that required him to procure 'any additional labour required for the purpose at his own expense'. He was obliged to be present on the links no later then 10.00 each morning, for which he was remunerated at the weekly rate of 10s.[215] This wage was similar to that received by an agricultural labourer at the time.[216] He received a total of £13 for his efforts in the course of the 1904–05 season.[217] Cost-cutting measures introduced at the AGM of 1905 as a result of a bank balance overdrawn to the sum £19 9s 10d, included the re-definition of some of the groundsman's duties, involving him in even more menial tasks.[218]

The record book of the Athlone Garrison Golf Club includes monthly accounts for the period between 1898 and 1902 that enable the detailed reconstruction of the financial affairs of the club. The minute book and financial accounts of the Westmeath County Golf Club also survive from 1904 to 1935. The first year for which a full financial record is presented in the Athlone Garrison minute book is for 1898.[219] In that year, the club suffered a loss of £6 9s 6d on the year's operations but began the year with a credit balance of £24 6s 1d. In 1898, the club gained its income from three sources. Membership fees were the most important and accounted for 59 per cent of total income. Male members paid a fee of

15s and females 7s 6d. Twenty-four males and thirteen females paid the full fee in 1898. The club endeavoured to maximise its income by making available different categories of membership and in particular attempted to encourage the short-stay army officer to become involved by offering weekly membership. A variety of other short-term membership fees that ranged from one week to a half season were also available. In September 1900 a variety of membership categories were defined and membership fees levied as illustrated in Table 8.[220] Entrance fees for competitions and sale of golf balls was the other means of raising income used by the club. Payment of the groundsman's wage constituted the main expenditure. He was paid a weekly wage of 12s 6d for a total of thirty-five weeks and a few part weeks that brought his take-home pay to £22 8s 6d for the year.[221] The club affiliated to the Golfing Union of Ireland and paid a subscription fee of £2 2s for 1897 and 1898.[222] This integration into the national system was extended still further in December 1899 when an entrance fee of £1 was paid to compete in the Irish club competition.[223] As mentioned earlier fees paid to the professional George Ferrie amounted to £4 13s 6d.[224] Rent of £5 10s was paid to J. Kilroy and £6 19s was paid out in prize-money for the various competitions organised during the year.[225] Maintaining a stock of balls (£12 8s 1d) that was available to members to purchase as well as expenses associated with club administration constituted the remainder of the expenditure.

Category	Cost		
	£	s	d
Gentlemen	1	5	0
Ladies		12	6
Gentlemen living >5 miles from links	1	0	0
Ladies living >5 miles from links		10	0
Monthly membership: gentlemen		2	6
Monthly membership: ladies		2	6
Ladies and gentlemen: one week			6

Table 8. Range of membership fees available in Athlone Garrison Golf Club, 1900 (Minute book of Athlone Garrison Golf Club)

The Westmeath County Club based at Mullingar also struggled financially on occasion. At this time the club had vacated the racecourse and was, since 1900, based in Mount Prospect on land owned by Mr Killian.[226] The income of £50 12s 6d for the 1904 season was composed almost totally of members' subscriptions and included a group subscription of £10 made by the officers of the Connaught Rangers. Expenditure for the season amounted to £69 8s 6d. The chief items of expenditure were rent of £15, groundsman's wages of £14 2s and a sum of £10 18s 6d paid to labourers.[227] At the annual meeting, held on 14 October 1905, the club was overdrawn by £19 9s 10d at the local bank.

Financial rectitude was paramount for the 1906 season. The services of the pavilion cleaning lady were dispensed with and the cleaning duties became part of the groundsman's duties. The secretary, P. J. Nooney, suggested that the amount of expenditure on the course was 'out of all proportion to its size'. In 1903, it amounted to £15 0s 6d and to £8 10s 3d in 1904; Nooney proposed that a sum not exceeding £3 would be spent on the course in the 1906 season. The groundsman was excused from piloting the boat across the canal for members and instead he was required to devote his time to working on the greens. A toll of one penny was charged to members using the boat that was now piloted by one of the caddies. The measures worked and the AGM of 1906 reported an income of £87 and an expenditure of £30 less. The overdraft had been cleared and the club was £10 13s 11d in credit.[228]

The picture that emerges from this fragmentary financial analysis is one that supports the conclusion of Tranter on his analysis of the financial circumstances of sports clubs in central Scotland. The more middle class a sport's membership, the more stable were its institutions and the less pronounced the fluctuations in their numbers.[229] The tennis and golf clubs established in Westmeath (with one exception), despite experiencing the occasional financial health-scare emerged at the end of the century as stable and established organisations. Access to bank overdrafts, the ability of members to afford increased membership fees, the facility to organise fund-raising events such as concerts, subscriptions sourced from benefactors, profits from organised competitions and financial retrenchment (if necessary), were factors in maintaining this stability. These clubs also provided the structure about which an important segment of the members' social life revolved. This emotional attachment was an extremely important factor in providing the incentives for members to make the necessary financial investment required to develop infrastructure and on occasion to maintain viability.

V

In the male dominant world of the Victorian and Edwardian era, the role of women was rigidly defined and confined almost exclusively to domesticity. The notion that men and women ought to inhabit separate spheres of existence was a fundamental tenet of elite and middle-class society. The public world of business, politics and leisure was considered appropriate for the male gender; for females, the private world of the home was the prescribed environment, where they would bear and raise children and provide a haven to which men would retreat from the pressures of public life. In practical terms, this meant that sport in general and competitive, team-based and mixed-gender sport in particular, was considered to be an unsuitable pursuit for women. Active participation threatened masculinity and femininity, as well as female domestic and procreative responsibilities. This ideology was sufficient to restrict women to a subordinate, minor and often derided sporting role. Therefore, for cultural, biological and social reasons the functions of the sexes were to be kept largely separate, according to the orthodoxy of the time. According to Hargreaves, the impact of the separate spheres of existence theory was such that women's participation in sport 'embodied the characteristics of passivity rather than activity, subordination rather than ascendancy': 'Women were obliged to show restraint, be refined and respectable, and confirm at all times the ladylike modes of behaviour prescribed for them.'[230] Those who sought social approval for their involvement in sport had to demonstrate that femininity and more active participation in physical activity were not incompatible.[231] It has been accepted that these societal attitudes were primarily responsible for the limited involvement of women in sport. However, Tranter has challenged this notion and is supported by Cartriona M. Parratt, who shows that 'some women were active, enthusiastic, and skilful participants who were drawn to the sport [hunting] by the enjoyment, the wholesomeness, even the nerve-bracing dash of danger'. Some women stepped outside the limits of conventionality and challenged the image of passive, fragile womanhood.[232] The performance of Westmeath women in the hunting field as documented in Chapter 1 epitomises this challenging of convention.[233]

Participation in philanthropic activities provided the main opportunity to upper- and middle-class Irish women to enhance and expand their public and social role. Social work, normally voluntary, ranging from house visitation to work in prisons, refuges or workhouses was viewed as a legitimate public occupation. Women established a myriad of philanthropic societies to cater for specific perceived needs and involvement in these organisations offered women a sense of identity and community, as well as a generating a sense of purpose and achievement, and allowed women to play a role in expressing their concern for the less fortunate in society.[234] This philanthropic desire was expressed in a sporting context, when a number of Athlone women were active in promoting and staffing a temperance tent at the Athlone races.[235]

The introduction of table tennis to the county provided the means for combining sports participation, organisation and the commitment to voluntarism. The novelty value associated with table tennis provided an opportunity for some women from landed families to organise tournaments of both a private and public nature for altruistic reasons. The sport was the ideal vehicle for showing that femininity and gentle physical activity were not incompatible. The Longworth Hall in Athlone was the venue for the first such tournament organised in February 1901. This event was organised to raise funds for the Westmeath stall at the Royal City Hospital Bazaar to be held in Dublin. The event attracted an entry of eighteen men and twelve women and raised a sum of £10 for the charity. A number of events were organised in the Moate district. Mrs Russell at her Lissanode mansion and Miss Fetherstonhaugh of

Grouse Lodge, promoted events. Mrs Barton of Mosstown promoted a competition that was held in the national school building in Moate.[236] Mrs Russell returned to Athlone and the Longworth Hall to promote a tournament in March.[237] A similar phenomenon was exhibited in Mullingar where a number of ladies of similar social status organised a 'ping-pong' tournament and an American croquet tournament at the grounds of the Westmeath Lawn Tennis and Croquet Club in aid of the Cigas Bazaar in Dublin.[238]

There is little evidence of women acting as patrons or as administrative officers. The Athlone Cricket and Lawn Tennis Club was exceptional as women were appointed to the main administrative positions of the tennis section of the club. Mrs Robson and Miss Haslam were elected treasurers and Miss Tighe secretary at the 1895 AGM of the club.[239] Women were active fundraisers for the initial tournament of the club. The club received subscriptions from the Misses Stokes and Mrs and the Misses Sheffield were also active in organising subscriptions. A member of the ladies' committee, Miss S. J. Smith, was responsible for collecting one-fifth of the entire amount collected by subscription.[240] The sole function of the ladies' committee established by the Garden Vale Club in 1895 and succeeding years was to provide refreshments at matches and club days.[241] The ladies' committee of the County Club in Mullingar had a similar function. These roles helped to emphasise what was regarded as the essential domesticity of the female.

Golf and tennis clubs actively encouraged women's participation by making available preferential subscription rates. The Athlone Cricket and Lawn Tennis Club in 1887 offered female membership at half the male rate.[242] This included a 50 per cent increase, on the previous season, an adjustment that was applied equally to both sexes.[243] Family participation was encouraged by the membership fee structure. Family membership for golf cost £2, gentlemen's membership £1 10s and female membership 15s at the Westmeath County Club in 1904.[244] The female golfers were not formally represented at committee level throughout the period of this study but there is no evidence in the minute books of either club significantly restricting female access to the courses. The Westmeath County Club organised a regular Saturday silver spoon competition for its members in which the lady members had the right to compete 'on every Saturday save the first Saturday of each month being the date fixed for Gentlemen's medal play'.[245] This is the only record of any restrictions operative against women members. The Athlone Garrison Club's competitions were open to all members, where Mrs Pearson was one of the lowest handicapped players.

The surviving minute books of the two main golf clubs in the county provide accurate evidence of female involvement in golf. The Westmeath County Club had thirteen female members in the 1904–05 season, out of a total membership of seventy-one.[246] In 1909 this had increased to forty-five from a total of 137, a proportionate increase from eighteen per cent to thirty-three per cent.[247] Eighteen of these women were married and at least twelve of them shared club membership with their husbands, an indication of the importance of shared family recreation. The female membership included eight family groups composed of seven mothers and daughters and one group of sisters. In the period between 1898 and 1901, twenty-five of the eighty-five members of the Athlone Garrison Golf Club were female, and seventeen of these women were married.

A feature of elite female involvement in tennis and golf was the extent to which a number of married women were active participants. As in central Scotland, active participation in sport was not restricted to unmarried females.[248] The active membership of the Garden Vale Croquet Club included at least ten married and eight single women, who participated in club competitions between 1898 and 1900. The lawn tennis equivalent had an equal distribution of single and active married women, but only four married women were involved at a competitive level; the remainder were involved in administrative and in particular shared responsibility for entertainment.

Cycling offered tremendous potential for liberation to middle-class females yet there is very little evidence of female participation in recreational or competitive cycling in Westmeath. Cycling offered females the opportunity to participate in active forms of recreation and was especially attractive to those who had never previously engaged in sport or pastimes. The bicycle represented the means by which girls could escape from chaperonage and other forms of control over their movements. It was, however, an opportunity that the women of Westmeath rejected at this time.

Female involvement in cycling was limited to passive participation as spectators who followed behind their male friends in carriages on their organised recreational outings.[249] The Athlone club in particular was especially anxious to increase female involvement. Upwards of fifty women were invited to the club's quadrille party in 1894 but, when only twenty-five acknowledged the invitation and twelve accepted, the club was forced to organise a bachelor party and smoking concert instead.[250] A motion was passed in 1896 that opened club membership to ladies but there is evidence of only one woman availing of this facility.[251] This was Miss Gladstone, who was an active participant in the club's outings and was proficient enough to cycle the thirty-five miles from Athlone to Mullingar in May 1896.[252] The members of the Athlone club were aware of the potential of the club for increasing social contact between young adults at a time when opportunities for meeting the opposite sex in an unsupervised setting were limited. Women were occasionally prepared to participate in the socialisation associated with cycling but were not prepared for active participation as cyclists.

A small number of Westmeath women became enthusiastic competitors in tennis, golf and croquet and, for a few, this competitive zeal was fulfilled by participation in regional and United Kingdom wide competition. In the period of this study there was no record of women competing in cycling but tennis, golf, croquet and table tennis inter- and intra-club competition featured women's events. In 1896, the Athlone Garrison Golf Club featured a mixed foursomes competition when Surgeon Major and Mrs Crofts defeated Lieutenant Thorpe and his partner in the final. The ladies stroke play competition of April 1898 attracted entries from seven ladies.[253] Miss Hodson, of the Garden Vale club, was the first tennis player to create an impression nationally, when she competed at the Fitzwilliam lawn tennis tournament, in May 1899. Her performance attracted the attention of the London journal *Lawn Tennis and Croquet*. According to this journal, Miss Hodson must be placed 'absolutely in the first class':

> She is very active and very steady: her style is easy, rather too easy in fact. If she took more pains in making her ground-strokes firmer and bolder and developed an overhand service she would be almost invincible.[254]

The 1899 success continued a trend begun the previous year. In September 1898, Miss Hodson was a winner at her host club's open tournament and earlier in the year she had been successful at open tournaments in Roscrea, Nenagh and Galway.[255] In the early 1900s, a number of Athlone ladies became part of the national croquet competitive circuit, a trend that began when Captain and Mrs Preston competed in the Irish croquet championships at Fitzwilliam in 1901.[256] The most successful of these was Miss Coote, daughter of sports evangelist Orlando Coote. In August 1901, she won the South of Ireland croquet championship.[257] In July 1902, Mrs Preston won the North of Ireland championship and Miss Coote the South of Ireland title.[258] According to one historian of the game, 'Nina Coote was a beautiful woman with large eyes and an aquiline nose and played with a rather wild vivacity that was in complete contrast to the more studied style of her closest rival.'[259] She won the Ladies' Open Championships in 1903 and 1905, a year in which she also won the mixed doubles, the Irish gold medals and the gold caskets.[260] She played with a golfer's wide swing and usually completed her games in record time although her inconsistent play also attracted attention.[261] Mrs Preston won the 1903 croquet championship of Ireland and defeated her club-mate in the semi-final. Miss Coote then went on to win the first-class singles handicap tournament at the same event.[262] In May 1903, Coote won the first of her English championship titles at Wimbledon, in an event that was contested by forty-three players. This victory meant the Garden Vale club members held the Irish and English championship titles.[263] The game was sufficiently popular with the ladies of Athlone that the club was able to travel to Banagher, County Offaly to challenge the local ladies in an inter-club event.[264] Clearly players such as these were far more than refining influences and decorative additions to the croquet lawns and were little concerned about displaying passivity or subordination.

The women who were actively involved in sport were those whose economic and domestic situation was such that they were free of any financial or time constraints that might have restricted their involvement. They were sufficiently independent to ignore contemporary ideas on the role of women in society. Mrs Edith Preston, whose achievements have been outlined above, was the wife of the resident magistrate, John Preston, and resided in a seventeen roomed, first class house in Athlone. A domestic staff of five female servants.– including governess, parlour maid, lady's maid, cook and house maid – managed the household chores and took care of the needs of the Preston's four children, aged between sixteen and eight in 1901.[265] This domestic and economic independence allowed Mrs Preston to travel extensively to compete in croquet events and in 1902 she recorded victories in Belfast, Mullingar, Tullamore, Cork, Dublin, Athlone and Chichester whilst her daughter was also successful in Tullamore, Dublin and Cork.[266] The Misses Hodson and Coote who also competed seriously at national level shared a landed-gentry background. These women were also free of any time or financial constraints that might have inhibited their participation.

VI

Golf and tennis clubs, with one notable exception, were permanent features of the Westmeath sporting and cultural landscape, during the period examined in this study. Ironically, cycling clubs, which required the least infrastructural investment, proved to be the transient organisations. The lifecycle of the cycling clubs' established in Westmeath in the 1890s extended no longer than five years. Cycling was popular in the 1890s, a popularity associated with its novelty value and its value as means of enhancing the status of clerks and shops assistants. Cycling clubs initial function was limited to the organisation of recreational outings to the rural surrounds linked to visits to places of historic and cultural interest. These outings attracted small numbers of members and so limited the social dimension of the activity. Socialisation required mass participation, which was never a feature of the Westmeath cycling club. This socialisation was an essential element of the sporting experience, as is abundantly clear throughout this study, and cycling's failure to develop this dimension was an important factor in club demise. The rapid development of the bicycle as a means of transport and as a work-related device effectively took the bicycle out of the leisure sphere and gave it a utilitarian purpose. The bicycle was no longer a status-enhancing accessory and therefore its popularity with the middle classes declined. The result was that the vocational group most closely associated with the bicycle at the end of the century, the RIC, also formed the strongest cycling club in the county.

In the hierarchy of social prestige associated with the clubs dealt with in this chapter, membership of a lawn-tennis club offered the highest status. There is little evidence of tennis bridging the gap between the upper and middle classes that Richard Holt identifies as one of the game's great virtues.[267] In so far as this happened the middle-class members attracted to the game came from a confined section of this group. The specifically middle-class Athlone club was short-lived, partly because its class structure proved to be a restrictive influence on its progress. The nature of its membership provided a barrier to its integration into the wider tennis networks and some of the people associated with this club found the Athlone Golf Club a more appropriate institution for recreation and socialisation. Golf, as it developed, increasingly became the preserve of the higher status professionals with doctors, lawyers and bank managers dominating membership lists. In Mullingar, special efforts were made to attract bank personnel to the game. Bankers, under the rank of manager or agent, were admitted at half the normal subscription rate in 1904.[268] As a winter activity its appeal to the sporting members of the landed gentry was limited. Hunting still remained the core activity for this group.

A small number of women of independent mind and means and with supportive husbands or fathers, defied the orthodoxy of the day, and stepped outside the bounds of domesticity and actively participated in lawn tennis and golf. The evidence from Westmeath on women's sports participation is similar to the findings of Neil Tranter in his Scottish studies, and would suggest that the behaviour of upper- and middle-class Victorian and Edwardian women, and the reactions of men towards them did not always conform to what was the desired ideal. The extent of female participation, as both players and spectators, their frequent shared participation with men, the competitive zeal displayed by some, and the extent to which married as well as single women took part, all suggest that the acceptance of the separate spheres lifestyle thesis was not universal. Similarly, based on male willingness to support female participation, their willingness to compete in mixed-gender events in tennis, croquet and golf, risking defeat by females in the latter two activities, and their practice of offering women preferential membership rates, would suggest that some middle- and upper-class males also rejected the prevailing orthodoxy.[269]

4. Cricket, 1850–1905

Cricket was the most important sport that developed in Victorian West-meath. It was the game that enjoyed the most continuity of play, and by the end of the century was the participant sport with the greatest popular appeal. Westmeath cricket in the period covered by this study, experienced an extraordinary metamorphosis that saw it transformed from being the preserve of the elite, to a sport in which the agricultural labourer was the main participant. Cricket did not decline as a sport in the 1880s, as is commonly perceived; in fact, the game experienced its most rigorous period of growth in Westmeath during the 1880s and 1890s. It became a sport with widespread appeal and an activity that allowed the workingman the opportunity of enjoying the sporting experience and its integral ancillary activities.

Irish historians have largely ignored cricket as a subject worthy of academic interrogation. Apart from a recent monograph, three important journal articles and local studies, the sport has remained unexplored in popular and academic journals.[1] This lack of analysis has allowed a number of accepted 'truths' to emerge on the role and importance of cricket in Irish society, which are unsupported by quantitative data. There is general agreement that cricket's popularity declined sharply after the 1870s, that it was confined to a narrow social elite and that its growth was associated with the military presence in Ireland. Historians who have commented on cricket's importance to Irish Victorian culture have identified the 1870s as the decade of the sports peak of popularity. Marcus de Burca considered that the rapid growth of the GAA brought to a halt the spread of cricket in rural areas where the game had gained a foothold.[2] Alan Bairner and John Sugden adopt a similar position and believe that the rapid growth that cricket experienced in the 1860s and 1870s was halted both 'as an indirect consequence of Land League activities and as a direct result of the GAA with its avowed policy to usurp such foreign games as cricket'.[3] They suggest that the activities of Land League protagonists soured relationships between sponsoring landlords and playing tenants and as a result the game withered and died. Neal Garnham, using a more empirical approach based on newspaper analysis and use of Lawrence's cricket handbooks, also identified a general decline in cricket during the 1870s.[4] In addition, Garnham suggests that in the years before widespread organised agrarian agitation landlords had either withdrawn their patronage of cricket or simply not offered it in the first place.[5]

A recent chronicler of the game, Gerard Siggins, has claimed that cricket suffered more than any other sport in the early 1880s as 'all was not well with Ireland'. Siggins claims that in the rural counties the land war was devastating for the game. He also identifies the upsurge in nationalism and the growth in interest in hurling and football as factors responsible for transforming 'cricket's role as a social glue' and as a result it 'rapidly turned to dust'. Competition from new sports was also an important factor in the game's decline 'but the changed political climate was most to blame'.[6] The importance of military garrisons in spreading the cricket gospel in Ireland is a popular theme in Irish sporting literature. According to Trevor West, cricket is the only sport that can be accurately referred to as a garrison game, 'for cricket clubs sprang up in remarkable profusion around the middle of the nineteenth century in the vicinity of army barracks or on the estates of the gentry'.[7]

Cricket has also been portrayed as the chosen pastime of the higher status social groups. Stanley Bergin and Derek Scott, writing in 1980, considered that 'whatever cricket was played in Ireland was confined essentially to the military, the gentry and members of the vice-regal or Chief Secretary's staff and household'.[8] The restricted popularity of Irish cricket was acknowledged by Lawrence in 1880 when he described cricket as dependent on 'the aristocracy and the well-to-do commercial class' rather than being the 'pastime of the masses, as it is in England'. He also suggested that the financial difficulties these classes were having at the time was responsible for their lack of support for the game.[9]

Patrick Bracken's study of cricket in Tipperary challenges several of these ideas on cricket's decline. Bracken identified a decline in cricket playing in Tipperary during and after the Land War, partly associated with withdrawn landlord patronage, a decline that levelled out in the years prior to and during the formation of the GAA. In the 1890s, the game was revived with renewed vigour, before declining in the 1900s.[10] In Westmeath, cricket experienced a period of growth between 1880 and 1900, and only began to decline in the early years of the new century. The sport was the only one within the county with widespread popular appeal.

As has been outlined in the Introduction, agriculture in Westmeath was dominated by the commercial grazing sector. This created a substantial reservoir of wealth in the county. The most immediate causes of the general economic depression in the late 1870s had a less serious impact on the Westmeath agricultural economy. Poor wheat prices and bad harvests, together with competition from cereals imported from America as well as the failure of the potato crop caused little distress in Westmeath.[11] Land League activities in Westmeath had little impact and according to one commentator the land war in the county 'was little more than an opportunity for verbal heroics on the part of a small but committed group of townsmen, priests and farmers; the history of the league in the county exhibited not the solidarity of the agricultural classes but the indifference of the majority of farmers to both nationalism and the wants and desires of labourers'.[12] What passed for Land League agitation in Westmeath from March to October 1881 amounted to little more than tenants offering their landlord Griffith's valuation and a coming to terms a short while later. Boycotts, evictions and sheriff's sales were rare occurrences. Settlements were reached through negotiation and compromise in the majority of cases. The involvement of most of the inhabitants of the county was to attend a Land League meeting and even then it is doubtful that more than a small minority attended such meetings regularly.[13]

There were several branches of the Land League formed in Kilkenny and many land disputes but the playing of cricket was largely unaffected by the unrest. Kilkenny cricket had progressed to the stage that most of the committed teams were largely independent of landlord support at the time of serious land league activity. Tullaroan was a cricket stronghold at this time and some of its cricket players were also land league activists. Henry D. Meagher for instance was elected assistant secretary of the Tullaroan branch of the Irish National League established in March 1884.[14]

II

The first formal game of cricket played in Ireland took place in the Phoenix Park in August 1792 between the Garrison and an All-Ireland selection. However, the sport made little progress until the 1830s when a number of teams scattered across the country played games against each other. Non-metropolitan centres of the game in the 1830s included Ballinasloe, County Galway, Kilkenny city and Carlow.[15] In Dublin, the Phoenix Club was founded in 1830, followed by the Trinity College Club in 1835 and the Leinster Cricket Club ten years later.[16] The Phoenix Club is generally considered to be the oldest in the country, pre-dating the Carlow County Club by one year; it has also been suggested that the latter club was founded in 1823 and that the Carlow landlord class introduced the game to Dublin. Carlow landlords were involved in the establishment of the Phoenix Club and in the 1830s the Carlow season always began with two games against the Dublin club.[17] By 1835, the Phoenix Club had secured its own ground south of the Grand Canal, behind upper Baggot Street and at this stage the club was strongly influenced by Lord Clonbrock, Lord Dunlo and John Parnell, who introduced cricket to Wicklow when he founded a club at Avondale.[18] By 1850, according to Trevor West, cricket had spread to the 'most unlikely parts of rural Ireland' and had gained a foothold in the larger towns, due to the combined influence of the gentry and the military.[19] Neal

Garnham has established that by 1871, cricket clubs existed in every county in Ireland.[20]

In the period between 1850 and 1879 cricket in Westmeath was restricted spatially and socially. It was confined to the main towns in the county, to three schools, to teams organised by members of the gentry and to the military regiments based in Athlone and Mullingar. Socially, the game was the almost exclusive preserve of the county's landed gentry and those who shared a similar background, such as the higher status professions and county administrators.

In the 1850s cricket was played sporadically with only seventeen games in total reported in the local press. The first recorded cricket game in Westmeath during the period of this study was played between Kilbeggan and the Vignoles estate at Cornaher in September 1852. This was followed by a return match in October.[21] Other matches were confined to games played by the County Westmeath Club against neighbouring County Meath and against various military regiments based in the county. Supportive gentry families hosted games, as at this stage the county club did not have a permanent venue. A two-day match with the Roebuck Club from Dublin was played on ground that bordered Lough Derravaragh where the hospitality of Sir Percy Nugent, 'the chief supporter of cricket in the county' was enjoyed.[22] In 1855–56 matches against Meath were played at Turbotstown, the seat of James Arthur Dease and at Baltrasna, the residence of Anthony O'Reilly, DL.[23]

In contrast, the 1860s was an extremely active decade with 244 games reported. This was followed by a sharp decline in the 1870s when only seventy-one matches were featured in the local press. This local pattern of chronological change was a reflection of national trends. Neal Garnham's analysis of Lawrence's incomplete data identified the late 1860s and early 1870s as the peak period of Irish cricket activity. The yearly variation in games played within the county for the period 1860 to 1879 is illustrated in Figure 14.

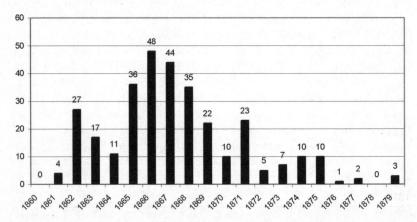

Figure 14. Cricket matches played in Westmeath, 1860–1879

These returns make it possible to gain an insight into the structure and organisation of cricket within the county at the time and the changes and continuities in the lives of those involved in the game. In the period between 1850 and 1879, thirty-nine different Westmeath combinations played the sport. Associations that represented the landed classes, ranging from the Westmeath County Club to teams representing individuals from this particular social group, dominated the scene. The Westmeath County Club activity peaked in the second half of the 1860s but from 1874 onwards neither Lawrence nor the local press contains any reference to County Club games for the remainder of the decade (Table 9). At this stage the club had procured its own ground, which was also used to host other sporting events. One of these events, a pigeon shoot advertised for January 1874, illustrates the extent to which county and military society was integrated, and the extent to which their sporting interests coincided. Members of the Westmeath Hunt Club, the Westmeath County Cricket Club, officers of the Westmeath Rifles and serving officers quartered in Athlone, Mullingar and Longford were eligible to compete.[24]

The Westmeath County Club's core playing membership was confined to a small number of individuals drawn from the ranks of the middle-ranking landed gentry. In this study the importance of individual influence to the promotion of sport is a recurring theme and, regardless of the social class involved, the impact of the enthusiastic individual key. The Westmeath club's most active period coincided with the residency of Major Moore at Mullingar. The small number of players involved meant that the club's existence was precarious. In 1869, for instance, 'owing to the absence from home of some of their best men they were not in any match able to bring their eleven together and in some matches not more than four or five men'.[25] In 1873, the 'Westmeath County Cricket Club could not get their eleven together for any of the matches they played . . . owing to the absence of some of their best men from home; they had consequently either to play short, or press emergencies into their stride.'[26] There is no record of County Club activity for the period between 1874 and 1880.

Year	Played	Won	Drew	Tie	Lost
1865	21	12	1	0	8
1866	26	21	2	0	3
1867	21	11	2	1	7
1868	15	9	4	0	2
1869	7	1	0	0	6
1870	7	1	0	0	6
1871	8	3	1	0	4
1872	2	2	0	0	0
1873	4	1	0	0	3

Table 9. Playing record of Westmeath County Cricket Club, 1865–1873 (*Lawrence's Handbook of Cricket* and *Westmeath Guardian* reportage)

When they were not active with the county team members of the landed gentry – such as Captain Nugent, Mr Hudson, Mr Hornridge, Major Moore, E. J. Cooper, Mr Fetherstonhaugh and the Honourable P. Greville-Nugent – organised their own matches. Demesne-centred combinations associated with the same individuals, such as those representing Calverston, Tyrrellspass, and Carrick, were also active at this time. Some Westmeath individuals interested in the sport also played with clubs outside the county.

Clubs were also established in the major urban areas during this period and are listed for Athlone, Mullingar, Kilbeggan, Castlepollard and Delvin. Three schools, Wilson's Hospital, Farra School and Ranelagh School, also promoted cricket as part of their curriculum. The Kilbeggan club was sufficiently well organised at this time to be able to hold an end of season game in 1862 between the first team and the second and third elevens of the club.[27] The popularity of the game in Kilbeggan was due to the influence of Tom Quinn, a property owner and land agent who was a native of the area. Quinn was a member of the Phoenix Club in Dublin and was, according to a contemporary commentator, 'the best bowler of his day. His batting and fielding were also good.'[28] Quinn was part of Charles Lawrence's All-Ireland XI of 1855 and an All-Ireland XXII that played against an All-England XI in 1860.[29] A club was established in Athlone in June 1871 with the MP for the town, J. J. Ennis, and Lord Castlemaine as patrons. The club's six-match programme embraced all the game's interest groups and included two matches with Roscommon county, two with the 98th Regiment and one with Ranelagh School. The club was strongly representative of the town's business interests.[30]

The opposition sourced for these games also provides an insight into the organisation and structure of the game at the time. The Westmeath County Club's main source of opposition was the military regiments based in Athlone or Mullingar followed by games with similar gentry selections. In the club's four busiest seasons from 1865 to 1868 matches were played against county teams including Wicklow, Meath, Cavan, Roscommon, Longford and Galway. Included in the Wicklow side that played in August 1865 was Charles Stewart Parnell, who was dismissed without scoring a single run.[31] This period of activity for the County Club included a week-long visit to Dublin where matches against the military, some educational institutions, the Vice-Regal Lodge, and leading clubs such as the Civil Service Club and the Phoenix Club were organised.[32] The landed gentry also dominated combinations that used non-county nomenclature as a means of identity, such as Summerhill (County Meath) and Edenderry (King's county). The Summerhill club was founded in 1863 and benefited from the patronage of Dr D. Trotter. He presented the members 'with an excellent piece of ground containing three acres that formed part of the gentleman's demesne'. He followed this the following year by erecting a 'spacious pavilion for the club'.[33]

A number of schools including Stoneyhurst College from Lancashire, Hollyville Pupils, St Stanislaus College and Sandymount were included in the competitive loop of the Westmeath County Club. In the early 1870s, according to Lawrence, many schools that had for years opposed school cricket as it 'distracted attention' from study were now amongst 'the liberal supporters of the game'. Public schools offered the advantage of a designated sports ground and a curriculum that placed an emphasis on sport for its health promoting value. Despite this, the game failed to prosper in the schools due to the very short summer term. The introduction of the Intermediate Education Act of 1878 reduced the school cricket season to just six weeks. 'Nothing', Lawrence reported, 'could be more injurious to the noble game.'[34] The Westmeath County Club played an annual match with the Jesuit St Stanislaus College at Rahan in the King's county close to the border of Westmeath. The college was noted for its cricket crease laid by Fr Wisthoff, who had come from Germany.[35] The restricted school summer term inspired some students to establish clubs in their home districts to satisfy their cricketing passions during the school holidays. The Clonmacnoise Cricket Club was founded in 1865 by the Charlton brothers, students of the Royal School, Banagher, 'in order to keep themselves in practice during the summer months.'[36]

In summary, the landed gentry and the schools that specialised in the education of their sons, dominated the game at this time. The most important sources of opposition for these clubs were the local military garrison clubs. Although the landed and associated classes may have dominated the game, cricket was not the exclusive preserve of these particular social groups. Urban professionals and merchants were

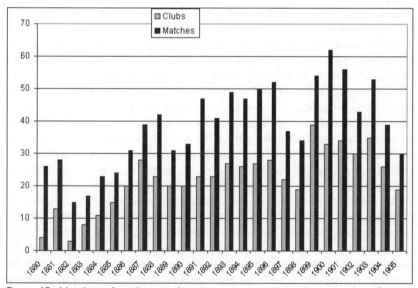

Figure 15. Number of cricket combinations active and matches played in County Westmeath, 1880–1905

becoming involved. Overall, in this period, Westmeath cricket conforms to the historical stereotype.

The years between 1880 and 1905 were the years of peak activity in Westmeath cricket, a time when the game was allegedly in decline nationally.

An examination of the number of games played and reported in the local press and the number of teams active has been used to measure the growth of cricket during this period. The pattern that emerges is illustrated in Figure 15. In the period 1880–1905, an incredible 1,003 cricket games were reported and, given the certainty of under-reporting, over 1,200 cricket matches were undoubtedly played within the county in this twenty-six year period.[37] Over 170 different civilian groups were identified as active at some stage during the period between 1880 and 1905.

The analysis established that a large proportion of clubs were ephemeral associations whose members came together for a single match and then dispersed. In the period 1880–1905, sixty-eight combinations are listed as involved in only one fixture and a further fifty-nine appeared in newspaper reports over two or three seasons. At the other end of the scale, twelve clubs were active over at least ten seasons. These clubs were properly established organisations that had a constitution and bye-laws, held annual meetings where officers for the season were elected, organised regular practice sessions and concluded the season with an annual ball. Many wore distinctive uniforms that emphasised their sense of collective identity and set them apart as a community of respectable athletes. The numbers involved in cricket in certain districts was such that twenty-five clubs had sufficient playing numbers to allow them to field an occasional second team or promote a juvenile section. The location of the most active of the clubs is illustrated in Figure 16 and their playing records are tabulated in Appendices 12, 13 and 14.

The 179 different civilian cricket combinations active in Westmeath in the period 1880–1905 can be divided into a number of categories; this classification system illustrates the broad appeal of the game at the time. One group, forming 16 per cent of the total, consisted of well-to-do individuals who assembled a group of their friends to challenge a combination formed by individuals of similar status. Twenty-eight different individuals organised these games the majority of which were once-off events. This group chiefly included landed estate proprietors such as Mr C. Clibborn and Mr F. W. Russell at Moate, Mr Murray at Mount Murray, Mullingar and Mr P. O'Reilly of Coolamber. They also included the selections of J. H. Locke, landowner and joint proprietor of Kilbeggan distillery and of the Church of Ireland rector Rev. H. St. George. This form of recreation was particularly popular with the O'Reilly's of Coolamber where regular games were organised, particularly with the Mullingar-based regiments. These matches brought together members of the local gentry, who formed part of the O'Reilly social circle for recreation and socialisation, in their natural environment

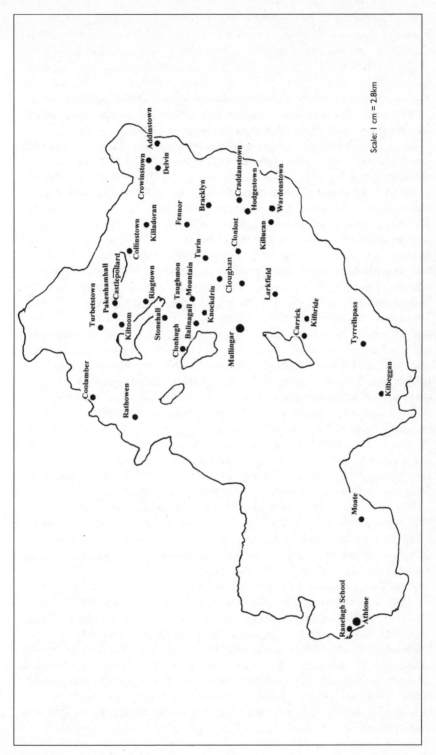

Figure 16.   Cricket playing districts in Westmeath, 1880–1905

of the landlord's demesne. Members of the Tottenham, Bond, Wilson, Murray and Dease families featured in August 1889, for instance, when Coolamber entertained the Royal Irish Rifles.[38] William Edward Wilson of the Daramona estate was another who used the cricket match as a focus of elite socialisation. On 7 August 1901 Daramona played a cricket match against the Turbotstown selection of the Dease family at Pakenham Hall and the return match was played the following day at Daramona where 'about sixty people attended to lunch and tea'.[39]

The elite Westmeath County Club represented the composite team of this particular group. The club was revived in April 1881 and claimed a membership of seventy. The club's old grounds on the outskirts of Mullingar were refurbished and Monday and Thursdays were established as practice evenings.[40] Officers of the Mullingar garrisons were admitted as honorary members.[41] The annual fee of one guinea, and the requirement of members joining after 1 May 1887 to also pay an entrance fee of one guinea, helped to regulate membership and finance the season's activities.[42] The renaissance season of 1881 was particularly active as the club played eighteen matches, winning ten, losing six with two games drawn.[43] This was the club of the landed gentry and their associates employed in local government posts, the higher professions and those involved in education at headmaster level. Newspaper reports identifying those who attended the annual meetings of 1881 and 1887, and the officer board elected in 1887, provide an insight into the socio-economic profile of the club membership. Detail on the officers in 1887 and their position in society is summarised in Table 10. Apart from the officers listed below, other landed family members associated with the club included J. C. Caulfield, W. Murray, H. P. Wilson and William Hodson. Local government officials involved with the club included M. F. Barnes, the deputy-sheriff; A.E. Joyce, the assistant county-surveyor; T.C. Foster, the headmaster of Farra School; T.A. Seagrave and bank-manger, E. C. Fitzpatrick also played.

The club began the 1892 season in serious fashion and employed a professional, Percy Muldowney, to manage the grounds at Ballinderry.[44] He was required to be in attendance every day during the season to bowl to members wishing to practise.[45] Muldowney then became an ubiquitous figure in Westmeath cricket and his name appeared on the team list of several clubs across the social classes.[46] The support of the members for the club, however, was less than total and an 1892 report suggested 'as was often the case in previous years, members of our county club were conspicuous by their absence, not withstanding the efforts of the hon. sec.'.[47] Despite the difficulties in organising members the club affiliated to the Irish Cricket Union and became involved in formal competition in 1895 when it unsuccessfully competed in the Leinster Junior Cup competition.[48] This was to be the club's penultimate season; after 1896 there is no record of the County Westmeath Club's existence.

Position	Officer	Local government post in 1887	Acreage of estate
President	G. A. Rochfort-Boyd	Deputy-Lieutenant	9,431
Vice-President	C. Brinsley-Marlay	Deputy-Lieutenant	9,059
Vice-President	Ralph Smyth	Deputy-Lieutenant	6,287
Hon. Secretary	Charles Tottenham	None	2,588
Asst. Secretary	Robert Harden	Clerk of the Union	Unknown
Committee	Colonel Vetch	Army officer	Unknown
Committee	Colonel Malone	Resident gentry	12,554
Committee	Philip O'Reilly	Deputy-Lieutenant	182
Committee	Wm.Fetherston-Haugh	None	871
Committee	John Lyons	None	1,357
Committee	Edmund Dease	None	2,315
Committee	John Hornridge	None	177

Table 10. Officers, local administration posts held and size of family estate, of committee of Westmeath Cricket Club in 1887 (*Westmeath Guardian*, 8 July 1887; *Return of owners of land, 1876; Thom's Irish Almanac and official directory of the United Kingdom*)

Another group of teams was directly associated with landed demesnes such as those of Lord Greville's Clonhugh demesne, Charles B. Marlay's Rochfort establishment, Tudenham Park of the Tottenham family, Killula Castle associated with the Nugent family, Lord Longford's Pakenham Hall and, in particular, the Coolamber estate of the most sports-obsessed of Westmeath's landed families, the O'Reillys. This group formed about 7 per cent of the total. These matches formed an important part of the social life of the landed gentry and were associated with sumptuous luncheons and musical entertainment provided by the regimental bands based in Athlone and Mullingar. At this level, the organisation of a cricket match was a good way of entertaining friends, neighbours, tenants and even labourers. After the match between the Pakenham Hall XI of Lord Longford's demesne and the Castlepollard Commercial Club in 1902, for example, the Countess of Longford invited all the players into the castle, 'where an excellently served tea was partaken of and a few hours spent in an enjoyable manner, songs, dances etc. making the time pass merrily'.[49] The composition of these teams tended to change as the century progressed and their social exclusiveness became considerably diluted. An examination of the names of those playing on some of these teams would suggest that apart from the local gentry, tenant farmers, demesne labourers and domestic staff were included in the selections.

Westmeath had a number of schools with similar characteristics to the English model of the public school and these formed 2 per cent of the total groups active. A more detailed examination of the role of sport in these educational establishments is undertaken in Chapter 5.[50] The

Ranelagh School Cricket Club featured in reports for ten of the years surveyed and the Farra School was also active. Cricket playing wasn't exclusively confined to the Protestant schools as the Irish Christian Brothers school, St Mary's College in Mullingar, also participated. A contemporary account of the game as played at Farra School illustrates its rudimentary nature and the problems associated with playing in poorly maintained fields. In Farra the 'cricket was never good and hardly popular'. The pitch consisted of stumps in a field and all the instruction given 'was to play straight-forward and low at balls that might be short'. When a 'sixer was swiped' it took 'half the other side to find the ball, so deep was the outfield in pasture unequalled for the production of beef and milk'.[51]

Teams associated with the workplace made up 3 per cent of the total. The distinction has been made between clubs organised and supported by management and proprietors and clubs formed by groups of men sharing the same workplace without employer support. Support of sport by paternalist employers was by no means unique in the Irish situation.[52] In Portlaw, County Waterford, the Malcomson Quaker family provided financial support to several social facilities that included the Mayfield Cricket Club, for the employees of their cotton plant, in the 1860s.[53] The support of the Herdman milling family for the Sion Mills Club in County Tyrone was crucial in establishing one of the country's more successful clubs.[54] In Westmeath, the Athlone Woollen Mills is worthy of particular note as the members benefited from the industrial paternalism of the proprietors. The Smith family organised a range of sporting and recreational activities for its employees and are considered in more detail in Chapter 5.[55] This was the only example of industrial paternalism operating within the county; the other teams with a workplace association were organisations founded from groups of men who shared employment networks. The Mullingar Mental Asylum XI, the United Banks XI, Shaw's XI and the Killucan (Railway) Station Cricket Club were examples of this type of team. The latter had sufficient members interested in the game in 1898 to organise matches between their first and second elevens and operated as a properly constituted club.[56]

As in other sports the voluntary associations fielded cricket teams as a means of broadening their social curriculum and as a method of providing paternalist guidance. Included in this category are the Athlone Brass Band XI, the Father Mathew Hall XI, the teams of Castlepollard, Killucan and Mullingar Workingmen's Club and the Catholic Commercial cricket clubs of Mullingar and Castlepollard. This group formed 4 per cent of the total.

Finally, the largest category of team identified from the newspaper survey represented the villages, parishes and townlands scattered across the county. These teams formed 68 per cent of the total that were active in the period. While some of these were certainly associated with landed estates their number and range is far too great for them to be

considered as gentry organised and supported teams only. Neighbourhood relationships were a crucial element in bringing men together to
play cricket, just as in an urban setting they brought men together to
play football between 1875 and 1900 in Birmingham, Liverpool, Blackburn and Stirling.[57]

Cricket's popularity in Westmeath with the farming and labouring
classes is explained by a number of factors. Firstly, the sport was practically free of any serious competition from other sports and therefore, in
rural areas, it offered the only opportunity to participate in organised
recreation. Time constraints, cost and social exclusion prevented access
to other forms of recreation. In the larger towns it proved similarly
attractive to the clerks and shop assistants whose social and economic
status excluded them from membership of tennis and golf clubs. The
identity of cricket was associated with the socially elite; the effect of this
was positive in that it presented the lower classes with an opportunity
to participate in a recreational activity associated with the rich and pow-
erful. As has been shown in Chapters 1 and 2 this was an important
consideration for the grazier farmers. The game was an ideal vehicle for
the pursuit of social respectability and at this stage was not associated
with a particular political or anti-national view.

The decline of the GAA after 1893 meant that rural dwellers had no
opportunities to participate in football. Even when football was popular it was essentially a winter–spring activity which complemented the
cricket season, and there was seasonal interaction between individuals
in both sports. The reaction of the Mullingar Football Club following
their victory in the Westmeath football championship in 1892 provides
a good example of this process. The members of the club announced
that they were retiring from football activities for the summer season
and instead re-assembled and established the Mullingar Cricket Club.
Membership of the club was designed to make it accessible to the less
wealthy employees. It required an entrance fee of one shilling, followed
by a 6d subscription for the first week, and 3d weekly thereafter.[58] A
four-month cricket season could be enjoyed for an investment of five
shillings in membership fees. The gentlemen of the County Club paid
eight times as much for their cricket pleasures.

Cricket was relatively cheap for participants. Rural clubs purchased
the necessary equipment, which was then communally owned, and this
reduced the cost of participation to the individual. This methodology of
organisation is suggested by the publication of an advertisement from
the Mornington Cricket Club in March 1904. Owing to a dispute
between members, the club offered for sale its equipment of two new
playing bats, two new practice bats, a set of wickets and balls that were
never used, a pair of shin guards and a new cricket book.[59] The more
elite clubs also used this method to organise their equipment. The
minute book of the Carrick-on-Suir Athletic, Cricket and Football club
from County Tipperary contains a number of references to decisions

made by the committee to purchase equipment, including 'a pair of match bats that were badly wanting', and later a match ball 'for the intended Rockwell engagement'.[60] Tennis clubs also purchased equipment for the benefit of their members although the players of Athlone Tennis and Cricket Club had this facility withdrawn in July 1886. A motion was passed that members buy balls from the club at half of the cost price, as over half of the balls supplied by the club were lost. It was believed that this change would 'encourage members to be more careful with club property'.[61]

Evidence of how clubs were organised, financed and managed is lacking for County Westmeath. Officers were elected annually and day-to-day management of club affairs was vested in a committee elected at the annual general meeting. The *Westmeath Independent* carried a report on the formation of the Ballymahon Club in 1865 and this offers an insight into the organisation of the early clubs of the landed gentry.[62] In addition to the general committee this club also elected a subscription committee and a playing committee. Individual patrons formed the lifeblood of all sporting clubs and events. The Ballymahon Club had a subscription list of twenty-one contributors who contributed sums that ranged from the £2 each subscribed by the King-Harmans to the 10s each donated by nine lesser landowners. The earlier examples from hunting highlighted the importance of individuals in sourcing funds for sporting organisations. The members of the Westmeath County Club identified this aspect of Major Moore's contribution to the club at his farewell testimonial in November 1866. He was fêted for 'not only procuring but generously contributing to the funds necessary for the maintenance of the club'.[63] In its first seven months of existence the Carrick-on-Suir Athletic and Cricket Club had an income of £81 6s.[64] The majority of this was provided by membership fees of £37 10s. Donations by various aristocrats and members of the landed gentry provided a further £11, and gate money and sale of cards for the clubs athletic sports amounted to £21.[65] Clubs of this stature were in a position to rent a playing arena and construct a pavilion, and investment in these items cost the club £32 over this period.[66]

Patronage was essential to the survival of the cricket club. The most important form of patronage was the provision of a suitable ground. It has been assumed that gentry patronage was central to the game's spread and survival but landlords were not the only source of patronage. The farmer who allowed access to his land was equally important, but suitable pieces of ground were sourced from a variety of individuals and institutions. The gentlemen of Athlone were facilitated for their return match against the Clonmacnoise XI in August 1867 'by the Colonel of the 2nd Queens who let them have the sick horse field for the day'.[67] Lord Longford provided the ground annually for the various Castlepollard teams.[68] Lord Greville defrayed 'the cost of the necessary appliances for the carrying out of the game', for the Clonhugh Club in the 1893 season.[69]

John Scally provided the ground for the Wardenstown Cricket Club for Sunday matches during the many years the club was in existence.[70] Ned Holdwright, a farmer, also provided a crease for the club.[71] The Kilbeggan Willow Club shared the use of a ground with the Belmont Club with the permission of Eugene Gannon.[72] James Cleary supported the Cloughan Club in a similar manner.[73] H. L. Pilkington, JP placed his grounds at the disposal of the Tyrrellspass team. The Killucan Station Cricket club benefited from the patronage of their president G. J. Boyan, PLG, who supplied 'liberal luncheon' and placed his grounds at the club's disposal for practice and matches.[74] The Kilbride National Cricket Club was based 'on the beautiful back lawn adjoining the ancient castle of Kilbride, the residence of Mr James King, JP'.[75] Clerical support was also forthcoming on occasions. The Wardenstown Cricket Club were beneficiaries of the support of the nationalist parish priest Fr Kelsh and his 'young curate' Fr Johnson. When the club played against the M. P. O'Brien's team from Edenderry, Fr Kelsh 'sent a handsome present on the occasion' and his curate 'contributed a bright one out of his purse'. The proprietor of the Wardenstown estate, Mrs Vandaleur, and the local doctor, Dr McGrane, also supported this particular occasion.[76]

III

Diffusion theory has been used in a number of studies to explain the introduction and growth of a sport to an area.[77] The theory can also be used to explain the spread of cricket in County Westmeath. Neighbourhood or contagious diffusion is one aspect of the theory, whereby an idea is introduced to an area and is then adopted by others in the locality. Hierarchical diffusion is also important. In this way a new idea spreads from the top of the hierarchy to the bottom, or from the most important members of society to the least influential.[78] Cricket was hierarchically diffused in Westmeath, in a manner that parallels the pattern identified by Hignell for the spread of cricket in Monmouthshire and by Clarke in Cornwall.[79] The Westmeath County Club was the earliest regular practitioner of the game in the county during the 1850s. The Kilbeggan Border Union club was also active throughout the 1850s and 1860s. In the 1860s, the game began to spread down the social ladder mainly as a result of the actions of the landed gentry. Members of the gentry who were particularly active in the game began to organise their own teams and also promoted country-house cricket. A number of reasons have been suggested to explain why the gentry arranged fixtures against teams from other estates and sides assembled by other gentlemen. The game enabled personal rivalries to be acted out in a risk-free environment and provided a means of entertainment, exercise and excitement.[80] Amongst the members of the gentry to organise their own sides at this stage were Mr Fetherstonhaugh, Captain Nugent, Mr Hornridge, Mr Hudson, Mr Dease of Turbotstown and Major Moore.[81]

Some of these individuals attributed a moral value to the promotion of the game and attempted to expand its participation base. In August 1862, Fetherstonhaugh attracted attention for 'encouraging among the young men in his extensive employment such a manly pastime as cricket'.[82] According to a report in Lawrence's handbook, his chief objective was the 'very commendable one of promoting cricket amongst the labouring classes of the locality, with a hope that it would tend to promote friendly feelings amongst all grades'.[83] James Perry made a similar intervention when he established the Belmont Club in King's county. In this district, cricket was unknown until the spring of 1864 when Perry got 'a few of the country natives to practise every fine evening and they liked the game extremely'.[84] The game was mainly played by the labouring class, whose chief defect was an

> absence of discipline and the presence of a person in authority was at first quite necessary to disallow the natural ardour for converting bats into the more genial shillelagh.[85]

At this time also a number of business people were involved in the game. William Kelly, manager of the Hibernian Bank in Mullingar, was one such individual; he occasionally organised his own side and also acted as secretary for the Mullingar club.[86] These individuals expressed their newly acquired wealth and rising social standing by becoming involved with cricket clubs in the towns, an activity that allowed them to rub shoulders with the leaders of local society and business.[87] Ambitious white-collar workers used the cricket club and other sports clubs as a means of social advancement and establishing their respectability.

The 1880s was the decade when shopkeepers, tenant farmers, lesser businessmen and commercial clerks became heavily involved in the game. Developments in Mullingar illustrate this aspect of diffusion where teams such as the Mullingar Commercial Club, the Mullingar Catholic Commercial Club, the Mullingar Wanderers and the Mullingar Shamrocks Club were founded by and catered for different social groupings. The clerks and shop assistants of the town's retail sector dominated the Catholic Commercial Club's membership. According to the *Westmeath Examiner* the club included young men who worked hard behind counters for six days a week and joined in the 'invigorating pastime' of cricket on their 'idle day'. Men who toiled 'over accounts' and those 'employed in other diverse occupations' were also members of a club that was 'open to all' classes.[88] The Mullingar Commercial Club was more elitist, and catered for the employer and professional classes of the town. The team that played in the August 1894 match against Ballymahon Cricket Club, for example, included three Shaw brothers of the retail family of Earl Street, Mullingar.[89] It also included E. S. Anderson, the sub-sheriff; Dr W. Midleton; J. Newburn, a farmer and land agent; A. D. Maxwell of the Ulster Bank and Percy Muldowney, the professional and caretaker of the County Club's cricket ground. The team for the return game also featured Dr Ledwith and T. C. Foster, headmaster of the Farra School.[90] Gradually, as the interest of the gentry in cricket declined the members of this club and social class began to feature regularly on the county cricket side. The Athlone Cricket and Lawn Tennis Club exhibited a similar socio-occupational structure.

The final stage of hierarchical diffusion occurred in the 1890s when the game became firmly established in the rural areas of east Westmeath, in particular, where it became the favourite sporting pastime of farmers and farm labourers. At this stage neighbourhood or contagious diffusion became important as the game spread through the rural districts. This development is best illustrated within the parish of Killucan where as many as seventeen different combinations were active at some stage in the period 1880–1905.

It is possible to illustrate with specific examples, the process by which cricket was hierarchically diffused, by tracing the means by which it spread from the exclusive Westmeath County Club, via the Castlepollard Club to the rural club of Ringtown (a team of farmers, labourers and skilled tradesmen). Individual influence was the crucial factor. The Westmeath County Club in the 1866–67 season included in its ranks J. R. Whitestone and E. F. Hickson.[91] These gentlemen were, in turn, two of the founders of the Castlepollard Cricket Club, the former acting as club captain and the latter as club secretary in 1867. The club, with a membership of thirty, was reported to have owed much of its success to the kindness of Whitestone, who worked to establish a first class club in the neighbourhood.[92] This club included in its ranks a tenant farmer, Denis Smith, who in turn established and provided support for the Ringtown Club and acted as its captain and patron by providing a suitable playing field in his 193 acre farm.[93] Smith had held the position of captain 'for many years' when he tendered his resignation in May 1892.[94] In 1899, a number of clubs were established in Castlepollard where cricket was reported to have 'taken a hold of the young men'. This began when the 'young labouring men' formed the Castlepollard Workingmen's Club (CWC) in July 1899.[95] A second club was started later in August when the Commercial Cricket Club was established. This club was 'composed chiefly of men who were debarred from joining the CWC, on the grounds of being non-workmen', but was 'in no way antagonistic' to the latter.[96] At the same time, the Pakenham Hall Club and the Kiltoom Club catered for the workers on the Longford demesne in Castlepollard.

IV

This model of diffusion excludes the military as an important agent of diffusion. The importance of the military, as cricket proselytisers, has been well documented but without any quantitative supportive data. In County Kilkenny, the military and local garrisons played only a minor role in the diffusion of cricket. There was only one military garrison in the county so the local gentry played a more important role in the spread of the game. In Tipperary some of the early teams originated in the military barracks at Nenagh, Templemore, Clonmel, Cahir, Carrick-on-Suir and later Tipperary.[97] The evidence from this study would suggest that military importance was limited and decreased over time. In the period between 1850 and 1879, 22.31 per cent of the games reported featured a military combination against a civilian selection, and 1.56 per cent of matches were inter-regimental. Of the 955 games documented for the period 1880–1905, 122 (12.77 per cent) involved garrison teams against civilian teams and another 22 games (2.32 per cent) were inter-regimental.[98] Military importance had declined completely after 1897, when the problems associated with the South African war resulted in the reduction in numbers of military personnel in Mullingar and Athlone. At this time also, soccer was considerably more popular with the Westmeath-based regiments, as will be seen in Chapter 6. In the period between 1898 and 1905, 355 games were reported in the county and only six of these involved teams representing military personnel. The variation in the importance of the military in providing opposition for civilian teams is illustrated in Table 11.

	1850–59	1860–69	1870–79	1880–89	1890–99	1900–05
Army opposition	6	37	15	57	60	10
Total games	17	175	61	268	444	283
% total	35.29	20.12	24.59	21.26	13.51	3.53

Table 11. Frequency of army combinations in opposition to civilian combinations, 1850–1905.

Athlone and Mullingar army garrisons were faced with a number of constraints that limited their role as cricket ambassadors. Army personnel had a full programme of summer manoeuvres that sometimes involved relocation to the Curragh or other areas during the cricket season. The 2nd Battalion of the Loyal North Lancashire Regiment, for instance, was stationed in the Curragh for their annual manoeuvres from mid-June until mid-August of 1895.[99] The frequent turnover of regiments also reduced the potential for ambassadorial impact. From April 1865 to January 1905, thirty-three different regiments were based at the Mullingar army barracks, giving an average tour of duty of fourteen months and two weeks.[100] Not all regiments embraced cricket with the same enthusiasm. Its popularity amongst soldiers, in the 1880s, was second to football, but it was particularly popular in Guards regiments mainly due to its place in the rural upper-class and public-school culture of aristocrats.[101]

Army personnel in Athlone and Mullingar played a facilitatory rather than a promotional role where cricket was concerned. The primary role played by military cricket teams in popularising cricket was to provide opposition to the elite county combinations or to the combinations of individual members of the landed gentry. In 1862, for instance, the Athlone garrison provided the opposition for the West-meath County Club and on three occasions; in 1871 the 97th Regiment featured on the list of opponents on four occasions; in 1892 the East Lancashire Regiment played matches against the Westmeath County Club on three occasions against the selection of Percy O'Reilly from Coolamber.[102] In the 1850s and 1860s prior to the development of a ded-icated cricket venue by the County Club, the availability of the army grounds was also an important factor in facilitating cricket matches. In return, cricket in a manner similar to hunting, presented army officers with an introduction and integration into county society. Teams from the lower orders of society also sourced army opposition. The working-class Athlone Woollen Mills team competed against the East Kent Regiment Band XI in 1893 and 1894 as well as a selection from the band of the Lancashire Fusiliers in 1895.[103]

Officers and soldiers were also recruited for representative sides assembled by members of the gentry. Corporal Woods and Private Clarke for example represented the County Westmeath Club in a game against Kilbeggan in which Clarke made over forty runs.[104] The gaiety of the occasion of several cricket matches was also considerably enhanced by the musical entertainment supplied by regimental bands. Military garrisons thus complemented participation, and elite participation in particular, in sport. Officers arrived in Mullingar and Athlone well versed in the sporting recreations of England and it was natural that they would have continued these recreations at their Irish bases. These recreational habits brought with them entry into county society and its social world.

V

Apart from the opportunity that the game presented to all classes to engage in sporting contest, cricket also played an important role in pro-moting social interaction between equals. Matches between civilian and military selections provided the focus of socialisation between members of county society. This dimension was most important for the West-meath gentry in the 1860s, with the annual week-long visit to Dublin that included a game against the Vice-Regal lodge, the social highlight. The club was founded in the mid-1850s by the liberal Earl of Carlisle, a genial bachelor noted for his generosity.[105] These games inevitably drew together the elite of Dublin and county society. In the 1864 match with Westmeath 'his excellency was in the scoring tent' and the 'usual vice-regal hospitalities were dispensed with'. The musical selection of the band of the 14th Regiment entertained 'a large collection of the fashion-ables'.[106] The social flavour of these occasions is suggested in the report of the activities that followed the game between Mullingar and Kil-beggan in June 1862.[107] After the game

> At seven o'clock in the evening the players, with other guests, to the
> number of forty, sat down to a sumptuous dinner – embracing all the
> delicacies of the season – provided by the Kilbeggan Club, with their
> usual and well known liberality. When ample justice had been done
> to the viands, the cloth was removed, and the 'rosy god' made her
> appearance. A variety of toasts – including the health of her Majesty,
> received with 'three times three, and one cheer more'. . . several
> songs were given in good style.

Social interaction was not limited to players as members of the local
gentry, army officers and females attended the elite matches. The
Westmeath–Kilbeggan game in 1862 attracted 'some of the elite among
the fair sex of the county' who 'graced the ground with their presence
and thus added much to the beauty of the scene'.[108] The match between
the Westmeath County Club and the Royal Irish Rifles in June 1890
took place in a field 'at the rere [sic] of the Asylum premises' during
which the band of the Rifles 'played a capital selection of music' and
from 'a spacious marquee' hospitality was dispensed in lavish
manner.[109] Members of the landed gentry organised some novelty
matches with a very definite social agenda in the early 1900s. A match
between the sporting spinsters and the bold bachelors was organised
at the Mullingar Polo grounds at an 'at home' given by Mrs Watson-
Murray. In this match the bachelors played left handed and batted with
broom-sticks 'alias pick handles'.[110] A year later many of the sporting
spinsters assembled at Knockdrin Castle where Miss Montgomery's XI
challenged the XI of Miss Levigne.

The role played by cricket, in providing a focus around which like-
minded people could assemble, declined in importance for the upper
echelons of society as the century progressed. However, its importance
increased for the less wealthy. As shown in earlier chapters, polo and
lawn tennis provided alternative seasonal social foci. At parish level, the
cricket club became the promoter of the social events which provided
celebratory focal points for rural communities. In the absence of other
social or sporting organisations, cricket clubs became the chief and
perhaps the only vehicle for formal occasions of social intercourse in
some rural areas. The annual ball, normally held towards the end of the
year, was the most important and elaborate of these events, but other
social events were organised in the course of a season. The Mount Street
(Mullingar), Turin, Killucan, Cloughan, Clonhugh, Killucan Station, Wardenstown and Ringtown clubs all organised dances, quadrille parties
and pre- or end-of-season balls during the 1890s and early 1900s.[111] A
variety of venues was used to stage these events including the Market
House in Mullingar, national schoolrooms provided by a supportive
parish priest, Workingmen's clubs' halls, farmers' residences and in the
case of the Clonhugh club 'the tastefully arranged barn' placed at the
'disposal of the committee by Lord Greville'.[112] The Killucan Station
Cricket Club in its first season held a quadrille party in the Rathwire

National School placed at its disposal by Fr Kelsh PP, and was attended by sixty-eight guests.[113] The Wardenstown Club's inaugural event in 1893 attracted eighty couples, who 'plied the light fantastic with vim and vigour until morning well had proclaimed its advent'.[114] Thirty-five ladies attended the Turin ball.[115] Food and refreshments were integral to these events and music for dancing was supplied by either local musicians or dance-bands hired specifically for the occasion, depending on the club's circumstances. The band of the Inniskilling Fusiliers provided the music for the Mount Street Club at which forty couples reportedly attended. These events provided a new secular ritual calendar and were important in maintaining club dynamics in a sport that was strictly seasonal.[116] Members were conscious of the importance of social occasions in establishing respectability. This awareness of the purpose of such events was clearly implied in the report of the Mount Street Club's ball of February 1900, which stated that

> As proficient and efficient as the Club showed themselves to be as wielders of the willow, in providing amusement and for a display of downright hospitality and good fellowship they are greater adepts.[117]

These social occasions were inspired by the annual hunt ball that provided the social highlight for the hunting community and their organisation was in part motivated by the desire for the members of these clubs to establish themselves as communities of respectable sporting gentlemen.

An examination of published lists of those who attended these events gives an indication of their appeal for the less exalted members of society and their importance in providing a social outlet for this group. The names of ninety-eight different people who attended the balls of the Ringtown, Turin and Cloughan clubs were published in the local press. It was possible to match fifty-eight of these people with completed census enumerators' forms from the 1901 census. The personal details of thirty single women who attended were established. They ranged in age from seventeen to thirty-six and had an average age of 24.62 years. These were some of the better-off females of the districts concerned, as thirteen (43 per cent) were from social class B and 11 (37 per cent) were from class C. These were farmers' daughters or were women who used some level of skill in their chosen occupation. Among these were women who worked as seamstresses or as dressmakers. Many of these were also farmers' daughters. Only four members of social class D attended. The personal biographies of twenty single male attendees were also constructed. Their age ranged from sixteen to thirty-eight years and they had an average age of 22.47 years.[118] The majority were farm labourers from social class D (50 per cent) with seven farmers' sons from class B (35 per cent) also present. A scholar, a shop assistant and a kennel-man were also present. Given the rigid social hierarchy that existed in rural areas at the time the social intercourse promoted by these events was likely to have been somewhat circumscribed. As one historian has suggested 'the widest gap in rural Ireland was that between the farmer and the landless labourer, and marriage rarely, if ever, bridged that gap'.[119]

Cricket also encouraged an informal socialisation that revolved around the game. Some sense of the fun and enjoyment associated with participation in the game is captured in a newspaper account of the journey made by the men of Ringtown to play a match against Stonehall. In July 1893, members of the club assembled on the shores of Lough Derravaragh to make the journey across the lake to play a match against Stonehall. Thirty-two members of the club climbed on board 'a large boat, kindly placed at their disposal by a local turf merchant'. After what was described as a delightful half-hour's sail, 'during which songs were sung and music rendered', the members arrived at the Stonehall grounds and dispensed with the challenge presented by the home team.[120] This image of a turf-boat full of singing and dancing young men from rural Westmeath on their way to a pre-arranged cricket game is one that is not normally associated with 'the quintessentially English game'. It was, however, very much the reality for the young men of the county, who throughout the 1890s used whatever transport was feasible to facilitate participation in their favoured sport. It is also an image that illustrates the role played by cricket in bringing much-needed colour and excitement to rural communities.

It was also a traditional part of the game to partake of liquid refreshments of the alcoholic variety in the course of the game, in particular between innings. This was an aspect of the game that concerned 'Short Slip' in a letter to the *Westmeath Guardian* in June 1888.[121] The letter emphasised the importance of continuing this tradition:

> It has hitherto been the custom with country clubs to provide luncheon and a half-barrel of porter for the visitors; which entailed expense to such a degree, as to deter clubs from engaging in no more than a few matches during a season. Now as a good many matches is what most players desire, I would suggest that the luncheon be left out, and a half-barrel of porter alone be supplied: each player providing his luncheon; which would be equally as satisfactory and a great deal cheaper than the other way.

The participation of marching bands, which became a particularly important part of the ritual of GAA matches, was also a feature of some working-class cricket matches. When the Wardenstown CC travelled to play the Castlepollard Cricket Club, for instance, they were accompanied by the Killucan Fife and Drum Band, who 'played spiritedly around the town and principal streets discoursing high class Irish numbers, prior to the match'.[122]

Cricket clubs did not confine their extra-curricular activities to the organisation of entertainment for their members and associates. A number of Westmeath clubs also became promoters of athletic sports events, ostensibly as a means of fund-raising for their primary activities, but their role in establishing status was equally important. Finance from these events was generated by charging entry fees to individual events, by levying fees on carriages and cars entering the grounds and by charging for entry to a reserved enclosure. The members of Mullingar Commercials Cricket Club held their inaugural sports on the grounds of the Westmeath County Club at Ballinderry in October 1885.[123] The first athletic sports meeting held in Delvin was organised by the members of the town's cricket club in October 1886.[124] The Moate Cricket Club athletic sports of September 1887 presented a programme of twenty events and featured an appearance by one of the outstanding middle-distance athletes of the day, Tom Conneff. The band of the Royal Dublin Fusiliers attended and provided the musical entertainment.[125] The opposite happened also on occasion. The members of the Mullingar Cricket Club decided 'that the most strenuous efforts be made to prevent the holding of athletic sports on our grounds at Ballinderry'. The members believed that the holding of the sports would result in very considerable damage to the grounds no matter what precautions were taken and as a result plans for the organisation of an athletics meeting had to be abandoned.[126]

VI

A detailed examination of the players who were involved in the game of cricket in the period between 1900 and 1902 was carried out with a view to establishing their social characteristics. The names of players appearing for twenty-two clubs listed in the newspapers were collated and analysed. The clubs included seven with a link to urban areas with the remainder representative of rural Westmeath. In total 227 players (73 per cent) out of a total of 312 were identified. The analysis of the members of these clubs by social class is illustrated in Table 12.

The ages of the sampled players ranged between fifteen and fifty with the majority, 66 per cent, aged twenty-five years of age or less. Cricket was the preserve of the young man with 45 per cent of the playing population aged between twenty and twenty-five years of age and a further 21 per cent were teenagers. Of the players aged over twenty-five years, 16 per cent were less than thirty and 19 per cent were aged thirty or over. The average age of the Westmeath cricket player was 24.63 years, but this figure is distorted by the presence in the sample of a few individuals in their late forties and early fifties; 45 per cent were twenty-two or under and if the cricket players aged thirty-one years and older are excluded the average age of the player is reduced to 22.53 years of age.

The game was also dominated by those of the Catholic faith, who formed 90 per cent of participants with members of the Church of Ireland accounting for 9.7 per cent. One person involved in the sport was returned as Wesleyan and there was also one Presbyterian. The sport was dominated by the single man with 90 per cent of the sample unmarried according to the information recorded in the census forms. At the end of the nineteenth century marriage brought new responsibilities, expenses and commitments for the cricket playing classes. The amount of money available for investment in social and recreational activities declined accordingly.

| | | SOCIAL CLASS | | | | |
	Sample	A	B	C	D	U
Belvedere	12	0	0	0	8	4
Boher	11	1	2	2	3	3
C'pollard Comm.	21	0	1	8	2	10
C'pollard Wolfe Tones	11	0	0	1	5	5
Clonhugh	16	0	1	4	8	3
Cloughan	21	0	7	0	1	13
Craddenstown	15	0	7	3	4	1
Delvin	11	0	1	3	5	2
Derryrow	15	0	5	0	8	2
Fennor	12	0	5	0	4	3
Kilbeggan	19	0	7	9	1	2
Kilbeggan WC	15	0	0	3	10	2
Kiltoom	13	0	1	0	10	2
Moate	15	1	2	5	3	4
Mount Street	13	0	1	4	2	6
Newtown	10	1	1	0	5	3
Pakenham Hall	15	0	1	2	9	3
Raharney	11	0	3	3	3	2
Stonehall	11	0	2	2	5	2
Turbotstown	11	0	0	1	2	8
Tyrrellspass	17	0	4	5	6	2
Wardenstown	17	0	8	2	4	3
Total	312	3	59	57	108	85

Table 12. Social classes of participants of selected cricket clubs in Westmeath, 1900–1902

Westmeath cricket in the early twentieth century drew its participants from across the social classes but was dominated by players from social class D, who formed 48 per cent of the total. Farm labourers dominated this category, a group that was close to the bottom of the economic ladder and one of the most disadvantaged groups in Irish society. Social classes B and C were almost equally represented and formed 26 and 25 per cent of the total respectively. Farmers' sons dominated the former group and made up 77 per cent of its total with farmers forming a further 19 per cent. Members of social class A, the group that introduced the game to the county and initially dominated it, had practically disappeared from the institutionalised club game and formed only 1 per cent of the total. This result is very different to Tranter's findings for central Scotland where around one-third of all cricketers came from social classes A and B and over half originated in social class C. Representatives from social class D formed a modest 7 per cent of the total in Tranter's sample group.[127]

The data also allows for a detailed analysis of the social profile of individual clubs and a number of general trends emerge. Teams associated with landed demesnes exhibited the greatest variation in religious belief as might be expected. Of the twenty members of the Church of Ireland involved in cricket, nine were associated with the Pakenham Hall combination of Lord Longford's demesne. Twelve members of the club were identified and nine of these were members of the Church of Ireland. The religious affiliation of the members had a significant impact on the social class of the team, but not in the manner that might have been expected. The majority of members, 71 per cent, belonged to class D, a product of the club's origin as one established by the Longford family to cater for the recreational needs of the big house employees. Three other members of the Church of Ireland were also associated with teams from the Castlepollard area. Robert Barton, a gardener, was a member of the Castlepollard Commercial Club and two members of the Kiltoom Club were also Protestants. Kiltoom was a village where employees of the Pakenham Hall estate resided. The three individuals from social class A were also members of the Church of Ireland: Captain Barton of the Mosstown estate, a 'land agent and captain', organised the Boher team and F. W. Russell, a 'gentleman farmer' was a member of the Moate Cricket Club. The other members of the Church of Ireland were from the Tyrrellspass region and included the Rev. McGinley, the only cricket-playing vicar active at the time and who was possibly the one who organised the Newtown team.

Clubs that catered for a more middle-class clientele included rural clubs, such as Wardenstown and Cloughan, which were dominated by farmers and the sons of farmers. Middle-class urban clubs included such clubs as the Moate Cricket Club, the Kilbeggan Cricket Club and the Mount Street Club of Mullingar. The Moate Cricket Club was the most stable and active of this type of club in the period 1880–1905. It was also a club that by 1901 had become more inclusive in terms of its social structure, and included members from social classes A and D. The club was first mentioned in match reports in 1884 and up to 1905 went unreported for games on only three years. The strength of the club was such that at the AGM of 1893 it was decided to field a second team under the captaincy of William Reid, a former student of Blackrock School, Dublin. Moate Cricket Club possessed the essential features that ensured permanency for the late-Victorian sports club, other than the social profile of its membership. It had a permanent and centrally-located venue at its disposal, which was maintained and improved during the course of the period under review. The grounds located in the Fair Green were considerably enlarged for the 1895 season, and the following season a pavilion was erected, on 'the east side of the ground, commanding a full view of the playing arena'. Tuesday and Friday practice sessions were a regular feature.[128] A new ground was in use for the 1900 season on the lands of W. C. Clibborn, JP, 'excellently laid out and if anything superior to the old ones'.[129] The club was able to boast, in 1901, that its 'roll of membership was never so extensive' and that it was 'in a more prosperous condition than heretofore'.[130] It included in its ranks 'a professional cricketer', Mr Frank Doran, whose brother fulfilled a similar function for the Ballinasloe Club in County Galway; both represented Connacht in inter-provincial competition.[131]

The social milieu of the club is evident from the spectators that attended some of its games and included the highest ranks of society. Lord Castlemaine, F. T. Dames-Longworth (HML), Thomas Maher and 'a large assembly of the elite of the County Westmeath and the King's county' attended the game at Tullamore in August 1892.[132] The more socially exclusive clubs played matches against clubs of similar status and the opposition featured during this period is indicative of the club's position in the social hierarchy. The two busiest seasons of the Moate club were in 1895 and 1898 during which eight fixtures were fulfilled in each season. In 1895, the club had games against the County Westmeath Club, two against County Longford, two against the officers of the Lancashire Fusiliers and a single game against Mr Locke's XI. In 1901 the core membership of the club was drawn from social class C. The club also included a domestic servant, a general labourer from social class D, as well as F.W. Russell in its ranks. The members of the club were older, having an average age of 26.6 years with a range that varied between seventeen and forty-eight years of age.

The rural clubs inevitably were formed from combinations of farmers, farmers' sons and farm labourers. Farmers and their sons and skilled tradesmen dominated the Wardenstown Club. Its playing membership ranged in age between nineteen and twenty-eight and had an average age of 23.54 years. Farm labourers, the group categorised as social class D, dominated a number of clubs. The identified members of the Belvedere team were all of this social class, five of whom were residents of the Rochfort demesne. This was the club of the Belvedere estate of Charles Marlay. The age of this group ranged between eighteen and thirty-nine and averaged 23.75. All were agricultural labourers and, with one exception, were single men. The Pakenham Hall and Kiltoom teams have already been mentioned and were directly associated with the Longford demesne. The ages of the former team ranged from an eighteen-year-old stable boy and domestic servant N. Crawford to a forty-four-year-old groom, William McCann. The average age of this team was high at 28.35 years. Kiltoom exhibited a similar social structure and included one of the oldest players sampled, fifty-one-year-old R. Scott, an unmarried farmer's son. This was also a team of single men and they had an average age of 26.27. Another club dominated by men from social class D was that of Stonehall. The age of the members, all unmarried, ranged between twenty-two and thirty-three and had an average age of 25.44. The Stonehall townland was the home of two substantial farmers, Jeremiah Gibson and William McLoughlin, who were involved in various forms of sporting recreation. McLoughlin was a subscriber to the Westmeath Hunt Club and Gibson was one of the chief organisers of the annual Crookedwood athletic and aquatic sports. It is reasonable to assume that the Stonehall cricket team consisted of labourers from their farms and benefited from the patronage of one or both of the landed proprietors.

VII

The recreational habits of the different social classes remain unexplored territory in Irish historiography and until additional quantitative studies of this type have been undertaken it will not be possible to contextualise the Westmeath situation. Reference has been made in the introduction to the specialised nature of the county's agricultural economy and this may have been a factor in the promotion of the game within the county. The Westmeath pattern of cricket is broadly similar to the pattern outlined by Bracken in Tipperary, although in the early 1900s in Tipperary, 'it was at the larger urban centres' that the game became focused, 'although some rural locations remained active for a while'. Unlike in Westmeath, 'gone were the days of the ad hoc townland or demesne teams'.[133] In Kilkenny the pattern was remarkably similar to that of Westmeath. The years between 1880 and 1893 were years of continuous growth and the game reached its peak of popularity between 1894 and 1900. In 1884 over thirty cricket teams were recorded as playing matches in the county and the number of teams peaked at fifty in 1896. In 1905 there were still thirty clubs active. It is also clear from O'Dwyer's study of Kilkenny cricket and the range of clubs involved that the sport was enjoyed by a similarly broad socio-economic constituency as in Westmeath.[134] The evidence that cricket was more popular in the broadest sense of the term, than has hitherto been accepted is conclusive. The popularity of the game in these counties may also be indicative of a strong regional demarcation for the game.

Cricket declined in popularity as a recreational activity for the landed gentry of Westmeath but this decline did not take place until the 1890s, almost twenty years later than is normally assumed. Members of this group did provide some of the patronage essential to the lower-class teams. As has been pointed out earlier, this decline was partly related to the popularity of polo within the county. The development of this game, initially at Mullingar and later at Moate and Castlepollard, provided the landed gentry and higher status professionals with a managed social and recreational outlet for the summer months that proved more attractive to the landed gentry than the peripatetic cricket. Tennis was also an alternative and provided a means of family recreation.

5. The embryonic GAA in Westmeath, 1884–1895[1]

The formation of the GAA in 1884 had little immediate impact in Westmeath. Cusack's 'prairie fire' didn't even singe the area. The movement was at its strongest in the county in the period 1890–1894 when a number of football clubs were active in the county and a county committee attempted to provide an organisational structure to the movement. Apart from a brief attempt to encourage hurling amongst the youth of Athlone there was no attempt made to introduce hurling to the wider county.

The Gaelic Athletic Association was established on 1 November 1884 at a meeting held in Hayes's hotel in Thurles, County Tipperary. Michael Cusack provided the motivating energy for the establishment of the new organisation and according to de Burca 'without him there would have been no GAA, certainly not in the 1880s'.[2] A multi-faceted sporting and professional career had convinced Cusack of the importance of revising the game of hurling and of the necessity to re-organise Irish athletics on a democratic basis and to control it through a national organisation.[3] Cusack's main support for the establishment of the new organisation came from a Carrick-on-Suir, County Tipperary, businessman and farmer, Maurice Davin. Davin brought social prestige and the status of a star athlete to the new movement. He was a member of one of Ireland's great athletic families. Three Davin brothers had won, between 1873 and 1882, twenty-six Irish athletic titles, which were organised by the Irish Champion Athletic Club, the organisation despised by Cusack.[4] Maurice Davin competed successfully in rowing, boxing and especially in the weight events in athletics.[5] His greatest athletic moment was in 1881 when he emerged from retirement and won both the shot and hammer titles at the AAA championships. His brother Pat, at the same championships, won the long jump and high jump titles, setting championship records in the process.[6] Davin's background was thus in the world of organised athletics, where rules and regulations mattered and the codification system developed in Britain held sway. Unlike Cusack, he felt that abuses such as gambling and cheating were not a problem for Irish athletics but was concerned at the decline of the traditional Irish events of weight throwing and jumping and was convinced of the need for games 'especially for the humble and the hard-working who seem now to be born into no other inheritance than an everlasting round of labour'.[7] As might be expected from someone of his background in

codified athletics, he wished to see proper rules drawn up for both football and hurling, declaring 'I would not like to see either game now as
the rules stand at present'.[8]

Despite the best intentions of both Cusack and Davin, much of the
initial history of the GAA involved a tripartite struggle for control of the
association's executive, waged between the constitutional nationalists,
the Catholic Church and the revolutionary secret society, the Irish
Republican Brotherhood (IRB). The national convention in January 1889
saw the culmination of the struggle for the control of the GAA conclude
with the IRB finally gaining control of the national executive of the association. De Burca interprets this as a reflection of the dominance of the
IRB at the grass-roots level of the organisation.[9] More realistically the
likelihood was that the IRB had managed to place its personnel in the
key county administrative positions.

Following the IRB takeover, the association was subjected to immediate clerical condemnation. Bishop Nulty of Meath (his diocese included
most of County Westmeath) and his priests launched an attack on the
GAA in all chapels on 21 July 1889. They outlined three problems
created by participation in GAA activities. Young men who travelled
outside their own parishes to play matches against other clubs were led
to drunkenness, they were introduced to secret societies and the priests
claimed to have evidence that the government was paying leading
members of the GAA to draw the members into secret work. Nulty
himself chose to speak in Navan, the county town of Meath, where he
prohibited the playing of matches outside of a parish because of the
increase in drunkenness and secret society activity.[10] That the leading
cleric chose Navan, rather than the cathedral town of Mullingar, to
deliver his homily is significant. The message from the pulpit was
intended for the parishioners of Meath but not Westmeath where GAA
activity was insignificant. At the time of the clerical condemnation only
three football games between Westmeath teams had been reported in
the local press. Based on the evidence contained in police reports, Nulty
and his clerics had very little cause for worry about secret society
activity, as the IRB was weak in Westmeath. The most significant GAA-
related IRB activity reported was at a football match held in Killucan in
March 1890, where the presence of a 'good many local IRB men' was
recorded; in the same month at two football matches played in Moate,
nothing of importance was observed by the police; at Mullingar, in
April, thirteen IRB men were reported to have attended a match.[11] A
similar report was made from Athlone in May, whilst in Killucan only
four IRB men were reported present in a crowd of over 400 people.[12]

II

Athlone, because of its central position, was chosen as a venue for some
of the initial tournament games that were important in the early stages

of the GAA. The new association was first brought to the attention of Mullingar readers of the *Westmeath Examiner* in January 1885.[13] The following week 'A lover of sport' played the nationalist card when he enquired if it was possible that the young men of Mullingar had 'not that amount of National Spirit which would induce them to preserve these games which are far and away superior to those brought to us by our English friends'.[14] A pessimistic response from W. D. Cleary, who was active in athletics, pointed out that 'Westmeath was uncivilized in athletics'. He asked where

> is our ancient wrestling arena, our hurling clubs, our dashing footballers, our unconquerable handball players, our weight throwers, and hammer slingers? They are gone, and I must say forever.

It is doubtful if they ever existed. Despite his pessimism Cleary was cautious about committing to the new association. He urged people to wait until 'after the meeting of the Irish athletics on 21st February'.[15] This was the meeting at the Wicklow Hotel, Dublin that established the Irish Amateur Athletic Association, an alternative athletic association to the GAA.[16] Inspired, perhaps, by the newspaper correspondence, some members of the National Workingmen's Club adjourned to Ward's field in Ballinderry (Mullingar) on 22 February 1885 and organised a 100-yards handicap race. On St Patrick's Day a more ambitious programme was organised for the same venue. A multi-dimensional tournament was held at Athlone on Easter Monday 1886, in which the feature event was a hurling match between Clara and Athenry.[17]

The progress of the GAA in Westmeath followed a different pattern to that experienced in other midland counties. In general terms, antagonism on the part of many bishops and priests, together with the friction between the Parnellites and anti-Parnellites, seriously weakened the GAA nationally for upwards of a decade.[18] The Westmeath pattern of development avoided some of this fallout. The organisation developed later and survived the damage that was inflicted on other areas by the IRB takeover and the fallout from the Parnell divorce case, with its associated parliamentary party divisions. Police reports document the decline of the GAA in the midland counties as being the result of these political developments. In December 1892, the RIC reported the existence of only nine clubs in Kildare, a decline from nineteen in December 1891 and thirty-eight in December 1890.[19] In Cavan, where the influence of the IRB was particularly strong, thirty-nine clubs existed at the end of 1891 but by the end of 1892 none existed.[20] A similar pattern existed in the other counties featuring in the midland crime branch special reports and is illustrated in Appendix 15. In contrast, the peak years of football activity in Westmeath, extended through 1892 when thirty-six football games were reported in the local newspapers and into 1893 when forty-nine were played.[21] This initial burst of enthusiasm did not survive beyond 1893.

The earliest and most active football clubs were located in the eastern section of the county. This district was familiar with a variety of sporting disciplines and contained individuals experienced in the organisation of sports events. There was also some tradition of folk football in the area. This version of football was primarily a game for large numbers played over large distances and involved the majority of the male population.[22] According to evidence collected by the folklore commissioners, games between teams of over 100 a side took place annually in Killucan 'without rules or referee and generally ended in a wrestling match'.[23] A branch of the new organisation may have been formed at Killucan in the early summer of 1885 although contemporary newspapers make no mention of the club's existence.[24]

Kinnegad was the early centre of the GAA in the county. Football was played regularly on an organised basis there from December 1887. The members of the Kinnegad Slashers club assembled each Sunday and played a match between two selections drawn from club members that were usually called the Liberals and the Tories. In May 1890, the club boasted of having played twelve matches in which they won nine, lost two and played one draw, scoring in the process 7 goals and 43 points and conceding only eight points.

Two other clubs existed in Westmeath in 1888. In August, the Delvin Emmet club was reported to have organised a tournament for the following month. In September, the Clonmellon Saint Patrick club was reported to be organising a similar event. There is no confirmation found in newspaper evidence that either of these tournaments took place. Two matches were also played between the Delvin and Kinnegad clubs.[25] Members of the Thomastown Rangers club began to hold regular practice sessions from February 1889.[26] Five years after the foundation of the parent body football began to make progress in the two main urban centres in the county. In Mullingar, the first branch of the GAA was formed on Thursday, 17 October 1889, when a football club was founded at a meeting held in Owen O'Sullivan's public house, Greville Street. The organisers of the meeting were Roland W. Moorwood and W. D. Cleary 'who canvassed the town and produced sinews of war'.[27] This was the same Cleary who had urged caution four years previously and who had in 1888 unsuccessfully tried to recruit members for a Gaelic Football Club. (Figure 17).

The thirty who attended the meeting agreed to establish a branch of the GAA in the town and the following Sunday the first reported football match in Mullingar was played at Ballyglass between teams selected by Moorwood and Cleary.[28] The *Westmeath Independent* reported on the formation of an Athlone GAA club in early January 1890. A membership of forty was reported that 'included some of the best athletes of the town and neighbourhood'. Officers were elected and an appeal was launched to the general public for subscriptions to purchase a set of jerseys.[29] Also in January, the new William O'Brien club was reported to

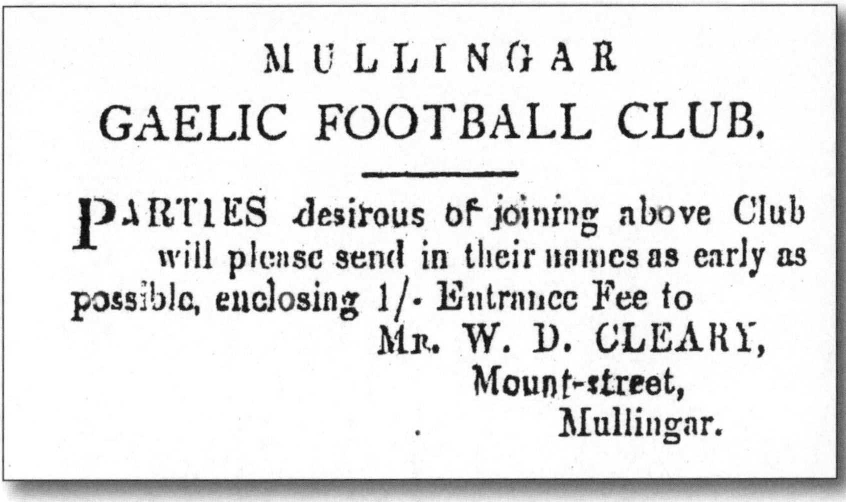

MULLINGAR

GAELIC FOOTBALL CLUB.

P ARTIES desirous of joining above Club
will please send in their names as early as
possible, enclosing 1/- Entrance Fee to
Mr. W. D. CLEARY,
Mount-street,
Mullingar.

Figure 17. Advertisement placed by W. D. Cleary in *Westmeath Examiner*, October
1888

have been founded in Moate. A membership of forty was claimed for
this club, which held regular Sunday practice matches, in a field provided by T. Kelly.[30] The Moate club was disadvantaged by the
antagonism of Canon Kearney and other clerics in the locality. In June,
Kearney preached against 'the disgusting sins of intemperance' and
warned his parishioners about taking part in football matches on
Sundays.[31] Given the level of clerical opposition, it was inevitable that a
second club would be founded that would have total abstinence from
alcohol as its basic principle; the Moate Shamrocks fulfilled this role.[32]
As 1890 concluded, football was played in Mullingar, Wooddown,
Athlone, Moate, Ballinahown, Killucan, Raharney, Rathowen and Kilbeggan. In January 1893, Rochfortbridge Erin's Hopes was founded
while in March, Gaulstown Park, Lovers of Erin was reported to have
affiliated to the county committee.[33] By 1894 young men in Ballynacarrigy, Ballinalack and Walshestown had experienced the novelty of
taking part in a football game. The geographic location of the main football playing districts is illustrated in Figure 18. Appendix 16 documents
the number of games played by these clubs in the 1890s.

The GAA was unique of the early Irish sporting bodies in that it
organised competitive games on a county basis. It established county
committees to organise county championship competitions and to
promote the playing of the games. In Westmeath, as clubs became more
numerous, moves were initiated to organise a county committee to
provide a management structure. This was not an IRB intervention or a
development imposed from outside the county, but originated in
particular amongst the members of the Mullingar Commercial Football
Club. In November 1890, the committee of the club placed advertisements in the three Westmeath newspapers calling on all clubs to

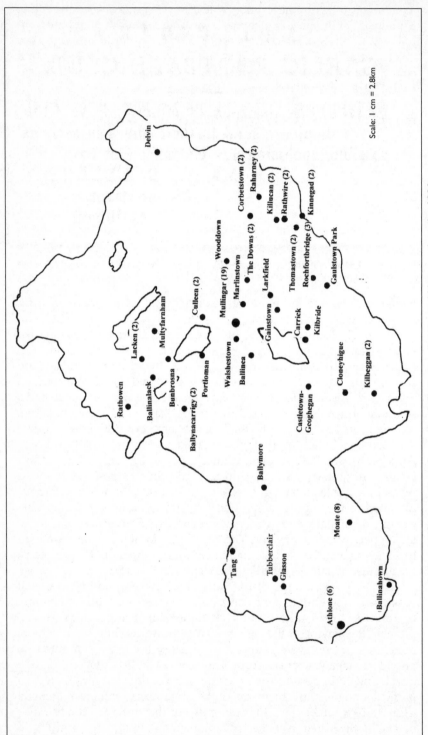

Figure 18. Location of main football-playing districts in Westmeath in the 1890s

'communicate with the Honourable Sec. Commercial Gaelic Club, Mullingar' to organise a meeting in order to establish a county committee.[34] Two weeks later, a *Westmeath Examiner* editorial supported the objectives of the Commercial club and commented that 'the want of a county council has perhaps a great deal to do with the present disorganised state of the county'.[35]

A county committee was eventually formed three months later, at a meeting held in the Lecture Hall, Mullingar, on 25 March 1891, and officers elected. Fr E. O'Reilly was appointed first president of the committee, Martin McGreevey vice-president, James Bennett (Kinnegad Slashers) was appointed treasurer, and James Murray (Mullingar Shamrocks) was elected secretary. Nine months after the pulpit condemnation, Fr O'Reilly now provided clerical credibility to the county committee. O'Reilly's willingness to allow his name to be used for promotional purposes in the new body meant that Church opposition to the GAA was ended in Westmeath. O'Reilly's involvement seems to have been brief as there is no report of the committee ever meeting. However, the association in Westmeath enjoyed at a minimum tacit Church support. Fr O'Reilly's appointment as president of the committee, despite the earlier surface opposition to the association, can only be understood in the context of clerical antagonism to Parnell.

Fr O'Reilly's involvement followed the order of December 1890 from Bishop Nulty to his priests to actively campaign against Parnell. Clerical opposition to Parnell was based on moral and political grounds as Parnell was 'stamped with the double [sic] crime, that of treachery, injustice and adultery.'[36] In a famous Lenten pastoral of 1892 Nulty condemned Parnellism as being the cause of more evil in its short lifetime than seven hundred years of English tyranny.[37] However, Westmeath local politics in Mullingar was complicated by a struggle for control between two rival nationalist factions. This struggle was between the Catholic Church and its political allies (chiefly the county farmers and shopkeepers), and the more radical young, educated, nationalist townsmen who challenged priestly hegemony in local politics and who became Parnellites. The battle for control was complicated by the personal antipathy of the two leaders of the groups, the Bishop, Dr Nulty, and John Hayden, the proprietor of the *Westmeath Examiner.* The fall of Parnell provided both factions with a national issue around which they could conduct their local struggle. Matters contested by the two factions ranged from clerical control of party funds, to the bishop's proposals for local sanitation. Throughout the 1890s the clericalists and anti-Parnellites maintained the upper hand in Westmeath politics and it was not until the end of the decade that the balance of power began to shift.[38] However, there is no evidence of this division being reflected in the organisation of the GAA. When disputes occurred there they related to intra-club and inter-club rivalries and concerned matters arising on the playing fields, as will be seen later in this chapter.

In November 1891, a new county committee met at Michael Doherty's licensed premises on Earl Street, Mullingar. Martin McGreevey chaired the meeting and Bennett and Murray were also present. The committee members covered a small area geographically and included J. Flynn (Kinnegad Slashers), James Mulvey (Mullingar Football Club), J. Coleman (Thomastown Rangers), A. Fitzsimons (Raharney Rovers) and Patrick Connell (Cullion Celtics). The composition of the county committee was, therefore, limited geographically to officers from the eastern half of the county; no representative from Athlone was present despite there having been considerable football activity in the town in 1890. The meeting passed a number of important resolutions aimed at providing an organisational structure to the association in the county. For example, a player who played with more than one club would be liable to suspension. In an attempt to force clubs to affiliate and exert control over the playing of games, a resolution was passed imposing suspension on 'an affiliated team kicking against a non-affiliated team'. Most importantly, the committee decided to organise a county championship. Clubs were required to have affiliated by 1 January 1892. The affiliation fee was set at ten shillings and clubs wishing to enter the county championship were required to pay an extra 2s 6d.[39] Later in an attempt to control the post-game drinking culture and reduce expenses for competing teams, President McGreevey prohibited receptions for championship matches, in February 1893.[40] By the time of the next meeting, held on 21 February 1892, nine clubs had affiliated.[41] Five of these teams were included in the championship draw made at the meeting. The desire of the Athlone members to become part of the Westmeath GAA community was essentially rejected at the meeting, as the club was refused entry to the championship on the basis that their entry fee postal order did not arrive in time.

The organisation of a championship provided a competitive alternative to the series of friendly games organised by the clubs themselves and proved to be extremely attractive to spectators. The championship of 1892, the first organised by the committee, was a tame affair and passed without major incident. The 1893 championship, however, was a tempestuous one, the fallout from which destroyed the organisational structure of the Westmeath GAA. Two of the leading clubs were lost to the game following incidents associated with the competition. One of the leading personalities associated with the organisational structure of the GAA also severed his association with the movement. Despite progressing smoothly to the semi-final stage, the 1893 championship would change with the meeting of the two Mullingar teams. Contemporary newspapers placed the blame squarely on a 'couple' of the Shamrocks players, for as the *Nationalist* reported, 'the larger number of the members of the team were [sic] actually disgusted at the conduct of a few'.[42] Violence throughout the match, and a controversial winning score that was followed by an assault on the referee, characterised the game.

The Mullingar captain, James Mulvey, was assaulted in the first half and fighting continued throughout the second half, almost without interruption. The most serious incident happened when Shamrocks scored a point after the referee had blown for a free. When he refused to allow the score 'the captain of the Shamrocks deliberately struck the referee with his clenched hand in the mouth.'[43] The losing Mullingar Shamrocks team objected to the result and appealed the decision of the referee to award the game to the Mullingar Football Club to the county committee. In the course of the unsuccessful hearing the President, Martin McGreevey, was assaulted by the captain of the Shamrocks team.[44] Having lost their appeal, the Shamrocks representatives informed the board members that they would be present and prepared to play on final day. This episode is important as it illustrates at least one example of how internal football matters damaged the local organisation.

The 1893 championship is significant in that it is the only occasion on which a Westmeath championship semi-final and final were played on the same day, 23 April 1893. This fixture was the cause of more dissent, especially from the Athlone club, and led to the exchange of viewpoints through the columns of the weekly national journal, *Sport*. The controversy surrounding the all-Mullingar semi-final and the possibility of trouble developing at the final made it difficult to obtain a venue for the games – 'those gentlemen who heretofore were so generous having to express their regret that their land was laid down for meadow' – but eventually John O'Connell obliged a deputation from the Mullingar Football Club and placed a field at Robinstown Levinge at the disposal of the county committee.[45]

Members of the Shamrocks club provided the stewards for the 1892 final to prevent spectators from encroaching on to the pitch; a year later the forces of the RIC, under the command of chief constable Reddington, were present to prevent members of the Shamrocks club from invading the pitch. In the semi-final, Athlone T. P. O'Connors beat the Wooddown Rackers 0–3 to 0–1; after an interval of one hour they lined out in the final against Mullingar Football Club. True to their word the Shamrocks players also prepared to take the field but were prevented from doing so by the RIC.[46] This co-operation between the RIC and the GAA is atypical and is an indication of how the GAA, as it initially developed in Westmeath, was in essence a sporting movement devoid of a political agenda. T. P. O'Connor's completed their double victory on a 2–3 to 1–6 scoreline, but one of the Athlone goals was bitterly disputed by the Mullingar side. Subsequent appeals to the county committee and to the Central Council failed to reverse the decision of the referee, Martin McGreevey, to award the game to the T. P. O'Connor's. Central Council did, however, decide to investigate the claim that the Athlone club had played under association rules after affiliation.[47]

Internal tensions associated with the breakdown of relationships between the Mullingar clubs and the fallout between the Mullingar

Football Club and the Athlone club, destroyed the infrastructure of the Westmeath GAA, and it was almost a decade before a new and effective county committee was established. Martin McGreevey was unfortunate to have been the referee in the disputed final, as well as being Mullingar Football Club and county president. He severed his connections with the GAA in the county and continued his administrative career with organisations such as the Mullingar National Workingmen's Club and the Holy Family Confraternity. Mullingar Shamrocks played only one more match following the events of 1892, and there is no record of the T. P. O'Connor's club again taking part in Gaelic football matches; as will be shown later in this chapter many of the playing members of the club were to become key members of the Athlone soccer clubs.[48] As a result of the internal wrangling only two clubs entered for the 1894 championship, Mullingar Football Club and Raharney Rovers, the final of which was a one-sided affair, won easily by the Mullingar Football Club.

III

The use of police reports as the main source of information on the early history of the GAA produces a profile that emphasises heavy IRB involvement. It also underestimates the amount of football that was played in an area. The police reports for Westmeath only identify nine active clubs in 1890.[49] Newspaper analysis provides evidence for many more football combinations. Between 1886 and 1900 seventy-three different combinations are recorded in the newspapers as having played a football match in Westmeath. The word 'combinations' is deliberately chosen; in many matches formally constituted clubs were not involved, but instead comprised ad hoc arrangements of people from one area challenging their peers in a neighbouring district to a football game. Of the different combinations recorded, nine of these represented the second or reserve teams of established clubs. Of these, Kinnegad Slashers on eight occasions, Mullingar Football Club on five, Mullingar Shamrocks on seven occasions and Thomastown Rangers on fourteen occasions had sufficient players interested in the game to field reserve teams. The number of games played between 1888 and 1899 is illustrated in Figure 19.

This hierarchical development of football clubs was the norm in other football codes and in societies very different to Westmeath. This was the pattern discovered by Metcalf in his study of soccer in the mining communities of East Northumberland.[50] Tranter, in his examination of football in central Scotland, discovered that at all levels soccer clubs came and went 'with the regularity of a yo-yo'.[51] There was generally a mass of ephemeral unaffiliated teams and a small number of semi-permanent, formally-constituted clubs that were affiliated to the county committee. The latter were integrated into the practices of modern sport; the members of the former group still displayed many of the

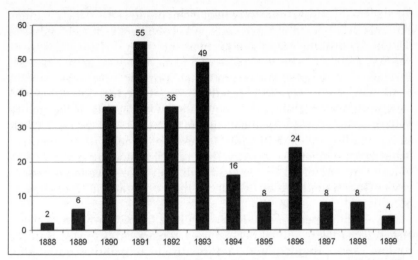

Figure 19. Number of inter-club football games played in Westmeath, 1888–1899

characteristics of pre-modern sport as defined by Melvin Adelman.[52] These 'pre-modern' contests were arranged by individuals directly or indirectly involved in the teams; the rules were likely to vary from one game to the next and from one locale to another; the competition between the teams was only meaningful locally and public information on the contests was likely to have been limited, local and oral.

In the formally-constituted group four distinct categories of football matches were organised. Intra-club games were the most common where the members assembled each Sunday and selected sides to compete against each other. These sides took various forms. In Kinnegad, throughout 1889, teams of members calling themselves the Tories and the Liberals played on a regular basis while matches between the married and single members occasionally interrupted the regularity of these games. In Athlone, the members of the T. P. O'Connor's club arranged games between the grocers' assistants and the rest, or between the natives and the outsiders. In Mullingar, the clubs tended to favour games played between selections made by the captain and the vice-captain. These games helped to train players in the basic skills and rules of the game and helped to maintain interest in the sport in the intervals between properly organised inter-club games. Despite being played between members of the same club these games often developed a sharp competitive edge that sometimes developed into violent confrontations, as suggested by the comments of the *Westmeath Nationalist* reporter following one of these practices between the members of Mullingar Football Club. He suggested that 'if teams kick as they did last Sunday they had better bring an ambulance wagon with them'.[53]

Challenge matches were organised normally between neighbouring clubs. Initiated by contact between club officers or club captains, or occasionally by means of challenges issued through the local press, these were the most common type of event organised. Of the 250 inter-club matches played in the county or involving Westmeath clubs, 94 per cent were of the friendly or tournament variety.[54] The setting up of one match usually resulted in a second game as it was common for the participants to engage in a return match, provided of course the first game was free of serious incident. Stronger, financially viable and more middle-class clubs were also invited to travel outside the county to participate in the tournaments organised by some of the established clubs. Mullingar Football Club, for example, made its competitive debut in September 1891 by travelling to Ballinasloe to participate in a tournament organised by the local club; they also travelled occasion-ally to Dublin to play matches, as did their occupational counterparts in Athlone.[55]

The establishment of a county committee in 1891 provided a short-term alternative to the ad hoc games arrangement. Clubs within the county were provided with a formalised competitive outlet but, unfortunately, this organisation did not survive beyond the early months of 1894.

Gaelic football was essentially a compromise game that combined elements of traditional folk football, soccer, rugby and Australian Rules with the intention of creating a distinctive football code.[56] All three foot-ball codes played in Ireland spuriously claimed to be the rightful heirs of the folk football tradition in the country. Gaelic football as much as soccer and rugby was the product of the Victorian shift towards rein-vention and codification.[57] Maurice Davin was probably responsible for the codification of the earliest rules. Davin's biographer, Ó Riain, has documented the intensive study of the rules of field sports made by Davin over the years as indicated by the numerous entries made in his notebooks and his accumulation of cuttings from newspapers and mag-azines on the emerging rules of rugby and association football.[58]

The game initially played regularly in Westmeath was in theory subject to the playing rules adopted by the association in 1889.[59] These rules were short and imprecise in relation to the management of the game. Despite their imprecision, the rules did contain the essential features of a modern codified football game: the boundaries of the playing area were defined, contending sides were to be equal in number and the method of scoring was defined. Thirteen rules in total were drafted and dealt with pitch organisation, the number and powers of match officials, the playing conventions of the game, methods of scoring and the type of playing gear to be used.[60]

The rules attempted to encourage a kicking game, as carrying and throwing were not allowed. Players could only catch the ball when it was off the ground but had then to immediately kick the ball or strike it with the hand. This rule helped shape an identity for Gaelic football; allowing a catch differentiated the game from soccer, catching followed by an immediate release distinguished the game from rugby. The restrictions on carrying the ball led to the introduction of a skill called dodging where the ball was hopped on the hand. In a match between the Shamrocks and Moate, the latter players were considered to be very useful 'in the art of dodging the ball on the hand and many a well intended kick from Mullingar was prevented by a Moate man stooping down and pushing the ball out of reach in another direction with his hand'.[61]

The scoring system in use at this time created a game that was attritional in nature. The victorious team was the one scoring the greater number of goals as the value of a goal outweighed any number of points scored. This system, allied to the crowded nature of the playing field, tended to encourage physical battles and defensive play. The basic tactic was to prevent the opposition from scoring a goal and if a goal was scored, then even the most tactically naive teams were aware of the importance of shoring up the defence. Poor quality fields, deep grass, unskilled practitioners, the winter playing season, heavy water-absorbing footballs, the crowded arena and use of footwear designed for everyday purposes all combined to ensure that scores were scarce. Thirty-six football games were reported in Westmeath in 1890; forty-one goals in total were scored but tw+enty-one of these were scored in five games leaving the remaining thirty-one games to produce twenty goals. On twenty-two occasions at least one team involved failed to register a score. In 1891, there was a more even spread of goals with thirty-five scored in the fifty-five games played; the same year twenty-seven teams failed to register a score.

An article in the *Westmeath Nationalist* in September 1891 illustrated some of the essential features of the game and provides a rare insight into how early football games were played. The author identified 'some very regrettable faults' evident in the way Westmeath teams played their football. Most Westmeath teams erred in the proper placing of men in the field and in the strict observance by the men of these positions. Related to this was the failure of players to carry out the instructions of the captain. In many cases he 'might as well have been bellowing at one of Stanley's dwarfs in distant Africa', and 'away goes Jack after his especial hobby, Tom after his, Jill after his and so on until all is confusion, and the game becomes one of a happy lucky sort'. The quality of the passing also attracted his attention. The author believed that the skill of accurate passing was one of the most important elements of success and could not be too much refined. The skill should be cultivated as much as possible with the feet. He wasn't impressed with the use of the hands for passing as 'it looks ungainly and is exceedingly dangerous to be continually reaching down and shoving the ball along with the hands'.[62] The essentials of good passing, and players maintaining their position, frequently came to the attention of contemporary commentators. One writer, in November 1891, wished that the Raharney Rovers 'would have a little more discipline, keeping their places properly in the field and practicing passing'.[63]

Football games at the time were very often shapeless masses of undisciplined players. This aspect of the game is featured in the report of the Shamrocks and Wooddown Rackers 'extra-ordinary' game, played in January 1892. It was 'really more of a hurry, scurry, rough and tumble game than anything else'. The lack of scientific play was regretted.[64] Despite the shapeless and shambolic nature of the game, few matches in Westmeath remained unfinished. Unfortunately, with no comparable information from other areas it is impossible to evaluate the typicality of the Westmeath situation. Problems developed when teams travelled outside their own districts to play in areas where a different code of rules might have existed. Problems might also develop when a referee unfamiliar with local practices took charge of a game, as happened when Cullion Celtics played the second team of Mullingar Football Club. The former disagreed with the interpretations of the Ballinasloe referee and walked off the pitch.[65] This problem with rules was not confined to Gaelic football but was also experienced by other football codes in their embryonic stages. Tony Collins has illustrated how a similar lack of familiarity with rules caused problems and disputes in rugby, particularly when clubs sourced opposition from outside neighbouring rugby playing areas.[66]

Such was the vague nature of early Gaelic football rules that confusion was inevitable. A core set of rules may have been generally known and taken for granted, but detailed rules for a game could be agreed between the rival captains on match day. Players were required to adapt quickly to any variations agreed by their captain, agreements which could be forgotten easily in the excitement of a keenly contested game. The 1891 championship match between Mullingar and Kinnegad Slashers for instance was 'played strictly in accordance to the Gaelic rules', with one exception when in the second half one 'of the Kinnegad team, who is stated to have formerly belonged to the "Clonards" hugged the ball under his arm and in right true rugby style ran towards the Mullingar goal'.[67] The following Sunday in Mullingar, Wooddown Rackers proved far too strong for the Rochfortbridge Erin's Hopes winning by 1–11 to 0–0 in a game that was 'impetuous fast and strong, but unscientific, rash and wanting in cultivation'.[68] The February 1893 county council meeting featured a discussion on rules and the President, Martin McGreevey, endeavoured to explain various rules to the delegates. He informed them that the old rules had been revised, but the officers had never received copies of them. It seems from the meeting that the journal *Sport* was the main vehicle for dissemination of information on rule changes.[69]

Problems with rule interpretation increased in scale when teams travelled outside the county for games. In July 1892, the Mullingar Football Club travelled to Clonturk Park in Dublin to compete in a festival of hurling and football. Following their match with Fontenoys members of the club passed a motion of condemnation 'at the transgression of the

Gaelic rules' by the Dublin team, and addressed their concerns in a letter to the editor of the *Freeman's Journal* and the national sports news-paper *Sport*. The principal objections were that the Fontenoys played in a style that was closer to rugby than Gaelic football and used tactics that included lying on the ball on the ground, head-butting from behind and holding the ball rather than releasing it as the rules required.[70] Similarly, when the club travelled to Dublin to play the Dunleary Independent club, they found the Adelaide Road venue 'rather small for a Gaelic match', whilst the second half of the match was 'simply indescribable as the Dunleary men began to play under rugby rules and they pulled down the visitors whether playing the ball with the hands or the feet'.[71] As will be shown later the T.P. O'Connor's club from Athlone faced similar problems when it travelled outside the county. The evidence suggests that different versions of Gaelic football were played which varied on a regional basis and teams, prior to matches, agreed on a com-promise set of rules to be used for a specific game.

The early version of football played in Westmeath was confined to the winter–spring period, with the majority of games taking place between November and May. An analysis of football matches played during the most active phase of activity in Westmeath, between 1890 and 1893, is illustrated in Figure 20. Of the 176 matches reported, 32 per cent were played during the months of November, December and January; 50 per cent between February and April. This preference for a time of the year when weather conditions were likely to be least favourable had a practical and theoretical basis. In a county where public recreational space was unavailable, football clubs were generally dependent on the support of a co-operative farmer for the use of a suit-able field. In winter months grass growth was dormant, so meadows

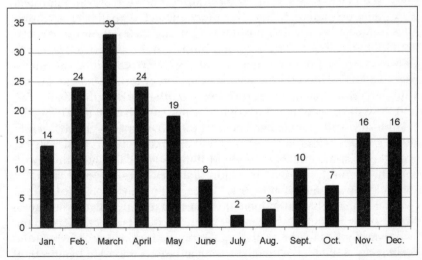

Figure 20. Number of football matches played on a monthly basis in Westmeath, 1890–93

weren't damaged by the action of over forty footballers confined to a relatively small area, nor did the spectators that crowded to some of the venues cause damage.

There was also a belief that the summer months were climatically unsuitable for football. Encouraging football in summer interfered with the promotion of athletics. This opinion was articulated at the Kerry GAA convention in January 1893 when attention was drawn to the increased popularity of summer football. Delegates complained that the activity 'injuriously affects athletic sports and prevents numerous promising athletes from devoting their full attention to training'. 'Hot boiling summer days are not conducive to the pleasure of vigorous pastimes, the continuous playing of which is certain to cause an enormous amount of *ennui*'.[72] An editorial in *Sport* in March of that year supported the idea. The editor believed that nothing was more 'likely to invite apathy and dislike for vigorous pastimes into the mind of a player than an hour's heavy play under the auspices of a scorching sun'. The player who rested for the summer would return with 'fresh energy and enthusiasm'.[73] Some Westmeath people shared this opinion. 'Sportsman', in his *Westmeath Nationalist* column, considered football out of place in the 'very hot weather we have had recently' and proposed cricket, 'ever so much a nobler game than the favourite lawn tennis', as the ideal summer game.[74] In June 1893, Ballinahown and Cloghan [King's county] played a game 'with the thermometer at ninety degrees'. In the reporter's consideration, football in 'such conditions is far more toil than pleasure', making it 'very difficult if not morally impossible to maintain anything like regular play'.[75]

Football was also seasonally confined in Westmeath because many of its practitioners, particularly those in Mullingar, enjoyed cricket. As has been seen in Chapter 3, some of these also found recreational fulfilment in summer by cycling. Many young men played football because it presented them with an opportunity of extending their sporting and social activities over the winter months. Mullingar Football Club was the winter version of the Mullingar Commercial Cricket Club. The Shamrocks Football Club was the winter extension of the Shamrocks Cricket Club. The club was first reported active on the cricket grounds in 1887 and it was involved in at least five matches each in 1888 and 1889. The relationship and interchange between the two games is clearly seen in the aftermath of the 1892 county football championship final. Having won the title, the members of the Mullingar Football Club announced that they would not play any more matches until the next season.[76] Instead they assembled at Michael Doherty's premises on 20 May 1892 'with the object of taking steps for the formation of a representative Mullingar cricket club'.[77] ('Representative' in this context referred to the two main football clubs, as the cricket eleven included members of the Shamrocks club.) Of the nineteen listed as having attended the meeting, nine had played in the football final. One of the outstanding football players, Charles Williams, was elected captain of the club. The desire for a representative team was confirmed when the Shamrocks football player and ubiquitous cricketer, Percy Muldowney, was elected vice-captain. James Mulvey, 'a man foremost in the promotion of every sport organised in town' and captain of Mullingar Football Club, was elected president of the new cricket club. The new club catered for those who were gainfully employed, as the entrance fee was set at 1s, although the introduction of a weekly contribution of 2d made club membership more accessible. However, players were responsible for their own travel expenses to matches. The Independent Wanderers also held a special meeting in May 1892 and decided to change the club to a cricket one for the summer.[78] A similar pattern existed in the Killucan district in the interchange between summer cricket and winter football in the 1890s. Hugh Fulham, who was captain of Raharney Rovers in the 1894 football final, was a familiar figure on the cricket circuit also. Frank Doran, the professional at the Moate Cricket Club, captained the Moate Gaelic Football Club in the first Westmeath football final in 1890.[79] The dual player was also common in Kilkenny cricket and hurling circles. The Tullaroan hurling team contained many of the same players as the cricket team. The early successes of the hurling team coincided with a time when players were also active cricket players. These included Henry J. Meagher, James Grace, Pierce Grace, Lar Coogan and John Morris. Matt Gargan, won five All-Ireland senior hurling medals between 1905 and 1913, and made regular appearances for different Kilkenny city cricket teams including the Marble City Cricket Club, Prospect Cricket Club and Elmville. In 1887 the Kells GAA club played a cricket match against Gaulstown of Tullaroan. The Seven Houses football club from the Danesfort district of Kilkenny won the Kilkenny senior football championship in 1896 with a team that included noted cricket players such as James and John Hughes, Pat Kinahan and Michael Drennan and then represented Kilkenny in the Leinster football championship.[80]

Gaelic football was played on Sundays, a decision considered by Neal Garnham to be crucially important in popularising the sport as 'it ensured that rural workers and urban white-collar workers such as shop assistants, who could not be assured of a day of rest on Saturdays, were able to participate'.[81] The notion of playing games on a Sunday, however, did not originate with the GAA, as Sunday had been well established as a cricket-playing day in Westmeath by the mid-1880s. Indeed Sunday was the established day to play a number of sports in nineteenth-century Ireland, and the use of Sunday increased accessibility to GAA sports. Sunday play also provided certain advantages in relation to the social dimension of the experience as it meant that the distance of the journey to the match meant that a legal drink was available to those who travelled.[82]

IV

The pleasure of kicking a heavy football around a makeshift football-field wasn't the only attraction provided by the early clubs. A common theme throughout this study has been the extent to which sports clubs 'provided for sociable activities as an intrinsic part of their growth' and the extent to which what John Lowerson has termed 'clubability', formed a core value of the institution.[83] The social activities organised around the football match were an important part of the culture of the stable GAA club. Travelling to and from the games provided some of the entertainment. In January 1892, Mullingar Football Club travelled out to Kinnegad to play the locals using 'two brakes, six cars and two traps'. On the outward journey 'music and songs whiled away the time in enjoyable style'.[84] The well organised clubs in Mullingar, Killucan and Athlone travelled by rail to compete in tournaments or friendly games. Mullingar Football Club's competitive debut was made at Ballinasloe in September 1891. The logistics of reaching Ballinasloe illustrate the benefits and some of the difficulties presented by the rail companies to the embryonic GAA. The Mullingar club conducted the negotiations with the rail company and attempted to organise a special excursion train to the Galway town. However,

> The company required the very large guarantee of £42 which of course could not be given. Even the generous offer on the part of the club to guarantee £20 failed to induce the directors to run a special excursion train, and so the members were compelled to accept the next best thing, and that was to travel down on Saturday night at single fare for the double journey.[85]

When the footballers arrived in Ballinasloe the reception party accompanied them to the Whelehan's Temperance Bar where they 'were provided with a sumptuous supper'.[86] On the Sunday morning the members made use of the available time to view the surrounding places of interest. After the games the 'festivities' began. 'Hall and club were thrown open to the visitors, and singing and dancing kept up till the departure of the Mullingar men by the morning mail.'[87]

There was a strong emphasis on socialising after games and, on occasion, before matches. This was an important part of Lowerson's clubability process and an important means of establishing a club's respectability. In May 1893, the Dublin club C. J. Kickham's travelled to Mullingar to play a match against the Mullingar Football Club. They arrived at the railway station where 'an enthusiastic crowd of local footballers and townspeople' met them. They were then escorted to the rooms of the Catholic National Young Men's Club 'where refreshments were lavishly provided and the best of good cheer was the order of the day for an hour or more'. Many of the Dubliners then took the opportunity to explore the two great attractions of Mullingar's hinterland,

and drove out to view either Lough Owel or Lough Belvedere.[88] This form of entertainment was still continuing in 1905 and the importance attached to this element of a club's activities is evident from the emphasis placed on its reportage in the press.

The importance of less formal socialisation is clear from surviving account material from a County Tipperary football (probably rugby football) team of the late 1870s, which provides evidence of the impact the social dimension had on club finances. The social aspect of this club absorbed the bulk of its finances once it had obtained its basic equipment. The Kilruane Football Club in 1876 purchased two footballs, a set of caps, several yards of tape and a book on football. The expenditure on these items amounted to £2 5s 9d, or 55 per cent of the total. The remaining expenditure was on the purchase of two half-barrels of porter and four gallons of ale. The expenditure on basic equipment would suggest that 1876 was the start-up year for the club as in 1877 the proportion spent on alcohol and lemonade had increased to 76 per cent. This was invested in the purchase of four barrels of porter, one gallon and one quart of whiskey, one gallon of malt and three-dozen bottles of lemonade. The final year of the accounts identify a similar pattern of expenditure on alcohol with transport also an important item for the 1879 season.[89]

Athlone T. P. O'Connor's began their campaign in fine social style, also against the Ballinasloe club. The Athlone National Band met the 'strangers' outside the town and escorted them to Mr Lennon's premises where pre-match refreshments were served. After the game the members of the Athlone club entertained the Ballinasloe members 'to a sumptuous repast in Mr. O'Sullivan's hotel, Connaught Street. Dancing was subsequently enjoyed and the strangers departed at 10.00.'[90] It wasn't unusual to have a team met at the railway station or on the outskirts of the town and accompanied to the football pitch or reception hall by one or more musical ensemble. This practice created a great sense of occasion, glamorised the participants, and was also a great publicity-generating device that drew the attention of the public to the event. Teams marching in military formation presented the footballers of the day with an opportunity to display publicly their orderliness, organisation and sense of mission.

Formal social occasions were also organised by clubs. Annual balls were held by some clubs and the departure from the club of a prominent member was marked by the presentation of a testimonial that usually included a social event. The Kinnegad Slashers had a membership sufficiently organised in the early 1890s to hold an annual ball at the local national school building, provided for the occasion by school patron, Fr Fitzsimons.[91] The support of the local cleric indicates clearly where the allegiance of this club rested. The 1893 occasion was attended by almost a hundred couples and 'the real old Irish jig, reel and hornpipe measures were indulged in to an advanced hour in the morning'.[92] The departure of J. J. Bergin, a founding member of both the Catholic

Commercial Club and the Commercial Football Club, was marked by a social event that included dance music provided by May Brothers, 4 Stephen's Green, Dublin.[93]

Those who played football in Westmeath in the early 1890s were participating in a recreational activity that had become fashionable within the county in a short time, an activity that promoted adventure and excitement for the individual in an often mundane society, and one that facilitated and encouraged social interaction between individuals of similar status. The choice of club name suggests that cultivating a nationalist identity or agenda was not a priority for the members of many of the Westmeath clubs. In the early 1890s it was traditional for clubs to proclaim their nationalism by choosing a name that honoured a contemporary national political figure or one that commemorated a major figure or major event from Ireland's nationalist past.[94] The thirty-one County Meath clubs identified in the 1890 special branch report examined by Mike Cronin all carried political names, and all related to the IRB faction in the county.[95] A similar pattern is evident from the names of the twenty-five clubs included in the special branch reports on the County Longford clubs. Nineteen of these clubs used names with nationalist connotations that embraced contemporary political figures and movements.[96] Four of the clubs opted for a title with a religious associatoin, the Ballymahon club immortalised local poet Leo O'Casey in their title while the Legan club appended 'sunbursts' to their title.[97] This policy constructed an identity for clubs that stressed and publicised their links as sportsmen to the nationalist mission, that embraced things Irish and rejected West Britonism.[98] Of the nine Westmeath clubs identified in the police reports only two were identified with contemporary political figures (T. P. O'Connor and William O'Brien) and only one with a contemporary movement (Rathowen Leaguers). Other appendages used included 'Shamrocks', 'Celtic', 'Emeralds', and proclaimed an Irish identity without any political or nationalist associations.[99]

The contention that the men of Mullingar Commercial Football Club were essentially involved in a sporting and cultural activity is reinforced by their participation in the coalition of interests responsible for the organisation of the athletics meet in Mullingar on 2 October 1893. The organisers of this event included representatives of the widest spectrum of socio-political opinion in the town. The meet was held under GAA and ICA rules; the organising committee was mainly composed of members of the Catholic Commercial Club and associates of Mullingar Football Club; military representative Captain Lewis (Adjutant, 9th Battalion Rifle Brigade) provided a liberal subscription as well as the ropes for the enclosure and tenting facilities; Colour-Sergeant Sparkes was granted permission to assist the committee in carrying out all field arrangements; Mrs Lewis presented the prizes; the band of the Loyal North Lancashire Regiment provided the musical entertainment and the socio-cultural ecumenism was appropriately concluded when Sergeant Lipsett of the RIC won the sixteen-pound hammer throw.[100] Police reports, always conscious of the political agenda, reported on the 1892 clubs as entirely non-political and composed 'chiefly of shop assistants who keep up the clubs for recreation purposes on Sunday'. In Athlone, the club was kept up 'for the pastime and not as a political club'.[101]

V

Mullingar Commercial Football Club was the first club established in the town on a formal basis. The initial meeting was held on 17 October 1889 at the licensed premises of Mr O'Sullivan, Greville Street. R.W. Moorwood and W. D. Cleary were the founding fathers of the club.[102] At least thirty people attended the initial meeting when it was 'unanimously' agreed to organise a branch of the Gaelic Association and on the following Sunday football was first played in Mullingar when two teams selected by the captain and secretary assembled at Ballyglass.[103] However, the new club almost imploded when an objection was made to the fact that some members had been elected on the field. A reconvened meeting was held which debated in detail the merits of the various football codes and eventually it was decided to establish a football club by a majority of fourteen votes to seven.[104] The name of this club, Mullingar Commercial Football Club, provides a clear indication of the socio-economic background of its members. The occupations of the original committee elected by the club are illustrated in Table 13. The club had a relatively short existence and in the course of its two-year history played six matches, winning only once.[105] This lack of success partly inspired the movement to amalgamate the Mullingar clubs.

Name	Position	Occupation
R. W. Moorwood	Captain	Retail trade
P. J. Shaw	Vice-captain	Grocer-publican family member
J. J. Geoghegan	Treasurer	Supervisor at Doyne's drapery store
M. J. Geary	Secretary	Shop assistant
W. D. Cleary	Committee	Publican
W. Fogarty	Committee	Unknown
W. Weymes	Committee	Member wool merchant family
J. J. King	Committee	Shop assistant at Shaw's
C. Beirne	Committee	Unknown
J. J. Bergin	Capt football team	Nooney's ironmongery employee
James Mulvey	Committee	Kellaghan's ironmongery assistant
J. H. Smith	Committee	Publican

Table 13. Occupations of officers and committee of Mullingar Commercial Football Club 1890

Civic pride, motivated by the desire to form a strong competitive club, capable of challenging for county championship honours was responsible for the establishment of Mullingar Football Club. Three clubs, Commercials, the Shamrocks and Newbrook Wanderers were active in the town in 1891 and in September, a committee representative of the three was established to explore the possibility of amalgamating the clubs. The idea was approved and the committee was empowered to decide on a name for the new club. A majority favoured the neutral name of Mullingar Football Club and this decision caused the Shamrock members to reject the proposal as they refused to accept any name other than their own. The lack of a political consciousness amongst the members of the Mullingar clubs was highlighted by the failure of the name Emmett to gain even a single vote. The new club included all the members of the former Commercials, almost all the Newbrook Wanderers and some members of the Shamrocks club. A membership fee of 1s as well as a weekly subscription of 2d was introduced for the new club, which adopted as its playing strip a red jersey with a green sash and red cap with a green overhanging tassel. In November, it was reported that membership of the club was 'pretty well on the century'.[106]

The appointed officers of the club in 1891 and 1892 were all involved in the commercial life of the town, generally employed as shop assistants and many were migrants.[107] The vice-captain, Joe Garry, was the exception, as he worked the family farm with his mother at Clonmore, on the edge of the town. President of the club, Martin McGreevey, was a native of Carrick-on-Shannon, County Leitrim and was an employee of Messrs Shaw's, one of the largest hardware, wine and spirits stores in the town. Both the captain and treasurer were employees of Peter Kelleghan's drapery store. Brett, the treasurer, was a Tipperary native and Mulvey, the captain, was from Longford. Secretary, Thomas Raftery, was from Loughrea, County Galway and had distinguished himself as a rugby player in his native county.[108] These officers, with the exception of McGreevey, combined playing with their administrative duties. The main employment represented was that of assistant in the drapery, iron-monger or pub trade.

The men involved in Mullingar Football Club were the leaders of their particular community. Many were important enough in their place of employment to represent their firm at formal occasions such as funerals. It was an era when young men working in white-collar occupations were becoming increasingly organised into social organi-sations that reflected the Victorian desire for self-improvement. The most popular club with shop assistants and clerks was the Mullingar Catholic Commercial Club, which was established in October 1890, with the objective of affording the members a means of 'social inter-course, mental and moral improvement and rational recreation'.[109] J. J. Geoghegan, a foreman in the ready-made department of James Doyne's drapery store, was one of those mainly responsible for the club's formation. The ambitious, status conscious, professionally upwardly mobile young men could socialise at the club with employer and employee and develop useful business contacts in the process. James Mulvey was the undoubted leader of this community and served in a variety of administrative and authoritative offices that included both the captaincy of the Mullingar Commercial Football Club and the Mullingar Cricket Club and secretary of the county GAA committee.

Much of the social life outside of sport was carried out in organisations that were associated with the Catholic Church and clearly proclaimed allegiance to the Catholic faith. A core group were founding members of the Mullingar Catholic National Young Men's Society. James Mulvey was elected treasurer and Patrick Brett secretary of the organisation. Clerical recommendation was responsible for the new club obtaining 'the largest of the front ground floor rooms' in Michael Doherty's Earl Street premises at a monthly rent of £1 5s.[110] The entrance fee of 2s 6d and a monthly subscription fee of 2s between 1 November and 1 May, and 1s for the remainder of the year ensured that membership was confined to those in regular employment and who enjoyed a comfortable living standard. The success of the new organisation was such that within a month its headquarters were re-located to the 'more commodious and suitable suite directly over the premises occupied by the Singer Machine Company'.[111] Many were also members of the Holy Family Confraternity, an organisation that mixed spiritualism, Catholic triumphalism, rational recreation and excursion. The rules of the confraternity required that the members engage in daily prayer, attend the bi-monthly meetings and receive monthly communion on the allocated Sunday. Fr Edward O'Reilly was spiritual director between 1883–1901 and he introduced public processions and excursions to different parts of Ireland. These normally concluded with athletic events that provided young Mullingar men with their first opportunity to compete in athletics. He also introduced a debating society to the organisation, established a library and secured a billiard table 'for the exclusive use of the members'.[112] The members of the Mullingar football clubs displayed very little interest in party politics. Patrick Brett was a notable exception. In 1893 he was present at the general meeting of the Mullingar National Federation.[113] Brett was one of the founder members with John P. Hayden, proprietor and editor of the *Westmeath Examiner*, of the UIL in Mullingar and combined an often-controversial business and political career in the town until his death in 1936.[114]

The second football club established in Mullingar was the Shamrocks club (the playing record of which has been described in detail earlier in this chapter). The core membership of this club had already been in sporting association through the medium of the Mullingar Shamrocks Cricket Club. The members decided to extend their seasonal involvement in sport in February 1890 by forming a football club. The new club included a broader social base than the Commercials club and was described by the *Westmeath Guardian* as a

> thoroughly representative and popular one. It embraces within its ranks the wealthy and humble, the business young man and the workingman, the employer and the artisan; all combined to promote the enjoyment of healthy and legitimate sport.[115]

Thomastown Rangers was the most active of the early rural clubs. Thomastown was a townland located within the civil parish of Killucan.[116] The story of the club is important as it illustrates how the early rural football clubs conducted their business. Although named Thomastown Rangers the club was a composite one that drew its members and supporters from a number of surrounding townlands. The club relied on local subscriptions to fund its activities. At the annual meetings of the club, committee members were elected from the adjacent townlands and these were the men charged with the responsibility of collecting subscriptions in their districts to fund the club for a season. The club was the most active of the early Westmeath clubs, taking part in at least twenty matches between March 1888 and December 1891. The club also had sufficient active members to field a reserve selection on fourteen of these occasions. After that date the club is recorded as having played only one additional match, the 1892 championship match against Mullingar Football Club. Members' tragedies were partly responsible for the club's demise. Club secretary Patrick Clinton died suddenly in December 1890 and the following October railway employee and playing member Laurence Brock was killed in a railway accident.[117] These tragic events changed the priorities of the club membership. Club funds were invested and members subscribed to erect graveyard monuments to the memory of the deceased members and the remainder of the funds on hand was donated to the father of Laurence Brock.[118] It was announced at the county committee meeting in January 1893 that Thomastown Rangers had amalgamated with neighbouring club, Raharney Rovers.[119]

Neil Tranter has identified the crucial significance 'of considerable numbers of private individuals willing and able to serve as patrons' to the development of institutionalised sport.[120] This patronage involved three basic types of assistance: donation of prizes for competitions, financial donations and, in the absence of public recreational grounds, the willingness of private landowners to grant sports participants access to land.[121] The latter was of crucial importance to the development of the early GAA clubs. The Cullion Celtics Club is a fine example of a club that depended on both monetary and facility-provision patronage. This club enjoyed the patronage of local landowner T. M. Reddy, who was active in hunting, racing and golf.[122] Reddy founded the club, supplied the members with a ball, gave them a field 'splendidly adapted for the purpose' and was prepared to pay any affiliation

fees required.[123] He also showed his support for the club by his presence, with his wife and daughter, at many of their games and by
making his house available on occasion for the post-match entertainment and festivity.[124] On occasions when Reddy travelled to Argentina
on business trips, instructions were given that 'the football club should
be accommodated in every reasonable way'.[125] The thirty-five members
who attended the annual meeting in October 1892 were informed that
they should feel especially grateful for 'the use of two fields, one for
practice matches and the other for [competitive] matches'.[126] This
largesse was provided at a time when some clubs struggled to gain the
use of one field for football purposes.

Obtaining the use of a suitable playing field was never a serious
problem in Mullingar, with at least six venues regularly used by the
clubs. The members of Mullingar Football Club showed their appreciation to Thomas Murtagh, who facilitated them by making available a
field at Springfield. In December 1892 he was visited at his home by the
club members and made a presentation of an 'exceedingly handsome
walking stick' made of 'polished ebony with silver band and Brazilian
horn handle'. The gesture of recognition proved worthwhile as in his
reply Murtagh informed the members that he was placing his house at
their disposal also.[127] Moate clubs, in contrast, had difficulty in accessing
appropriate playing fields, mainly because of the opposition of Canon
Kearney, who opposed football playing on a number of occasions
because of its associations with alcohol consumption.

The most important club in the western half of the county was the T. P.
O'Connor's club, established in December 1889 in Athlone. E. Doyle was
appointed captain, J. O'Flynn was elected secretary and R. Johnstone as
treasurer. The secretary reported a membership of over forty 'including
some of the best athletes of the town and neighbourhood'.[128] The choice
of name suggested a club with politically conscious members but it also
celebrated a local success story. T. P. O'Connor was an Athlone native
and a *Daily Telegraph* journalist who was elected MP for Galway in 1880
and for Liverpool in 1885, a position he retained to his death in 1929.[129] In
the opinion of the police, the T. P. O'Connor club was 'kept up as for the
pastime and not as a political club'.[130] The club elected as president,
Charles O'Donoghue, Ballinahown Court, a member of a leading
landowning family in Westmeath.[131] O'Donoghue provided financial
support to the club and also supported the club by attending some of the
more important matches. This club depended on the same economic constituency as the Mullingar Football Club for its membership with one
notable difference. Members such as M. O'Flynn, T. Hogan, E. Foy, E. J.
Doyle and J. Monahan were the sons of important and successful
Athlone businessmen. Mullingar Football Club catered for employees;
the T. P. O'Connor's club core membership consisted of employers' sons.

The competitive history of the T. P. O'Connor's club is important, as
the vicissitudes experienced by the club illustrate in stark detail many of

the difficulties experienced by the early GAA in achieving standardisation and compliance to an administrative structure. A Westmeath football championship was played in 1890 in which four clubs competed and was eventually won by the Athlone club in unsatisfactory circumstances (the Moate club walked off the field upset by the partisanship of the supporters).[132] The next important occasion for the club was in August 1890 when the members travelled to Dublin to play the Isles of the Sea in a tournament game. Having led by 0–1 to 0–0 at half-time the club managed to lose the match by 6–11 to 0–2.[133] Problems with the referee, it seems, were responsible for this debacle. The Athlone men were so upset by the decision to allow the first goal scored by the Dublin team that 'they stood up and let goal after goal pass them'. The *Westmeath Independent* reported that the Athlone men were not prepared for the foul play indulged in by their opponents.[134]

Athlone's problems continued in 1892 when permission to affiliate to the Westmeath county committee was refused, as their entry fee allegedly arrived late. Instead the club affiliated in Roscommon and represented Connacht in the All-Ireland championship semi-final match against Dublin (played 19 March 1893). Midway through the second half an incident occurred that resulted in the Athlone team leaving the field. This followed an incident in which a Dublin player 'ran the length of the field and struck J. Monahan of Roscommon almost breaking his jaw'. Despite Athlone objections, Dublin was awarded the match and another perceived injustice was added to the Athlone list. The final problem happened within a matter of weeks, when the club was required to travel to Mullingar to compete against the Cullion Celtics in the county championship and then return the following week to play in the championship semi-final and final. The 1893 final ended in controversy with the Mullingar Football Club disputing the final score despite the fact that the referee was Martin McGreevey, who was both president of the Mullingar club and of the county committee. The Mullingar club contested the decision of the referee to award the game to the Athlone club to the highest level of the Association. The departure of the T. P. O'Connor's club from the GAA, 'owing to the unfair treatment to which they had been subjected', was announced in December 1893. Now titled the Athlone Association Football Club 'they bid fair to add many new triumphs to their record'.[135] On St Stephen's Day, 1893, the Athlone Association Club played Bohemians in a friendly game. Ten of the eleven players were former prominent football players with the T. P. O'Connor's club. This changeover energised Athlone soccer and introduced a new competitive dimension to the sport.

The story of the T. P. O'Connor's club is important as it encapsulates many of the non-political difficulties that confronted the early association. In four of the most important games played by the club two were unfinished and two ended in controversy. The lack of a nationally accepted, clearly defined set of rules applied consistently by referees familiar with their content, caused difficulties on the occasions the club travelled to Dublin. Parochialism prevented their acceptance into the Mullingar dominated county committee and it was the failure of that body to recognise their championship victory of 1893 that precipitated their withdrawal from the GAA.

VI

A social profile of Gaelic footballers active at this time was constructed by compiling a list of 198 players involved in the game. Their identities were investigated by using information contained in the enumerators' forms of the 1901 census and also using information extracted from newspaper reports. It was possible to identify 120 (61 per cent) individuals, a number large enough to reach some general conclusions on the social status and personal circumstances of the earliest footballers in Westmeath. The information is illustrated in Table 14. Seven clubs were used to compile this profile and included urban (77 players) and rural (121 players) organisations.

| | | SOCIAL CLASS | | | |
| | | B | C | D | U |
	Sample				
Corbetstown Home Rulers	24	8	I	7	8
Kinnegad Slashers	34	12	4	4	14
Raharney Rovers	21	2	2	6	11
Thomastown Rovers	23	11	0	6	6
Wooddown Rackers	19	9	I	2	7
Mullingar Football Club	43	2	20	6	15
Athlone	34	4	12	I	17
Total	198	48	40	32	78

Table 14. Social classes of footballers in Westmeath, 1892

Members of social classes B and D dominated rural clubs. Those who identified themselves as farmers or farmers' sons in 1901 were the most active football players in 1892 and formed 55 per cent of the identified rural total. Farm labourers, who formed social class D, were the next most active category and accounted for 35 per cent of the group. In the urban areas, football was most popular with members of social class C and especially the white-collar representatives of the clerk or shop assistant group, who formed 53 per cent of the urban total. The remainder of this class were employed in various trades such as butcher, carpenter, wood-turner and tailor. The evidence here suggests that the formation of the GAA did not result in the sudden liberation of the poorer sectors of Irish society to the recreational fields, as farmers and their sons significantly outnumbered farm labourers. Nevertheless, some progress had been made in meeting Davin's desire to provide games for the 'humble and the hard-working' men that would provide an alternative to the 'everlasting round of labour'. In Mullingar, six members of the unskilled or general labourer category were active with the club.

As with other team sports, football was the reserve of the young man.[136] The age ranged between thirteen and thirty-three years; the average age of a rural football player in 1892 was 20.67 years. The uniformity in the average age of the football player was remarkable as the average age of the Mullingar player was 20.7 years, with his Athlone equivalent aged 20.56 years. Forty of the group were less than twenty years of age; thirty were aged between twenty and twenty-four; seventeen between twenty-five and twenty-nine and only two were over thirty.[137] The age profile also implies that these were mainly single men. In 1891, only three out of a total Westmeath male population of 3,798 aged between fifteen and twenty years of age, were married. Of those aged between twenty and twenty five, only 4 per cent were married.[138]

VII

This chapter has illustrated how the failure of Gaelic football and the GAA to maintain its progress in the county after its initial success was partly because of the failure of the internal management structure and the refusal of clubs to accept the decisions made by the controlling authority. This is not surprising, given the circumstances of the time. The ability to accept the authority of a controlling body required a political maturity in the sporting sense that had not yet been reached. The survival of a county committee required the achievement of consensus. Clubs were required to sacrifice their individual interests to the overall benefit of the game within the county. Despite the existence of rules and a hierarchy of officials to enforce them, ultimately within the county this consensus was not maintained. The two Mullingar clubs in particular refused to accept the county committee's decisions and this resulted in the Athlone club abandoning football in favour of soccer, and the disappearance of the Shamrock's club.

Codification was one of the characteristics of the transformation of sport from the pre-modern to its modern manifestation. As a process it was a slowly evolving one and the achievement of uniformity of rule interpretation and acceptance was protracted. Men with minimum experience of involvement in competitive sport or whose previous experience was in recreational cricket were expected to compete in a game in which the codes showed considerable geographical variation. In the interim, disputes on rules and regulations were common and retarded the development of the football game. Disputed scores and illegal tackles were important in damaging the development of the early GAA in Westmeath. Problems with rule interpretation proved particularly difficult for the T. P. O'Connor's club in Athlone. The experience of the core group of this football club, when they opted for soccer, illustrates the importance of a widely understood and established set of rules and regulations. The group made the transfer without difficulty and became one of the most successful clubs in Leinster in the early 1890s. The development of soccer and the impact of this transfer on the development of the 'association game' will be considered in the next chapter.

6. The development of soccer and rugby, 1875–1905

The decline of Gaelic football provided a major boost to soccer in Athlone. A core group of young middle-class commercial men became involved in the game and provided the stability and continuity that enabled the sport to progress and become a competitive sport. Athlone became a centre for the sport but its popularity both as a participant and spectator sport fluctuated during the period of this study. Rugby development was far more circumscribed and was confined to a narrow base provided by the Ranelagh School in Athlone and the Farra School in Bunbrosna, a district located a few miles outside Mullingar. The presence of a hockey-playing military regiment in Athlone introduced hockey to the town but this sport failed to sustain itself on a long-term basis.

The early history of soccer in Ireland has recently been subjected to a detailed analysis by Neal Garnham, who explores its introduction and development as well its socio-economic context in a manner similar to the important studies of soccer in England by Mason and Collins's exploration of rugby. Garnham's work on Irish soccer provides the most comprehensive analysis of the development of any sport in Ireland and examines the development of the game, club origins and their role in the promotion of the game, the social characteristics of the players, the structure and behaviour of the Irish football crowd, as well as the political difficulties experienced by the sport that resulted in division and the establishment of two controlling bodies.[1]

Soccer on a formal basis was first played in Ireland on 24 October 1878 when two Scottish clubs, Caledonians and Queen's Park, played an exhibition game at the grounds of the Ulster Cricket Club in Belfast. This match was organised by a Belfast drapery store manager, J. A. McAlery, who was reputedly introduced to the game while on honeymoon in Scotland.[2] The following spring a team of Belfast players contested a friendly game with the Lenzie Football Club from Stirlinghsire. The popularity of rugby and a difficulty in obtaining suitable playing grounds provided obstacles to the immediate adoption of the game in Belfast but in the autumn of 1879 the Cliftonville Club was formed from members of that club's cricket section. This manner of development in a sport is common. New sports clubs or clubs that adopted new sports often had their origins in existing sporting or social organisations. In April 1880 there were 'four thoroughly organized Clubs playing Association rules only', active in Belfast while there were 'several others occasionally practising them'. Moyola, based in Catledawson, Knock (Belfast) and Banbridge Academy in County Down, had joined Cliftonville as association football clubs and in the first season of their existence twenty-three soccer games were played in the region.[3] The game was also introduced to the Irish midlands as St Stanislaus College in Rahan had formed a soccer club.[4] The college was involved in cricket so the opportunity to include a new sport on the curriculum that catered for the winter recreational needs of the boys was likely to have been welcomed.

The final component in the creation of an Irish soccer infrastructure was put in place on 18 November 1880. A meeting of Belfast clubs, instigated by the Cliftonville Club, was held at the Queen's Hotel and the IFA was formed to organise, govern and promote the association game.[5] Soccer spread slowly and its regional penetration was confined. In 1890, regional associations had been established in the counties of Derry, Antrim, Down and a mid-Ulster association had also been formed from the clubs in north Armagh and adjacent areas. A total of 124 affiliated clubs existed at this stage. A Leinster Football Association was founded in 1892 and in October 1901 the Munster Football Association was established and affiliated to the IFA.[6]

II

Organised soccer was first introduced to Athlone in January 1887. Orlando Coote, a man who possessed aristocratic credentials of the highest order, was responsible for the initiative that brought the game to Athlone. His brother, Algernon, was a graduate of Eton, Cambridge and Trinity Colleges and although no information is available on Orlando's education, undoubtedly (given his background), he received an English public-school education where he would have been exposed to the ideals of muscular Christianity and the games ethic that was common in these institutions.[7] Coote's career in Athlone as a pioneer of sport and his involvement in its administration indicates a familiarity with a variety of sports and their operational codes. His was a ubiquitous presence in the Athlone sporting world, as his name was associated with tennis, hockey, rowing, yachting, cycling and coursing. Coote had family connections with the Roscommon area and was employed in Athlone as a land agent, one of the traditional sources of employment favoured by the younger sons of landed-gentry families.[8]

Coote established a soccer club in Athlone in January 1887 and, according to the *Westmeath Independent*, he founded 'successful clubs in Castlerea and other places he resided'.[9] Mr S. Wilson provided the use of his large field 'the entrance to which is from Northgate Street, opposite the Town Hall'.[10] The game in its initial manifestation in Athlone was an elitist activity. Training sessions, entrance fees and the organisation of games confined involvement to those who were financially secure and time rich. Members were required to subscribe 5s to join the club, the initial training session was timed for 3.00 on Monday afternoon and the earliest games of the club were played on Wednesday afternoons. Travel to games in Dublin and participation in the post-match socialisation required disposable income and so further restricted potential membership. The membership fee, however, remained constant, as seven years later it remained at 5s. A non-playing membership of 2s 6d was also available.[11] The new club was also closely associated with the Ranelagh School, which supplied officers, players and a new playing pitch when Wilson's field was 'vacated in favour of the Rugby fraternity as the Ranelagh pitch was more suitable to skilful ground football'.[12] The school ground from that time became the venue for the most important games played by the club and other Athlone-based clubs during the period of this study.

The office holders and the membership of its early committees are indicative of the initial gentry and upper-middle class influence. Those elected to office in 1887 and 1888 were drawn from the upper echelons of Athlone society. Orlando Coote and H. Milligan were elected captain and secretary respectively. P. B. Treacy was appointed treasurer and the committee consisted of M. Geoghegan, T. Langstaff, J. Hodson, W. Jeffers and Captain Inglis. Coote and Hodson represented the landed gentry. H. Milligan and M. Geoghegan were members of two of Athlone's leading business families. The Milligan family owned one of the town's leading drapery and millinery stores and Geoghegan's family were proprietors of the Prince of Wales Hotel. Captain Inglis was elected to the committee in 1888 as a representative of the Royal Artillery, while Langstaff and Jeffers were teachers at the Ranelagh School.[13] The treasurer, P. B. Treacy, was associated with the same community and was employed in Athlone as the petty sessions clerk.

The Athlone Association Football Club had an active first three months of existence, during which time seven matches were organised. The first match was played on 9 February 1887 when Orlando Coote captained the club in a scoreless draw against Castlerea, a club also founded by Coote. Two games were played against the military teams of the Royal Berkshire Regiments and the Royal Artillery. A match was played against Ranelagh School as well as games against a Trinity College team and a selection of Dublin AFC that included 'four first eleven Trinity men and four first eleven Dublin AFC men'. Castlerea also provided the opposition for the final game of the season.[14] Seventeen different players were used, and eleven of these were either teachers or students of the Ranelagh School. This relationship continued in 1888 when, in the first game of the season, six players from the school represented the club against Dublin AFC.[15] Orlando Coote was part of this team that also included two members of the military, Captain Inglis and Lieutenant W. N. Bolton. The club remained active throughout 1888 and 1889 but from April of that year its rate of activity declined and only one game was played in 1891 and 1892. The playing record of the club in its first three seasons is summarised in Table 15.

At this stage soccer in the county was informal, devoid of structure and formal competition, and restricted to a narrow Athlone-based social group. In this phase of development friendly matches were organised through personal contact within a socially restricted network. The four leading Dublin clubs were formed from similar social groups. The Dublin University Club and the Leinster Nomads, despite the name, were privileged to have access to private grounds. Bohemians played in the polo grounds and had the use of one of the gatekeepers' lodges as changing rooms, while the Nomads 'dressed in the comfortable surroundings of P. S. Fleming on Sandymount Green'.[16]

	Played	Won	Drew	Lost
1887	7	5	0	2
1888	9	3	2	4
1889	10	5	1	4

Table 15. Record of Athlone Association Football Club, 1887–89
(*Westmeath Independent*)

III

The Ranelagh School was one of the most important centres of education in Westmeath and was one of three schools in the county that equated to the English model of the public school. Ranelagh School and Farra School (Bunbrosna) were under the patronage and superintendence of the Incorporated Society for Promoting English Protestant Schools in Ireland. This society supported six Irish schools.[17]

Initially, sports participation in schools was seen simply as a way of filling the days of pupils and as a means of diverting them from less acceptable pastimes. This attitude was refined and the promotion of games was seen as essential because of their health promoting virtues. Farra and Ranelagh schools in their advertisements emphasised the role games participation played in this process. In Farra 'the greatest possible care was bestowed upon the health and domestic comfort of the Pupils' and as a means to this end 'cricket and other outdoor games were encouraged'. Ranelagh School advertised a situation that was 'most healthful', with a playground that was large and well adapted for school games, to which great attention was paid by the principal.[18] According to the principal, Mr Bailie, there was a 'wholesome rule' in the school that required all boys at the school 'to go out two days a week and take their turns at the games, whether cricket, football or hockey' and 'this involvement accounted for the excellent health of the boys'. He had also constructed at his own expense an 'extensive shed' for use as an indoor playground during unfavourable weather conditions.[19] The school endeavoured to develop muscular as well as mental power, according to Bailie in his 1890 end-of-term address, a time when the school had 119 pupils on its roll.[20] The numbers enrolled had grown steadily since 1880 when there were sixty-seven boys in the school (forty-eight boarders and nineteen day boys), of whom three were Catholics. Seven years later there was a total of 117 boys in the school, the vast majority of whom were Protestants, with a few Wesleyans and Presbyterians and seven Catholic dayboys.[21]

In the 1890s muscular Christianity had become part of the ethos of Irish educational establishments.[22] This was based on the belief that physical activity played a crucial role in developing Christian gentlemen. Participation in sport taught courage, self-reliance and helped character building. As a result, schools under the control of Catholic religious also involved their students in soccer playing. In 1903, St Mary's Intermediate School in Athlone (managed by the Marist Brothers) played matches against the Ranelagh School.[23] In 1905, the Mullingar Christian Brothers School was involved in matches with the Franciscan College in Multyfarnham. The latter school was particularly active in 1904 and 1905 and competed successfully in a junior tournament organised by the Mullingar St Patrick's club.[24]

Despite its initial association with the soccer code, the Ranelagh School's chief sporting interest was in rugby football. Irish connections with English public schools were instrumental in the introduction of rugby to Ireland. Former pupils of these schools who attended Trinity College introduced the sport to this country. In 1854, some former pupils of the Rugby and Cheltenham schools in England formed a rugby club at the university. Over the next five years the Trinity club's rugby activity was confined to internal games with students forming makeshift teams organised on the basis of places of birth, places of education, alphabetical identity and involvement in other sports. Two members of the Trinity club formulated rules for the game in October 1868. The first ever recognised international match took place in 1871 and in February 1879 a unified Irish Rugby Football Union was formed to manage and promote the game.[25] Trinity graduates played a key role in the diffusion of rugby outside the metropolitan region.

This link was crucial to the introduction of rugby to the Farra and Ranelagh schools; the two headmasters who promoted sport in the schools, T. C. Foster and Robert Bailie, were both Trinity graduates.[26] A Trinity education presupposed attendance at a public school where the two gentleman were likely to have experienced the games ethic of these establishments. These influences were reflected in the policies they pursued as headmasters. The first recorded rugby game in Westmeath was played between the two schools at Farra, on 25 February 1879 and was, appropriately, drawn.[27] This game came a year after both Bailie and Foster were appointed headmasters at Ranelagh and Farra schools respectively.[28] Teams for these games combined masters and students and for the initial game T. C. Foster captained the Farra side; four years later he was still 'A1' at fullback against the Royal School, Cavan.[29] In the 1885 game between Farra and Ranelagh, the latter included 'four masters and two past men'.[30] These matches brought organisation and regulation to the normal football games that were played in the Farra School. In many ways these resembled the practices of folk football games. According to a contemporary pupil 'fierce, often venomous games of football' were popular in the school. The football played recognised 'no rules, no bounds except a lake or a river', and was likely to 'rouse, mad, wild passion in the players'. Games were played with one half of the school taking on the other in a style of rugby that 'was only less a scrimmage than the other sort, contemptuously described by us as the kind the soldiers played'.[31]

From 1879 both schools organised regular games with schools of a similar ethos and also maintained the link with Trinity by organising games with the college. Farra School, until its closure in April 1898, offered a comprehensive rugby programme and the school was one of seven entrants in the inaugural Leinster Senior Schools Cup in 1887.[32] In 1892, the Farra School twice played games against Cavan Grammar School and the Trinity College 2nd XV, against Longford 1st XV and Portora Royal School from Enniskillen, County Fermanagh. The school also competed in the Leinster Schools Cup and beat Dundalk in the first round but lost to Blackrock College in the final.[33] Ranelagh School had a similar programme and in the 1889 and 1890 seasons also played eight matches against selections from Galway Grammar School, Birr, Portarlington and Longford.[34]

Despite the popularity of rugby in the schools, the game did not transfer to the civilian population. Only one reference to rugby in Mullingar was discovered in the course of this research. This was in December 1880 when the Farra School defeated a Mullingar selection. The Mullingar team were reported to be playing their first match and the report concluded that 'it should be mentioned that the Mullingar team played two men short'.[35] The absence of local opposition was discussed at the AGM of the Farra club in September 1885 and was considered the 'one great drawback' to the promotion of rugby, as 'competition in such a game has certainly a very beneficial effect, particularly in a school team'. This was at a time when 'almost every village in the county has had its cricket club'.[36] The relative isolation of Farra from Mullingar, its nearest urban centre, may partly explain why rugby diffusion failed to take place. This does not apply to Athlone, where Ranelagh School was at the centre of various recreational activities and initiatives. Both schools were primarily boarding schools where students were educated in isolation from the local communities and, on completion of their schooling, progressed to university or pursued careers in places where their influence as rugby missionaries may have been important. The absence in both towns of a rugby-playing army regiment was also an important factor in the failure of rugby to develop a profile of any significance. The critical mass of boys educated at public schools was never assembled in Mullingar or Athlone and therefore the game never captured the public imagination at any stage during the period covered by this study. The only regiment associated with rugby was the Lancashire Fusiliers, who were based in Athlone from 1896 to 1897. The regiment established a rugby club in February 1897 that was made up of the unit's officers and men. Richard Adamson was the only civilian involved. The club unsuccessfully contested the first Connacht Rugby Cup final, but the sport seems to have disappeared following the departure of the regiment.[37]

The Lancashire Fusiliers were also associated with the most serious attempt at developing hockey in Athlone in 1897. Prior to this, occasional games between military and civilian teams were reported.[38] On 30 September 1896 the Athlone Garden Vale Hockey Club was formed with Lieutenant E. C. Brierley elected captain; Orlando Coote accepted the position of secretary and treasurer. The club affiliated to the Irish Hockey Union (IHU).[39] This club was very active in its initial season and filled a vacuum that existed following the changed circumstances of the Athlone Soccer Club. The players included some of Athlone's original soccer players and the competitive loop of the club also included Trinity College. A shortage of local opposition and the difficulty in attracting strong opposition to Athlone meant that the club travelled to Galway and Dublin for competitive games. Matches against Palmerston, Trinity College, Donnybrook and the Galway club were played on a number of occasions.[40] Eight matches were played in the club's first season and only losses to Donnybrook and the Cork clubs blemished the record.[41] Inevitably hockey was added to the recreational curriculum of the Ranelagh School and following the departure of the Fusiliers, the Athlone club became more closely identified with the school.[42] The school entered for the Irish junior hockey cup in 1898 and included Hodson and Adamson of the Garden Vale Club in its selection.[43] Hockey provided an outlet for Orlando Coote to expand his career as a sports administrator. In October 1898 the Connacht Hockey Union was formed and Coote was elected vice-president. At this meeting nine clubs, including the Athlone Ranelagh Club, entered the Connacht hockey league.[44] The following year Coote was elected to the positions of secretary-treasurer, was chosen as a delegate to the IHU and appointed a selector for the Connacht provincial team.[45]

The cult of games in both schools also extended to the promotion of athletics. Annual athletics meets were organised from 1885 in Ranelagh and 1886 in Farra.[46] These events generally consisted of standard foot races and other track and field fare, as well as a number of novelty events to encourage wide participation. The 1889 Farra sports promoted events open to the entire county that had previously been confined to residents in the immediate locality of the school. This meet

was noteworthy as it marked the first reported competitive performance of Walter Newburn, who finished second in the senior boys
220 yards race.[47]

IV

Involvement in soccer was not wholly limited to those associated with
Ranelagh School at this time. The working classes were also involved in
soccer in the early 1890s in Athlone. Tony Mason, in his study of English
soccer, has identified the workplace as a source of origin for football
clubs and this was also of some importance in Ireland.[48] Two of Ireland's
most prominent clubs had their roots in the industrial heart of Belfast.
The Distillery club was originally formed in 1879 from employees of
Dunville's distillery while the Linfield club was formed from the
workers at the Ulster Spinning Company's Linfield Mill. Both clubs
received encouragement and material assistance from their employers.[49]
A small-scale example of this industrial paternalism took place in
Athlone. The Athlone Woollen Mills was the largest industrial establishment in the county at this time. The employees of this particular firm
benefited from the paternalist approach of the proprietorial Smith family
to industrial relations. Sport was included amongst the range of benevo-
lent interventions promoted at the factory. Cricket, athletics and soccer
were encouraged and this recreational paternalism included the promotion of an athletic meeting in 1886, which claimed to be the first held in
the area that provided the working classes with an opportunity to
compete. The programme included a girls' race that attracted an entry of
eleven.[50] Earlier in the year a football match under GAA rules was also
played between the woollen mills and the sawmill employees.[51]

According to a contemporary newspaper report, the management of
the factory was based on the principle that 'all work and no play makes
Jack a dull boy'. The employers organised annual dance parties and
soirées, granted the usual popular holidays and supported excursions
such as an 1892 visit to Dublin.[52] Soccer was part of the sporting programme available for the workers and between 1892 and 1894 the
Athlone Woollen Mills played a number of matches against military
combinations. However, reports of Athlone Woollen Mills participation
in soccer do not appear after 1894. Smith's benevolence and interventions on behalf of the Athlone working classes continued, however, and
in 1896 he financed a temperance hall in the town dedicated to Fr
Mathew. This hall was opened on 1 November 1897 and was the
seventh such hall associated with the various temperance societies in
the town in the Victorian period.[53] The Fr Mathew Club was a typical
Victorian self-help organisation and provided a variety of activities
designed to improve mind and body in an alcohol-free environment. In
the first year, it was claimed that almost 13,000 were served at the café
and 2,000 books were borrowed from the library, which provided a

range of both light and serious reading. The hall was 'fitted out like a gentleman's club' and had available several newspapers as well as 'two beautiful billiard tables'.[54]

V

The organisation and management of soccer in the Athlone district was altered fundamentally in the 1893–94 season. This development resulted from the decision of the T. P. O'Connor's Gaelic Football Club to withdraw from the GAA. This body of experienced and competitive footballers switched their allegiance to the soccer code and the impact on the Athlone Association Football Club was dramatic and immediate. The club now involved itself in national competition and its social composition changed from one dominated by public-school representatives to one that catered for the middle-class clerks and shop assistants of the town. This group were experienced Gaelic footballers and the success enjoyed by them in their adopted code is indicative of the extent to which the essential skills of both codes were transferable at this stage.

The changed circumstances are reflected in the attendance at the 1894 annual meeting. Orlando Coote maintained the connection with the original committee and was elected president. R. Jeffers was elected to the committee and preserved the linkage with the Ranelagh School. P.V. C. Murtagh, a lawyer, J. Radden, an engineer, and P. B. Treacy, the petty-sessions clerk were also elected to the club committee. The remaining sixteen who attended the meeting were associated with the town's business community (as illustrated in Table 16). Shop assistants and clerks constituted the main core of the playing population of the club at this time. Fifteen different players were used in the 1894 and 1895 Leinster junior cup finals and it has been possible to identify eight of these. All were engaged in white-collar occupations including shop assistants, commission agents, loan officers and clerks. Of these Edward Foy, Michael O'Flynn, Thomas Hogan, Jim Monahan and Jim Campbell were members of prominent Athlone business families. Maurice Norton, the goalkeeper on the 1894 team, obviously believed that an association with a successful soccer team was of some commercial value as he advertised his newly established victualler's store in Wentworth Street using the headline 'footballer'. The close association between the commercial sector of the town and association football at this time was further solidified by the use of the rooms of the Commercial Club in Excise Street as an entertainment venue for travelling teams.[55] Apart from the commercial dimension, the club at this stage also had a strong neighbourhood identity with Connaught Street and Church Street particularly well represented. Neighbourhood association was an important factor in the formation of British football clubs, the members of which were, as Holt has observed, 'probably childhood playmates who graduated from street games to street teams'.[56] Some of those involved in the Athlone Association Football Club at this time may have shared similar childhood experiences and, of course, graduated from Gaelic football to soccer.

Name	Nature of business	Address
Campbell, J.	Grocer & spirit dealer	Connaught Street
Connell, H.	Grocer & spirit dealer	Church Street
Conway, J.	Rate collector	Unknown
Conway, M. J.	Rate collector	Unknown
Doyle, E. J.	Grocer & spirit dealer	Connaught Street
Foy, E.	Pawnbroker	Church Street
Geoghegan, M., TC & PLG	Hotel proprietor	Church Street
Gladstone, R.	Grocer & spirit dealer	Queen Street
Hannon, W., TC	Grocer & spirit dealer	Connaught Street
Hogan, T. J.	Stationer	Church Street
Macken, J.	Grocer & provision dealer	Mardyke Street
Milligan, H.	Milliner & draper	Church Street
Monahan, J.	Publican & earthen-ware dealer	Connaught Street
O'Flynn, M.	Grocer & spirit dealer	High Street
Smith, H.	Athlone Woollen Mills	Devenish Court
Turkington, J.	Baker & game dealer	King Street

Table 16. Names, businesses and places of residence of those attending AGM of Athlone AFC, October 1894 (source of occupations: *Slater's Directory*, 1892, 16–19)

Participation in more meaningful competitions than the friendly games was made possible through affiliation to the new Leinster Council, established in 1892. This body organised a new competition, the Leinster Junior Cup, for which Athlone was one of fourteen entrants and the only one from outside of Dublin city.[57] A respectable standard of soccer was played in Athlone at this time. This was developed from interaction with, and exposure to army skills and expertise as well as the football skills and competitive instincts developed on the Gaelic football fields. The quality of play is indicated by the fact that the club was successful in its competitive debut, winning the Leinster Junior Cup in the 1893–94 season. In this competition, Dublin clubs – the GPO, the Nomads, St Helen's and Britannia – were defeated without the concession of a goal. The following season was equally successful as Britannia, Bohemians and the GPO were beaten as the title was defended.[58] The promotion to senior football that followed these successes proved to be less successful. A journey to Belfast to play Glentoran in the Irish Senior Cup resulted in a 7-1 defeat. However, Hibernians from Dublin were beaten 2-1 in the Leinster Senior Cup semi-final; this competition ended for the Athlone club with a 2-1 final loss to Bohemians.[59]

Former Gaelic football players dominated the Athlone Football Club in its two most successful seasons. In the four matches played in the Leinster campaign of 1893, seventeen different players were used. Eight of these had played on the T. P. O'Connor's club team in the P. W. Nally memorial tournament mentioned in the previous chapter. The 1893 soccer season concluded with an exhibition match played on St Stephen's day between Athlone and Bohemians. Ten of the Athlone team were former T. P. O'Connor's players. Apart from the transferability of skills, this example of football crossover from Athlone illustrates the concept of football as understood by its participants as a recreational activity devoid of political connotations. Gaelic football playing at this stage, despite the best efforts of the GAA at national level, had yet to be equated with a nationalist identity in Westmeath. The men who transferred their football allegiance in 1893 included Parnellite nationalists who at the conclusion of the P. W. Nally memorial game joined their supporters and marched to Glasnevin to place a wreath on Parnell's grave.[60]

VI

The importance of the military in popularising certain sports is a recurring theme in Irish sports history and the introduction of soccer to the county provides an opportunity to examine the validity of the thesis as it relates to that particular sport.[61] Garnham concludes from his investigation that in the early years of association football's development in Ireland, the military were important in the game's diffusion and in setting standards of play. This worked in a number of ways. Soldiers serving in Ireland provided recruits for many of the early Irish clubs, and also became some of the early Irish professional players. Irishmen in the British military services took up the game and occasionally returned to Ireland bringing knowledge of the game with them. Military teams played matches against local civilian teams who were often short of opposition. However, as Garnham points out, the role of the military as soccer ambassadors varied over both time and space. In certain areas a number of sources of tension existed between military sides and their civilian counterparts.[62] Earlier chapters of this book dealt with elite socialisation between military officers and landed interests as mediated through the vehicle of sport. Soccer in Athlone was responsible for considerable interaction between the rank-and-file soldiers and the middle and lower classes of the town. Although Burke details a number of incidents, some serious in nature, between the civilian population and Athlone-based soldiers, the relationship between soldiers and civilians was generally good. This was confirmed by a police report of October 1899 which stated that 'the town people have always been on good terms with the military'.[63] Evidence from Church of Ireland marriage registers support this contention and suggest that there was considerable social intercourse between soldiers based in Athlone and

Mullingar and women who resided in the vicinity of the army bar-racks.in these towns. The register of St Peter's Church records 247 marriages between 1851 and 1870 and eighty-three percent of these were between a local woman and a soldier based in the Victoria Bar-racks. In the period between 1880 and 1905 an additional 142 marriages took place and eighty-four percent of these were between soldiers and civilian women. St Mary's Church hosted 227 marriages between 1851 and 1905 and thirty-eight per cent of these were between soldiers and local women. The same period at Mullingar's All Saint's Church fea-tured 101 weddings with seventy percent between soldiers and Mullingar women.[64]

The earliest reference to soccer in the county provides a classic example to support the notion of military involvement in the promo-tion of the game, as it included an inter-regimental game, an offer to play games against civilian sides and a willingness to explain the rules to the uninitiated. In November 1878, the *Westmeath Guardian* adver-tised a match in Mullingar between the Beverley Rovers and the 1st Battalion of the 15th Regiment, in the 'field adjoining the Barracks, on Wednesday 20th November'.[65] Spectators were promised that the rules of the association as 'played throughout the United Kingdom would be carried out', and they would also have the 'opportunity of impressing the technicalities of the game on their mind'. The Battalion members also announced their willingness to meet any team in a friendly match at any time during the season and 'to give every infor-mation on the rules of the game'.[66] Unfortunately there was no further report of this game and newspaper references to soccer in Mullingar are scarce for the 1880s and 1890s.

An analysis of newspaper reports of games played in the period 1887–1905 provides evidence that the military played an important role in soccer's development in the county. This role involved providing opposition for the local civilian clubs, particularly in Athlone. Inter-regimental games provided public demonstrations of the codes and skills of the game and developed its public profile. In the period 1887–1905, 241 games were reported in the local press and 119 (49 per cent) involved a military team. Of these 119 games, forty-nine were intra- or inter-regimental ones. The military involvement was relatively contin-uous over the period, as can be seen from a few examples of the playing records of regimental teams. The soccer club of the Athlone based Royal Artillery concluded its 1891 season with a record of five wins and two losses in seven games in which they scored twenty-six goals and con-ceded twelve.[67] Between October 1904 and December 1905 the team attached to the Connaught Rangers played at least twenty-four games while based in Mullingar.[68]

This period of intense military involvement in soccer, both locally and at regimental level, coincided with a time when the promotion of phys-ical fitness through involvement in sport became important in army training. The importance of sport to the lives of soldiers is reflected in regimental newsletters and journals, which are dominated by sports reports and debate.[69] According to Campbell, the amount of time and energy spent by soldiers on football, as compared to time spent on regimental duties, was far more than one would normally expect for mere leisure time. Soccer was the most popular sport in the late Victorian army and it has been suggested that the popularity of a sport was influenced partly by where a regiment was from and partly by the preference of the officers.[70] Tournaments at the company level were organised in order to identify and train younger players for selection on the regimental teams.[71] Games of this category were common in Athlone and Mullingar and were important in popularising the game. On occasion, they provided an entertainment package that included music provided by the regimental band. The October 1890 game in Mullingar between the East Lancashire Regiment and the Grenadier Guards attracted a large number of spectators, including 'a number of the poor demented inmates of the Institution'. Music provided by the 'Lilywhites' band entertained spectators throughout the game.[72] In February 1893, the South Lancashire Regiment hosted a three-day tournament in Athlone, which included the other local participants, the 2nd Battalion of the East Kent Regiment (Buffs), Ranelagh School and Athlone Football Club.[73] In April, the final of the regimental shield between G and D companies of the South Lancashire regiment attracted an 'immense crowd of spectators'.[74] The various football interests in Athlone maintained contact and occasionally came together and formed composite teams to play against each other. A number of these games were played in March and April 1892. On St Patrick's day, an Athlone selection of footballers played Ballinasloe in a rugby game and this was followed in April by two soccer matches that were organised as result of a challenge delivered by the Athlone clubs representing soccer, rugby and football to the RIF.[75]

The military also influenced the development of the game by providing players to local teams, although in Westmeath this was an occasional occurrence. In the early years in Athlone, the club benefited from the skills of two members of the Wiltshire Regiment. Captain Inglis and Lieutenant Bolton were regulars in the 1887–88 season and featured in the lists of goal scorers.[76] Driver Jackson, reportedly a former Blackburn Rovers player, was another whose talents were used by the civilian side and he was included in at least one match in the initial and successful Leinster Junior Cup campaign.[77] The T. P. O'Connor's football club also used his talent when it played in Dublin in the P. W. Nally memorial tournament.[78] In that particular game, Jackson 'wore a red and white patched jersey' as opposed to the rest of his colleagues who were 'beautifully attired in their sea green jerseys'. With his colleague (soon to be prominent soccer player), O'Flynn, he 'elicited the repeated plaudits of an admiring concourse of spectators'.[79] His Royal Artillery regiment publicised their willingness to play any team in the Athlone hinterland under association rules. Soldiers Barrett and Armstrong of the Connaught Rangers were members of the Mullingar St Patrick's team on occasion also.[80]

At a time when access to a suitable playing field was not always possible the contribution of both the military and Ranelagh School in making available recreational space was also significant in the promotion of soccer and indeed other sports. The Queen's Meadow in Athlone was the property of the War Office and was maintained to a high standard. Civilians had access to this ground for football and cricket games, 'permission for same being made in days and at times on which the ground is not otherwise engaged'.[81] The Ranelagh school grounds were used for all the important soccer matches played in the period of this study.

There is no clear point of origin for the introduction of soccer to Mullingar, and it cannot be credited to individual initiative similar to that of Orlando Coote. As described earlier, the game was certainly played by military personnel based in the town and the early newspaper reports of the game refer to matches between various companies from the Mullingar regiments. In 1883, the *Westmeath Examiner* advertised a match between the 5th Northumberland Fusiliers and the Mullingar Club but unfortunately, like the example quoted above, there was no follow-up report.[82] The first reported game between civilian teams was played between the Victors and the Green Road and took place in October 1893 and was refereed by Daniel Earl of the Mullingar Football Club.[83] The only properly constituted soccer club that developed in Mullingar during the period of this study was the St Patrick's Club, an organisation that oscillated between playing football and soccer in the early years of its existence. It was active in football from 1896 and in soccer from 1899, playing both codes during a season.[84] This code switching was common at the time and not unique to Westmeath. The Cookstown Swifts Club began in football but switched to soccer because of the lack of local opposition and then, like Athlone's T. P. O'Connor's, turned to rugby in the 1890s after losing an appeal to the IFA over a contested cup-tie. Another example was the Laune Rangers Football Club in Kerry, which originated as a rugby club.[85] Cavan's first soccer team, the Belturbet Red Stars was formed in 1893, partly from former members of the Rory O'More football club. In 1902 Belturbet Red Stars and Rory O'More's Gaelic football club united as Belturbet United Gaelic and Soccer Club and in tournaments held in 1900 and 1901 in Cavan it was usual to have games in both football codes.[86]

At this stage compliance to a single code in team sports had yet to develop. For at least twenty years after the formation of the GAA there was continual crossover between team games such as cricket, soccer and football in Westmeath. The changed circumstances that introduced demarcation lines in sport will be examined in the next chapter.

Military influence was probably important in introducing the young men of the St Patrick's Club to the soccer game. Some members of the club resided in Patrick Street, Mullingar.[87] This street was located close to the military barracks and it is reasonable to conclude that young boys in the area would have discovered the game by watching the soldiers play. The club eventually opted for soccer, having switched football codes for a number of seasons, and affiliated to the Leinster Football Association in 1903. This was the club's busiest season and the seven games contested included first-round defeats in both the Leinster Junior Cup and All-Ireland Junior Cup competitions.[88] The 1904 competitive season ended with a 5–0 home defeat to the Athlone team in the Leinster junior cup and the match report gives an indication of the poor quality play of the Mullingar team. According to the reporter,

> Mullingar had plenty of vigour but lacked every other quality. Mullingar lacked every essential that goes to make a successful team. Their combination was nothing while their play around goal was ridiculous. The most magnificent opportunities being thrown away by them and in point of lasting powers they simply were not in it.[89]

This series of defeats, coupled with an incident in a St Stephen's Day match in 1905, when a Dublin player accidentally suffered a broken leg, ended the activities of the St Patrick's Club. A new club, Glenmore, was formed from the same core group of players, and this club played a number of friendly games in 1905.[90] At the same time, both Athlone clubs re-constituted themselves with the formation of the Connaught Wanderers and the Rebel clubs, both of which affiliated to the Leinster association for the 1905–06 season.[91] Although the St Patrick's Club may have eventually opted for soccer, individual members of the club continued to play Gaelic football. Newbrook Wanderers, a team that included eight members of the St Patrick's soccer club, won the first football tournament organised in Mullingar in 1903.[92] The players included James Reynolds, the captain of the St Patrick's Football Club and H. Stenson, the vice-captain.[93]

VII

The fragmented nature of soccer development in the Athlone district is illustrated by developments following the successful 1894 and 1895 seasons. The Leinster senior cup final defeat was followed in early 1897 by a 13-5 defeat by the Lancashire Fusiliers; these reverses seem to have dimmed the enthusiasm of the members for the game.[94] The period between 1896 and 1900 was dominated by military games, with eighteen of the thirty-three matches played in Athlone inter-regimental. There is also evidence of the game developing in the rural hinterland of Athlone, in Glasson, Blary, Drumraney, Coosan, Bealnamullia, Tubberclare, Auburn and the Moydrum districts.[95] A number of games between clubs in these districts were reported. These were attractive in

rural areas where public sources of entertainment were rare and reportedly over 1,000 spectators attended the 1898 St Patrick's Day game
between the Glasson Young Ireland and the Blary McBride club. Some
of these clubs used a naming policy that had nationalist connotations;
Daniel O'Connell, Major John McBride (for his efforts in the Boer War),
Wolfe Tone and the Young Ireland movement were all memorialised by
these rural clubs. The use of nationalist icons by young men playing
soccer would suggest that the game at this stage had not developed a
particular political identity. That this also happened with cricket suggests that the process whereby certain games became politicised was a
post-1900 development. The post-1903 growth of cultural nationalism
and the Irish-Ireland movement, with its associated GAA development,
provided a football alternative for the young men of these districts.
Coosan, Tubberclare and Glasson clubs affiliated to the GAA in 1905
and thus ended the possibility of soccer becoming popular in rural
Westmeath.

The relatively inactive period between 1896 and 1900 was followed
in the early 1900s by a remarkable escalation in soccer activity in
Athlone. This was fuelled by the emergence of a new team, the Athlone
Junior team. At the end of October 1902 this club had played thirteen
games and remained unbeaten.[96] In April 1903 this run had extended
to thirty games with twenty-three wins, five draws and two losses
recorded, in which 109 goals were scored.[97] The club was financially
stable and its popularity in Athlone was reflected in the £9 5s 6d that
was contributed by the townspeople at the end of the 1902 season. The
club members adopted a relatively professional approach in their
preparation for matches. They worked on developing fitness levels and
included regular Tuesday-night runs in their training schedule. The
club also promoted the game and helped its own finances by making
available weekly, 'at a nominal' sum, their clubrooms to the Shamrock
team, which was also formed at this time. The Ranelagh school
grounds were placed at the club's disposal for cup games and, Mr
Bailie, the principal of the school, was appointed club president for the
1902–03 season.[98] Inspired by the Juniors' performances, the original
and successful Athlone team of the early 1890s also returned to competitive soccer in October 1902.[99]

Athlone at this stage had three civilian teams (the Shamrocks team
was active from October 1902) and, with two military garrisons based in
the town, soccer dominated as a participant and spectator sport.[100] The
1902–03 season was particularly busy and featured a regular programme
of soccer from October to April. The number of active teams in the district meant that double-header and triple-header Sunday programmes
were organised. The Athlone Juniors played twice on the same day
against a team from Kiltoom and a Coney Island selection in May
1902; in October, as part of a triple bill, the Shamrocks XI played the
Athlone Junior team and an Artillery team in successive games. This

was followed by a game that featured the re-formed Athlone Senior team against an Artillery selection. These events proved very attractive to the Athlone public and on this occasion, 'Shortly after 1 o'clock spectators were to be seen, filing into the grounds and before the second match was completed the town had emptied itself of the majority of its inhabitants, leaving the streets almost deserted.'[101] November featured two further double bills and in December a triple-header was held and the month concluded with a Leinster Junior Cup game between the Athlone Junior team and University College.[102] At this stage the *Westmeath Independent* reported that

> The grand old game of association football seems to have taken complete sway in Athlone and both players and public have become almost entirely fascinated by it; this most manly sport has taken a firm root in the minds of the sports loving public of Athlone.[103]

The major public holidays of St Stephen's Day, St Patrick's Day and Easter Monday in Athlone featured soccer games as the main source of entertainment. GAA organised games at this time had little impact in the town and a Westmeath championship football game in May 1904 drew derision from some. According to the *Westmeath Independent*, 'there was undoubtedly a disposition on the part of very many to ridicule and make little of the Gaelic Game'.[104] Soccer never attained the same popularity as a spectator sport or as a vehicle for participation in Mullingar. Football and hurling tournaments provided sporting spectacles from 1903 onwards. In April 1905, following a badly-supported soccer game staged at the Showgrounds in Mullingar, the *Midland Reporter* claimed that hurling and football had 'certainly killed the imported game in the County Westmeath and cricket this summer is bound to follow its friend, Association, into the oblivion from which it should never have emerged'.[105]

VIII

A detailed examination of the 105 players who participated in soccer in the period 1900–1904 was undertaken to establish a socio-economic profile of those involved in the game. Seventy-five of these players were identified in the census material. This gives a sample of 71 per cent and is large enough to be representative of the group as a whole. The findings of this analysis are illustrated in Table 17. Urban soccer attracted participants particularly from social class C (67 per cent), with individuals from social class D also well represented. The absence of representatives from social class D in the rural districts is particularly noteworthy. Twenty-one individuals out of twenty-five who represented Glasson in soccer in the period 1900–01 were identified. Landowners or tenant farmers dominated the group as fourteen were farmers' sons and three were farmers. Three farm labourers and a tailor completed the group, which had an average age of 21.5 years.

	Mullingar	Athlone	Rural	Total
Sample	30	50	25	105
Identified	18	36	21	75
B		4	17	21
C	12	24	1	37
D (rural)			3	3
D (urban)	6	8		14

Table 17. Social classes of Athlone and Mullingar soccer players, 1900–1904

In Athlone social class C had the greatest representation. This category included occupations such as a coach painter, victualler, plumber and carpenter as well as white-collar workers such as clerks and shop assistants. In Mullingar the skilled tradesmen involved included a cycle repairer, a boot-maker, a tailor and a printer's compositor. The West-meath situation whereby the majority of soccer players (67 per cent) were from social class C is similar to the results of Tranter's sample from central Scotland and the findings of Ian Nannestad in Lincolnshire. In central Scotland, in the period 1880–83, 73 per cent of footballers were from social class C whilst the same group formed 61 per cent of the total in Lincolnshire.[106]

The age of the Westmeath soccer player ranged from fifteen to thirty-four and the average age of a Mullingar player at 21.88 was younger than the Athlone player (23.22 years). The difference in average age reflects the fact that the Athlone sample includes a number of individuals who were active in the game since 1894. Amateur soccer at this level was overwhelmingly the preserve of the young and single man as only two Athlone based individuals from the total sample were married. The relative youth of the players partly explains this conjugal status but also was a product of their economic circumstances. Marriage brought new responsibilities, family commitments and expenses, and the amount of disposable income available for investment in social and recreational activities became circumscribed. Remarkably, the average age of a Westmeath soccer player (22.6 years) is almost exactly the same as the average age of the Irish professional (22.7 years) discovered by Neal Garnham in his study.[107] The conjugal status of the players, however, was significantly different as 35 per cent of Garnham's sample study were married. Payment for playing football, for those in receipt of it, provided a substantial supplement to the weekly wage or provided a notable increase on the average weekly wage if employed by a club full-time. The economic situation in Belfast also facilitated the combination of marriage, family, work commitments and football. Comparatively low accommodation costs in Belfast and greater availability of employment for female dependents there, meant real domestic incomes in Edwardian Belfast were comparatively higher than elsewhere.[108]

The unskilled urban labourer, at 26 per cent, was significantly represented in the Westmeath sample and the involvement of the unskilled labourer was far greater than his counterpart of central Scotland or in Lincolnshire, where only 6 and 5 per cent respectively were involved.[109] The proportion is, however, smaller than that discovered by Garnham, where 36 per cent were unskilled labourers. This difference again illustrates the importance of the wage earned by the footballer in Belfast in maintaining an involvement in soccer. More striking was the homogenous nature of the religious affiliation displayed by the Westmeath group; all of those sampled were members of the Catholic Church. The total absence of Church of Ireland members from the sample is a measure of the changed circumstances of the Athlone club once the formative links between the sport and Ranelagh School personnel were severed. Members of the Church of Ireland were of a higher social status and found sporting fulfilment in the more elitist recreational activities such as lawn tennis, croquet and golf.

IX

In conclusion, the withdrawal of the T. P. O'Connor's club from GAA activities and the decision of the members to concentrate on soccer transformed the socio-economic constituency of that sport in Athlone and changed its competitive ethos. The development of soccer was facilitated by the presence of the army garrison in the town. Army teams provided quality opposition, knowledge of the skills and tactics of the game and information on the rules of play that had become standardised over time.

The most important factor responsible for a strong soccer culture in Athlone, however, was that a small core of middle-class businessmen (who were members of some of the town's leading commercial families) transferred their allegiance from Gaelic football to soccer and maintained their support for the game into the early 1900s. Michael Mullen, in his explanation of what he terms the 'bifurcation of Irish sport', suggested that class leadership in Irish sport fell to the Catholic petit bourgeois, 'a stratum in the 1880s unimpressed by British sport and committed to its opposition'.[110] This was not how Athlone developed its soccer culture. It was the members of this 'petit bourgeois' class that were responsible for the strength of the game there. The school, the army and the GAA crossover were also important ingredients. This type of class support for either football code was absent in Mullingar, as many of those initially involved in the GAA were migrants to the town and had moved elsewhere by 1900.

The development of rugby presents elements of the classic British model of sports diffusion. Headmasters Bailie and Foster were public-school graduates who attended Trinity College and on graduation introduced rugby to their schools at Ranelagh and Farra respectively following their appointments. However, further diffusion failed to happen and rugby's popularity remained within the boundaries of the schools, whose activities were restricted to a network of similar institutions.

7. Cultural ferment and the re-emergence of the GAA, 1900–1905

The period 1900–05 saw the re-emergence of the GAA on an institutional basis within the county, a development partly influenced by political and cultural nationalism. The GAA at national level was reorganised at this time, administration was improved and a provincial structure established. Hurling was introduced to the county, Gaelic football was revived and the formation of football and hurling clubs challenged the role of cricket in providing a recreational outlet for the labouring classes of the county. There was also a spatial dimension to the emergence of the post–1900 GAA as a comparison of the maps that illustrate the location of clubs in the 1890s and 1900 indicate. North Westmeath, where there was little evidence of GAA activity in the 1890s, was now an area where several clubs, in both hurling and football, were active.

The late 1890s witnessed a revival of political nationalism, associated with the 1798 centenary celebrations, the Boer War, the extension of elected local government throughout Ireland, a franchise extension and the emergence of the United Irish League (UIL). The UIL was designed to reconcile the various parliamentary factions by uniting them around a new programme of agrarian agitation, political reform and home rule.[1] According to one analyst the decade was, 'despite a superficial appearance of passivity a period of intensive political organisation'.[2] In the years between 1890 and 1910, according to Garvin, Irish parliamentary forces were outflanked by societies often unsympathetic to representative politics. The break-up of the Irish National League that followed the Parnell downfall, permitted organisations to emerge that captured youthful imaginations. Trade unions and cultural nationalist movements such as the Gaelic League and a revived GAA were the beneficiaries of this process.

These political and cultural organisations advocated conflicting national ideals. Nationalist critiques of UIL agrarianism were common. Between 1900 and 1905 the most prominent voices of critique came from the proprietors of two national weekly newspapers, the *United Irishman* and *The Leader*. In the former, Arthur Griffith promoted separatism in terms of Parnellism and artisan traditions of self-help; in the latter D. P. Moran harnessed cultural nationalism to an aggressive form of nationalism aimed at young Catholic professionals who were 'more numerous and confident and less deferential than their predecessors'.[3] These two journalists, who reacted against the perceived stagnation of national life, became the chief spokesmen for a young Catholic intelligentsia. They translated the evolutionary ideas of the cultural revivalists into economic, social and political programmes for the regeneration of Ireland as a modern urban civilisation.[4]

Griffith's newspaper articles were multi-themed, but for the purposes of this study, his attitude to sporting activities is of interest.[5] Griffith perceived soccer and other sports identified as foreign, as the snobbish pretensions of middle-class West Britons or as the commercial pastimes of degraded English lower classes. Participation in these, he argued, endangered national virtues through socialisation with anti-national elements. For Griffith, GAA amateurism was truly patriotic, but his belief in centralism led him to claim that the GAA was ruined by a parliamentarian-inspired devolution of authority, from executive to county committees.[6]

D. P. Moran, who began publication of his weekly, *The Leader*, in September 1900, was 'the major figure of the politico-cultural revival'.[7] He was the chief architect of the expansion of the language campaign into a general Irish-Ireland movement that allied the Catholic educated classes with reformist and neo-traditionalist clergy against Protestant hegemony in Ireland, paving the way for the creation of an essentially Gaelic Catholic identity.[8] He denounced British mass-culture as corrupting and degenerate, ridiculed snobberies and West Britonism among the Catholic middle-classes, criticised the Irish Party as hypocritical and ineffective and 'called for self-reliance and a producerist ethos driven by pride in Irish distinctiveness'. Catholicism underpinned Irish distinctiveness in Moran's view.[9]

The ideas of Griffith and Moran had considerable impact on the Gaelic League and it became an umbrella organisation for a range of interests and underwent a dramatic expansion in branches and numbers between 1900 and 1906.[10] The organisation was founded in 1893 as a non-political, non-sectarian organisation dedicated to the preservation and revival of the Irish language and the 'celebration of, and if possible the resuscitation of, traditional dress, dances and customs'.[11] The rapid growth experienced by the League in the early years of the new century transformed the movement and it became more Catholic, less Dublin oriented and more clericalist.[12]

National trends were replicated in Westmeath and increased political enthusiasm was reflected in the rapid growth of the UIL. Individual membership increased from 1,433 to 2,875 and the number of branches increased from twenty-six to forty between 1900 and 1906.[13] Cultural nationalism was the ideological force that impacted most significantly on social life in Westmeath between 1900 and 1906. Gaelic League branches in Westmeath were first established in the early 1900s. The Mullingar branch was founded on 24 February 1901 at a public meeting that was, according to the hyperbole, 'marked by an enthusiasm of a kind never before witnessed in Mullingar'.[14] Members of the town's business community, clerks and shop assistants dominated a meeting chaired by the parish administrator, Rev. E. O'Reilly, who delivered the keynote address.

Inconsistency characterised the performance of the Gaelic League in Mullingar in the early years. The initial enthusiasm was short-lived and in its first two years the organisation had little impact.[15] However, an editorial in the *Westmeath Examiner* in April 1903 suggested that circumstances were about to change, as there was 'arising in Mullingar a strong wave of public opinion in favour of the revival of the Gaelic tongue and the Gaelic tradition'.[16] Crucially, the importance of extending the programme of the Gaelic League beyond the language, literature and music instructional classes was signalled. The aims of the organisation would be best achieved, it was argued, by developing 'the social side of the Irish character'. The Gaelic revival had been most successful 'in areas where pleasant social functions, reunions, gatherings of students, Irish concerts, Irish dances, Gaelic Clubs', were combined with the language classes.[17] This editorial was inspired by the first public performance of the Mullingar Brass and Reed Band at which support for the ideals of the Irish-Ireland movement came from the commanding officer of the 1st Battalion of the Connaught Rangers. Colonel Moore addressed the bandsmen and assembled audience and suggested that if they

> Would be really Irish, and have their art really Irish, they would have to adopt the whole Gaelic tradition, speak the Irish tongue, read Irish books, and learn Irish songs, instead of using English musical or literary importations . . . if the bandsmen wanted to be really Irish, they must quit using the language of the foreigner and speak and express their ideas and feelings in that old tongue in which are enshrined the thoughts and traditions of the Gael.[18]

A public meeting was later held to consider what steps could be taken to help the Gaelic movement in Mullingar and the arguments of Colonel Moore were expanded to include the notion of boycotting certain events. Moore suggested that they should encourage Irish music, Irish songs at concerts, and 'absent themselves from such concerts as would not include Irish songs'.[19]

This meeting was followed by a third and more expansive attempt to launch the Gaelic League in Mullingar. Women were invited to join and in a matter of weeks, twenty girls and thirty boys regularly attended language classes. A second branch catering for the national teachers of the town was also established.[20] A branch was established in Athlone in October 1902.[21] Irish language classes were organised from December 1903 in Castlepollard. Peter Nea, a native of the district and a member of the McHale Branch of the Gaelic League in Dublin, was an influential proselytiser in this district.[22] A branch of the Gaelic League was established in the town in November 1904. The movement was particularly strong in the Milltown parish, located six miles to the west of Mullingar. There the branch secretary was the primary school teacher, John Casey, who was a native Irish speaker from Kerry. The Milltown Gaelic League branch members enhanced their language classes by including Irish songs and dances in each class 'so that business and enjoyment go hand in hand'. Approval of this diversification was qualified as members were also cautioned that a Gaelic League branch was 'a school for the education of the people on Irish-Ireland lines and is not to be considered a dancing hall or a mere place of amusement'.[23]

The emphasis on a broader programme of activities introduced a new element of entertainment to Westmeath. These were the *aeridheachta*, open-air festivals of Irish singing, recitation, dancing and music, and they formed a very important element of the social landscape of the county during the summer months of 1904 and 1905, and played a crucial role in the promotion of a cultural nationalist agenda. The Milltown branch of the Gaelic League pioneered the local prototype of this event. This was held on Sunday 28 June 1903 and was attended by 'roughly speaking 4,000 persons of all classes, religions, professions and trades'.[24] Irish traditional singing and recitations, Irish dancing competitions and displays, piping and instrumental music were featured. The most spectacular *aeridheacht* was held in Kinnegad on July 2 1905 'for the glory of God and the honour of Ireland'. The event was organised by the local branch of the Gaelic League with profits generated directed to the funds for the building of the new Catholic Church in Kinnegad.[25] The positive relationships between the Catholic Church and the elements of the Irish-Ireland movement, including the GAA at this time, are clear from the ways in which Catholic Church personnel also used the popularity of football tournaments as fundraising ventures for their building programmes. Tournaments were organised in Rathwire and Clonard in November 1904 and March 1905 to help finance the repair of the village churches.[26]

II

Cultural nationalism had a significant impact on the development of sport within the county. Participation in sport became a vehicle for the expression of national identity and the promotion of what were considered to be Irish sports was central to the creation of an Irish-Ireland. Hurling in particular found favour with Gaelic League activists for whom the myth of its prehistoric origins proved particularly attractive. The corollary also pertained. Games perceived as British were challenged and their supporters were stigmatised as West Britons, a badge of identity designed to undermine support for these games, given the ethos and culture of the day. The promotion of the concept of an Irish-Ireland and the targeting of West Britonism by the *Midland Reporter* newspaper especially, and to a lesser extent by the *Westmeath*

Independent and the *Westmeath Examiner,* were important in creating the climate that undermined support for cricket and sports tainted with an anti-national identity. Cricket, the most popular sport in the county, became a specific target of attack and vilification. This phenomenon wasn't universal however. Cricket playing in Kilkenny for instance was never classified as an anti-national activity and the sport was never classified as a 'foreign' game in the county. The *Kilkenny People* founded in 1893 was the main nationalist newspaper and it carried comprehensive cricket reports that were value free.[27]

It was not just participation in the sport that concerned the cultural nationalists. There was also a reaction against the cultural trappings and fraternisation that accompanied cricket and soccer. Concern about the impact on the 'national virtue' that socialisation with what were considered to be anti-national elements was articulated nationally and locally. Activities and events inherent in soccer and cricket were condemned as promoting notions of servility, subjection and allegiance to the alien power in Ireland.[28] The Gaelic games columnist of the *Westmeath Independent* provided a clear definition of this position when he outlined the negative impact such associations had on the youth of Athlone:

> We do not find fault with soccer and rugby as such. They may be more scientific than Gaelic or they may not. That is not our contention now but every Nationalist must object to the surroundings in which they are played. Their atmosphere is one thing which tends to degrade and anglicise the Irish mind. We have soldiers of all sorts and shapes participating in them. At the big matches we have the blaze of the military band, the 'God-Save-the-King element' and all the snobocracy baring their heads in acknowledgement of their own degradation. Those are the elements we object to. We do not like to see our fine Irish youths making acquaintance of the British recruiting sergeant and cultivating the acquaintances of England's soldiers . . . We only want to emphasise that the Irish games are for the Irish, the former ones for the foreigner and that it is only by depending on ourselves in the regions of sport as well as in everything else we can become really Irish. Certainly we must keep our young men from coming in contact with the barrack-room and by having them on the Gaelic field, there will be little inducement held out to them to go there.[29]

The *Midland Reporter* was in the vanguard of promoting Irish-Ireland and targeting the West Briton. The newspaper conducted a serious assault on cricket's credibility throughout 1904 and 1905. The playing of cricket and West Britonism were equated. The cricket-playing West Briton was attacked and the newspaper developed a speciality in the baiting and taunting of Westmeath cricketers. They were deliberately targeted and tainted with the brush of anti-Irishness. Areas where cricket was popular were pilloried for their lack of national fervour. 'The muddied oafs and flannelled fools' from the district of Cloughan were a particular target because of the 'strong love for the game of the Saxon'.[30] Cloughan, and other cricket-playing districts, was identified as an area that was hopeless from the national point of view. According to the columnist this was all that could be expected from

> any body of young men who call themselves Irishmen, when they are continually truckling to the *seoiníns* and their importations. Cloughan and Kilbride, Stoneyford and the Mountain Parish are simply useless so far as Ireland is concerned. The great object of the young men in these places is to change the townlands, and make them assume the appearance of districts in the England that they love.[31]

In June 1905, when the 'West Britons' of Mullingar arranged a cricket match against a Dublin team, they had 'to requisition the Cloughan worthies to show off their skill with the bat and ball. Cloughan is a disgrace to the county of Westmeath, and all the young nationalists to whom I have been speaking had nothing but words of contempt for these degenerates.'[32]

Clubs such as Kilbeggan, Multyfarnham and Rathconrath that had not affiliated to the GAA were identified as the 'black sheep' of the county, 'stuck in the mire' without any 'ambition for honours ' and 'absolutely no use to either themselves or the GAA'.[33] The news that the men of Kiltoom village had decided to affiliate a hurling team was greeted with the announcement that a funeral would be held 'over what is left of the remains of cricket'. The interment was to be carried out at Moyne 'by the few sole survivors of the old Saxon cricket that exist there'.[34]

Another tactic adopted was to ridicule the standard of play that was found 'in the few benighted districts in the country, where alleged cricket clubs' existed. In these clubs, according to the *Midland Herald*, not one of them knew how to play the game properly:

> One single cricketer from England would beat the massed teams of the county, and would have by long odds, a higher score to their credit, than the whole crowd . . . Poor creatures, they are more to be pitied than blamed. They are incapable of thinking for themselves, and like a moth round a candle, they hanker after English ideas, although their limited intelligence does not permit them to imitate.

The local nationalist press also used cartoons to lampoon the county's cricketers and followers of targeted British sports. The *Midland Reporter* specialised in this form of attack but the *Westmeath Independent* also used the occasional cartoon. The portrayal in Figure 21 is a fine example of the type used. In it the caricatured *seoinín* implores the woodman to spare the tree that represented the chief elements of West British culture accompanied by a note of approval that 'the uprise of Westmeath in

Figure 21.   Lampooning of West Britonism by means of cartoon (*Midland Reporter*, 15 September 1904)

regard to Hurling, Gaelic Football and the holding of Aerideachta, etc., had been something phenomenal and is full of promise for the future'.[35]

In the Athlone district, where soccer was more popular, questions on the respective skill levels of the two most popular football codes were debated and these were extended to give them a political application. According to the *Westmeath Independent,* those who categorised Gaelic games as rough and savage activities devoid of skill, tact, manliness and fair play were using similar arguments to those used by Unionist opponents of Home Rule. They implied an inability to manage affairs 'in matters so trivial as sports and games' and undermined any claim to be able to do so in 'serious matters'. The same article emphasised the necessity for an Irish organisation to manage sport for the Irish people. According to the writer, nationalism and support for British games were incompatible, for 'a soccerite, a rugbyite, is scarcely a Home Ruler'.[36]

III

Hurling was a stick-and-ball game for which its supporters claimed a pedigree that extended back to prehistoric times. This mythology established a status for hurling as the most Irish of games and made it an ideal vehicle for promotion by Gaelic League activists. The mythological referencing of hurling in prehistory has been used as evidence for the existence of the game 'as a distinctively Irish pastime for at least 2,000 years'![37] The first recorded mention of the game allegedly dates it to a legendary battle fought at Moytura, County Galway in 1272 BC. It supposedly played a central part in the prehistoric Tailteann games and featured in the legends of Cuchulainn, who earned his name and reputation through his hurling exploits. The reality, as Comerford has pointed out, is that stick and ball games were found in many ancient and later cultures and that a number of modern codified forms have evolved including cricket, hockey, shinty and hurling, to mention only team sports.[38]

In the early modern period, versions of the game were so popular that the authorities made some attempt to control it.[39] By the eighteenth century two regional versions of the game existed in Ireland. A winter version of the game was played in the northern half of the country that had some of the characteristics of modern hockey in that the ball could not be handled and was played with a narrow wooden stick. A summer version was played in the south of Ireland. It was a handling and carrying game played with a soft, animal-hair ball. This game enjoyed gentry patronage and was a spectator and gambling sport associated with fairs and other public gatherings.[40] By the mid-nineteenth century hurling had declined so sharply that it survived only in the hinterland of Cork city, in south-east Galway and in a district north of Wexford town.[41]

There are some brief references to the early existence of the game in areas of Westmeath. The poetry of Laurence Whyte provides circumstantial evidence that hurling was played in the Ballymore district of County Westmeath in the early eighteenth century. His poem *The Parting Cup* concerns itself with the vicissitudes of a substantial Westmeath tenant farmer. The sporting prowess of the family was celebrated in the verses as one that 'seldom did refuse a summons, to play at football or at Commons'.[42] A series of articles published in the *Westmeath Independent* in the 1930s featured the reminiscences of Michael Kilkelly of Athlone. He recalled some of the outstanding players who featured in matches that were played in the Big Meadows in the 1860s. In these games the hurley was not made from ash but 'crabtree, blackthorn, whitethorn, and kinds cut from hedges' were used.[43] Hurling did not feature in the initial version of the GAA in Westmeath in the 1890s. It was more difficult to organise and promote than football or cricket, as it required specialist equipment for each player. It required that each player develop a great range of skills under the pressure of the attention of a direct opponent. It required the knowledge and experience of a practitioner of the game from one of the strong hurling counties to introduce the game to the virgin hurling territory of Westmeath.

In Mullingar, the temperance club was part of the broad cultural nationalist movement. St Mary's Temperance Club, established in 1896, was one of the most active clubs in the town and was popular with the young male lower-middle-class Catholic clerks, shop assistants and artisans of the town. This was an ultra-Catholic organisation that required public proclamation of adherence to the faith and the temperance cause. The club members promised to abstain from alcoholic liquor for five years, attend the bi-monthly meetings of the club and receive communion wearing the society's ribbon and medal on the first Sunday of each month.[44] Clubs that combined religious observance and temperance were required to provide entertainment if they were to compete with the conviviality of the public house. These activities were also used to promote the temperance agenda. Temperance society members in Mullingar had access to reading rooms and snooker tables along with the opportunity to participate in amateur theatricals and to join the Brass and Reed Band. They were also provided with the chance to compete in sporting pastimes in both an indoor and outdoor setting.

Membership overlap between the Mullingar branch of the Gaelic League and the Temperance Club and considerable coalescence of ideals was a characteristic of the time. The promotion of temperance was included within the Gaelic League ambit whilst the St Mary's Temperance Club contributed to the development of nationalism by the staging of plays with a nationalistic theme. These shared aspirations were responsible for the formation of the first hurling club in Westmeath, when the St Mary's Hurling Club was founded on 27 February 1902 with a claimed membership of forty. The members held their first practice match on 16 March 1902.[45] In January 1903, influenced by the contemporary cultural ethos, a more positive Irish identity was formulated when the name of the club was changed to the Mullingar Shamrocks Club. The formation of a hurling club within the temperance organisation enhanced the standing of the members as cultural nationalists.

The Temperance Club provided the social network around which the first hurling club was established in Mullingar but there were other significant influences involved. The expertise was provided by the arrival in Mullingar of some individuals familiar with the game and, according to one source, was particularly due 'to the teachings of a Limerick player who formerly belonged to the Croom team in that county'.[46] Employment-related networks were also important. At least six of the members were employees of the Shaw family firm, where not alone did they share employment but they also inhabited the same place of residence.

Hurling was next established in Castlepollard where five cricket clubs were active in the period 1899–1902. Similar circumstances to Mullingar were responsible for the introduction of the game to the town. This time the pioneer was Patrick Corcoran an employee of Hennessy's grocery store. Corcoran was a native of Tipperary and reportedly was a 'warm exponent of all old Gaelic games and pastimes, especially hurling at which he was adept'.[47] He had been four years resident in Castlepollard in November 1903 when the Castlepollard Hurling Club was established.[48] Over twenty players regularly practised at this time, with the group dominated by 'commercial men' who were employed in Hennessy's and Gibney's retail outlets. The Castlepollard Cricket Club provided a nucleus for the hurling club as a number of cricketers reportedly enrolled shortly after its establishment.[49]

Once introduced to north Westmeath contiguous diffusion was responsible for the spread of hurling in other districts close to Castlepollard. The formation of Ringtown, Delvin, Simonstown Gaels and the Kiltoom Cruickilawee Rovers hurling clubs quickly followed. With the exception of the Delvin club, the Gaelic League activist, Peter Nea, was influential in their formation. He combined enthusiasm for the ideals of the Gaelic League with the promotion of hurling. According to the *Midland Reporter* he was the 'pioneer of everything Gaelic in this part of Westmeath'. He was 'accountable for starting the Sarsfields, the Myles O'Reilly's, and then came the Cruickilawee, and last, but not least, the Simonstown Hurling Club'.[50]

The importance of the Gaelic League in the promotion of hurling wasn't unique to Westmeath. After 1900, a number of GAA clubs were affiliated in Dublin that were directly linked to the organisation. Teachers, clerks and civil servants were attracted to the Dublin GAA, having been exposed to nationalism through the Gaelic League. Most of these clubs chose names that related to Ireland's mythological past rather than opting for names that celebrated either constitutional or physical force nationalism.[51] The Saint Laurence O'Toole branch of the Gaelic League was founded on 8 February 1901 and in October a hurling club was formed among its members. The middle-class structure of the club is suggested by the inclusion in its ranks of 'a pioneer of the Abbey Theatre', a sculptor member of the Royal Hibernian Academy (RHA), a number of teachers, a sailing enthusiast, a ship's engineer and a builder.[52] A similar phenomenon has been documented in Derry where Gaelic League associates were active in starting hurling clubs wherever they had Irish language and literary classes. The Gaelic League developed rapidly in the north-west of Ireland and, owing to its influence, a hurling league that brought together teams from three counties was organised in 1903.[53]

The cricket clubs of north Westmeath proved to be an important source for practitioners of the newly introduced stick and ball game. Cricket clubs themselves did not take on the game but provided a source for recruits, who under the influence of the culture of the time, wished to cross over to the GAA fields. The Ringtown Hurling Club was

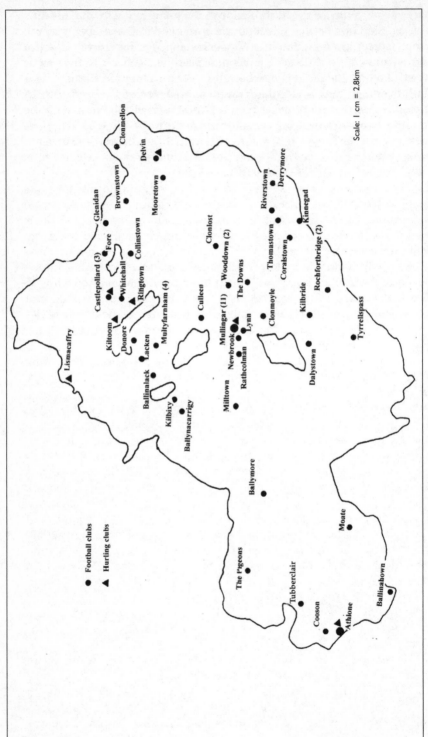

Figure 22. Hurling- and football-playing districts in Westmeath, 1900–1905

founded in February 1904 and shared a direct lineage with the area's cricket club. It benefited from the patronage of landowner Denis Smyth JP who had acted as captain and main patron of the cricket club for many years. Smyth always placed the 'back field' at the disposal of the hurling club for practice and games.[54] The village of Kiltoom was located close to Castlepollard and was the estate village for the labourers of the demesne of the Earl of Longford. The Cruickilawee Rovers club was centred on the village and was formed from the members of the village's cricket club in March 1905.[55] The Castlepollard and Delvin hurling clubs 'were old friends since the days of cricket in Westmeath' and a similar claim was made for the Simonstown Gaels Club when it affiliated.[56] The distribution of hurling and football playing districts is illustrated in Figure 22. Hurling thus used an existing network of social, territorial and work-related loyalties and in the process created a new recreational and cultural identity. Familiarity with a stick and ball game (cricket), hand-eye co-ordination, an individual resident in the district with knowledge of the skills of the game, a pre-existing social or work network and the influence of a Gaelic League activist were the important factors in the promotion of the game. The Irish-Ireland movement, as mediated by Gaelic League activists, provided the catalyst that initiated the process.

IV

The revival of Gaelic football in Westmeath occurred in a number of stages. Initially, groups of men came together to play games on an ad hoc basis. This was followed by the organisation of Gaelic football tournaments and eventually the GAA was formally instituted in Westmeath, with the formation of the county committee. Following the post-1894 decline of the GAA in the county, occasional Gaelic football games were organised and it was one of the combinations involved in this informal football network that was instrumental in the move to re-establish the institutional GAA in Westmeath. Again the impetus came from those who were already members of a social and sporting organisation. Towards the end of 1899 attempts were made by the members of the Mount Street Cricket Club to revive football in Mullingar. The club members played football as a means of engaging in a recreational activity and maintaining social networks over the winter months. At the end of the cricket season 'in order to keep their limbs in practice' they turned their attention to their favoured winter football game. The editor of the *Westmeath Examiner* supported the initiative of the Mount Street men but also suggested that football was 'a game more in keeping with Irish character than cricket which is positively English'. Football was identified as the national game. In a *Westmeath Examiner* article that strongly echoed the famous letter of Dr Croke of December 1884 it was argued that[57]

> If latter day Irish young men would try to preserve these games they
> would be doing a wonderful service to their country. For next to lan-
> guage the distinctive games of a people are the purest indication of
> their nationality. Therefore it is not out of place to ask the young men
> of the present day of this county to do everything in their power to
> preserve the national games, and to foster them, and neither is it out
> of place to ask grown men to lend in every way their sympathy and
> support to such an ideal, in order that these pastimes may have a
> counteracting effect to the Anglicising inroads that have been made,
> and the influences that have been at work to Anglicise our people, in
> whose minds English ideas have almost displaced those in the old
> fashion which were the pride and glory of our forefathers, and the
> proud characteristics of a race which though conquered could never
> be vanquished.[58]

Despite the availability of a modern enclosed venue at the Horse
Show Grounds, team sport in Mullingar at this time was poorly developed. A letter published in the *Westmeath Examiner* in December 1902
suggested that the town was one where games such as 'cricket, football,
hurling, handball, hockey and many others, which afford ample recreation to one and all' were 'conspicuous by their absence' and that in
games promotion the town was 'the most backward in the Emerald
Isle'.[59] The same edition of the newspaper carried the news that the
Mount Street football team had been reorganised for the new season
and were ready to receive challenges from all country teams. At a
meeting held at the Market House on Sunday, 14 December, the club
was reconstituted and became the Young Ireland club. The name change
is indicative of the change in political outlook that had taken place in a
few years and further evidence of the change is contained in the statement made by the Mullingar Young Ireland club that called for the
establishment of a county committee. The statement concluded by
noting that 'it would indeed be a great thing if the county clubs would
put more dash and spirit into the movement now on hand, and let other
counties see that Westmeath, if but slowly is surely trying not to be
behind time in the Gaelic revival'.[60] Nothing developed from this call.
Friendly and tournament games were played in the absence of a county
committee structure that might have organised more competitive fare.

The promotion of Gaelic football received a boost in April 1903 when
the Brass and Reed Band sponsored a tournament in Mullingar. Seven
entries were received for the competition and Rochfortbridge Warriors
and Wooddown Rackers entered from outside the Mullingar area. Based
on the entries, Mullingar Shamrocks, Cullion Celtics, Railway Stars,
Newbrook Wanderers and Independent Wanderers as well as the Young
Ireland team played Gaelic football at some level at this time in
Mullingar and its environs.[61] The final was played on Sunday 28 June
and attracted a large crowd to the Horse Show grounds despite the
counter attraction of the 'great concert and competitions at Milltown'.[62]
The winners were Newbrook Wanderers and although Gaelic football

clubs were evolving, the practice of interchange between practitioners of the two main football codes continued. The successful Wanderers team included many members of St Patrick's Association Football Club. Of the thirteen members of St Patrick's soccer club represented at the funeral of Joseph Garry, eight had played in the football final for New-brook Wanderers.[63] The successful team included James Reynolds, the captain of St Patrick's AFC and H. Stenson, its vice-captain.[64]

Inspired by the success of the summer competition, the Young Ireland club in October 1903 announced plans for the holding of a monster Gaelic tournament, 'in order to promote our Gaelic pastimes in the County Westmeath and place it on a proper footing with its neigh-bouring counties'.[65] An exclusion rule applied to this tournament and all soldiers, sailors or association players were debarred from taking part. The inclusion of this rule was a reflection of developments at national level within the GAA, but may also have been an attempt to force the members of St Patrick's club to affiliate to the GAA. A third tournament, organised in 1904, provides a clear indication of the growing popularity of Gaelic football in the Midlands and the commercial possibilities of this growth. The tournament featured a business involvement in the promo-tion of the game that provides an early example of brand imaging in association with a GAA event. Mr G. H. Goodwin, the district manager of the Irish Provident Assurance Company, provided a 'beautiful cup' for competition between the county champion football clubs of his district.[66]

In the southern section of the county similar developments were taking place. Football was played in the Athlone area for the first time in almost a decade in February 1902, when an Athlone team (which included a number of members of the Athlone soccer team) challenged a team from Athleague, County Roscommon.[67] Shortly afterwards an attempt was made to start a hurling team in Athlone.[68] J. J. Walsh inspired this move. He explained that while numerous games were played in Ireland 'with few, if any exception, they were styled West British'. The formation of a hurling club was 'best calculated to properly meet the crush of West British games and amusements'.[69] The club played at least one friendly game against the local football club.[70] Walsh's untimely death in early 1903 was to delay the development of a hurling club in the town until late 1904. The popularity of soccer in Athlone at this time has been documented in the previous chapter, and a number of new clubs were established and older institutions revived.[71] In 1904 a soccer match between Athlone and the Bohemians 'B' team from Dublin was the major St Patrick's Day attraction and was attended by a crowd of 'several thousand'. This was followed by a dance at Longworth Hall attended by the visitors.[72] Despite the popularity of soccer the develop-ment of the GAA in Athlone reportedly made 'prodigious strides' in 1904. Thirty-eight members attended the AGM of the Athlone GAA club held in November 1904. It was decided to amalgamate the hurling and football clubs and they were placed under the control of a single committee. The football club continued to use the title of the Athlone Volunteers and the hurling section adopted the title St Ciaran's. As the year ended 'new players are turning up while the older members are becoming more and more imbued with an enthusiasm for the pastimes of the Gael'. A new field was obtained and the club planned to enclose it. A football tournament was organised by the club 'for a set of jerseys of Irish manufacture' aimed at spreading the game amongst the juveniles of the district. This was a competition confined to boys aged less than fifteen years old and to schools within a ten-mile radius of Athlone. Each school was allowed to select five non-school-attending boys. The hurlers and footballers of Athlone were also now engaged in regular evening practice.[73]

The impact of the growth of nationalism in the re-emergence of the GAA in Westmeath is reflected in the naming policy of the new clubs. It is also indicative of the extent to which football and hurling had now become politicised in Westmeath. The clubs adopted a policy that established their position in the Irish-Ireland community and the members adopted names that embraced the local and the national. The first part of the name established a territorial link with the parish, urban area or townland. This was accompanied by an appendage that embraced the political and historical or established a link to Catholicism by including the name of a national or local saint or church figure. This aspect of club development is illustrated in Appendix 17. The names were drawn mainly from nationalist history and contemporary political figures were ignored with the exception of O'Growney, who was commemorated by the Castlepollard football club.[74] Catholic identity was emphasised by the choice of St Patrick, St Ciaran and St Fintan as the names adopted by the Derrymore, Athlone and Lismacaffry clubs respectively. The majority of clubs constructed an identity that linked their members as sportsmen to the nationalist mission, to the embracing of things Irish and the rejection of West Britonism in a manner that was remarkably different to the Westmeath clubs of the 1890s.[75] This phenomenon was also manifested in the use of songs celebrating the cause of Irish nationalism or commemorating the achievements of major figures in Irish nationalist iconography in the post-game social setting. The entertainment that followed the football game between the Dublin club, McBride-Mitchell's and Westmeath, played in May 1905, for instance, included the singing of songs such as 'Wrap the green flag round me', 'The thirty-two counties' and 'A nation once again'.[76]

Cultural nationalism was also associated with a growth in the number of musical bands of the brass and reed variety, a development that facilitated and was facilitated by the popularity of hurling and football tournaments. The relationship became transposed when the Mullingar Brass and Reed Band became the first promoter of a football tournament in the town, a tournament that began the process of reconstituting the GAA in the county. GAA tournaments provide an ideal occasion for musical combinations to display their talents and provided an additional layer of entertainment at the venues. Some of these provided a comprehensive entertainment experience. The Brass and Reed Band's football tournament final featured entertainment provided by two Mullingar bands, the Brass and Reed Band and the Irish National Foresters Fife and Drum Band (INF).[77] A tournament held at Rochfortbridge in November 1903 had as its feature event a football match between the Rochfortbridge Warriors and Cullion Celtics but also included two donkey races, an athletics programme and during the intervals 'the Milltown Pass Fife and Drum Band played a choice selection of Irish airs'.[78] The Mullingar Shamrocks and Clara hurling game featured entertainment by two bands. Clara arrived at Mullingar railway station accompanied by their own band where they were met by the Mullingar INF band, which escorted them to O'Connell's hotel. After the refreshments both bands played the teams to the Dublin Road grounds of Mullingar Shamrocks.[79] This aspect of Gaelic games promotion – providing a broad entertainment package that was good value – was recently recognised by Neil Garnham as an important factor in explaining the early success of the GAA.[80]

The Irish-Ireland movement was exclusionist and the GAA at national level introduced a series of rules which evolved between 1901 and 1905 to exclude those who supported games defined by the association as foreign. These rules reflected the national mood. The introduction of the exclusion rules has been variously interpreted. W. F. Mandle has linked the upturn in nationalist sentiment in the GAA to the influence of the IRB, who he believed had returned to the GAA in an attempt to re-establish itself. In an overstatement of the extent of IRB involvement and a failure to take into account the prevailing cultural nationalist mood, Mandle has suggested that 'there was not a man who meant anything in the organisation of the GAA who was not of the Brotherhood'.[81] The increased support offered by the GAA for nationalist causes has been correctly identified by Paul Rouse as a reflection of the increased nationalist enthusiasm within Ireland as a whole.[82] When individuals such as Michael Cusack, T. F. O'Sullivan, Maurice Moynihan and Dan Fraher delivered trenchant speeches, at an annual GAA congress, which supported a variety of nationalist issues and causes, they spoke in harmony with the credo of an increasingly broad sector of Irish society and one that increased rapidly in importance in the new century.[83]

Other organisations were similarly influenced and reflected the spirit of the age. In the early 1900s, the world of Irish dance was convulsed with a debate conducted through the columns and letter pages of the Gaelic League newspaper on which dances were acceptable as Irish. The attempt to define a canon of Irish dance precipitated 'a cultural civil war with dance as the arena of combat'.[84] The outcome was that four- and eight-hand-reel figure dances were excluded from Irish dance competitions because of their supposedly foreign origins.[85] In excluding certain activities as foreign, nationalists were engaging in a process of invention. Definition of the nation by selective rejection was one of the key ways in which nationalists contributed to nation invention.[86]

The upshot of this nationalist fervour was that the GAA had in place by January 1906 a rule that specifically excluded certain individuals from membership and prevented its members from participating in sports defined as foreign. The principle of what became popularly known as the 'ban' was established at the national convention of 1901 when county 'committees were empowered to disqualify and suspend members of the Association who countenance sports which are calculated to interfere with the preservation and cultivation' of national pastimes. Over the next three years the rule evolved, so that by 1905 GAA members were forbidden by rule to play or promote the games that were defined as foreign. These were cricket, rugby, hockey and soccer. Police and military were also excluded from membership of the GAA.[87] The Westmeath county committee adopted the rule at its annual meeting held in early February 1905.[88]

The impact of this ban at a local level is difficult to assess, particularly as its implementation was confined to the final years of this study. In Kilkenny the number of active cricket teams declined from thirty teams to twenty-one between 1905 and 1906. After this date the game was still widely played in the county. O'Dwyer concludes that the 'ban undoubtedly had an effect on the number of cricket teams although many players continued to play both cricket and hurling'. This was facilitated by rural anonymity with players generally not known outside their native parishes.[89] In Tipperary, according to Bracken, its introduction 'was the death knell for cricket'.[90] Bracken equates the decline of rural cricket with the introduction of the ban. However, the cultural milieu of the time was more important in establishing loyalties than any institutionalised restriction. Initially in Westmeath, the implementation of the GAA ban reflected a mood rather than defined or prescribed an attitude. GAA clubs in Westmeath that included soccer players in competitive games went unpunished by the controlling body. Moate Football Club, who objected to the inclusion of a soccer player in the Cullion Celtic team that defeated them in the Young Ireland tournament, lost their case despite the strong evidence they presented. At this stage there was no period of exclusion that a returning player of 'foreign sports' was required to serve before becoming eligible to participate in GAA games. Athlone were ordered by the county committee to re-play their hurling championship match against Ringtown in 1905 as they had included a soccer player but on appeal to the higher authority of the Leinster Council, the secretary ruled that the player had 'a perfect legal right to play as he had not played soccer since November, 1904'.[91] Mobility between the sports concerned certainly decreased but the possibility of interchange was lessened by the reduction in the number of cricket clubs and the changed seasonality of Gaelic sports.

V

The establishment of a county committee in 1904 brought an organisational structure to the playing of football and hurling in the county.[92] The establishment of this committee, unlike what happened in the 1890s, was not totally a grass-roots response by the newly emerging clubs but was orchestrated partly by the officers of the recently established Leinster Council of the GAA. The episode illustrates the importance of the improved administrative structures to the re-emergence of the GAA in the early 1900s. The provincial councils, which were to become the corner stones of the GAA's administrative structure, were established between 1900 and 1903. According to Eoghan Corry the establishment of the provincial councils solved most of the organisational problems of the GAA 'with apparent ease'.[93] Marcus de Burca identifies the annual congress held in September 1901 as the occasion where this process of improved organisation began. At this congress, Jim Nowlan of Kilkenny was elected president and Luke O'Toole of Wicklow as secretary, two officials from 'a group of younger men determined to rejuvenate the Association'. In several areas also the GAA received a welcome and a badly needed infusion of new ordinary members from the ranks of the Gaelic League.[94] The playing rules of both hurling and football had been revised a number of times since the 1880s and this process had produced games that were safer, less physically intense, more attractive to players and spectators and with more clearly defined and understood regulations.[95]

The impetus to set up a Westmeath county committee followed from a meeting of the Leinster Council held in Mullingar in January 1904. At this meeting Joe Robins of the Young Ireland club and A. Conniffee of the Shamrocks club were empowered to call a meeting and establish a county committee. The meeting was held on 27 February, at which the committee was founded.[96] This committee provided a management structure for the county's GAA activities. Formalised competition was introduced with the establishment of championships in both codes from 1904. Four clubs entered the 1904 hurling championship and seven in that of 1905. The football championship attracted an entry of seven and eighteen clubs in 1904 and 1905 respectively.[97] The management of these competitions formed the main business of the county committee. Draws were made and fixtures set. Objections to claimed illegalities were investigated and judgements handed down. Financial solvency was a critical factor in the survival of the sporting club and the county committee made some attempt to assist in GAA clubs' finances. At the second meeting of the county committee held in early April 1904, it was decided that gate receipts for county championship matches were to be divided equally between the host club, the county committee and the competing teams. The exclusion rules were also adopted as part of the county byelaws.[98]

The role of organised competition in popularising sport has been well documented.[99] Participation in competitions provided an added layer of meaning to a club's *raison d'être*. Club members now had the opportunity of making a contribution to the promotion of local identity. Cricket remained a recreational activity and failed to develop a competitive structure within the county. GAA players and clubs were integrated into the practices of modern sport; the members of cricket clubs still displayed many of the characteristics of pre-modern sport as defined by Adelman.[100] The many combinations that existed in Westmeath played casual cricket on an intermittent basis and were transient organisations. Players had few opportunities to develop their skills on an ongoing basis or construct meaningful achievements on the field of play.

The change in the relationship between the four main team-sports in terms of games played between 1880–1905 is illustrated in Figure 23. In the period covered in this study, 1905 was the watershed year in the relationship between the sports. In that year, Gaelic football was the most popular game played with eighty-nine games reported, and was the sport's busiest year in the county since the formation of the GAA in 1884. More significantly, the number of hurling matches played outnumbered soccer and cricket matches. The change in the respective popularity of the sports happened quickly, as 1900 was the year of cricket's peak in popularity in terms of games played. The playing

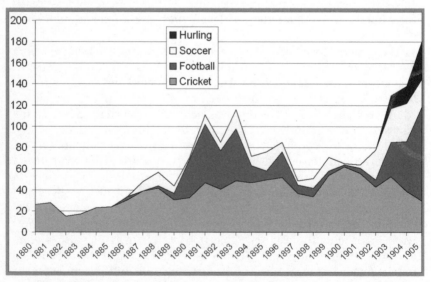

Figure 23. Number of games played in cricket, football, hurling and soccer in County Westmeath, 1880–1905

records of hurling and football clubs at this period are illustrated in Appendices 18 and 19.

There was also a significant change in the playing season of football (and hurling) and this change also challenged cricket's dominance. In Chapter 5, it was shown that football was essentially a game played over the winter and spring months with 81 per cent of matches played between November and April in the period 1890–93. An analysis of football matches played between 1904 and 1905 shows that football was now an all-year round activity but with a significant peak in the March–July period, as illustrated in Figure 24. From 1903 to 1905 the proportion of games played between November and April was reduced to 47 per cent. This change in seasonality challenged the dominance of cricket by providing a competitive alternative to recreational cricket over the summer months.

Despite the favourable cultural climate many GAA clubs still struggled to survive. Financial difficulties and the loss of key personnel presented insurmountable obstacles for some clubs. The Brian Boru club from Ballymore competed in the Young Ireland football tournament as a gesture of support for the venture but were unable to meet their commitments to a replay: 'No funds were on hands to defray expenses.' The distance to Mullingar, the difficulty in securing conveyance, 'the generally bad state of the weather and principally the absence of funds provided insuperable difficulties'.[101] The officers believed that 'the general members of a country club, like Ballymore, cannot well contribute the necessary amount to keep funds to working level'.[102] The episode illustrates the class dimension to the successful management of Westmeath sport. At the same time as the Ballymore footballers could not afford to travel to Mullingar, the members of the

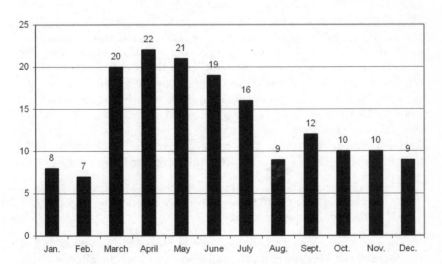

Figure 24. Monthly variation in number of football games, 1904 and 1905

Westmeath Golf Club were comfortably able to raise sufficient funds to erect a clubhouse at their Prospect course.

The fate of the Mullingar Young Ireland club provides a clear example of the potential for transience that was latent in the sports club that catered for the lower social orders. The tournament hosted by the club in Mullingar in February 1904, its affiliation to the GAA at national level and its influence on the establishment of a county committee were instrumental in the establishment of a formalised structure for the GAA in Westmeath. Despite the fact that the club was financially viable, with a credit balance of £14 at the end of 1904, the season was the last of the club.[103] Heavy defeats, particularly in the Goodwin Cup against Cavan when the Mullingar players received a number of serious injuries, were partly responsible for undermining the interest of the members.[104] Death and migration deprived the club of its key officers. The president of the Club, Joe Garry was killed in a train accident in September 1903.[105] Young player and treasurer and community leader Jack Dunne died in December 1904 after a short illness.[106] Club captain, and chairman of the county committee, P. Murphy, as well as others, migrated.[107] The end result was that the most influential club in the formative period of the GAA in the early 1900s did not affiliate in 1905 and a new club, the Mullingar Football Club, was formed in June 1905.[108] Other clubs failed for more mundane reasons if we are to believe the newspaper rhetoric. According to the *Midland Reporter* the Gainstown GAA club failed when members were seduced to play cricket by copious supplies of porter from a nearby 'rancher's' pub.[109]

Patronage was still critical to the survival of the GAA club and the provision of a suitable playing pitch was the most important support provided. Those whose cultural and political ethos was non-nationalist sometimes provided this patronage. C. G. Adamson of Lacken Lodge, for instance, 'gave the use of a field to the Tubberclare [*sic*] Football Club for as long as they needed it'.[110] The Longford family were one of the leading unionist families in the county who provided significant sporting patronage to members of their own class, as was seen in Chapter 1. This, however, did not prevent the family from supporting the Castlepollard Hurling Club. The members of this club in appreciation of this support, decided to present the Countess of Longford with 'an Irish camán made from ash grown in Pakenham Hall.' Suitably inscribed on a band of silver inlaid on the handle was:

> In consideration of her ladyship's thoughtfulness to the hurling club
> in erecting seats for their accommodation as well as leaving a field at
> their disposal all the year round.[111]

Mullingar GAA clubs had the use of the Horse Show Grounds but the Shamrocks Hurling Club developed their own Gaelic Grounds by renting a suitable field from Mr Killian. The inclusion of two stonewall jumps in the venue made the Horse Show Grounds rather unsuitable for play.[112] P. Flanagan, proprietor of the sawmills, facilitated the playing of football games in Moate. Cullion Celtics still benefited from the patronage of T. M. Reddy and as a result were the only early-1890s club that returned to the scene in the 1900s. This topic was a regular concern of the 'With the Gaels' columnist of the *Westmeath Independent*. In his opinion 'the difficulty in procuring a suitable grounds was the cause of breaking up some excellent teams'. Farmers and others who shared nationalist principles 'often showed little sympathy with the hurlers and footballers'. He suggested that an enclosed venue where an admission fee could be charged was essential to survival. The fact that the members of the GAA 'were wage earners' made it hard to understand 'how the large expenses for balls, jerseys, travelling etc. can in all cases be met'.[113] The Clonown club attempted to deal with the funding problem by organising a raffle in 1906, with first prize a suit of tweeds.[114] The Athlone club obtained the use of Mr Farrell's field for the 1905 season, which was located a 'convenient distance from the town and therefore a rallying point.' The club was able to report 'a very substantial credit balance' for the 1906 season.[115] The venue was developed to the extent that it was chosen to host the 1904 All-Ireland semi-final in May 1906 and catered for a crowd of 10,000.[116]

VI

A detailed examination of the players who were involved in football and hurling clubs in the early 1900s was carried out in order to establish a social profile of GAA practitioners at this time. The names of players appearing for six hurling clubs listed in the newspapers for the 1903–05 period were collated and analysed. These clubs were equally balanced between rural and urban and included St Ciaran's Club, Athlone, Mullingar Shamrocks, Ringtown Myles O'Reilly's, Castlepollard Sarsfields, Simonstown Gaels and Delvin Hurling Club. In total 124 names were listed and eighty-two were positively identified representing 66 per cent of the total. The results of the analysis of the members of these clubs by social class is illustrated in Table 18

The social status of hurling players was more confined than that of the county's cricketers. The majority of hurlers, 48 per cent, were from social class C. A further 35 per cent, mainly farmers' sons, were from class B. Only one in six (17 per cent) of all hurlers were farm- or unskilled-labourers and these were members of the Delvin and Ringtown clubs. White-collar, lower middle-class, socially ambitious shop assistants and clerks dominated the game, particularly in its urban setting.

The typical hurling player was also slightly older than his cricket-playing counterpart with an age that ranged between fifteen and thirty-four. In 1905, the average age of a Westmeath hurler sampled was 24.96 years of age. With the exception of the Delvin player, who averaged 22.42 years, the average age of the individual player of the other clubs displayed a remarkable consistency and ranged between 25.33 and 26.12 years of age. Despite the importance of some knowledge of the skills of the game, 81 per cent of the players were natives of Westmeath with players from twelve other counties represented in the sample. The Mullingar Shamrocks club players displayed the greatest diversity of origin with eight counties represented apart from Westmeath. Clerks and shop assistants who found employment in Mullingar dominated the club. As with the other team sports that catered for the lower social classes, hurling was the preserve of the single man, with 99 per cent of players unnamed.

| | SOCIAL CLASS | | | |
	B	C	D	U
Delvin HC	8	0	6	4
Simonstown Gaels	4	0	1	3
Castlepollard HC	1	15	2	7
Athlone HC	3	5	0	10
Mullingar Shamrocks	6	17	1	13
Ringtown HC	7	2	4	5
Total	29	39	14	42

Table 18. Social class of County Westmeath hurlers, 1903–1905

The dominance of social class C and the low level of representation of social class D is a product of culture and finance. The appeal of the Gaelic League was mainly to the lower middle classes and was particularly attractive to shop assistants, clerks and teachers for recreation and socialisation. It also fulfilled needs that were partly psychological.[117] The dominance of members of social class C in the Westmeath hurling community suggests that the ideology of the Gaelic League had significant impact in producing urban-based hurlers. Individual biographies support this suggestion. Patrick Brett, the President of the Mullingar Shamrocks hurling club, was one of the few individuals involved in 1902 who had been involved in the original version of the GAA in the early 1890s. Since that time he had progressed in his business career, advancing from shop assistant to the proprietor of a drapery store in Mullingar. For much of that time Brett had no GAA involvement. It was only when the post-1900, Gaelic League-inspired cultural nationalist movement began that he rediscovered his zeal for hurling and football. Hugh Burke held important administrative positions in both organisations. In 1903, he was secretary of the Gaelic League branch and vice-president of Mullingar Shamrocks hurling club.[118] Newly qualified Athlone lawyer, J. J. Walsh, was an advocate of the Gaelic League and was in the process of establishing a hurling club at the time of his death. The role Gaelic League activist Peter Nea played in the promotion of hurling has been outlined earlier in this chapter. The Gaelic League had little impact on or appeal for the general labourer or unskilled labourer in the urban areas; this group were deprived of the cultural capital that encouraged young men to participate in hurling.

This exclusion also had an economic dimension. Hurling was a game that required some financial input as individual equipment was required to play the game. Hurleys had to be purchased and were liable to be broken in the course of a game. Cricket was far more accessible to the labourer as one communally-owned bat was sufficient to allow a match to take place. Shop assistants, clerks and teachers were financially more secure and their working environment allowed for ease of organisation. Working in offices, workshops and shops meant constant contact with fellow workers, customers and neighbours.[119] The close relationship between shared places of employment and residence has been pointed out earlier in relation to the Mullingar and Castlepollard clubs.

In football the situation was somewhat different. In this examination, a database of 201 football players who represented ten rural clubs in a championship game between 1904 and 1905 was constructed. The identities of 141 (70 per cent) of these were established. In addition, a database of 165 urban players was compiled of which ninety-five (58 per cent) were identified. The players involved ranged in age between fifteen and thirty-four years of age and had an average age of 23.57. The rural clubs were dominated by farmers' sons and farm labourers who form social class B and D respectively. Farmers or farmers' sons formed 50 per cent of the total and farm and general labourers 40 per cent. Thirteen footballers (9 per cent) were from class C, where skilled tradesmen dominated. Six of these were attached to the Riverstown Emmett club and included three Leech brothers, who were returned as sailors and worked as boatmen on the Royal Canal. In contrast, footballers from social class C dominated the urban sample forming 61 per cent of the total, with class B at 23 per cent next in importance. Over half of this group were farmers' sons who were members of the Athlone Volunteer club. The average age of the urban footballer at 23.52 years was similar to his rural counterpart. With regard to religious affiliation and conjugal status footballers were almost homogeneous. Nine footballers were married and only three members of the Church of Ireland were evident from the sample. The analysis of the members of these clubs by social class is illustrated in Table 19.

In both the urban and rural situation football had a greater significance in catering for the recreation of the general and farm labourer. Given the social structure of rural Westmeath and the isolated nature of farm-based employment, it is suggested that there was a work related dimension to the composition of the rural football club. Farm labourers who were involved in football clubs may have been employed on the family farm of the farmers' sons who were involved in the same club. Of the urban clubs, the number of labourers involved distinguishes the Moate and the St Patrick's clubs. The cost factor allowed farm labourers to become more involved in football than hurling as the purchase of personal equipment was not an essential requirement for participation.

| Club | SOCIAL CLASS | | | |
	B	C	D	U
Rural Clubs				
Ballymore	12	1	1	7
Cullion Celtics	5	1	5	14
Collinstown	5	2	6	3
Coosan	11	0	2	3
Derrymore	4	0	9	5
Graftonstown	3	2	7	6
Lacken Rovers	6	0	6	5
Riverstown Emmetts	7	6	11	8
Tubberclair	12	0	4	4
Thomastown Rovers	6	1	6	5
TOTAL RURAL	71	13	57	60
Urban Clubs				
Athlone Volunteers	8	17	1	29
Moate	5	8	14	10
Mullingar Young Ireland	1	25	1	14
St Patrick's	1	9	6	16
TOTAL URBAN	15	59	22	69
Total	86	72	79	129

Table 19. Social class of footballers in Westmeath, 1898–1905.

VII

This chapter has offered a different perspective on the development of sport at the local level to that presented in other chapters of this study. The revival of the GAA and its associated games of hurling and football emerged as part of the cultural nationalist movement that became important in post-1900 Ireland. The spread of the GAA from 1901 onwards, as de Burca has correctly identified, was part of the general revival of the nationalist movement that began around this time.[120] This movement towards the creation of an Irish-Ireland had a significant impact on the recreational habits of the young men of County Westmeath. Hurling and football provided an opportunity for the young men of the county to engage in a sporting activity that was politicised and for some rural residents provided the opportunity to engage in an alternative recreational pastime to cricket. This had the additional attraction that involvement enabled participants to define themselves as Irishmen. The formation of hurling and football clubs also provided those who may have been excluded from the cricket community an opportunity to engage in sports. Cricket's dominant position in rural Westmeath was challenged and overtaken, in particular by football, in 1905. The ranchers who provided some of the essential supports for the game were subjected to an intense period of land agitation involving cattle driving, the prevention of the letting of grazing land and boy-cotting between 1906 and 1911, and this further eroded support for the game. The most active warrior in the 'ranch war' was the agrarian radical, Laurence Ginnell, who was MP for Westmeath North between 1906 and 1918 and the architect and public advocate of the cattle driving policy. Westmeath led the way in this campaign.[121]

Maurice Davin was the least politically motivated of the founding fathers of the GAA and became involved in the new organisation in 1884 for sports-related reasons. He believed there was a need to provide an opportunity for labourers to participate in organised sport.[122] This group formed the majority of the constituency that benefited from the growth of cricket in Westmeath between the decline of the GAA in the post-1894 years and its re-emergence in 1903. There is evidence from this analysis that this group may have been disenfranchised in a sporting context by the post-1900 developments. Although the GAA at national level, by including two disparate sports under its organisa-tional umbrella, unwittingly created a movement that catered for the recreational needs of the lower middle and working classes, the evi-dence from Westmeath suggests that the latter group were significantly outnumbered. Representatives from social classes B and C, dominated by farmers' sons and white-collar clerical workers and shop assistants, dominated the GAA playing cohort. These classes formed 71 per cent of the combined total of Westmeath hurlers and footballers, with class D forming 29 per cent. Cricket at this time catered chiefly for the farm labourers of social class D and as Vincent Comerford has perceptively suggested 'the disappearance of horizontal divisions within Cusack's organisation was to take time'.[123] Cricket maintained a presence in rural Westmeath and in the 1920s a Westmeath cricket league was organised with seven teams affiliated.[124]

8. Spectator sport, 1850–1905

The previous chapters of this book have dealt with the development of sport from the perspective of individual participation and examined the evolution of the institutions that facilitated personal involvement. Despite the number and variety of sporting disciplines that developed in Victorian and early Edwardian Westmeath, direct participation in sport was very much a minority involvement. The mass of the population at this time experienced the sporting occasion as spectators. People of all classes attended sports events in Westmeath in large numbers and with increased frequency as the century progressed. They were attracted by the prospect of enjoying sporting competition but also by the multi-faceted nature of the entertainment available. The main event provided the infrastructure that supported a variety of ancillary events that added to the entertainment experience. Musical entertainment, eating and drinking opportunities, participation in illegal gaming, carnival type attractions and freedom from the restrictions of convention were some of the ancillary attractions available at a sporting event.

When English visitors Mr and Mrs Hall visited Ireland in 1840 they found two aspects of the contemporary social scene worthy of comment. They believed that 'no people in the world have so few amusements as the Irish', particularly 'as drinking and fighting' had been abolished. 'The absence of the accompanying stimulus' also meant that 'dancing and hurling' had become equally neglected.[1] This observation by the Halls identified an important pre-Famine change taking place in popular cultural practices. Popular occasions of entertainment such as fairs and patterns and the more private occasions of celebration and excess such as weddings, wakes and funerals had been curtailed considerably. Clerical and magistracy opposition, improved standards of literacy and education, the coming of the railway, the introduction of effective policing, the suppression of illicit distillation and the calamity of the Famine were all factors that contributed to the decline in traditional popular recreation.[2] John Keegan, who was a native of Streamstown, County Westmeath, and was employed by the Ordnance Survey made a similar observation to that of the Halls'. In December 1846, he was based in the Moate district and noted that 'the wakes and funerals are not attended as formerly and the same ceremonies observed' and further commented that 'as far as a dance, hurling or football, the people seem to have forgotten there were ever such amusements'.[3]

Ó Cadhla, in his study of the St Declan pattern phenomenon at Ardmore, County Waterford, concluded that 'the increased value attached to literacy, restraint, sobriety and Victorian respectability undoubtedly began to peripheralise many aspects of nineteenth-century vernacular culture, if not stigmatising them'.[4] The most notorious festival of excess was the Donnybrook fair. This was the chief carnival of the citizens of Dublin and was, according to its leading chronicler, 'a byword for revelry and riotous behaviour'. The fair was a late 1850s victim of Victorian respectability.[5] The concept of the fair was transformed from a multi-faceted cultural and economic event stretching over a period of days to a one-day event the primary purpose of which was commerce, revolving around the buying and selling of farm animals. As Malcolm has indicated, the number of fairs held in Ireland increased significantly between 1840 and 1900 but their annual distribution changed drastically, with the traditional seasonal pattern of fair organisation practically disappearing. Athlone in the early nineteenth century was the venue for three-day fairs in January, March, May and August, all of which were also associated with important religious feast days. In 1900, Athlone fairs had become monthly one-day commercial events with the exception of the January and September fairs, which lasted for two days.[6]

The other great public occasion of celebration and carnival that had attracted mass gatherings, was the pattern. A pattern was a fixed annual event, the primary purpose of which was to celebrate the day of the local patron saint with penitential and devotional acts.[7] The range of ancillary activities associated with these patterns were similar to those at the fairs and has been well documented in particular for the patterns of St Kevin at Glendalough, County Wicklow and for St Declan at Ardmore.[8] Patterns were described in the 1870s as events that the majority of adults could remember but had by this time fallen largely into disuse. Clerical condemnation and opposition succeeded in suppressing a number of the gatherings altogether and imposed some degree of control on the behaviour seen at others.[9] In the diocese of Meath, which includes much of County Westmeath, Bishop John Cantwell was active in attempting to modify the combination of ritual observance and boisterous behaviour that the pattern had come to represent. Cantwell was active in the immediate pre-Famine and post-Famine period.[10]

The primary opposition of the Catholic Church was based on its belief that these events included many non-Christian features. Patterns (and wakes) provided the occasion for various forms of perceived misconduct – principally drunkenness, sexual immorality and brawling – which the church authorities found particularly disturbing.[11] The successful suppression of pattern festivals took place in the context of the broader changes taking place in popular attitudes and behaviour, when a whole range of traditional beliefs and practices were abandoned.[12] Changes in the social structure of rural Ireland were accompanied by improved living standards and exposure to new cultural influences and

new models of behaviour. 'The result was the adoption of new standards of respectability and decorum, and these inevitably brought with
them the decline of many of the less inhibited amusements of the Irish
countryside and the modification of others'.[13] In the second half of the
nineteenth century, with the curtailment of the traditional forms of
popular entertainment, access to a sports event – and the racecourse in
particular – provided for many the primary occasion of public entertainment and celebration.

II

Large crowds of people attended sports events in Westmeath especially
in the 1890s and early 1900s. Approximately fifteen events within the
county were organised annually at this time where the reported attendance was numbered in the thousands. The racecourse, the makeshift
athletic arena, the Athlone regatta and the football field formed cross-
class, multi-dimensional entertainment venues that offered the
additional advantage of granting free entry to the majority of spectators
throughout the nineteenth century. The precise size of a particular crowd
or the exact proportions of class representations within it remain a matter
of speculation. The numbers reported in attendance at events would
suggest that the lower classes formed the majority of the crowd and that
they lived within the immediate catchment area of the venue. Unlike
Tony Mason for Glasgow, Neal Garnham for Belfast or Neil Tranter for
Cappielow, the analyst of the Westmeath sports crowd has no casualty
list from which to extract quantitative detail on the social status or the
age and gender composition of the spectators in attendance.[14] The only
incident that might have produced such a report happened at Moate
races in 1889 when the makeshift grandstand collapsed without any
serious injuries occurring.[15] Had such been the case, the incident would
have been of little value in revealing anything about the classes of people
in attendance as the grandstand was occupied only by members of the
aristocracy and landed gentry or their social equals. Newspaper reports
provide the only attendance estimates available and are likely to be
exaggerated. Reports on race meetings, for instance, tend to describe
each meet as attracting a larger attendance than that of the previous
year. Nevertheless, regardless of the accuracy of estimates, there is no
doubt that Westmeath sports meetings were popular sporting and social
events attracting large crowds of all classes to the host venues. Race
meetings were the most popular occasions but the Athlone regatta, athletic sports, football and soccer matches also succeeded in attracting
large attendances.

Westmeath race meets, in particular, were popular events drawing vast
crowds of spectators. It was suggested that 15,000 people attended the
Mullingar summer meet of 1892.[16] The attendance in 1894 was described
as a record one while the 1899 report of the *Westmeath Examiner* on the

Mullingar meeting featured the highest reported attendance at any sporting event in the county when both the reserved and unreserved enclosures were reportedly thronged with the estimated 30,000 spectators.[17] The 1893 revived Athlone race meeting was attended by 12,000 people.[18] Severe weather conditions impacted directly on attendance on occasions. The Athlone meet of 1894 attracted an estimated 6,000 as deplorable weather prevented several thousand 'holiday seekers' already present in the town from going out to the course.[19] A race meet held at Moate in 1889 was attended by between 6,000 and 7,000 people.[20] Proximity in timing to other local fixtures was believed to be responsible for the reduced attendance of between 2,000 and 3, 000 people at the 1894 meet.[21]

Regattas were a regular feature of the Athlone sporting calendar during the period of this study. Two types of event were held. The yachting events held on Lough Ree were long established and more exclusive and formed a seasonal and aquatic parallel to the Mullingar polo culture. Rowing regattas were held between the two bridges of Athlone and provided free entertainment to the masses in much the same manner as a race meeting. Race meetings and regattas shared many organisational similarities. They were organised by a committee, funded by subscription, with control and adjudication the responsibility of the stewards. The programme of events was modelled on the race meet, a reserved enclosure was available for social segregation and musical entertainment was mandatory. The typical regatta programme consisted of eight to ten rowing events conducted on the river Shannon and novelty events such as climbing the greasy-pole, duck hunts and swimming races were often included and added to the entertainment.[22]

A fireworks display at the end was a unique aspect of the regatta experience. In keeping with the local dimension of the 1887 regatta, the organising committee hired William Jones of Connaught Street to provide the display rather than follow the usual practice of employing a Dublin expert. On this occasion 'the Shells, Rockets, Maroons, Pieces and Fountains were excellent, and the success of the Big Balloon drew forth hearty cheers'.[23] 'Not less than ten thousand people', according to the *Westmeath Independent*, attended this event, while only a 'few dozen' were present at the start of the boat club regatta.[24] In 1887 Athlone went 'regatta mad' and three regattas were organised within a fortnight of each other. The annual regatta became the 'people's regatta' because of an internal dispute within the boat club on the question of hiring musical bands. The boat club also organised a regatta and the Athlone sailing regatta was also held.[25]

Other sporting events also proved attractive. Football games in the early 1890s were popular events. An 1888 GAA tournament organised in Athlone attracted a crowd of 9,000 to 10,000, encouraging the *Westmeath Independent* reporter to record that 'never have we seen the thoroughfares of this ancient and historic town so crowded with pedestrians, young and old, rich and poor, and all apparently in the best of humour'.

A Westmeath football championship was played in 1890 and over 2,000 were reported to have attended the final in Athlone despite the 2d entrance fee.[26] The first match of the 1892 championship between Mullingar Football Club and Thomastown Rangers attracted an attendance of 'something like 4,000' spectators; the semi-final between Mullingar Shamrocks and Raharney Rovers was played before a crowd of 2,000 people and according to the *Westmeath Nationalist* 'there was certainly no less than 6,000 spectators present' at the final. On Sunday 19 March 1893 Mullingar Football Club played Killucan in a match at the Wooddown Rackers pitch, which was attended 'by a contingent of enormous proportions' from the town. Before the game 'vehicles, bicycles, pedestrians, of all sorts and conditions might be seen tending hurriedly towards the point of concentration at Wooddown'.[27] The most important GAA matches hosted in the county were the All-Ireland hurling and football semi-finals played in May 1906. These were the penultimate rounds of the 1904 championships as the GAA national championships were hopelessly behind schedule at the time. A crowd of between 10,000 and 11,000 attended and reminded the reporter 'of those monster meetings called by O'Connell in the pre-Emancipation days'.[28] Soccer, as documented earlier, also enjoyed great popular appeal in Athlone.

Athletics meets also attracted large numbers of spectators. An improbable 6,000 people reportedly attended the Ranelagh School athletic sports in July 1889.[29] The Athlone Bicycle Club in the 1890s promoted an athletic meet that attracted between 4,000 and 5,000 people to the 1893 event.[30] Crookedwood is located about five miles from Mullingar and from 1893 was the venue for a sports meet that included aquatic, athletic, equestrian and cycling events. The Crookedwood sports of 1899 were attended by 'thousands of spectators' that included representatives of 'many classes and districts' from Westmeath and other counties.[31] Substantial numbers attending sports meetings was not confined to the later decades. The Garrycastle race meeting (1857–68) was a popular event. A two-day meet survived until 1866 at which attendance on the first day always exceeded the second day and which was also influenced by the month in which the event was held. The races attracted an attendance of between 7,000 and 8,000 in 1861.[32]

The annual races organised by the County Westmeath Polo Club provide an exception to the large attendances reported at other events. The relative isolation of the Ledeston venue and the elitism associated with the sport marginalised its popular appeal. The races normally brought the polo season to a close and as one report noted a 'polo race will always partake more of the nature of a social than a great public function', where 'the rank and fashion were largely in evidence'.[33] The emphasis was as much on the entertainment as on the racing and club members and individuals took advantage of the occasion to entertain friends. In this way, the races fulfilled a similar purpose to the annual hunt club steeplechase and point-to-point race meetings. At the 1901 event, for instance, 'hospitality was liberally dispensed by the members of the club in the pavilion and also by Mr Boyd-Rochfort, J. H. Locke and others'.[34] Musical entertainment provided by the band of the Mullingar-based regiment was a consistent feature of these races.[35]

The most basic level at which women participated in sport was as spectators and their presence at sports events, particularly at race meetings, was documented from the early 1850s. Special provision was also made at some venues to cater for the needs of the upper-class women. The infrastructure of the Mullingar venue built in 1852 included a reserved enclosure in which at least three distinct areas were made available for patrons, namely the grandstand, the area reserved specifically for the use of ladies and the carriage enclosure. Early newspaper reports make continuous reference to the 'portion of stand reserved for ladies', with the earliest such reference dating to the meet of 1852.[36] Twenty-one years later, the policy continued at the venue where a 'portion of the stand was carpeted and reserved for ladies'.[37] The pavilion at Ledeston of the Westmeath County Polo Club also included a marquee reserved specifically for ladies.[38]

Descriptions of the presence of the 'fair sex' in the grandstand are common and are usually dealt with in condescending and chauvinistic terms. Reports emphasising their visual impact on the occasion or as adding decorative effect were the norm and there is very little evidence of women being serious participants in a sporting occasion. The description of the women who were present at the revived Kilbeggan meeting of 1901 is typical of the type:

> On the grandstand the ladies clustered, their bright costumes and the varying colours of their dresses spreading brightly up the stand's terraced steps, and making it like a sloping bank of many-hued flowers or a hill-side where many bright-plumed birds were at rest.[39]

At the same Kilbeggan meet the reporter commented that female 'smiles and comments and chit-chat are always welcome' and 'their merry ringing laughter indispensable rippling cadenzas to the merry music of the holiday spirit'.[40] Females attended the Rathowen races in November 1901 with 'a reckless disregard to the fate of the curls of their feathers and the havoc which rain and mud usually play with feminine attire generally'.[41] Women from all classes attended the races and were present in greater numbers in the unreserved section of the racecourse where free access to the range of ancillary activities proved attractive to all. Huggins estimates that females formed about 10 per cent of the crowd attending a race meeting, a calculation based on an analysis of crowd pictures from the *Illustrated London News* and on paintings of racecourse crowd scenes.[42]

The extent of female active participation in the range of events is unclear but in Athlone in 1899 'one saw flitting continuously' between the weighing room and the enclosure 'the brightest garments and the most up-to-date hats, and it was wonderful to notice how keenly these fair admirers of equine sport looked for the winners'.[43] At the summer meet in Mullingar in 1904 the ladies 'flitted about like butterflies, laying their odds, and discussing the points of the runners with quite as much knowledge as many of the sterner sex'.[44] Regardless of the extent of the active involvement and the reporters' chauvinism, it is clear that for a particular class of Westmeath woman attendance at a race meeting was central to their lifestyle and provided an occasion for display and conspicuous consumption.

Women also attended cricket matches regularly where on occasion special provision was made to cater for their needs. Kilbeggan was one of the early centres of the game in the county and the club's games attracted female spectators from the higher social classes. At the 1862 match against Mullingar 'some of the elite among the fair sex of the county graced the ground with their presence' and added 'much to the beauty of the scene'; an 1863 match against Geasehill (King's county) also attracted 'a number of the fair sex'.[45] At the match between the Westmeath County Club and the East Lancashire Regiment in 1892 a marquee was provided for the ladies, 'a large number of whom graced the proceedings with their presence'.[46] The attendance at cricket matches was not limited to elite women. Cricket was the most popular game in the county in the 1890s and women were amongst those who attended the matches. When Cloughan played Crowenstown they had more attention 'paid to them than there was to the cricket ball'.[47] The presence of 'the fair sex' at football matches was also frequently noted.[48]

The presence of children at sporting occasions was also noted. The *Westmeath Independent* reporter, in a somewhat jaundiced fashion, recorded their attendance at the Athlone races of 1895:

> Children as many as could be kept within bounds, were stowed away in every corner, and as many as could not be thus disposed of, ran in and out in all intricate spots, crept between people's legs and carriage wheels and came forth unharmed from under horses hoofs.[49]

Medical officers at Mullingar Lunatic Asylum also used the sporting occasion as an intervention to relieve the monotony for some of those detained in the institution. Dr Jameson Dwyer used the racecourse for therapeutic purposes. The report of the Newbrook Harriers Sportsman's races of 1883 recorded the presence of a number of afflicted persons from the Lunatic Asylum.[50] Dr Finnegan organised the attendance of some patients at the cricket match between the Westmeath County and the RIR in 1890.[51] Earlier in the year, at a football match between Mullingar Commercials and Raharney Rovers, the attendance included 'a number of the poor inmates of the Lunatic Asylum, who under the convoy of the attendants, Dr Finnegan, with his usual kindness allowed to be present'.[52]

The majority of people who attended sporting events for the period covered by this book did so free of charge. The Mullingar spring race meet of 1903 was the first to impose a general 6d admission charge. Prior to this only those wishing to enter the reserved enclosure were required to pay an admission fee. Admission fees to reserved enclosures where patrons paid for the privilege of a better vantage point, comfort and access to food and drink were often structured as the following unsystematically-compiled samples illustrate. The organising committee of the Killucan Steeplechases of 1882 charged a 6s fee for carriage entry, 2s 6d for cars and a similar fee for admission to the stand.[53] Four years earlier Percy Nugent Fitzgerald promoted a steeplechase at Newbrook (Mullingar) and charged a 7s 6d entry fee to the grandstand and was heavily criticised for his efforts.[54] There was a 2s 6d entrance charge to the boat-house grounds for the Athlone regatta of 1872.[55] Advertisements for the Athlone Bicycle Club's second annual sports meeting in 1893 at the Queen's Meadow informed patrons of the availability of a reserved area that provided seating and tents for drinking and refreshments, which could be accessed for the fee of 1s. In 1896 a general admission fee to the field of 6d was imposed as well as a 1s fee to the enclosure. In return patrons could enjoy cycling, athletics and tug-o-war competitions as well as the musical recital of the band of the Lancashire Fuisiliers.[56] An individual wishing to enter the enclosure for the Athlone regatta in 1906 could do so on the payment of 1s or a family ticket could be purchased that admitted three non-subscribers for 2s 6d. Those who subscribed 10s to the event's funds were entitled to a family ticket free of charge.[57] Entrance to the enclosure for the Rathowen races in June 1904 was 6d whilst in 1890 the standard entrance fee for carriages of 5s, 2s 6d for cars and 10s each for tents was levied.[58] The rules of the INHSC forbade the levying of an admission fee to a hunt club promoted point-to-point meet so that events of this nature organised by the County Westmeath Hunt Club or its south Westmeath equivalent still offered free entertainment for those interested. The majority of newspaper advertisements for sports events examined for the period of this study carry no information on admission fees. Organising committees depended on subscriptions sourced and entry fees to cover the cost of the event.

Competitive soccer matches played in Athlone charged gate-money. Entry to the Leinster senior soccer cup final between Athlone and Bohemians cost 6d on the day (17 March 1896) but pre-purchased tickets could be had for 4d.[59] The policy of charging to attend local GAA games became standardised in the early 1900s. Prior to this a fee was levied occasionally to defray costs. The initial Westmeath football final was held in Athlone between Athlone and Moate in May 1890. A 'nominal' 2d admission was charged to defray expenses and to prevent overcrowding.[60] In January 1895 a game between 'the champions of Westmeath and the champions of Longford', took place and the Mullingar club members decided to cover some of the expense involved in organising the game by 'charging 2d each for admission to the game', a sum 'that was very freely paid'.[61] This wasn't always the situation, as there seems to have been some resentment amongst intending patrons of GAA games at having to pay to gain entry. The first two games of the Young Ireland club's 1903 tournament ended in draws and it was suggested that the results were fixed to generate finance for the promoting club. The club captain, P. Murphy, was emphatic in rejecting this notion and in a letter to the *Westmeath Examiner* he suggested that 'those that instituted this charge against us are of the type that would go around by Saunderson's Bridge or elsewhere before paying three-pence to see any sport'. The club were 'prepared to pay half expenses of the four teams, which means a decided loss to our club instead of a benefit, as those low-minded people imagine'.[62]

The reluctance to pay admission fees and the activities of the 'ditch breakers' was a constant theme of the 'With the Gaels' columnist in the *Westmeath Independent*.[63] The GAA county committee at its April 1904 meeting put regulations in place for the division of gate receipts. Income from county championship matches was to be divided equally between the host club, competing teams and the county committee.[64] At this stage an admission charge of 3d became standard.[65] Therefore, after 1900 those who wished to view GAA games were required to pay some sort of tariff, a requirement that might have excluded the poorest members of society from watching the games. These charges were imposed at a time when the average agricultural summer wage in the Mullingar district ranged from 1s 6d to 2s per day and from 2s to 2s 6d in the Delvin area for 1901.[66]

III

Large-scale attendance at a sports meeting and at a race meeting in particular was in many ways a product of the railway age. As has been shown earlier Westmeath's railway infrastructure was particularly comprehensive and linked the two main urban centres with all areas of the state. The internal rail linkages were also widespread. The holding of the Garrycastle race meet coincided with a time when Athlone's rail links were developed to connect the town with all parts of Ireland. The permanent venue for the Mullingar races was chosen for the access it provided to the newly built rail terminal and the earlier meets were promoted by the holder of the franchise for the saloon at the station. Improved transport infrastructure considerably enlarged the catchment area for potential spectators.

Rail companies exploited the commercial possibilities of racing events. The MGWR Company organised a special from Galway for the 1859 Garrycastle meet. Special rates were available at stations between Dublin and Killucan on the early morning scheduled service from Dublin for the 1860 meet. Also the company organised a special train from Mullingar. A train from Roscommon reportedly brought 300 passengers to this meet.[67] According to the *Freeman's Journal*, Athlone from an early hour was filled with visitors from Dublin, Westmeath, Roscommon and Galway with 'the ordinary and special trains of the Midland and the Great Southern and Western branch line from Tullamore bringing hundreds to the scene'.[68] The Great Southern and Western Company issued first- and second-class return tickets at single fares for its ordinary trains connecting several Kildare towns as well as Geasehill, Portarlington, Tullamore and Clara to Athlone.[69] In 1861, the 'facility which railway communication afforded was . . . made fully available' and the trains of the various servicing companies brought 'an influx of visitors never equalled within the precincts' of the 'old and historic course'.[70] The 1864 meet was according to the *Westmeath Independent* report 'as eagerly attended as we have seen' and 'the special trains of the Midland and Southern railway completely flooded the town with strangers and gave employment to the host of jarveys who reaped a rich harvest in conveying them to the racecourse'.[71] The MGWR company policy had developed by 1866 to provide a service that was impressively comprehensive. The company organised three special passenger trains with '1st, 2nd and 3rd Class Carriages' from Mullingar, Galway and Castlerea. Special fares were available that provided 'tickets at a single fare for the double journey'. The MGWR offered special rates to passengers on its special and scheduled services from a total of twenty-two different stations in Westmeath and the west of Ireland in addition to Dublin and the stations between Enfield and Killucan 'both inclusive'.[72]

Rail transport was organised to carry passengers to Mullingar race meets from the date of the completion of the connection with Dublin in October 1848. References to crowd size emphasised the numbers of spectators carried to the venue by rail. The report on the 1849 April meeting makes reference to the arrival of a special train from Dublin. In April 1851 it was reported that 200 spectators travelled by rail.[73] The 1860 attendance 'was very large, the trains from Dublin and Longford and Cavan being heavily freighted'.[74] The 1865 *Westmeath Guardian* report claimed that the specials of the MGWR carried 6,000 passengers from Dublin, Ballinasloe, Cavan and Longford.[75] Three years later, the MGWR was reported to have carried almost 7,000 people to the first day of the meet and 2,000 on the second day.[76] The absence of a direct rail link to a course was perceived to have a negative impact on attendance at Kilbeggan. The village was located almost half-way between the stations of the MGWR and those of the GSWR and the small crowd attending the 1902 meet was linked to the absence of a direct railway link to the course, 'the attendance depending more on the neighbourhood than any where else – such as indeed as is almost always the case with meetings not held directly on the railway lines'.[77]

The directors of the MGWR and the Westmeath Race Company Limited established a very close working relationship, to the mutual benefit of both organisations. This culminated in 1902 when two 'commodious, safe and well ordered' railway sidings that gave rail travellers direct access to the Mullingar racecourse were opened. The Dublin express train, the Kildare and Clara trains, the Athlone train and a Clonsilla (Dublin) special servicing intermediate stations arrived at one of these platforms. The second platform catered for the Cavan, Longford and Hill-of-Down specials.[78] This advance eliminated one of the image problems associated with the Mullingar racecourse; it had been perceived to be an 'unpleasant journey from the railway station to the course'. Mullingar was now a far more attractive venue for Dublin race followers. It was possible to make the return trip to Mullingar from Dublin and include the races in a time of five hours. Dubliners were now reported to claim that it was at least as convenient to 'take a day at Mullingar races as at Baldoyle or Leopardstown'.[79] The construction of the sidings also allowed, the development of a cheap system of public transport to operate from within the town eliminating some of the racketeering practices of the jarvey men who operated between the railway station and the Mullingar course. A special train from Mullingar to the course that charged all-in fares of 1s and 6d for first- and third-class carriages was introduced.[80]

Other sports events also benefited from the railway infrastructure. In 1893 'each succeeding train from Tullamore, Clara, Moate, Roscommon and Ballinasloe were crowded with excursionists' arriving in Athlone to attend the athletics and bicycle sports. Close to 200 people paid the return fare of two shillings and travelled from Athlone to Mullingar to the second leg of the county senior hurling final in February 1906 and enjoyed the privilege of being played through the town by the Brass and Reed Band as they made their way to the Horse Show Grounds venue.[81] The rail links also facilitated the attendance of large numbers at the various regattas held in Athlone over the period. In 1901, spectators from Mullingar, Moate, Tullamore, Clara, Ballinasloe and Ballymahon arrived by rail.[82]

Those who chose not to avail of the railway system or who lived close to the designated venue requisitioned other modes of transport. Supporters of the Athlone races and regattas availed of river transport. The Shannon Development Company, for example, ran a special steamer from Portumna, Banagher and Shannonbridge to Athlone. About 120 people travelled by steamer to the 1899 races that were staged once again at the 'historic' Garrycastle course.[83] 'Numbers came in boats from the islands of Lough Ree, and the districts bordering the Shannon on the Leinster and Connaught side' to the regatta in 1901.[84] Those attending the Kilbeggan race meet of 1905 were inconvenienced by 'the dearth of cars' and the resulting profiteering in which 'pretty stiff prices were given for seats from Mullingar to and from Kilbeggan, as far as 10s being taken and offered for a single seat'.[85] The Athlone football team travelled to Moate in May 1904 by brake with 'a string of side cars, and traps, even horse crates, followed, and after them in grand array a long line of cyclists'.[86] Other means of transport were becoming more common. Sir Richard Levinge's party arrived at Kilbeggan in 1905 by motorcar. On the same day, the approach roads were 'literally covered with cyclists, gay young men and buxom females pedalling along, and whiling the time away with merry jokes, unmindful of the slight inconveniences caused by the dust'.[87]

Contemporary newspapers provide some detail on the place of origin of those attending events. The catchment area was greatest for those attending race meets. The central location of the two main urban areas of the county, Mullingar and Athlone, gave them access to vast hinterlands that by the end of the century were almost nationwide in extent. Kilbeggan's zone of influence was restricted by its lack of a direct rail service as Horsleap, Tullamore, Mullingar and Castletown-Geoghegan were the nearest settlements with railway stations. The numbers attending would suggest that the majority came from the immediate vicinity of the venue and from the towns served by a railway link to the host venue. Over 450 patrons who used the Hill-of-Down station, as well as large numbers from Longford, Cavan, Athlone, Tullamore, Dublin, Galway, Tuam and Clara attended the 1902 Mullingar races. At the 1904 Mullingar June meet, visitors were seen in great numbers from Longford, Cavan, Meath, Kildare as well as from all parts of Westmeath and many parts of Roscommon. The Dublin visitors were much more numerous than on any previous occasion and according to the *Westmeath Independent* 'Dublin sent about twice as much as in previous years'.[88] At the 1906 summer meet specific mention was made of the number of Belfast and Enniskillen visitors.[89] Moate races attracted the majority of its spectators from the Athlone area as they used the direct rail link with the town. Many from Athlone were also reported to have pooled their resources to hire brakes and cars and 'drove to the course by road enjoying the landscape scenery on the route'.[90]

IV

We have to rely on newspaper reports for evidence of the class structure of the spectators in attendance at a sports event. It is clear that throughout the second half of the nineteenth century spectators at Westmeath sports events were drawn from all sections of the community, from the aristocracy to the landless labourer, from the industrial proprietor to the factory worker, 'from the blue blood aristocrat to the thread-bare mendicant'. 'The upper ten and the lower five, with the intermediate numbers' were all assembled at the sports venue as the century ended.[91] This social mix applied to race meetings in particular. The Mullingar race meet of 1850 was principally attended by the middle and humbler classes in which 'the grey coats greatly outnumbered all the rest'; in 1851 the 'frieze-coated peasantry, who conducted themselves in the most peaceable manner' formed the majority.[92] The attendance of those who worked regular hours for a living, especially in the urban centres of Mullingar and Athlone, was facilitated by their place of employment normally closing for business at midday. In 1889, when the Ranelagh School sports were held it was considered a 'gala day' in Athlone. 'Business people suspended transactions for the day, employees sought for and were granted a day's holiday'. All employees of the Athlone Woollen Mills were granted a half-day to attend and compete in that firm's annual sports.[93] The principal merchants of Athlone gave their employees a half-day to allow them attend the annual Athlone Bicycle Club sports.[94] In 1894 'the majority of the business houses were closed at 12.30 o'clock, including the Woollen Mills and Saw Mills, in order that the employees in these concerns might have a holiday in order to enjoy the sports on the Bushfield course'.[95]

Race meetings were anticipated with eagerness by all social classes and contemporary newspapers made frequent reference to the cross-class appeal of the racecourse. The Westmeath Hunt Sportsman's races of 1888, for example, were reported to have attracted an immense attendance, comprising the leading county families, the military, the shopkeepers and traders and the agricultural community.[96] Twenty-five years earlier, at Mullingar, the races attracted the same heterogeneous crowd. The *Westmeath Guardian* reported that 'in front of the stand house a considerable space was covered with the carriages of and equipages of the gentry, a long line of tents occupied their appropriate spaces and every elevated spot was crowded with the farming and working classes, who assembled in much larger numbers than in years past'.[97] The *Irish Sportsman* in July 1875 reported that 'with all ranks and classes of Irishmen steeplechasing is a favourite amusement. The farmer never can get his men to work upon a holiday or when there is either a funeral or a steeplechase within ten miles of them. The women look forward to a race with as much interest as the men.' This report also suggested that attendance at race meetings and other sports events was a significant part of the courtship ritual. According to the reporter 'the course is the scene of many courtships and there are sundry adjournments in the evening from the *tents* to the priests' *house*'.[98] This aspect of the sporting occasion frequently attracted comment. At the Athlone regatta of 1850 'there was a sunshine of soft smiles and bewitching glances to disarm the heart of its ire' and 'many a heart passed from its possessor's control to be chained as captive to the dark eye of a lovely gal'!![99] Almost twenty years later at Crookedwood athletics sports 'male lovers and admirers of noble and manly sports' were accompanied by 'a large contingent of their own lovers and admirers'.[100]

As a venue, the racecourse combined the social, the sporting and the economic. Arguably the social dimension dominated, as the pleasures that the experience offered to the majority were those of the playground or carnival. The wealthy and the aspiring looked to the balls and the ordinaries, especially in the early period of this study when two-day meets were common, the rest looked to the occasional holiday they could risk taking, to the free excitement of the races themselves, to the display of wealth and privilege, to frequenting the drinking booths and the multiplicity of entertainment on the course.[101] An ordinary was held each evening of the Westmeath steeplechases at the York Hotel in Mullingar in 1850.[102] At the opening meet at Thomastown in 1857, 'immediately after the first race a sumptuous *dejuner* was given by the hospitable and sporting owner, Thomas M. Naghten ... to which over two hundred persons sat down, every delicacy was provided and champaign [sic] flowed *ad libium*'.[103] Balls were also an important element of the culture of the regatta in the 1850s. The 'equatic [sic] gentlemen' who attended at Lough Ree in 1853 were 'most sumptuously entertained by the Lough Ree Club, at Madam De Ruyter's Railway Hotel, where every delicacy of the season was provided and wines of the choicest vintage' on the eve of the regatta as well as on each evening that events were held. On the Wednesday of the regatta the 'Club Room at the Railway Hotel was thrown open and ... some 120 of the rank, fashion and beauty of the town, garrison and neighbourhood, assembled in the Hall'.[104] For one unsympathetic local observer the racecourse presented a venue for 'buffoonery, deception, double dealing and disorder', a day when there seemed to be 'a traditional licence for indulgence'.[105] Attending a race meeting provided the masses with one of the few sources of release from the grinding hardship of rural life. The lack of excitement and glamour in the lifestyle of the rural population continued after 1900, a fact that was recognised by the reporter of the *Westmeath Independent* who reported on the Garrycastle meet of 1902.[106] The writer recognised that one of the functions of a race meeting was to brighten 'the hum drum every day life in the country'.

People of all classes may have attended sports occasions but they did not associate freely inside the grounds. The 'frieze coated peasantry' may have shared the same arena in Mullingar in 1850 and 1851 as social luminaries such as the Earls of Bective and Clonmel, Lord Longford, Lord St Lawrence, the Honourable W. Hutchinson, as well as a host of landed gentry and army officers, but the social and recreational experience were extreme opposites.[107] Social mixing was limited and closely regulated. Racing crowds were heavily segregated, an aspect of course management that helped to reinforce social hierarchies. Throughout much of the century the use of a grandstand and carriage enclosure was the chief instrument of segregation. Even the smallest of local meets provided, at a minimum, a makeshift grandstand constructed on a temporary basis. At the end of the meet, the construction was dismantled and the timber stored for use the following year. The constructions occasionally collapsed endangering the life and limb of the occupants. At the Mallow, County Cork, autumn meet in 1867, the structure collapsed when it was crowded with race watchers, fortunately without serious injury to any of the occupants.[108] At the inaugural Moate meeting of 1889 the grandstand collapsed, again without serious consequences.[109] The operation of the reserved enclosure was an important means of fundraising for organising committees. The income from the grandstand at Moate in 1890 amounted to £20 15s in addition to £6 2s paid for entry to the carriage enclosure. The expenditure on timber for the course was £7 2s and the cost of erecting the stand amounted to £3 8s so that even for the smaller venues the grandstand was an important revenue source. The Athlone income from grandstand entrance fees in 1895 provided 33 per cent of the total revenue raised. This enabled race committees to introduce a system of segregation by price, by providing a comfortable viewing place to those who were able to afford the privilege. Food and drink prepared to the highest of professional standards was available, at the more important events, usually in an area beneath the grandstand.

A survey of lists of attendance allows those present in the enclosed arenas to be identified. At the apex were the chief aristocrats of Westmeath and surrounding areas. Viscount Avonmore, 'who had the previous evening come up the river on his yacht' headed the list of attendees at the Athlone athletic sports and rowing matches in 1877.[110] The 1894 Athlone meet attracted Lord Castlemaine and his party as well as the Earl and Countess of Clancarty and Lord Crofton. Representing the next level of the social hierarchy were some of the leading landed-gentry families of County Westmeath. These included parties representing two of the county's largest landowning families, Charles O'Donoghue and E. Dames-Longworth. Army officers based in the locality were also present, as well as those from local landowning families who held service titles. However, the published list (numbering fifty in total) of those attending the Athlone meet of 1894 was dominated by the members of the professions and commercial classes. Doctors, solicitors, auctioneers, merchants, grocers and publicans were well represented, as well as three newspaper proprietors. Some of these local commercial men were active politically and five of those listed held office as town commissioners.[111]

Events organised by the Westmeath hunt clubs or polo clubs featured reserved enclosures that were more socially exclusive. The Westmeath Polo Club races based in the club's grounds at Ledeston were a socially exclusive private event. The attendance at the 1893 event included representatives of most of the leading gentry, military and aristocratic families in the eastern half of the county, headed by the proprietor of the town, Lord Greville.[112] The establishment of the identities and professions of those present in the enclosures challenges the contention of Vamplew – made in relation to British flat racing – that 'the respectable middle class would not go racing'.[113] Certainly the evidence from this study is that the most respectable of the middle classes went racing and as has been shown in Chapter 2, were actively involved in race promotion, organisation and management. Some of those who were present in the grandstand may have been there, as Vamplew suggests because of the opportunity that was presented to mix with the aristocracy and gentry. 'They went wearing their social blinkers, not seeing the baser turf follower, but focusing on those attenders with whom they wished to be identified.'[114] The legal profession was one of the great growth professions of the last quarter of the nineteenth century, when much business was generated from legal requirements consequent on the introduction of a variety of new land legislation. The landed classes also provided auctioneers with much of their lucrative business through the sale of estates and annual stock clearance auctions. Many of the professional classes present in the grandstand were there as business associates of the landed elites. Presence in the social circle of the grandstand confirmed and solidified social and economic networks.

Race meetings provided an opportunity for the county gentry and army regiments to entertain their social equals. This entertainment was carried out in the vicinity of the reserved enclosure. At the Athlone races it was customary that 'the officers of the regiment had a marquee in the enclosure, as also had the officers belonging to the Artillery, at both of which numerous guests were entertained during the day'.[115] At the south Westmeath races of 1897 officers of the Royal Highland Artillery and the York Regiment joined forces to provide luncheon 'in a very spacious marquee'.[116] The following year, the Athlone-based military regiments attended en masse and fulfilled their entertainment duties to the full. The Connaught Rangers had a 'special tent erected on the field in which everything desirable for the entertainment of their friends was provided'.[117] At the same meet, Lord Castlemaine entertained visitors in a marquee especially constructed for the purpose. At Athlone in 1899 it was Mr Taylor of the Shannon Development Committee that provided the hospitality. Iced drinks and refreshing teas were provided which 'reduced the heated man to a normal state'.[118] Captain Honourable Greville Nugent entertained his friends to *recherché* luncheon during the day at the Westmeath Hunt Club races of 1873. The 23rd Fusiliers and 8th Hussars entertained at the same meeting.[119] At the Mullingar autumn meet of 1898 the stewards provided luncheon for a large number of visitors in the paddock while on the course Mrs Fitzgerald entertained her guests.[120] Whiskey distiller, J. H. Locke entertained a number of visitors at Kilbeggan in 1901 along with 'rendering valuable assistance in keeping the course clear of pedestrians'.[121]

The policy of entertaining guests at a race meeting was displayed on a most impressive scale at the Westmeath Hunt Club's point-to-point meet held at Clondaliever on 15 March 1904. This lavish entertainment recognised the changed power structures of rural society and the necessity for the members of the Westmeath Hunt Club to exercise diplomacy to guarantee access to hunting territory. The meeting publicly acknowledged that 'it is not the farmer who is complimented by the hounds passing over his land but the Hunt who are obliged'.[122] Harry Whitworth, MFH, provided the hospitality in his marquee, which had table accommodation for 200 people at a sitting. Whitworth was anxious to 'publicly and collectively as well as individually acknowledge the thanks he felt as well as the greater number of the Westmeath Hunt members to the farmers for allowing the hounds to cross freely over their lands'. The firm of Mr M. P. O'Brien of Edenderry and Mullingar provided the catering and was prepared to cater for over 1,000 people in the course of the day and 'a good stride towards that number was made before the day was out'.[123]

Presence at a race meeting fulfilled a number of sporting and social functions. No doubt many attended for the excitement presented by watching how the horses coped with the challenge presented by the various steeplechase courses. A day spent racing offered relief from the pressures and stresses of daily life. 'Men of staid capacity, business men forget their occupations, and for the time are entirely concerned in those smaller intricacies of life.'[124] Attendance at local race meetings also served important social functions for members of the gentry and the aristocracy. It enabled them to reinforce their position in the social hierarchy. Their demonstration of conspicuous consumption, ritual and display reminded the local community who was at its head. This was where, as an observer noted, 'the fashionably dressed, if not gaudily decked knots of people consumed confectionery and sipped champagne in barouches, as if absolutely oblivious to the fact that the world was not made for their express benefit'.[125] Arrival at the course by coach was an important part of this display especially in the early years of this study.[126] At the inaugural Newbrook meeting in 1852 the number of cars, carriages and vehicles of every description was noteworthy but it was 'the beautiful drag of G. A. Boyd Esq. and its four magnificent horses' that attracted most attention.[127]

The racecourse was a venue where a hierarchy of social and economic networks operated. The nature of these networks changed over the century. Members of the gentry, aristocracy and military gentlemen from a similar milieu initially dominated the enclosed areas but as the century progressed the grandstands and enclosures were increasingly populated by middle-class members of the professions and business community. Social networks publicly manifested at the racecourse were continued after the meeting as private entertainment remained an important part of the race meeting experience. This aspect of entertainment is well described in the diary of a young Catholic middle-class lady, Mary Anne Power, from Carrick-on-Suir, County Waterford. In her diary she describes being at Temple Mungret, County Limerick and her attendance at the races and the range of social activities associated with them.[128] During the Punchestown race meeting, the big houses of Kildare and surrounding counties provided hospitality and accommodation to landlords and their families who had to travel long distances. For the meeting in April 1880, for example, the *Leinster Express* listed sixteen houses from which almost 400 guests left on one day to attend

Punchestown.[129] Outside the reserved arenas, the racecourse was also an important meeting place where people attended with the expectation of meeting family members and friends.

V

An ancillary range of activities, both formal and informal were supported by the core sports business of the event. These provided much of the attractions for the masses and were standard fare at any event where large crowds assembled in the Victorian period. Even the small country meets featured a wide range of attractions and they may have been proportionally more plentiful at these venues, where control was likely to have been less stringent and the audience less sophisticated and worldly-wise. At Kilbeggan in 1903, for instance, 'the tents, shooting galleries, roulette tables, card tables, and all the other integral portions of a racecourse ensemble were in evidence'.[130] In 1895, at Athlone, 'gipsy girls hooded in showy handkerchiefs issued forth to tell fortunes and ventriloquists and conjurers counted the likely sixpences long before they were earned'.[131] The 'brethren who generally frequent gatherings of this description' provided the entertainment at the 1888 Castlepollard meet. The range of attractions included aunt Sally, the swing boats 'patronised on a large scale by those who wished to enjoy the sensation of flying through the air for a short space of time', roulette and the penny show with its 'usual concomitant of burlesque'.[132] The 1904 Mullingar summer meet attracted

> the usual battalions of nomads in the shape of tinkers, armless and blind men (or shall we say alleged?), fiddlers and fluters, thimble-riggers, fortune-tellers, card-trick men, and, no doubt, a liberal sprinkling of the fraternity who have been given the happy designation of 'the light fingered gentry'. Every species of attraction in the range of the juggler's art also seemed to be provided and money was made and lost in a variety of bewildering ways.[133]

The inaugural Moate race meet of 1889 also attracted the full complement of attractions. The unenclosed area was occupied by the 'stalls of the itinerant vendors of oranges, cakes and sweets', as well as the

> The knife, the card, the trick-of-the-loop, and the gun-men also managed, unobserved by the police to trade a little in their peculiar lines and as to musicians they were also in abundance and between the races played for the accommodation of lads and lassies who beguiled away the time by the exercise of the light fantastic.[134]

Cardsharps of all kinds and the thimble-riggers with their tin cups, dried peas and horny thumbnails found racecourses, especially the rural ones, an ideal venue for their trade, where they could take advantage of country people who probably only attended a few local meets

Figure 25. Summary justice is dispensed to the three-card trick man at the Mullingar races.

and were easily duped by the slickness of the promoters of these games and the encouragement of their accomplices (Figure 25).[135]

The list of fairground type attractions available at the 1899 Athlone meet was extensive and 'exotic'. As well as the standard roulette and thimble-riggers, there was 'the figure of a soldier attired somewhat after the fashion of a Turkish Bashi bazank', to which spectators invested the sum of one penny for the opportunity to throw three balls at 'his much abused head'. Behind another screen of canvas were figures in 'male and female guise deriving melancholy consolation from two short pipes and apparently sympathising with each other on the ill-treatment of fate'. There was also the representation of 'some birds of foreign plume one of which presented the investor of a penny with his or her fortune, or an outline of his or her future life'. Most novel of all was a line of instantaneous photography by means of which, on putting a penny in the slot the investor received a portrait of his or her 'future husband, wife or mother in law', according to the slot selected. Letters from sweethearts were also supplied for the same moderate contribution.[136]

Illegal gaming activities were not always confined to the unreserved sections nor was the appeal of these activities confined to the unsophisticated masses. In Moate in 1889, for instance, 'some of the extensive gamblers, the wheel of fortune and *rouge et noire* people' were admitted to the private enclosure in front of the grandstand. Their presence provided an additional opportunity for the grandstand patrons to become involved in unregulated gambling and to engage in a form of conspicuous consumption to the benefit of the games promoters, who, according to the *Westmeath Independent* reporter, 'literally coined during the day, their tables bending down with gold, silver and copper won from the unlucky gamesters'.[137] In 1890, also at Moate, 'betting men and roulette men were present in the reserved enclosure in the same numbers as are present at the Curragh and other principal races'. There 'the itinerant gamesters made large odds on the speculation of their dupes'. Those who gambled included 'the son of a lord, a D.I. of the Constabulary and many members of the RIC.'[138] At the 1891 meet it seemed that the band of professional betters and roulette table owners had combined and succeeded in 'filching from the pockets of the guilded every spare sovereign, shilling or half-penny'.[139] Again 'the son of a lord, the daughter of do [sic], the sons of do [sic] and the male and female gentry of the district were engaged at playing and they left behind them all their cash and patience'.[140] At the revived Athlone meeting of 1899 the roulette promoters were also present in the 'sacred precinct' of the grandstand. Here the roulette provided entertainment at the intervals between the races and 'around the tables were seen many of the smart set'.[141] Illegal gambling opportunities were not confined to the course. Mullingar railway station was also used as an arena for the promotion of games. The commentator of the national journal *Sport*, took issue with the 'scandalous manner in which the railway platform at Mullingar was allowed to be crowded with roulette tables and the like', making the platform both difficult and dangerous to cross.[142]

Musical entertainment was also a significant feature of the sporting occasion. Its importance to the culture of tennis has been illustrated in Chapter 3. An event of significance could not proceed without the inclusion of music. This was included specifically to entertain those who frequented the reserved enclosure and music also provided entertainment between events. For most of the Victorian period this was provided by the military bands based in Athlone or Mullingar. The programme was dominated by classical music and contributed a sense of formality to the occasion and established status for the event. Newspaper reportage of the entertainment fulfilled a similar function. At the 1850 Westmeath Steeplechases at Mullingar, 'a portion of the band of the 85th Regiment' entertained whilst at the Athlone regatta of 1851 'the band of the 9th Regiment went up from Athlone on the Avonmore steamer and played on the shore during the day'.[143] The band of the 71st Highland Light Infantry gave a 'splendid performance of some of the most select pieces and polkas'.[144] The people's regatta of 1887 in Athlone featured musical entertainment provided by 'three excellent bands', which performed 'a variety of national and operatic airs'.[145] In 1903, at Crookedwood, the band of the 6th Battalion Rifle Brigade entertained. Earlier that week the Westmeath RIC Cycling and Athletic Club's sports could afford the luxury of having two bands present when the Mullingar Brass and Reed Band and the Band of the RIC performed.[146] The 1893 revived Athlone race meet featured the band of the Buff's Regiment.[147] In Rathowen, in 1901, it was the village fife and drum band that provided the musical entertainment at a race meet organised 'to raise funds for necessary repairs to the Catholic Church'.[148] The itinerant musicians who frequented such events entertained those excluded from the reserved enclosures. The post-1900 cultural nationalism expansion in Westmeath featured the revival of brass and reed bands. Sporting occasions provided an opportunity for these ensembles to display their abilities and in 1904 and 1905 the Mullingar Brass and Reed band performed at the Crookedwood Sports.[149] The performance of brass and reed bands were an essential feature of GAA tournaments as shown in the previous chapter.

The availability of alcohol was a critical factor in determining the success of sporting occasions. Alcohol consumption was an attractive part of the day's festivities and the granting of space to a publican at the event was an important source of finance for the meet organisers. This importance can be illustrated by the surviving minute book of the Carrick-on-Suir Athletic, Cricket and Football Club founded in 1879,[150] the club which included in its membership Maurice Davin. The club in preparation for its proposed athletic meeting planned for Easter Monday 1880 sought the views of the club president, H. L. Briscoe, on the question of the supply of 'refreshments' on the day. Briscoe requested that no drink be sold and as a result the committee decided that 'the selling or the allowing the selling of drink on that day be dispensed with'.[151] The meet was poorly supported and the committee appointed a delegation to meet with Mr Briscoe to 'explain the advisability of having refreshments on the course on the day of the next meeting'. Briscoe's approval was obtained and the sale of alcoholic drink, excluding whiskey and brandy, at future sports meets was allocated by means of tender. J. Winchester's tender of £5 to supply refreshments in the reserved enclosure and William Hearn's tender of £4 to supply the unreserved enclosure for the October meet were accepted.[152]

Drunkenness associated with sporting occasions encouraged the morally outraged to vent their disapproval in the local press. A letter writer to the *Westmeath Guardian* in September 1899 objected strongly to the hosting of sports events on the Sabbath Day and the associated heavy consumption of alcohol.[153] The writer felt that it was time that public opinion was brought to bear before it was too late:

> To stamp out such desecration on the Sabbath as is barefacedly carried on Sunday after Sunday in several villages in Westmeath, or else we may expect before long to have a 'Paris at Home.'. . . It is a well-known fact that these sports are got up for a purpose in nearly all cases by the proprietors of country public-houses, not to

encourage sports, but to encourage a horrible 'tap-room traffic' and increase the sale of porter . . . How they must chuckle with delight when they know how successful they have been in grabbing the surplus of Saturday night's pay, heedless of the cries of starving children and the wants of a poor care worn mother.

The *Westmeath Independent's* 'man in the crowd' encountered drinking tents around the course at the Athlone 1899 meet, 'each choke-full of customers, all of whom seemed to be excessively thirsty, judging from the avidity with which they consumed porter, ale, whiskey and other inebriating fluids, and the eagerness with which more was demanded and consumed'.[154]

The Athlone regattas also provided opportunity for indulgence. An insight into the cultural practices associated with these events is provided by a report on the two-day event of 1856. On the first day

> By six-o-clock, the greater portion of the spectators had returned to their houses; but we regret to learn that up to a later hour, or rather early in the morning the tents were occupied, as the night passed in scenes of drunkenness and debauchery too often attended on these events.[155]

In 1863 'foot-racing, leaping, and climbing and other games on shore' closed the days amusements. 'Delicacies' were on sale from a string of tents at which 'pigs trotters, grilled eels, gingerbread were not the least conspicuous in the bill of fare'. 'The curling smoke from the "hole in the sod" told the tale of "hot taters" or toddy.' Despite the fact that the tents 'afforded every requisite for stimulating a row' and were crowded for the day, 'Paddy probably with the fear of the Peelers before his eye, kept his hands quiet' but 'kept his feet employed elsewhere'. 'The "thumper on the flure" and the drone of the pipes indoors gave evidence that he was welting it to his heart's content.'[156]

On some occasions these attractions were the only ones that interested the spectators. At Derravaragh Lake in 1872 the regatta was only a secondary attraction as 'the proprietors of a couple of drinking booths, Aunt Sally, and roulette tables, by far, received the greater share of the time and patronage of the holiday makers who amused themselves in jig dancing in addition to imbibing the wares'.[157] William Bulfin documented the same phenomenon in the early 1900s in Athlone, where the gentry 'took the slightest interest in the races any more than the classes'.[158]

VI

Reports on the conduct of the spectators were generally positive, with the inclusion of comment on the good order in which an event was conducted an almost regular feature. The inclusion of such commentary is in itself a reflection of the extent to which the perception existed that disorder was a problem associated with the sporting occasion. So also was the heavy police presence at many race meetings. In general, over the period of this study, the number of prosecutions reported was small in proportion to the reported attendance and the number of events held. Quantification of the extent of sports-related crime is an impossible task. Newspaper reports on prosecutions heard at the local petty sessions and higher courts provide the main source of evidence relating to such occurences. There is no guarantee that court hearings were regularly reported or that detail on the minor occasions of crime were included in the reports. Rates of prosecution owed as much to the intensity and sensitivity of policing and to the definition of crime as to levels of lawbreaking.[159] Newspaper reports on disorder at a venue are less frequent after the early 1850s. The Athlone Regatta of 1850 was well ordered except 'for a few blows on the course, some old grudge settled in the fashion for which Paddy is proverbially famous'. At the 1852 event 'everything passed off quietly' with the 'exception of a few drunken skirmishes and some broken heads usual at the winding up of such amusements'.[160]

The racecourse provided a convenient venue for the ritualised communal violence associated with the faction fight. Faction fighting has been variously interpreted as mass hooliganism or as a means of expressing class resentment, but according to Ó Cadhla, faction fights were also strongly symbolic, especially when they coincided with the great events of the ritual year in vernacular culture. The Garrycastle meeting was a noted occasion for faction fighting in the 1860s. Fighting involved considerable ritual: convention established the ground rules for an event. A commemorative article published in 1899 suggested that 'the race day was made the occasion for the healing of old scores, real or imaginary, and the giving of a few too'.[161] According to this report, fights were initiated when the factions marched to the racecourse headed by their respective leaders. When the signal for the fight to commence was given, both sides 'had at one another with a degree of vigour and determination which one would expect to witness in the case of two armies fighting to decide the fate of a dynasty'.[162] The Garrycastle faction fighters originated from the Drumraney, Ballinahown and Glasson districts and were known as the 'Shanbeens' and the 'Keils' or the 'black feet' and 'white feet'.[163] The last year of the Garrycastle meet was 'disgraced by a faction fight of more than ordinary fierceness'. Faction fighting was 'a cult of the disenfranchised', according to Ó Cadhla, that allowed fighters access to an alternative world 'from that of their meagre daily allotment of work and subservience, a world in which any individual worker could embrace values and standards that might redefine him in terms of both personal accomplishment and factional honour'.[164]

Disorder and violence in the streets and access roads at the conclusion of a day's racing provided problems for the organisers and the enforcers of law and order. At the Westmeath Hunt Club races of 1892 drunkenness on the course was unusually absent, but 'the same could not be said of the streets as great numbers displayed unmistakable signs of having imbibed "not freely but too well" the majority being of the class who travel from one racing meeting to another'.[165] Stabbings, assaults on policemen and beating a man about the head with a stick were among the incidents reported before the courts. The 1868 Garry-castle race meeting was particularly riotous. Twelve were charged with disorderly conduct, nine members of a family from Bloomhill, King's county were charged with rioting at the racecourse as a result of a family feud and eight were charged with assault on a sergeant and party of the 2nd Regiment who were manning a military picket on the race-course road.[166] Large crowds assembled in a relaxed environment provided opportunities for pickpockets and the possibility of business for prostitutes. 'Professional' pickpockets travelled from event to event in search of easy pickings. The theft of a gold watch and chain from the pocket of Mullingar publican, John Rainey, at the spring races of 1905 resulted in the conviction of two Dublin pickpockets who were sen-tenced to eighteen months and twelve months imprisonment with hard labour. They were convicted despite the fact that the watch and chain were never recovered.[167] At least one woman was convicted of 'loitering in the streets of Mullingar for purposes of prostitution'.[168]

The 1873 Mullingar meet provided a case against John Gavan, who was charged with having assaulted and severely wounded on the head, with a stone, a corporal of the 23rd Welsh Fusiliers. The fact that he found 'his mother and sister drunk and fighting in a ditch by the road-side' and that his sister was in the company of a soldier did not save the defendant from a heavy fine or prison sentence in default.[169] The events of 1881, in Mullingar, provide the most extreme example of public disorder recorded following a race meeting. A number of distur-bances had taken place at the racecourse during the day including an incident in which a number of individuals were arrested and charged with a range of offences that including civilian assault, assault on a soldier, assault on a policeman ('cursing the Queen and assault', 'throwing stones at the police') and being drunk. Atypical were the events that occurred on the street that evening. An affray occurred in which soldiers and civilians united in common purpose against the police authorities. The police had attempted to arrest some soldiers of the 105th Regiment who had spent the day drinking at the races. They resisted arrest and found support from some local civilians. Police bay-onets were drawn and approximately

> fifty of the soldiers and a crowd of country people gathered around the police in menacing attitudes and at the same time addressed them in most opprobrious epithets. One of the soldiers struck a mounted policeman's horse a severe blow with a stick and on being arrested, the civilians retired behind a farm house, from which they hurled volley after volley of stones at the police. A couple of the con-stabulary were severely injured.

Troop reinforcements were drawn from the Mullingar army barracks to quell the disturbances and at the petty sessions court two soldiers were sentenced to six months imprisonment with hard labour and a third to two months with hard labour.[170] (In what was a particularly violent occasion, evidence was also presented that police intervention prevented the development of a faction fight between men from the Curraghmore area of Mullingar.[171]) This was not the only occasion when disorderly behaviour did not confine itself to over-exuberant civilians. The *Westmeath Examiner* report on the Westmeath Hunt races of 1888 drew attention to the 'disgraceful conduct of a few men who belong to the Royal Irish Rifles', then stationed at Mullingar. 'Their conduct was bad in the extreme, and deserves attention at the hands of their officers, more especially at the hands of the Colonel who is popular with those of the people with whom he mixes.'[172]

The 1894 Athlone meet provided a large number of candidates for the local petty sessions court, although the *Westmeath Independent* reporter was comforted by the fact that the twenty-seven who were arrested were 'not in any way identified with our town or its surroundings. The offenders were for the most part tramps or suspected pickpockets, who got drunk out of spite for losing their expected profits on drink.' So many were arrested for drunk and disorderly offences and 'undecent [sic] language' that the cell accommodation in the Brawney barracks was inadequate to cater for the offenders, so that 'the bedrooms of the RIC, the kitchen and other available locked up apartments, were utilised'.[173] Some of the itinerant vendors and gamesters found themselves arrested for practising their trades on the streets on race evening. In 1889 at Athlone, Peter Doyle was arrested for playing the three-card-trick outside the Palace Bar on the night of the races and was sentenced to fourteen days imprisonment. James Dinegan from Mullingar and a 'trick of the loop' exponent had a very successful day at the races but his alcohol-fuelled celebrations ended with an attack on an arresting constable which was punished with a six-month's imprisonment.[174]

Welching bookmakers were also part of the racing scene ('an ever-recurring nuisance' according to the *Midland Reporter*), and instances of duped punters were reported in the contemporary press.[175] These were bookmakers who accepted bets from punters, often at particularly attractive odds, but disappeared with the punters' cash during the course of the meet. Two incidents were reported from Athlone in 1901. A bookmaker operating within the enclosure absconded after the end of the third race with fifteen guineas of the punters' cash. 'The man in the crowd' who reported for the *Westmeath Independent* invested 'a winning but modest sum in the first race' but on returning to collect his winnings all that remained of the 'refinedly-cruel bookie was a tattered account-book, a square yard of green baize and a mineral water case'.[176] John Garland, who claimed to be a Manchester bookmaker, attending the Westmeath Polo Club races in September 1899 was not as lucky, as

he failed to make his escape from Mullingar. Garland had miscalcu-
lated the odds on one of the winning horses at the races and in 'a fit of
temporary absent mindedness was leaving the course without fulfilling
his engagements' when 'some parties interested doubted the purity of
his intentions and forcefully detained him'. Saved by the intervention
of the police, Garland later turned up at Mullingar railway station
where he was detained for assaulting a railway official and being
drunk and disorderly.[177] The former offence earned him a sentence of
one month in prison with hard labour and for being drunk and disorderly he was fined five shillings.[178]

The most serious incident of sports-related crime occurred at the
Crookedwood sports meeting of 1898. John Gaffney was charged before
the Grand Jury at Mullingar with having 'unlawfully, feloniously, wil-
fully and with malice afterthought killed and murdered Daniel
McKeown'. The charge followed the death of McKeown as a result of a

Figure 26. Trouble for a welching Bookmaker

stabbing incident on the road outside the sports ground on the evening of 21 June 1898, after both men had spent several hours consuming alcohol. Gaffney, in evidence to the magisterial enquiry, explained that he was attacked as a result of his friendship with a water bailiff and produced the knife to defend himself while he was assaulted several times by McKeown. Gaffney pleaded not guilty but in the course of the trial changed the plea to manslaughter. The mitigating circumstances and the suggestion that Gaffney's difficulties arose from his friendship with an individual associated with the legalities of rural life impressed the presiding judge to the extent that he imposed a particularly lenient sentence of twelve months' imprisonment.[179]

A similar stabbing incident with less serious consequences happened at the 1899 sports and resulted in a magisterial investigation following which Michael Connor, Kiltoom was charged with 'unlawfully and maliciously wounding with a knife, Thomas Delamere, from Lacken, Multyfarnham, on 27 June at Crookedwood'.[180] Connor was a gardener employed by Lord Longford. This incident happened following an evening spent drinking at the tent of John Gaynor. A row that involved 'eight or twelve people' ended with the stabbing of Delamere. Both parties made their escape on Lough Derravaragh in two separate boats before they were ordered to return to shore by policemen present. Medical evidence described Delamere's wound as 'a clean cut wound on the head about an inch long', which did not present any great threat to his future welfare. The Resident Magistrate Mr P. D. Sullivan returned Connor for trial to the Quarter Sessions despite the fact that the case was 'clearly one of circumstantial evidence'.[181]

This racecourse and associated sports-venue-fuelled violence was not a particularly Westmeath or national phenomenon. Wray Vamplew has documented the extent to which race meetings and other sporting events were frequently scenes of violence in Britain. He exonerated the criminal element for much of this violence and blamed the troubles on a notoriously rowdy and aggressive British working class. 'Violence seemed to be an inevitable accompaniment of any event attended by the less respectable of working men'. The ready availability of sex, alcohol, gambling and the activities of the criminal fraternity served to aggravate the situation.[182]

VII

Management and organising committees, stewards and the forces of law and order adopted various approaches to improve the conduct of sport and its spectators. Wray Vamplew has identified five major methods of crowd control in operation by the end of the century. These included improvements in the conduct of the sport, improvement in the organisation of the events, segregation within the crowd, control of ancillary activities and the use of control agents.[183] Although Vamplew's research was confined to British sport, Irish organising committees adopted similar strategies. In Chapter 2 the methods by which the Turf Club and the INHSC extended control over all aspects of Irish racing and how steeplechasing became increasingly codified was outlined. Evidence of malpractice (such as foul riding) enraging spectators or of spectators interfering in a race is rare in Westmeath. Evidence of the abandonment of football games because of violence is similarly difficult to find. Reference has already been made to the abandonment of the 1890 Westmeath football final when the Moate team left the field because of the partisanship of the Athlone supporters. The riding of Frank Mitchell on The Admiral at Cullion in 1891 was a rare example of a crowd taking exception to a jockey's performance in which an incensed 'mob invaded the tent, abused the officers and otherwise misconducted themselves'.[184]

One of the greatest difficulties faced by race committees and stewards on race day was maintaining order during a race, as it was common for excited spectators to crowd on to the course, particularly as a race reached its final stages. In an era when the use of flags was often the only means of identifying the course and the use of a roped home straight the most permanent means of course identity, the tendency of spectators to crowd onto the course in the excitement of a finish represented a real threat to the safety of spectators, horses and jockeys. The lack of a race-viewing etiquette amongst the public reached a tragic conclusion at the Castlepollard meet of July 1887 when a widow called Jane Kiernan was knocked down by two horses as they passed the finishing post and died a number of days later as a result of the injuries received.[185] Organising committees designated personnel to keep the course clear. At hunt club events the huntsman and his support staff often fulfilled this duty. The 'mounted artillery kept the course clear' in Athlone in 1900.[186]

Interference in the actual running of a race was occasionally reported. The Glynwood Cup was one of the feature events of the Garrycastle meet. In 1868, Christopher Usher, the jockey of Souvenir, one of the favoured horses for the event, was a victim of such interference. On the second round of the race, he was approached by a man with a 'large stick which appeared to be a young tree'. A blow aimed at the jockey missed its target but connected with the horse, forcing it to stagger and lose the prestigious race. As a result Red Tape, the property of John Malone, succeeded in winning the trophy for the third successive time.[187] Encroachment, rather than player violence, posed problems at football matches and indeed at race courses also. In the era of the unenclosed venue the playing or racing ground tended to get smaller as excitement mounted. The military authorities at Athlone, in an attempt to deal with this problem, erected a boundary of stakes and ropes around the football enclosure at the Queen's Meadow in order 'to keep the ground for the players'.[188]

The control of ancillary activities was the most important restriction introduced at the local level. In particular the consumption of alcohol was regulated. Race organisers had to balance the importance of finances raised from the sale of drinking booth space against the potential destructive impact of drink-fuelled feuds on the good order and reputation of an event. Measures introduced to control drinking varied over the course of the half-century. Clerical intervention was important at various times in the fifty-five years covered by this book. The intervention of one of the most important power brokers in the Moate district, Canon Kearney, led to a total ban on the sale of intoxicating liquor at the Moate meeting between 1889 and 1898. This ban impacted on attendance, with contemporary reports attributing the reduced attendance at the 1890 meet to the ban. However, this restriction had a positive impact, as the good order and discipline displayed during the day was attributed to the fact that 'no refreshment tents were allowed on, even for the sale of mineral water'.[189] The importance of drink to the carnival of racing was evident in the town of Moate as Canon Kearney's ban extended to the sale of alcohol in the town on race morning. According to one report the town 'appeared to be in mourning and not rejoicing over the races', and 'publicans and other establishments had their shutters up and strangers asked who of importance is dead'.[190] The reporter commented, oblivious to the irony involved, that 'the course and its surroundings, crowded with spectators had no excitement thanks to Canon Kearney'.[191] The ban on the sale of alcohol in the town, however, did not survive. In 1894, on the morning of the races

> The licensed houses were crowded with holiday seekers who appeared at the time to have a superabundance of cash and to spend same without any compunction of conscience in honour of the races.[192]

Kearney was not the first cleric to take action to prevent the sale of alcohol at a Westmeath race meet. In 1840, there was no whiskey sold on the Mullingar course as 'Father Masterson made sad havoc amongst the bottles and jars'.[193] The organisers of the 1868 Mullingar event recruited the moral authority of the Catholic Church. At Sunday services clergy directed their congregations to abstain from intoxicating drinks and quarrels. The advice had an impact as the meet passed without serious incident.[194]

Race committees tacitly accepted the problems of alcohol sale and the necessity for its control by approving the establishment of temperance booths on the courses. In the 1890s, in Athlone and Mullingar, temperance clubs were active in providing an alternative to the beer and spirit booths. In Athlone, the Fr Mathew Club established a booth where 'a bottle of lemonade and cup of tea and a sandwich', were available. This served the needs of those who objected to the sale of strong liquor and those who refused to 'consume the minerals and cakes vended by the nomadic tribes'.[195] In Mullingar, following the commercialisation of the sport, the National Workingmen's Club, prompted by Catholic curate,

Rev. P. Barry, provided a temperance marquee at Newbrook. Fr Barry suggested that a marquee that supplied a 'good drink of spring water made palatable by an ingredient' such as 'limejuice syrup' would provide a viable alternative to the places where 'spirituous liquors were sold' and patrons 'exposed to grave temptations'.[196] The initiative was re-ported to have been a total success and was continued in later events.[197]

Another important control measure was magisterial intervention. On occasion magistrates handed down exemplary sentences to send a message that future examples of drunken rowdiness would not be tol-erated. This policy resulted in two women who were charged with assaulting a partly blind man on the road home from the Loughegar races of 1879 being sentenced to two months imprisonment with hard labour. The resident magistrate, Captain Barry, pointed out that 'the magistrates were determined to put a stop to such conduct as this, which frequently occurs at races'.[198]

Magistrates and police combined to regulate the number of drinking-booth licences issued, to limit the hours when the booths were opened and to refuse licences to those who had been convicted of breaches of the licensing laws. Athlone solicitor John Gaynor was one of the main personalities involved in the promotion of the Garrycastle races and he experienced the full rigour of the legal authorities' concerns when he applied, on behalf of the race committee, for temporary licences for eight publicans who sought permission to erect tents for the sale of drink at the races of 1899. The presiding RM, Captain Preston, decreed that only those who could use their power properly would be granted licences. Three of the applicants were refused because of convictions for minor (non-racing) breaches of the laws over the previous years and a fourth was refused as he had been prosecuted on three occasions but not convicted. The four licence-holders were restricted to selling drink between the hours of twelve and six and permission was accompanied by a stern warning from the Magistrate that

> Those who have these licences should be very careful as to whom they serve drink, as if there is any drunkenness in future I would be opposed to the granting of any licence at all.[199]

Police maintained vigilance on race day and ensured that the temporary licence holders did not abuse their privilege.[200] The cautious approach to the issuing of licences to sell alcohol had its impact on the good order and control at the Athlone races. The 1902 meeting was distinguished by 'practically the entire absence of disorderliness'. 'There was not a single unseemly incident to interrupt the harmony and good-fellowship that prevailed amongst the crowd.'[201] An incident at the Mullingar races in 1902 became somewhat of a local cause célèbre when the publicans, John and Margaret Gonoud, were charged and eventually fined £1 for serving alcohol to an already intoxicated person and for permitting drunkenness on their premises at Newbrook.[202]

The maintenance of good order at the racecourse became a commercial imperative from 1890 onwards, when the Mullingar races were promoted by a limited company specifically incorporated for the purpose. The company invested all profits up to 1903 in ground and course infrastructure. Once enclosure was completed there was a threat to gate receipts if crowd disorder and on-course annoyance deterred paying customers from attending. Prior to enclosure the company increased the police presence by organising a battalion of the Dublin Metropolitan Police to maintain order inside the course.[203] The Mullingar RIC were responsible for maintaining order outside the venue and on race days maintained a high-profile presence on the road from the railway station to the racecourse. This policy, not surprisingly, met with the approval of the local press. The *Westmeath Examiner* comments on the 1898 summer meet:

> Under the supervision of a large contingent of the Metropolitan Police, the order of the course was well maintained, not a hitch occurring to mar the harmony or enjoyment of the occasion whilst the RIC as regulators of the heavy traffic on the road to the course could not be excelled.[204]

In the new century, evidence from the newspapers strongly suggests that the racecourse behaviour of the 'general public' had improved considerably. According to reports 'drunkenness seemed to be scarcely present at all, clamour and fights and indifferent language were also entirely absent on the (Mullingar) course'. The good order and decorum evident in the ring was replicated 'in the betting and other pursuits of the public outside'.[205] The final stage in the modernisation of racing in the county was achieved in Mullingar in 1903 when work on the boundary wall was completed and, from the spring meet of April 1903, an entry fee of 6d was charged with 'no change given at the turnstile'.[206] Racing at Mullingar was now commodified and commercialised, fundamentally changing the relationship between spectators and the race company. As paying customers, spectators now expected minimum standards of comfort when attending a race meet. Enclosure enabled the most extreme form of segregation to be introduced (the exclusion of undesirables from the venue). The impact was immediate as at the summer meet of 1903 spectators were relieved of 'the torment of tramps and others begging on the course'.[207] Again the response of the local media was positive; the *Westmeath Examiner* reported that at the 1905 summer meet there 'was not one row or sign of disorder, and the conduct of the thousands of people assembled was highly credible in every way'. Enclosure according to the report aided 'good order and real enjoyment of sport and has helped to bring about a vast change from what was experienced previously, when brawls and the annoyance of all sorts of nomads were naturally to be faced, as on other open courses and were unpleasant experiences of the day's outing'.[208] 'The enjoyable character of a day at the races on any part of the course is now clearly realised whilst rows, riots, bad language and drunken brawls are practically a thing of the past on such occasions.'[209]

VIII

In conclusion, it is clear that sports events in the county were capable of attracting large crowds, in some cases proportionally larger crowds than those (reportedly) attending events of national importance. It has been suggested that crowds assembled at a function were of two types: those that were spectators of an event and those that were participants in an event.[210] Spectators at a sports event embraced both of these aspects. They participated in many of the ancillary events, both formal and informal and some of dubious legality, that were a by-product of the core business of the occasion. These activities provided much of the attraction of the occasion for the masses. The development of rail transport was crucial in transforming sports events into mass appeal events. This travel facility brought tremendous potential for personal liberation, albeit on a temporary basis. It made possible personal indulgence outside residential territorial boundaries and brought liberation from the arbiters of social convention and respectability. Perhaps the real attraction of races and other sports events was that they provided an arena where this sense of liberation could be achieved.

Epilogue

The key finding emerging from this study is the extent to which sporting involvement was a product of the class structure of Westmeath society. Developments within the county were typical of those in the wider world as the most recent study of Victorian sport has claimed: 'Victorian sporting experience was largely a product and a reflection of social class . . . class was a major fault line in sporting culture.'[1] In Westmeath, social class largely determined the type of sport played as well as the age, gender and conjugal status of the individual involved. The detailed social analysis of sportspeople in Westmeath from 1850 to 1905 has revealed that in general, different classes were involved in their own specific sports and that participation by the unskilled and semi-skilled in the new 'commercial sports' (developed from the 1880s onwards), was non-existent. Table 20 summarises the social class characteristics of the individual participants in the main sports examined in this study and provides the quantitative evidence for conclusions relating to the class characteristics of the different activities. The illustrated pattern has been examined in depth in the individual chapters and the sample size is sufficiently large to formulate valid conclusions.

| Sport | Sample | SOCIAL CLASS | | | | Average age |
		A	B	C	D	
Cricket (1900–02)	227	1.30	26.00	25.12	47.58	24.63
Cycling (1891–98)	48	20.84	14.58	64.58	0	27.72
Football (1892–1905)	357	0	37.53	31.37	31.10	22.07
Golf (1904)	83	86.77	12.02	1.21	0	39.68
Hunting (1900)	114	86.84	13.16	0	0	44.67
Hurling (1904)	82	0	35.37	47.56	17.07	24.96
Polo (1905)	70	100.00	0	0	0	46.51
Soccer (1900–04)	75	0	28.00	49.33	22.67	22.55
Tennis (1890–1901)	92	96.73	1.09	2.18	0	38.55

Table 20. Social classes of individual participants of main sports

Hunting was totally dominated by members of social class A until the mid-1880s when a number of wealthy 'bona fide' farmers became eligible and accepted as members of the Westmeath County Hunt Club.

Sports such as polo, golf and tennis remained the almost total preserve of the aristocracy and gentry and the members of the higher status professions comfortably positioned in social class A. This finding is remarkably similar to that of Tranter for central Scotland despite the different structures of the economies of the two districts.[2] The social origins of cricketers were the most varied of the sports examined. Cricket underwent the most extraordinary metamorphosis during the period of this study, as it changed from an activity confined to the landed gentry in the 1850s to one in which all classes participated by the end of the century, and was dominated by the farm labourers of social class D. It was the only sport availed of by all classes, although by the end of the century gentry participation was limited to individual challenge or novelty events. Cycling's appeal for the lower middle classes is confirmed by the evidence from Westmeath where over six out of every ten cyclists, mainly shop assistants and clerks, were members of social class C. It also had some appeal for the higher status professionals of social class A. The physical contact sports of football, soccer and hurling drew roughly 70 per cent of their participant base from classes B and C. In the urban context, these were the shop assistants and clerks and the skilled tradesmen while in the rural context class B was dominated by farmers' sons whose economic status and flexibility of work arrangements allowed greater freedom to participate in sport than the labourers of class D. The evidence suggests that GAA sports did not provide the same recreational opportunities for the labouring classes as supplied by cricket. The implication of this finding from Westmeath for both the history of the GAA and the wider history of recreation is a topic worthy of further investigation.

Social class also influenced the average age of participants and their conjugal status. The average age of the participants and the age range they exhibit suggests that for some from social group A involvement in sport and ancillary socialisation was lifelong. These individuals, by means of their wealth, social status and educational backgrounds, were able to access age-appropriate sports. For instance, 77 per cent of the hunting subscribers identified in 1900 were married. At the other end of the social scale, sport was overwhelmingly the preserve of the young and single man. The conjugal status was partly a product of the age profile of the participants. Delayed marriage characterised the demographics of nineteenth-century rural Ireland.[3] The age-profile of hurlers, footballers, soccer and cricket players was of the age-group that remained largely unmarried. In Westmeath in 1901, only one individual from a total of 3,210 in the15–19 age-group was married and of the 20–24 age-group only 2.67 per cent were married.[4] Marriage brought responsibilities and new financial obligations to a group with limited disposable income and lifestyle decisions had to be made that restricted recreation, a process that did not impact on the higher social classes. In Belfast, 35 per cent of the young men who played professional football for remuneration continued their involvement in the game after marriage.[5] Clearly, the financial implications of marriage impacted on the lower social classes' lifestyle choices.

Tennis, of the sports examined in this study, was the one that displayed the greatest devotional identity with individual membership confined almost exclusively to members of the Church of Ireland community, in which several of the participants were active in church administration. Golf was far more accessible to the Catholic professional and the denomination formed 42 per cent of the identified sample. There was a strong Catholic presence amongst the hunting community throughout the period.[6] Cricket almost exactly replicated the religious structure of the population as a whole in the county. In general, the religious mix exhibited by the participants in the football codes and hurling is comparable with the religious make-up of the social classes who were the main participants.

The sports club provided the institutional framework around which sporting participation was managed and organised. In numerical terms, the sports club was the most important vehicle for socialisation and the maintenance of social networks in the county. They heavily outnumbered self-help organisations, voluntary, temperance and political societies.[7] A key finding of this study is the relationship between the lifespan of a club and its financial circumstances. This is also a function of the class structure. Essentially, clubs with a more middle-class membership were more stable institutions and fluctuation in their membership was less pronounced.[8] The clubs established in Westmeath that catered for the recreational pleasures of the upper and middle classes had emerged at the end of the century as stable and established institutions. The members could afford the financial investment to acquire a specialised permanent and privatised location that was specifically used for sport and ancillary entertainment, develop a basic pavilion, employ a caretaker or maintenance person to maintain the facilities, and on occasion, hire professional expertise to teach the basic skills of the sport. Financial problems experienced by these clubs could be overcome in a variety of ways, including increased membership and entrance fees, sourcing donations from wealthy patrons, the operation of bank overdrafts, retrenchment, and in the case of the Westmeath Hunt Club, the recruitment of a wealthy benefactor as master. Inability to gain access to an appropriate venue or the loss through migration or death of key individuals was also critical in bringing about club demise. These factors in particular were important in the demise of several clubs that catered for the sporting interests of the lower social classes.

This examination of Westmeath sport has provided important insights into the recreational habits of women. Social class was critical in influencing participation. Although the numbers involved were small and confined to the upper and middle classes, some Victorian and Edwardian Westmeath women were more dynamic and active participants in sport than the accepted norm would permit.[9] There is evidence from Westmeath that women participated in at least fourteen different sports, including individual sports such as archery, athletics, tennis, badminton, table-tennis, golf, croquet, cycling; field sports, such as hunting, fishing and shooting, and team sports such as hockey and as a novelty event, cricket.[10] Divorcee, Mrs Locke, and her two daughters, Mrs Batten and Flo Locke, were competent point-to-point riders and had a number of winning rides to their credit.[11] It has also been suggested that one Westmeath lady was responsible for the intro-duction of archery to Ireland.[12] In some of the activities women were competitively involved and the range of disciplines involved demanded various degrees of courage, stamina, strength and skill from the participants.[13] Women were full and active participants in hunting and were frequently commended for their ability. Stamina, strength, skill and courage were all required in the high-speed chases that epitomised the hunt and several Westmeath women established their status as high-calibre sportswomen in these chases. Undoubtedly, the suggestion of Hargreaves that the sportswoman at the end of the century was a submissive creature who avoided over-exertion and bodily display and 'represented the embellishment of man', typified the involvement of many Westmeath women in sport, but some were also active and competitive and were prepared to travel extensively to satisfy their competitive instincts.[14] These were the women whose per-sonal circumstances allowed them to ignore contemporary attitudes and restrictive conventions.

Tony Collins has suggested in his study of rugby league football that 'periods separated by relatively short spans of time can be profoundly different, especially as perceived by the participants themselves, a fact which is especially true of late Victorian sport'.[15] A similar summation can be used in relation to the GAA evidence that has emerged from this study. The foundation of the GAA in 1884 was partly inspired by the contemporary demands for legislative independence and land reform and represented an attempt to establish an Irish model for managing, codifying and promoting athletics, football and hurling. The split in the constitutional nationalist movement, difficulties arising from the takeover of the association by the revolutionaries of the IRB and associ-ated Catholic Church opposition, contributed to the demise of the GAA in the early 1890s. The GAA collapsed because it was devoid of any cul-tural support-structure to counteract the loss of political stimulation. More practical considerations such as difficulties with the codification process and an unwillingness to accept the authority of controlling com-mittees were also extremely important.

A decade later, circumstances had changed dramatically and the GAA re-emerged, buoyed by the development of cultural nationalism that promoted the concept of Irish-Ireland. This study has identified the importance of this development in Westmeath and its impact in creating a sense of national identity in which the playing of games identified as Irish was centrally significant. The Gaelic League played a key role in the creation of this sense of identity and personnel associated with the organisation were important ambassadors of hurling for certain districts in the county. Hurling and football challenged the dominance of cricket in rural Westmeath. The latter activity was now disadvantaged through its strong negative associations with West Britonism. Hurling in Ireland is regionally demarcated and the extent to which this is a product of the presence or absence of a Gaelic League activist is also an area worthy of further investigation. Discontinuity is a key feature of GAA history, and the evidence presented in this study would suggest that the long-term impact of the post-1900 cultural nationalist inspired movement, is of greater significance than the events of the 1884–94 era. The real water-shed in GAA inspired recreational practice is a product of the revival of the organisation and not of its inception; in Westmeath 1905 is the key year in this revival.

The important role played by military garrisons in the promotion of Irish sport has been a recurring theme in the limited analysis devoted to Irish sports history. This perception resulted in cricket and soccer in par-ticular achieving a popular identity as garrison games. Generalisations on the ambassadorial role of the military in recreational matters have been made without any supportive quantification. The conclusions from this Westmeath study are based on empirical data. Army officers used sport as a means of achieving integration into the social networks of local landed society that allowed them to continue uninterrupted a lifestyle that revolved around participation in field sports in particular. Military importance in local cricket declined as the century progressed and by the time cricket was targeted for its anti-national characteristics, army involvement had virtually ceased in the county. Soccer had replaced cricket as the popular sport with army personnel. The presence of two garrisons in Athlone played a crucial role in the popularisation of soccer in that town in the 1890s. Their role in the diffusion of the codes and regulations of the sport and its tactical nuances was critical. Army teams provided regular opposition for civilian teams and as a result, Athlone teams competed without rancour and successfully at provincial level in the 1890s. Disputes created by unfamiliarity with Gaelic football codes precipitated the decision of the core group of Athlone soccer players to withdraw from the GAA in 1893.

Players for golf, tennis, cricket and soccer teams were occasionally recruited from regiments in Athlone and Mullingar. Army officers were recruited to the post of MFH, the most important position available in nineteenth-century sport. Clubs also benefited financially from military association. Regimental donations and the subscriptions of individual officers were important sources of finance for race and regatta organ-isers as well as polo, hunting, tennis and golf clubs. Specific fundraising events such as drama promotions were organised by regiments. At the

most basic level, regimental bands provided much of the musical entertainment that was an integral part of the sporting occasion.

The centrality of sport in creating a social life for its practitioners is
clearly evident from this study. Sport became the conduit for socialisation that took place outside the boundaries of the field of play and
provided an 'after life' beyond the sporting event. The winter months,
for landlords and their families, were dominated by hunting. The
central importance of hunting to the lifestyles of the elite is clear from
Lady Fingall's statement that 'if you didn't hunt in Meath you might as
well be dead'.[16] The winter social diaries of hunting devotees revolved
around hunt meets, point-to-point and race meets, attendance at social
occasions hosted at the residences of similarly-minded families, culmi-
nating in the hunt ball, the annual social highlight for county society.
From the 1880s polo enabled a similar process of socialisation to continue over the summer months for many of the hunting fraternity. The
new sports of the 1880s and 1890s provided an additional layer to this
process. The development of tennis made possible the arrangement of a
summer social calendar that was inclusive of all family members and
was a critical factor in its popularity among the landed gentry at the
time. John Lowerson has highlighted the importance of this aspect of
sport for the middle classes but it was important for all classes that were
involved in recreation. The social activities organised around the football match were an important part of the culture of the stable GAA club.
One of the attractions of football, when it was introduced to the county
in the 1890s, was that it allowed participants to maintain and extend
social networks that had been developed over a summer of cricket
involvement. The post-match meal and entertainment were central elements of the early football clubs' activities, particularly the more
successful ones, and may have had a limiting effect on membership.
Participation in these rituals, as well as transport costs to away matches,
required that those involved had some disposable income available for
investment in recreation. Cultural nationalists of the early 1900s found
the socialisation associated with cricket and soccer objectionable; as
Patrick Maume has suggested they 'endangered national virtue through
socialisation with anti-national elements'.[17]

This book examines sports development in a society characterised by
declining population and absence of significant industrialisation. Neither
of these factors proved inimical to sporting development. Nor was
peripheral location an obstacle to sporting innovation and opportunity.
The landed gentry of social class A as members of 'a supra-national class'
embracing the whole of the British Isles were quickly introduced to the
latest recreational innovation. Mobility was a characteristic feature of this
class and evidence from surviving diaries confirms this facet of gentry
lifestyle and illustrates the variety of recreational activities experienced
by individuals from this class on their frequent trips to England.[18] Such
was the commonality of interest between the leading elements of society

that developments in Westmeath were similar in many instances to UK-wide recreational and sporting developments. Geographic peripherality provided no barrier to recreational progress as can be seen from the range of sports that developed, the impact of codification, the increased commercialisation of sport and the central role of sport in the socialisation process. The range of sports institutionalised in club form is illustrated in Appendix 20.

Many people in the period covered by this book experienced sport as spectators and the multi-dimensional importance of this outlet in the lives of the different classes is clear. In the second half of the nineteenth century (with the curtailment of the traditional forms of entertainment), access to a sporting event and to the racecourse in particular provided one form of popular entertainment and celebration. The racecourse was a cross-class, multi-dimensional entertainment venue that offered free entry to the majority of spectators. Race meetings provided the excitement of the races, carnivalesque celebration, displays of wealth and privilege, opportunities for drinking and faction fighting, and the opportunity to experience a variety of formal and informal entertainment. For one local observer the racecourse was a venue for 'buffoonery, deception, double dealing and disorder', a day when there seemed to be 'a traditional licence for indulgence'.[19] The course provided relief for the masses from the hardship of rural life and brightened 'the humdrum every day life in the country'.[20]

The impact of sport on the business and economy of the county is an aspect that is worthy of further examination. As the surviving quantitative data is imprecise and fragmentary, it is impossible to determine the exact amount of capital invested in sport, the number of people employed and their earnings. Nevertheless, it is possible to make some evaluation of the economic importance of sport. Sport was potentially profitable to several sectors of the embryonic sport industry according to Huggins.[21] In Westmeath, the increased importance of sport as the century progressed amplified its economic significance. The development of commercial sports provided new retail opportunities for owners of drapery, hardware and ironmongery stores. By the end of the century at least one specialist bicycle store had opened for business in both Athlone and Mullingar. Newspaper proprietors' advertising revenue increased. Any attempt to interfere with the sanctity of hunting was normally challenged by newspaper letters from apologists that stressed the economic importance of the sport to the county. In 1897, it was estimated that £12,050 was annually expended on hunting alone. This excluded the actual cost of living and rent of people settled in the county and the contribution made by people who lived in the county because of the quality of its hunting. In fifty years, in excess of £600,000 had been invested in hunting in the county, it was claimed. Horses regularly hunted had their value increased. The annual Horse Show, the hunt ball and the three race meetings owed their origin and maintenance to hunting, in addition to 'the profits made and the money circulated by horse breeding, training and selling'.[22] In 1902, T. F. Levinge estimated that both directly and indirectly the expenditure on hunting was between £20,000 and £30,000 annually in the county.[23] A number of people were employed to service the growing needs of sports-club members and participants. A. J. Pilkington and James Cheshire earned a living as horse trainers. At the time of his retirement in 1900, Will Matthews earned £250 annually as huntsman to the West-meath Hunt Club. Angling and in particular fly-fishing associated with the rise of the May-fly, brought visitors to Mullingar to enjoy the sport on Lough Owel and Lough Ennell.[24] Less formal employment was available to golf caddies, golf-course attendants, stablemen, hunt ser-vants such as earth-stoppers, boatmen and builders, yachting hands on the Shannon and Lough Ree, ticket collectors at race meetings, and tradesmen who prepared temporary stands for sporting events.

In attempting to gain an insight into the role played by sport in the recreational habits of all sections of Westmeath society during the Victo-rian and early Edwardian periods, the evidence produced in this study contributes to the historiography of Irish sport and sport in general. It is the first study to examine empirically sports development and partici-pation rates in the Irish context, at the level of the county.[25] Until we have more detailed local studies of the type attempted here it will not be possible to make quantitative generalisations on the characteristics of Irish sporting development. The absence of local and regional studies of Irish sport has more than likely distorted the true picture of the nature of Irish sports development. Meaningful qualitative second-order com-parative study must depend on carefully researched local studies.[26] The research of a number of such studies can provide the foundation mate-rial for the national synthesis of Irish sports history.

Notes and references

A NOTE ON SOURCES AND METHODOLOGY

1 For a general review of the importance of the newspaper and other media to sport in Victorian times see Mike Huggins, *The Victorians and sport* (London, 2004), pp. 141–66. For a more specific examination in an Irish context see Paul Rouse, 'Sport and Ireland in 1881', in Alan Bairner (ed.), *Sport and the Irish: histories, identities, issues* (Dublin, 2005), pp. 7–21.

2 The *Westmeath Guardian* was published between 8 January 1835 and 19 October 1928. The *Westmeath Independent* was first published in 1846 and is still published today. The *Westmeath Examiner* was first published on 23 September 1882 and it also still survives, while the *Westmeath Nationalist and Midland Reporter* began publication on 30 April 1891 as an anti-Parnellite, pro-clerical newspaper to provide an alternative voice to the pro-Parnellite, anti-clerical *Westmeath Examiner*. It continued as the *Midland Reporter and Westmeath Nationalist* from 23 September 1897 until 21 September 1939 when it ceased publication. With the exception of the *Westmeath Independent*, where some issues are missing for the early 1880s, a continuous run of the other papers was available and they were interrogated for the purpose of this study.

3 *WG*, 5 November 1886.

4 *WG*, 2 September 1887.

5 *WE*, 9 September 1893.

6 *WI*, 25 December 1897.

7 See in particular Peter Hart's, *The IRA and its enemies: violence and community in Cork, 1916–1923* (Oxford, 1998). Hart used information from the 1911 census forms to establish the social composition of the IRA in Cork. See also Michael Farry, *The aftermath of revolution: Sligo, 1921–23* (Dublin, 2000), who compiled similar reconstructions.

8 Form A recorded the household data, giving details of individual persons in each house, including their names, their relationship to the heads of households, place of birth, age, marital status, religious profession, occupation, education and ability to speak the Irish language.

9 Neil Tranter, 'The chronology of organised sport in nineteenth-century Scotland: a regional study. Patterns' in *International Journal of the History of Sport*, vol. 7, no. 2, 1990, pp. 188–203.

10 *Sport*, 23 December 1893.

11 Neil Tranter, 'The social and occupational structure of organized sport in Central Scotland during the nineteenth century', in *International Journal of the History of Sport*, vol. 4, no. 1, 1987, pp. 308–9.

12 W.A. Armstrong, 'The use of information about occupations', in E.A. Wrigley (ed.), *Nineteenth-Century Society* (Cambridge, 1992), pp. 191–310.

13 Thomas Hunt, 'The development of sport in Westmeath, 1850–1905', Ph.D thesis, De Montfort University, Leicester, 2005.

14 *Census of Ireland*, 1901, 64.

INTRODUCTION

1 W. F. Mandle, The *Gaelic Athletic Association & Irish nationalist politics*, 1884–1924 (Dublin, 1987), p. 14.

2   Neil Tranter, 'The chronology of organised sport in nineteenth–century Scotland: a regional study, I. Patterns', in *International Journal of the History of Sport*, vol. 7, no. 2, 1990, p. 188.

3   Neal Garnham, *Association football and society in pre–partition Ireland* (Belfast, 2004), pp. 7, 43.

4   Neal Garnham, 'Accounting for the early success of the Gaelic Athletic Association', in *Irish Historical Studies*, vol. xxxiv, no. 133, May 2004, p. 65.

5   William A. Menton, *The Golfing Union of Ireland, 1891–1991* (Dublin, 1991), p. 17.

6   Chris Glennon (ed.), *90 years of the Irish Hockey Union* (Naas, n.d.), p. 66.

7   Garnham, *Association football*, pp. 6–13.

8   Census of Ireland, 1881 [C–3042–VII], p. 869; Census of Ireland, 1901 [Cd 847.–IX.], p.vii; Census of Ireland, 1911 [Cd. 6049–X], p. vii. The percentages are based on those over five years of age in the early census years but in 1911 the percentage was based on those over nine years of age who could read and write.

9   Garnham, *Association football*, pp. 8–13. Tom Hunt, 'Mullingar sport in the 1890s: communities at play', in Mary Farrell (ed.), *Mullingar: essays in the history of a midlands town in the 19th century* (Mullingar, 2002), p. 3.

10 J. R. Hill (ed.), *A new history of Ireland 1921–1984* (Oxford, 2004). In addition to the political history, the work contains chapters on the economy, literature in Irish, literature in English, the visual arts, two chapters on music, the mass media, education, emigration and women.

11 For a detailed review of the recent academic writing on the growth of the GAA see Mike Cronin, 'Fighting for Ireland, playing for England? The nationalist history of the Gaelic Athletic Association and the English influence on Irish sport', in *International Journal of the History of Sport*, vol. xv, no. 3, 1998, pp. 36–56. Also Mike Cronin, *Sport and nationalism in Ireland, Gaelic games, soccer and Irish identity since 1884* (Dublin, 1999), pp. 90–111. Also Neal Garnham, 'Accounting for the early success of the Gaelic Athletic Association', pp. 65–78.

12 Another curiosity in this respect is that the best works of analysis of GAA history have been the work of scholars who have been based outside Ireland. W. F. Mandle is an Australian, Mike Cronin and Neal Garnham are English historians.

13 W. F. Mandle, 'The I.R.B. and the beginnings of the Gaelic Athletic Association', in *Irish Historical Studies*, vol. xx, no. 80, 1977, pp. 422, 432.

14 W. F. Mandle, 'The GAA and popular culture, 1884–1924', in Oliver MacDonagh, W. F. Mandle and P. Travers (eds.), *Irish culture and Irish nationalism* (London, 1993), pp. 105, 111.

15 W. F. Mandle, *The Gaelic Athletic Association & Irish nationalist politics*.

16 Ibid., pp. 13–14.

17 Mike Cronin, *Sport and nationalism*, p. 100. Cronin considers this to be the most important work ever produced that details the history of the GAA.

18 W. F. Mandle, 'Sport as politics: the Gaelic Athletic Association 1884–1916', in R. Cashman and M. McKernan (eds.), *Sport in history* (St Lucia, Queensland: University of Queensland Press, 1979), pp. 99–123.

19 Conor Cruise O'Brien, 'Foreword' in *The shaping of modern Ireland* (London, 1960), p. 16.

20 L. P. Curtis Jnr, 'Stopping the Hunt, 1881–1882: an aspect of the Irish Land War', in C. H. E. Philipin (ed.), *Nationalism and popular protest in Ireland* (Cambridge, 1987), pp. 349–401.

21 J. W. H. Carter, *The Land War and its leaders in Queen's county, 1879–82* (Portlaoise, 1994).

22 Richard Davis, 'Irish cricket and nationalism', in *Sporting Traditions*, vol. X, no. 2, 1994, pp. 77–96.

23 Neal Garnham, *Association football and society in pre–partition Ireland* (Belfast, 2004); Alan Bairner (ed.), *Sport and the Irish: histories, identities and issues* (Dublin, 2005).

24 Mike Cronin, 'Writing the history of the GAA', in *High Ball: the official GAA monthly magazine*, vol. 6, no. 6, June 2003, p. 53.

25 Paul Rouse, 'Why Irish historians have ignored sport: a note', in *The History Review*, xiv, 2003, p. 68.

26 *Census of Ireland, 1901. Part 1. Area, houses and population: also the ages, civil or conjugal condition, occupations, birthplaces, religion and education of the people. volume 1. Province of Leinster, No. 10. county of Westmeath*, [Cd. 847. IX]. 1901.

27 Ibid., p. 1.

28 S. Lewis, *Topographical dictionary of Ireland*, vol. ii (London, 1837), pp. 223.

29 *Census of Ireland*, 1901, p. 1.

30 Stephen A. Royle, 'Small towns in Ireland, 1841–1851', in Howard B. Clarke, Jacinta Prunty and Mark Hennessy (eds.), *Multidisciplinary essays in honour of Angret Simms* (Dublin, 2004), pp. 544–49.

31 Ibid., pp. 557–8.

32 Small towns in this instance are defined as those that had a population of less than 10,000.

33 *Census of Ireland*, 1901, p. vii.

34 *Slater's directory, 1894*, p. 16.

35 Alan Bairner, 'Ireland, Sport and Empire', in K. Jeffrey (ed.), *An Irish Empire? Aspects of Ireland and the British Empire* (Manchester, 1996), p. 61. D. Hannigan, *The garrison game: the state of Irish football* (Edinburgh, 1998). Trevor West, *The Bold Collegians: the development of sport in Trinity College, Dublin* (Dublin, 1991).

36 Apart from the military barracks both towns had union workhouses and Mullingar was also the location of the District Lunatic Asylum.

37 W. E. Vaughan and A. J. Fitzpatrick (eds.), *Irish historical statistics: population 1821–1971* (Dublin, 1978), p. 32. Athlone's population increased from 6,199 in 1851 to 6,617 in 1901. The population in 1881 was 6,755 and in 1891 it had declined slightly to 6,742. Mullingar's population decreased from 4,817 in 1851 to 4,500 in 1901. The town's population was in a greater state of flux as between 1881 and 1891 it had increased from 4,787 to 5,323.

38 John Burke, 'Victorian Athlone, the struggle to modernise an Irish provincial town', unpublished MA Thesis, Galway–Mayo Institute of Technology, Galway, 2004, pp. 96–100.

39 Ibid., pp. 100–101. On at least two occasions in 1861 and 1891 the population of Mullingar was inflated when census day coincided with a fair day in the town. The 1861 increase was estimated at 'upwards of 600' according to the census report. See *Census of Ireland, 1891*, p. 889.

40 Andy Bielenberg, *Locke's Distillery, a history* (Dublin, 1993) provides a comprehensive study of the fortunes of Locke's distillery.

41 David S. Jones, 'The cleavage between graziers and peasants in the land struggle, 1890–1910', in Samuel Clark and J. S. Donnelly jr (eds.), *Irish peasants, violence and political unrest, 1780–1914* (Wisconsin and Manchester, 1983), p. 374. For a detailed analysis of Athlone's demographics see John Burke, *Athlone in the Victorian Era* (Athlone, 2007), pp. 10–21.

42 *Agricultural statistics of Ireland, 1871*, lxxviii: *Agricultural statistics of Ireland, 1902, General abstracts showing the acreage under crops and the number and description of livestock in each county and province, 1901–1902* [Cd 1263], 661, p. 14.

43 *Farming since the Famine: Irish farm statistics 1847–1996*, (Dublin, 1997), pp. 200–201. See also Burke, *Athlone in the Victorian Era*, pp. 96–102.

44 The grazing business encountered periods of crisis such as those between 1866–68, 1884–47 and 1891–96.

45 *WG*, 14 November 1872.

46 *Agricultural statistics of Ireland, 1902*, p. 20.

47 *Return of untenanted lands in rural districts, distinguishing demesnes on which there is a mansion, showing: rural districts and electoral divisions; townland; area in statute acres; poor law valuation; names of occupiers as in valuation lists*. H.C. 1906, C.177, pp. 182–92.

48 Terence Dooley, *Sources for history of the landed estates in Ireland* (Dublin, 2000), p. 14.

49 *Agricultural Statistics of Ireland, 1902*, pp. 10–13. King's county contained 493,263 acres, Longford, 257,770, Roscommon, 607,002 and Cavan 467,025 acres.

50 National Archives (NA), CSO papers, report of Captain Butler, December 1882, registered papers, 1888/20736.

51 *WE*, 15 February 1890.

52 Fergus Mulligan, *One hundred and fifty years of Irish railways* (Dublin, 1990), pp. 67–69.

53 Ruth Illingworth, 'Transport, 1806–1905', in Mary Farrell (ed.), *Mullingar*, p. 140. *WG*, 5 October 1848.

54 Ernest Shepherd, *The Midland Great Western Railway of Ireland: an illustrated history* by Ernest Shpeherd (Earl Shilton: Midland Publishing Limited, *c*.1994), p. 17.

55 Illingworth, 'Transport', p. 141.

56 Kevin O'Connor, *Ironing the land: the coming of the railways to Ireland* (Dublin, 1999), pp. 84–87.

57 *Thom's Irish almanac and official directory of the United Kingdom of Great Britain and Ireland for the year 1897* (Dublin, Alexander Thom, 1890), p. 1247.

58 O'Connor, *Ironing the land*, p. 83. The GN & WR was heavily backed by the MGWR. Burke, *Athlone in the Victorian Era*, pp. 90–96.

59 Ibid., p. 90. All these trains served Mullingar.

1. The Community of the Hunt, 1850–1905

1 J.P. Mahaffey, 'The Irish Landlords', in *Contemporary Review*, vol. xli, 1882, p. 162; Elizabeth, Countess of Fingall, *Seventy Years Young* (Dublin, 1991), p. 98.

2 *WG*, 22 April 1858.

3 *WI*, 2 November 1895.

4 Curtis, 'Stopping the Hunt'. See also Carter, *The Land War*, pp. 223–32.

5 *Waterford Daily Mail*, 22 September 1881.

6 *Agricultural statistics of Ireland, 1902*, pp. 14–16. The eight counties were Dublin, Kildare, Meath, Cork, Limerick, Tipperary, Antrim and Down.

7 *Agricultural statistics of Ireland, 1871*, p. lxvi: *Agricultural statistics of Ireland, 1882*, p. 14; *Agricultural statistics of Ireland, 1891*, p. 62. In 1871, 7.4 per cent of horses were used for recreational purposes; in 1881, 6.46 per cent and in 1891, 6.77 per cent.

8 *Agricultural statistics of Ireland, 1902*, p. 20. The corresponding figures for King's county were 82, for Roscommon 66, for Cavan only 12 and for Longford 19.

9 Iris M. Middleton, 'The origins of English fox hunting and the myth of Hugo Meynell and the Quorn', in *Sport in History*, vol. 25, no. 1, April 2005, pp. 1–16.

10 Muriel Bowen, *Irish hunting* (Tralee, 1954), p. 154.

11 In the eighteenth century and the first half of the nineteenth century families such as the Pakenhams, various branches of the Fetherstonhaugh family, the Tuites and Murray family possessed private packs, amongst others.

12 *WG*, 4 May 1854.

13 *WG*, 18 May 1854.

14 R. Carr, *English fox hunting* (London, 1976), pp. 114–15.

15 The establishment of a subscription pack did not end the era of the privately supported pack within the county. At different stages during the half-century, despite the difficulties and expense involved, some individuals possessed the necessary resources to maintain a variety of private packs.

16 *WI*, 11 November 1854.

17 Edmund F. Dease, *A complete history of the Westmeath hunt from its foundation* (Dublin, 1898) p. 44. For detail on spectacular chases enjoyed by members ot the Westmeath hunt see pp. 34, 39, 89, 106–7, 137.

18 *WG*, 28 February 1878.

19 *WG*, 10 December 1880.

20 Bowen, *Irish hunting*, p. 195. B. M. J. Fitzpatrick, *Irish sport and sportsmen* (Dublin, 1878), p. 160.

21 Dease, *Westmeath hunt*, p. 44.

22 Ibid., p. 44.

23 *WG*, 24 April 1891.
24 Dease, *Westmeath hunt*, p. 134.
25 Fitzpatrick, *Irish sport*, p. 166.
26 *WE*, 20 February 1897.
27 *WG*, 8 November 1878. Those who joined the field at the Killare crossroads were rewarded with a chase that lasted 'fully an hour and a half' at which Lord and the Ladies Churchill were present at the finish.
28 *WG*, 27 February 1880. The Empress failed to appear.
29 *WG*, 5 November 1886.
30 *WI*, 26 February 1898.
31 *WE*, 13 February 1904.
32 For a Kerry perspective see Valentine M. Bary, 'The hunting diaries (1863–1881) of Sir John Fermor Godfrey of Kilcoleman Abbey, County Kerry', in *Irish Ancestor*, vol. xi, 1979, pp. 107–19, and vol. xii, 1980, pp. 13–25. The County Kerry proprietor of a private pack, Sir John hunted during the 1863–64 season, which stretched from October to April, on sixty-three occasions. In this season, January was his most active month when he hunted on fourteen occasions with an incredible seven different packs. Ten years later in a rain interrupted season Sir John managed only forty-five outings.
33 VO District of Mullingar, electoral division of Multyfarnham, 1860–1940, valuation lists No. 37, revision 1, 1897–1907. Moore farmed 162 acres of land valued highly at £129 17s at Rathganny with buildings valued at £20 13s 35.
34 WCL, Hunting register for the season, 1879–80.
35 WCL, The sportsman's game book, 1879–88.
36 WCL, Hunting register for the season, 1880–81.
37 NA, Valentine McDonnell Papers; The fox-hunting diary, 1901–02, Business records Roscommon 11/3. See also David Seth Jones, *Graziers, land reform and political conflict in Ireland* (Washington, DC, 1995), p. 149.
38 Jones, *Graziers*, p. 15.
39 *British Hunts and Huntsmen* (London, 1911), p. 411.
40 Ibid., pp. 411–12. His brother was even more active and as well as participating with the same Irish hunts he also saw action with the Warwickshire, the North Warwickshire, the Atherstone and the Pytchley hunts.
41 David Carradine, *The decline and fall of the British aristocracy* (New Haven and London, 1990), p. 15.
42 It is impossible to quantify with total accuracy the structure of a hunting field. While newspaper accounts of hunting activity are abundant only the well known members of hunting society are identified and lists of participants inevitably conclude with the 'etc.' abbreviation, creating the impression that the account is somewhat incomplete.
43 Dease, *Westmeath hunt*, p. 147.
44 Paul Connell, *The diocese of Meath under Bishop John Cantwell*, 1830–66 (Dublin, 2004), pp. 126–27.
45 J.D. Campbell, '"Training for sport is training for war": sport and the transformation of the British Army, 1860–1914', in *International Journal of the History of Sport*, vol. 17, no. 4, 2000, p. 23.
46 Campbell, 'Training for sport', pp. 23–4.
47 K. Jeffrey (ed.), 'The Irish military tradition and the British Empire' in *An Irish Empire? Aspects of Ireland and the British Empire* (Manchester: Manchester University Press, 1996), pp. 105–06.
48 Dease, *Westmeath hunt*, pp. 133–4.
49 Westmeath Hunt Club Financial Records from 1890–91 to 1900–01 (hereafter WHCFR). Dooley, Terence, *The decline of the big house in Ireland, a study of Irish landed families 1860–1960*, (Dublin, 2001), p. 58. A list of 112 subscribers to the Limerick Hunt in 1879 included only six army officers.
50 *WG*, 7 March 1867.

51   *WG*, 1 November 1877.
52   *WG*, 9 March 1888.
53   *WG*, 24 May 1896.
54   Minutes of Westmeath Hunt Club (Hereafter WHMCMB), 31 January 1889.
55   WHCFR.
56   General Sir Alexander Godley, *Life of an Irish soldier* (London, 1939), pp. 14–16. Godley was a member of a Killegar, County Leitrim family.
57   *The Lilywhites' Gazette*, 1 August 1890, vol. viii, no. 8. I am indebted to Neal Garnham for drawing my attention to this reference.
58   *WG*, 13 May 1875.
59   *WG*, 13 January 1893.
60   WHCFR.
61   WHCFR, 21 January 1897.
62   *WG*, 8 March 1889. Tom Hunt, 'Mullingar sport in the 1890s: communities at play', in Farrell (ed.), *Mullingar*, p. 5.
63   *WG*, 31 March 1864.
64   *WG*, 7 November 1879.
65   Mark Bence-Jones, *Twilight of the ascendancy* (London, 1987), p. 1.
66   *WG*, 5 November 1886.
67   WHCFR. They included the Misses Hall, Quinn, Reynell and Greville as well as Mrs Dease, Mrs J. Fetherstonhaugh, Mrs Greville, Mrs Lewis, Mrs Malone, Mrs Smyth, Mrs Barnes, and Mrs C. Fetherstonhaugh.
68   *WG*, 26 January 1906; 9 February 1906, 23 February 1906, 2 March 1906; on these occasions twenty-five women out of a field of seventy-three, thirty-nine out of ninety-one, twenty out of sixty-five, fifty out of 120 respectively hunted.
69   A copy of this collage is available at the local history room at the Westmeath County Library headquarters in Mullingar.
70   Fingall, *Seventy years young*, pp. 130–35.
71   Godley, *Irish soldier*, p. 14.
72   *British Hunts and Huntsmen*, pp. 415.
73   The dangerous nature of hunting is evident from the fact that five individuals were killed in the Westmeath hunting fields in the period covered by this study. Perhaps this should not occasion any great surprise given the number of deaths that have occurred in the modern sport of three day eventing where in the past decade a number of top class competitors have been killed competing in the cross-country section of the event.
74   *WI*, 1 March 1873. Also, Dease, *Westmeath hunt*, pp. 74–75, 89–90. The MFH at this time was Captain Reginald Greville who served as master in the 1872 and 1873 hunting seasons. He was also one of the leading gentlemen jockeys in the United Kingdom at the time. In March 1878 Greville was killed riding a horse called Longford at Sandown Park. Details of Greville's riding career under the pseudonym St James are contained in Appendix 4.
75   *WG*, 24 November 1882.
76   *WG*, 5 November 1886. The brush was presented to the first rider present at the kill.
77   *WG*, 18 November 1887.
78   *WG*, 2 February 1894.
79   *WG*, 26 February 1898.
80   Dease, *Westmeath hunt*, preface.
81   NLI, Reynell Papers: The Diary of Laeda Reynell, 1862, P.C. 601(II). *WG*, 23 February 1906.
82   The wives and daughters totalled thirty-three.
83   *WE*, 18 November 1905.
84   WHCMB, 17 November 1887 and 1 December 1887.
85   It was possible to identify the year of birth of twenty-five of the subscribers and the exact age average was 37.8 years of age.

86 Dease, *Westmeath hunt*, pp. 131–33. WHCFR, based on the list of subscribers for the 1900–1901 season.

87 *WI*, 19 February 1870.

88 This was exactly the same as the amount of land the members of the Queen's county club owned in that county. The Queen's county membership also included thirty-three magistrates, twenty-seven grand-jury members and twenty-two freemasons. See Carter, *The Land War*, pp. 224–45.

89 *Landowners in Ireland: return of owners of land of one acre and upwards in the several counties, counties of cities, and counties of towns in Ireland*, [C–1492] Dublin, 1876, pp. 82–86.

90 T. K. Hoppen, *Elections, politics and society in Ireland, 1832–1885* (Oxford, 1984), p. 121.

91 At this time the county contained ninety-five estate owners who owned over 1,000 acres of land and another seventy-nine individuals possessed estates between 500 and 999 acres.

92 Dease, *Westmeath hunt*, p. 131.

93 The Diary of William Edward Wilson of Daramona, January 1889–January 1908. In 1898 for instance he went shooting on 16, 29 August; 1, 3, 17, 20 September; 12 October and on 1 and 22 November. I am grateful to Ms Joan Keary from Streete for alerting me to the survival of the Wilson diary.

94 *Astronomical and physical research at Mr. Wilson's observatory, Daramona, Westmeath*, unpaginated and undated.

95 Wilson diary, 13 August 1898. Information on the value of subscriptions and number of subscribers to the Westmeath Hunt Club for the period 1890–1902 is documented in Appendix 5.

96 WHCMB, 12 May 1877, 26 October 1877, 21 March 1878.

97 D. C. Itzkowitz, *Peculiar privilege: a social history of English fox hunting, 1753–1885* (London, 1977), p. 157.

98 John Lowerson, *Sport and the English middle classes, 1850–1914* (Manchester, 1993), p. 33.

99 F.G. Aflalo (ed.), *The cost of sport* (London, 1899), p. 151.

100 *WE*, 6 March 1897.

101 Dooley, *Sources for the History of Landed Estates*, p. 11.

102 *A return showing according to provinces and counties the number of cases in which judicial rents have been fixed by all the methods provided by the Land Law Acts for a first and second statutory term, respectively, to 31 December 1902 with particulars as to acreage, former rents of holdings, and percentages of reductions in rents HC 1903, vol. lvii, 91*, p. 374. For a similar analysis of the situation in the neighbouring county of Meath see, Terence Dooley, '"A world turned upside down": a study of the changing social world of the landed nobility of County Meath, 1875–1945', in *Ríocht na Midhe, Records of Meath Archaeological and Historical Society*, vol. XII, 2001, pp. 188–227.

103 *Return of payments made to landlords by the Irish Land Commissions pursuant to the first and sixteenth sections of the Arrears of Rent (Ireland) Act 1882, HC, 1884, lxiv*, p. 107.

104 Lord Longford was a subaltern in the 2nd Life Guards and the Honourable Edward Pakenham was in the Coldstreams.

105 WHCMB, 23 January 1890.

106 WHCFR.

107 WHCMB, 1 December 1898.

108 WHCFR.

109 WHCFR.

110 Dooley, *Big house*, p. 64.

111 Bence-Jones, *Twilight*, pp. 53–56.

112 The more up-market Kildare Street Club was by far the most popular. Thirteen of the eighteen were members of this club while only five joined the Sackville Street Club. More subscribers were members of London clubs than Dublin clubs,

indicative perhaps of the extent to which London, as opposed to Dublin life dominated the mental and social world of these members.

113   Dooley, *Big house*, p. 63.
114   FL. Figures based on an analysis of the following membership ledgers held in the Freemason's Library: Ledger 1–199 (1760–1860), membership of Mullingar lodge number 131, unpaginated; Ledger 95–188 (1860–1900), membership of Mullingar lodge number 131, pp. 289–293; membership of lodge number 123, the Albert Edward lodge, Mullingar, p. 226; membership of lodge number 124, Castlepollard, p. 235; membership of lodge number 101, Athlone, pp. 49–53.
115   *WG*, 7 April 1893.
116   Ibid.
117   Curtis, *Stopping the hunt*, pp. 351–4.
118   Patrick Fagan, 'Thomas Dease, Bishop of Meath, 1622–1651: his life and times', in *Ríocht na Midhe, records of Meath Archaeological and Historical Society*, vol. xvii, 2006, p. 77.
119   Michael Wheatley, *Nationalism and the Irish Party, provincial Ireland 1910–1916* (Oxford, 2005), pp. 75–76. Patrick Maume, *The Long Gestation: Irish nationalist life, 1891–1918* (Dublin, 1999), p. 237. Sir Walter was educated at Downside and was heavily involved in hunting, shooting and racing. He was a member of the Reform Club, the Turf Club, United Services, St Stephens Green, and Kildare Street Clubs, a director of the MGWR and Northern Insurance as well as being involved in the running of the *Freeman's Journal* before 1916. He was defeated as an independent nationalist candidate for Westmeath in 1918 and subsequently served as a Free State senator and a governor of the Bank of Ireland.
120   Andy Bielenberg, *Locke's Distillery, a history* (Dublin, 1993), pp. 63–4.
121   Ibid., pp. 66–68. John Edward's wife was one of Westmeath's leading hunting women and enjoyed the distinction of being one of the first women to drive a car in Westmeath.
122   *Sport*, 16 June 1900.
123   Moyvoughley Historical Committee, *Moyvoughley and its hinterland* (no place of publication; [1999] this date based on information from county library), p. 110.
124   Bielenberg, *Locke's Distillery*, p. 68.
125   *WG*, 26 December 1890.
126   Senia Pašeta, *Before the revolution: nationalism, social change and Ireland's Catholic elite, 1879–1922* (Cork, 1999), pp. 83–5.
127   *WN*, 24 November 1892.
128   *WE*, 15 April 1899.
129   In 1896 he rode the winner of the Westmeath Hunt Club welterweight race on Larkfield, the property of Captain Lewis. Subsequently he rode each year and in 1899 he won the Westmeath lightweight cup on his own horse, Diversion. In 1904 at the Westmeath Hunt races he was the first winner of the Harry Whitworth cup valued at 100 guineas, piloting his own horse Little Boy to victory.
130   *British Hunts and Huntsmen*, p. 419.
131   Dease, *Westmeath hunt*, p. 130. 'Bona fide' farmers is the phrase that was used when it was proposed that farmers be admitted as members of the Westmeath Hunt Club in December 1887. The member who proposed the motion was probably being unnecessarily verbose as the intention was to admit tenant farmers as members of the club which prior to this was the exclusive preserve of members of the landed gentry and professionals from a similar background.
132   WHCMB, 15 December 1887.
133   *WI*, September 1893.
134   Dease, *Westmeath hunt*, p. 110.
135   Jones, 'Cleavage', pp. 404–5.
136   *Moyvoughley and its hinterland*, pp. 108–13.
137   *WG*, 2 February 1865.
138   *WG*, 1 February 1866.

139   *WG*, 26 January 1871.
140   Ibid.
141   *WG*, 8 March 1889.
142   *WG*, 3 February 1905.
143   Dease, *Westmeath hunt*, p. 70.
144   *WG*, 1 February 1872.
145   *WE*, 14 May 1898.
146   WHCMB, 9 September 1882.
147   *WG*, 9 February 1905.
148   Dease, *Westmeath hunt*, p. 68.
149   Rev. Randall McCollum, *Sketches of the highlands of Cavan* (Belfast, 1856), p. 252.
150   Tony Collins and Wray Vamplew, *Mud, sweat and beers, a cultural history of sport and alcohol* (Oxford, 2002), pp. 69–70.
151   Dease, *Westmeath hunt*, p. 13.
152   NLI, Reynell Papers, 'The diary of Laeda Reynell', 1862, P.C. 601 (II).
153   Harry M. Sargent, *Thoughts upon sport* (London, 1894), p. 291.
154   Aflalo, *Cost of sport*, pp. 297–9.
155   *WG*, 5 April 1887.
156   Jack Leonard, 'Polo in Ireland', in Noel Phillips Browne (ed.), *The horse in Ireland* (London, 1967), p. 179. Brian Smith, *The horse in Ireland* (Dublin, 1991) p. 283.
157   Leonard, 'Polo in Ireland', p. 180.
158   Ibid., p. 181.
159   *British Hunts and Huntsmen*, p. 310. Watson founded the Freebooters team.
160   Ibid., p. 310.
161   Ibid., p. 310.
162   *WG*, 15 April 1881.
163   *MR*, 22 March 1900.
164   *WE*, 7 May 1905.
165   *WI*, 14 March 1903.
166   *WE*, 6 August 1904.
167   *WE*, 29 July and 5 August 1905.
168   NLI, Minute book of Irish County Polo Club Union (ICPCU), Ms. 16,830.
169   Minute book of ICPCU; *WE*, 29 August 1903.
170   Leonard, 'Polo in Ireland', p. 181.
171   Bill Mallon and Ian Buchanan, *The 1908 Olympic Games; results for all competitors in all events with commentary* (Jefferson, NC, 2000), pp. 205–7.
172   *Irish Field*, 22 August 1903; 29 August 1903; 20 August 1904.
173   *Irish Field*, 9 May 1903.
174   Dease, *Westmeath hunt*, p. 102.
175   *WG*, 7 May 1920.
176   *WG*, 10 June 1887.
177   *WG*, 14 August 1885.
178   *WE*, 21 May 1892.
179   WCL, *Rules and byelaws of the Westmeath Polo Club, 1905* (Mullingar, 1905), pp. 7–8.
180   Hugh Dolan (ed.), 'County Carlow Polo Club' in *Carloviana, journal of the old Carlow society*, vol. 30, 1983, p. 11.
181   WCL, *Rules and byelaws, 1905*, pp. 7–8. Membership of the elite Hurlingham Polo Club in London cost £5 5s at the time. (Aflalo, *The cost of sport*, p. 299).
182   WCL, *Rules and byelaws of the Westmeath Polo Club, 1911* (Mullingar, 1911), pp. 5–6.
183   *Rules and byelaws, 1905*, p. 3.
184   Ibid., p. 4.
185   Ibid., p. 3.
186   Calculation based on the average age of forty-seven members.
187   This is the nearest available subscribers list for comparison.
188   *Lawrence's handbook of Cricket in Ireland*, 1878, p. 19.

189   *WE*, 22 August 1903.

190   *WG*, 10 July 1887.

191   *WG*, 26 August 1881.

192   *WG*, 20 September 1895. See *WG*, 22 July 1892 and 22 September 1893 for particularly comprehensive attendance lists which included representatives of numerous landed families in the county.

193   *WE*, 28 September 1901.

194   The programme presented by the band of the East Lancashire Regiment at the 1892 meet is representative of the musical entertainment presented.

CATEGORY	TITLE	COMPOSER
March	The Duke of York	Paget
Overture	The Ruler of Spirits	Weber
Quadrilles	Covent Garden	Coote
Valse (Militaire)	The Grenadiers	Waldteufel
Fantasia	Paul Jones	Planquette
Valse	Unter den Linden	Gingl
Selection	Maritana	Kappey

WG, 22 July 1892.

195   *Vanity Fair*, 23 August 1896.

196   *Irish Field*, 29 August 1896.

197   R.V. Comerford, *The Fenians in context: Irish politics and society 1848–82* (Dublin, 1998 edition), p. 236.

2. HORSERACING DEVELOPMENT, 1850–1905

1   Harman Murtagh, 'Horse-racing in Georgian Athlone', in *Journal of the old Athlone society*, vol. ii, no. 6, 1985, p. 85.

2   Fergus A. D'Arcy, *Horses, Lords and racing men: the Turf Club, 1790–1990* (The Curragh, 1991), p. 16.

3   Stan McCormack, *Against the odds, Kilbeggan races, 1840–1994* (Kilbeggan, 1995), pp. 15–20.

4   D'Arcy, *Horses, Lords and racing men*. This work examines the history of the Turf Club and its role in managing flat racing over a 200-year period.

5   Guy St John Williams and Francis P. M. Hyland, *The Irish Derby, 1866–1979* (London, 1980); Guy St John Williams and Francis P. M. Hyland, *Jameson Irish Grand National: a history of Ireland's premier steeplechase* (Dublin, 1995); Colonel S. J. Watson, MBE, MA, *Between the flags: a history of Irish steeplechasing* (Dublin, 1969); John Welcome, *Irish horse racing, an illustrated history* (London, 1982).

6   Wray Vamplew, *The Turf: a social and economic history of horse racing* (London, 1976). Mike Huggins, *Flat racing and British society 1790–1914: a social and economic history* (London, 2000).

7   John Tolson, 'The Railways and Racing', unpublished PhD thesis (De Monfort University, Leicester, 1999).

8   Iris Maud Middleton, 'The developing pattern of horse racing in Yorkshire 1700–1749: an analysis of the people and the places', unpublished PhD thesis (De Monfort University, Leicester, 2000).

9   McCormack, *Against the odds*, pp. 21–23; pp. 25–37; p. 39.

10   No race meets were held in Athlone in 1897 and 1904.

11   *WE*, 16 March 1889.

12   *WG*, 26 February 1857, 26 March 1867.

13   *WG*, 21 March 1890. The first event was confined to gentlemen who had hunted with the harriers during the previous season with the second event confined to farmers who had hunted with the harriers or whose lands had been ridden over.

14   *WG*, 21 March 1890.

15   Dease, *Westmeath hunt*, p. 89.

16   *WG*, 4 April 1879.

17   *WG*, 22 April 1887.

18   Watson, *Between the flags*, pp. 132–33.
19   *WE*, 5 March 1904.
20   *WG*, 10 February 1893; 7 April 1893 for Rathowen and Dalystown charges.
21   *WE*, 12 April 1890.
22   Ibid.
23   D'Arcy, *Horses, Lords and racing men*, p. 213.
24   The names of these individuals were extracted from the newspapers and their occupations identified from their stated occupations in the 1901 Census returns.
25   Huggins, *Flat racing*, p. 32.
26   *WI*, 24 May 1866; *WG*, 28 May 1873.
27   R. Munting, *Hedges and hurdles: a social and economic history of national hunt racing* (London, 1987), p. 31.
28   *Racing Calendar*, 1858, pp. 33–34. The Naghten estate was located in County Roscommon.
29   *Racing Calendar*, 1859, p. 83; *Racing Calendar*, 1869, p. 63.
30   The 1866 race, for instance, placed an additional penalty of 7lb on a horse winning a race valued at £50 and a 14lb penalty on a horse winning a race of value in excess of £100.
31   Huggins, *Flat racing*, p. 35.
32   *WG*, 28 April 1864. In 1864, for example, three-year-old horses carried 9st weight, four-year-olds 10st 10lb, five-year-olds 11st 4lb and horses aged six and upwards carried 11st 7lb.
33   Huggins, *Flat racing*, p. 35.
34   Jeremiah Sheehan, *South Westmeath, farm and folk* (Dublin, 1978), pp. 48–52. Twenty years later he owned an estate of 13,432 acres that provided him with an estimated annual rental of £9,000.
35   Sheehan, *South Westmeath*, p. 206.
36   *WI*, 25 April 1863; *Irish Times*, 22 April 1863.
37   *WI*, 31 March 1860.
38   Ibid.
39   *Racing Calendar*, 1866, p. 40.
40   *Racing Calendar*, 1865, p. 50; ibid., 1866, pp. 78–9; ibid., 1867, p. 86; ibid., 1868, p. 64.
41   *WI*, 26 April 1862.
42   *Racing Calendar*, 1858, p. 33.
43   *Racing Calendar*, 1859, p. 66; ibid., 1867, p. 77.
44   *WI*, 29 March 1862.
45   *WI*, 26 April 1862.
46   *WI*, 31 March 1860.
47   *WG*, 28 April 1864.
48   Sixteen owners from Galway and the same from Roscommon raced horses at Garrycastle.
49   R.V. Comerford, 'Tipperary representatives at Westminster, 1801–1918', in William Nolan (ed.), *Tipperary: history and society, interdisciplinary essays on the history of an Irish county* (Dublin, 1985), p. 331. *Irish Times*, 17 May 1865.
50   *Irish Times*, 23 May 1866.
51   *Racing Calendar*, 1858, p. 307.
52   Dease, *Westmeath hunt*, p. 57.
53   Dooley, *Big house*, pp. 59–61.
54   *Return of land owners*, p. 318.
55   *Racing Calendar*, 1857, pp. 8, 34, 47, 55, 71, 125, 127–8, 290.
56   *Racing Calendar*, 1860, pp. 240, 245.
57   Ibid., 1860, pp. 272, 284, 288.
58   *Return of land owners*, p. 304.
59   *Racing Calendar*, 1860, p. 259.
60   Diarmuid Ó Cearbhaill, 'The Colohans – a remarkable Galway family', in *Journal of the Galway archaeological and historical association*, vol. 54, 2002, pp. 121–126.

61 *Returns of land owners*, p. 300. Ussher also competed nationally and was a member of the original regulatory committee of the INHSC.

62 U. H. Hussey de Burgh, *The great landowners of Great Britain and Ireland* (London, 1883), p. 124; *Return of landowners of Ireland* (Baltimore, 1988), pp. 295, 320.

63 Fitzpatrick, *Irish sport*, pp. 205–07.

64 *WI*, 26 April 1862.

65 *WI*, 30 April 1864.

66 *WI*, 11 May 1865; *Irish Times*, 10 May 1865.

67 *WI*, 24 May 1866.

68 *The FJ*, 23 May 1866.

69 *WI*, 25 May 1867.

70 *WI*, 13 May 1899.

71 Wray Vamplew, *Pay up and play the game, professional sport in Britain, 1875–1914* (Cambridge, 1988), p. 266. See D'Arcy, *Horses, Lords and racing men*, for incidents of violence at Newcastle, County Limerick race meets in 1867 that led to the abandonment of the meet, pp. 191–92.

72 *WI*, 13 May 1899.

73 *The Freeman's Journal*, 23 May 1866.

74 *Irish Times*, 30 April 1868.

75 D'Arcy, *Horses, Lords and racing men*, p. 176.

76 Ibid., p. 1.

77 Ibid., p. 181.

78 Ibid., pp. 183–4.

79 Ibid., pp. 184–5.

80 Ibid., pp. 186–7.

81 R. Munting, *Hedges and hurdles, a social and economic history of national hunt racing* (London, 1987), p. 22. Watson, *Between the flags*, pp. 58–9. The *Steeple Chase Calendar* was dedicated to one of the most important figures in Irish hunting and steeplechasing, the Marquis of Waterford. As well as the suggested rules and regulations the volume also records results of all steeplechases run in England since 1826 and in Ireland since 1842.

82 Munting, *Hedges and hurdles*, p. 72.

83 Welcome, *Irish horse racing*, pp. 46–47.

84 *Racing Calendar*, 1866, pp. lxiv–lxxxv; ibid., 1877, pp. lxxxi–cxxii; ibid., 1894, pp. lxxxv–cxix; ibid., 1905, pp. cix–cxvi.

85 D'Arcy, *Horses, Lords and racing men*, p. 206.

86 Ibid., p. 213.

87 Garnham, *Association football*, pp. 53–61.

88 James Walvin, *Leisure and society, 1830–1950* (London, 1978), p. 68.

89 Charles P. Korr, 'West Ham United Football Club and the beginnings of professional football in east London, 1895–1914', in *Journal of Contemporary History*, vol. 13, no. 2, 1978, pp. 211–32.

90 Tony Mason, *Association football and English society 1863–1915* (Brighton, 1980), pp. 37–49; Vamplew, *Pay up and play the game*, pp. 77–87; also Vamplew, 'The economics of a sports industry: Scottish gate-money football, 1890–1914', in *Economic History Review*, vol. 35, no. 4, 1982, pp. 549–67.

91 *WE*, 1 February 1890.

92 *WG*, 9 January 1891.

93 John Bateman, *The great landowners of Great Britain and Ireland* (London, 1879), p. 195. The 1876 return of owners of land in Britain and Ireland recorded Greville as the owner of 9,783 acres, 2 roods and 23 perches in Westmeath. This estate included the town of Mullingar. The town was purchased from the Earl of Granard by Colonel Fulke Southwell Greville in 1859. In general terms the Greville family were regarded positively in Mullingar. An article in *The Times* of 23 September 1869 credited the then prosperity of the town to Greville's policy of giving long leases to the Mullingar shopkeepers. This allowed them the security of investing in

improvements in their shops and according to the reporter provided an example of the benefits that would follow from tenants gaining security of tenure. In July 1883 Lord Greville was honoured at a major banquet held at St Mary's College, Mullingar and attended by Dr Nulty, Bishop of Meath. At the banquet Dr Nulty in his address promised 'that Lord Greville's tenants would be willing to defend himself or his property even at the cannon's mouth' (see *WG*, 27 July 1883). See A. P. W. Malcomson, *The pursuit of the heiress, aristocratic marriage in Ireland 1740-1840* (Belfast, 2006), p.100–101, for Fulke Southwell Greville's introduction to Westmeath society. He married Lady Rosa Nugent in 1840, daughter of the first and last Marquess of Westmeath and purchased his Westmeath estate for 'something like £125, 000' which provided a rental income of £5,720. He was elevated to the peerage in December 1869 by the Liberals and died in 1883 and was succeeded by his eldest son Algernon William Fulke Greville (1841–1909).

94 VO, Valuation lists; county of Westmeath, district of Delvin, Electoral division of Killulagh, 1860–1936. Valuation list number 15, 1884–1898 revision, 15 (Gigginstown); 27 (Rickardstown).

95 Fergus D'Arcy and Con Power (eds.), *Leopardstown Racecourse, 1888–1988, a centenary commemoration* (Dublin, 1988), p. 6.

96 *WE*, 15 February 1890.

97 Vamplew, *Pay up and play the game*, p. 79.

98 *WE*, 1 February 1890.

99 *WG*, 9 January 1891.

100 *WG*, 19 February 1892.

101 *WG*, 30 May 1890.

102 *Sport*, 12 August 1890.

103 *WG*, 19 February 1892.

104 *WG*, 14 June 1896.

105 *WG*, 6 June 1894; see also Hunt, *Mullingar sport*, pp. 10–11 for clerical opposition to the holding of the 1895 horse show on 15 August.

106 *MR*, 12 April 1900.

107 *WE*, 9 September 1905.

108 Ibid.

109 *WG*, 2 March 1906.

110 VO, Valuation lists: county of Westmeath, district of Mullingar, electoral division of Mullingar rural, number 34, 1891–1904, pp. 15.

111 *WG*, 4 March 1906.

112 *WG*, 30 May 1890.

113 *WG*, 19 February 1892.

114 *WG*, 3 February 1893.

115 *WG*, 27 January 1894; *WN*, 1 February 1894.

116 The list of subscribers for 1893 was unpublished.

117 *WG*, 30 May 1890.

118 *WE*, 7 June 1890.

119 *WG*, 6 October 1894; 2 August 1895; 11 September 1896; *WN*, 22 July 1897; *WE*, 10 September 1898; *MR*, 3 August 1899; *WE*, 4 August 1900; 7 August 1904.

120 *WE*, 2 August 1900.

121 *WG*, 19 May 1893.

122 Ibid.

123 *WN*, 1 February 1894; 26 March 1896.

124 *WG*, 22 February 1895.

125 *MR*, 20 July 1901.

126 *WE*, 15 March 1902; 14 March 1903.

127 *WE*, 14 September 1904.

128 *WE*, 11 March 1905.

129 *Sport*, 10 June 1905.

130 *WE*, 6 June 1903.

131 *WE*, 5 April 1905.
132 *WE*, 10 June 1905.
133 *WG*, 2 March 1906.
134 *Racing Calendar*, 1904, pp. 128–9; ibid., pp. 151–2; ibid., pp. 146–8; ibid., pp. 145–6; ibid., pp. 141–5.
135 *WE*, 6 June 1903.
136 Vamplew, *The Turf*, p. 53.
137 Fergus D'Arcy, *Horses, Lords and racing men*, pp. 144–152.
138 Tranter, *Sport, economy and society*, p. 34.
139 Dennis Brailsford, *Sport, time and society: the British at play* (London, 1991), p. 69.
140 Tolson, 'Railways and racing', p. 352.
141 See Introduction, pp. 1-2, 9–10.
142 *WG*, 25 April 1850. Costello in November 1849 offered visitors to the town fair the 'provisions and comforts of a first class hotel, combined with economy and attention. . . . Wines, spirits, liqueurs, cigars etc. of the most choice deasciptions [sic].'
143 *WG*, 9 May 1850; 17 April 1851; 1 May 1851.
144 *WG*, November 1852.
145 *WG*, 28 October 1852.
146 *WG*, 4 November 1852.
147 Ibid.
148 *WG*, 16 May 1872; 5 June 1873; 28 May 1874.
149 *WG*, 24 May 1877.
150 Dease, *Westmeath hunt*, p. 88.
151 *WG*, June 13 1878.
152 *WG*, 2 June 1882.
153 Mike Huggins and John Tolson, 'The railways and sport in Victorian Britain: a critical reassessment', in *The Journal of Transport History*, vol. 22, no. 2, 2001, p. 103.
154 D'Arcy, *Horses, Lords and racing men*, p. 145. Rail sponsorship began in June 1844 when the Dublin & Drogheda railway company added twenty-five sovereigns to a sweepstake handicap at Bellewstown, County Louth.
155 Ibid., p. 149.
156 *WG*, 7 April 1853.
157 D'Arcy, *Horses, Lords and racing men*, p. 149.
158 Ibid., p. 146; *WG*, 30 September 1887; G. A. Boyd Rochfort at the time of his death in 1887 had been vice-chairman of the MGWR for nearly twenty years. This relatively small sponsorship compared to the total prize-money available was proportionately greater than in mainland Britain where the respective proportions amounted to only 0.11 per cent and 0.04 per cent respectively for the years 1874 and 1901; see John Tolson, *Railways and Racing*, p. 142.
159 *WI*, 22 April 1899.
160 Seventy-nine per cent of those identified as residents outside the county only competed once or twice at the meet. The great majority of those unidentified also made only single entries to the meet.
161 Sargent, *Thoughts upon sport*, p. 141.
162 Smith, *The horse in Ireland*, p. 210.
163 The list included C. J. Blake from Maryborough; F. F. Cullen based at the Rossmore Lodge, the Curragh; Michael Dawson, Rathbride Manor, the Curragh; H. E. Linde, Eyrefield Lodge, the Curragh; J. J. Maher, Tara, County Meath; Denis Shanahan, Straw Hall, the Curragh; G. L. Walker, Balrath, Athboy, County Meath and Captain (later Major) Dewhurst.
164 Based on an analysis of the lists of subscribers to the Westmeath Hunt Club for the period 1890–1901.
165 *WE*, 27 May 1905.
166 *WE*, 11 June 1904.
167 Ibid.
168 *The Irish Field, 9 July 1904, 23 July 1904*. Reid farmed 150 acres 1 rood and 30 perches

that had a valuation of £98 and carried an annual annuity of £62 4s 10d under the terms of purchase under the land acts. In the two years prior to his death, he had invested £500 in improvement of the land and premises (He also owned a small farm at Bracknadevia of 8 acres 2 roods). Like many of his fellow farmers who were involved in racing Reid was also a cattle and sheep farmer as included in the sale of his estate were 61 cattle as well as 30 sheep and lambs along with 15 horses. The lands were sold at auction for £1,880 with the horse realising 516 guineas.

169   *Return of owners of land*, p. 85.
170   *Walford's county families of the United Kingdom, a royal manual of the titled and untitled aristocracy of England, Wales, Scotland and Ireland* (London, 1915), p. 985.
171   *Sport*, 21 January 1898.
172   Aubrey Brabazon, *Racing through my mind* (Ardmore, 1998), p. 2.
173   *WN*, 27 April 1893. His mare, Gentle Annie, captured the Metropolitan Plate at Baldoyle, the Grand Stand Plate at Cork and the second Coyningham Cup at Punchestown.
174   *British Hunts and Huntsmen*, p. 417.
175   Ibid., p. 418.
176   Ibid., p. 418.
177   *Sport*, 5 March 1892.
178   *Irish Field*, 12 November 1898.
179   *Royal Commission to inquire into horse breeding in Ireland, 1898 [C.8651, 8652], xxxiii, 261, 295*, pp. 50–51.
180   Williams and Hyland, *Irish Grand National*, pp. 46-7. Mitchell's chief success happened in 1894 when he rode and trained The Admiral to win the Irish Grand National and the prize of £245, a nice reward for an owner who had never previously won a stake of more than £25.
181   *Racing Calendar for the year 1892*, 1893. The horse was raced at Attanah (Queen's Co.), Birr, Loughrea, Ballina, Castlebar, Boyle, Rathkeale, Slane, Tuam, Ballinrobe, Claremorris, Carrickmacross, Athenry, Carnew, Kilkenny, Listowel, Lismore, twice at Dundalk and at Mullingar; pp. 2, 34, 63, 69, 75, 76, 98, 105, 120, 128, 131, 140, 151, 157, 182, 192, 200, 219, 221 and 232. Details of prize-money won on p. 271.
182   *Racing Calendar*, 1894, p. 291.
183   Information gathered from speaking to grandson and niece on 25 October 2002.
184   *Sport*, 23 December 1899.
185   *Census of Ireland 1901*, Enumerators' forms; VO, Valuation lists, county of Westmeath, district of Mullingar, electoral division of Portloman, revisions of 1893–1907, p. 47.
186   VO, Valuation lists, county of Westmeath, district of Mullingar, electoral division of Portloman, 1860–1936, No. 40 (1893–1907 revision), p. 47.
187   *Census of Ireland, 1901*, Enumerators' form.
188   Other women who raced horses at Mullingar included Lady Clancarty on four occasions, Mrs N. J. Kelly and Mrs Stackpoole on two occasions. Mrs Stackpoole was an Ennis resident whose late husband was heavily involved in steeplechasing and hunting and had maintained his own harrier pack in County Clare.
189   Bill Curling, *The Captain: a biography of Captain Sir Cecil Boyd-Rochfort, royal trainer* (London, 1970), pp. 4–5.
190   *Sport*, 16 June 1900.
191   Ibid.
192   *Census of Ireland, 1901*, Enumerators' form.
193   Bielenberg, *Locke's distillery*, pp. 62–3.
194   McCormick, *Against the odds*, pp. 208–9.
195   *WG*, 18 May 1896.
196   *WG*, 18 May 1900.
197   *WG*, 18 August 1901.
198   Vamplew, *Pay up and play the game*, p. 104.

199   Ibid., pp. 103–8; see also Huggins, *Flat racing*, pp. 52–3 for the expense involved in racing.
200   In 1890, for example, the average prize-money available per horse racing in Britain was £213 compared to £36 in Ireland; this differential was continued to 1905 and although the difference was reduced from £149 to £47, the average Irish prize-money available was still extremely small.
201   *Sport*, 15 December1894.
202   *Irish Field*, 12 November 1898.
203   Wray Vamplew, 'Horse-Racing', in Tony Mason (ed.), *Sport in Britain: a social history* (Cambridge, 1989), pp. 227–8.
204   Huggins, *Flat racing*, pp. 51–2.
205   Ibid., pp. 54–60.
206   *Leicester Weekly Post*, 25 May 1878. At a bankruptcy court Sir Walter Nugent explained how he had lost £60,000 through gambling and that it had cost him 'a great deal more by borrowing'.
207   Huggins, *Flat racing*, pp. 79–80.

3. COMMERCIAL SPORTS, 1880–1905

1   Hiner Gillmeister, *Tennis: a cultural history* (New York, 1998), pp. 172–7.
2   Helen Walker, 'Lawn Tennis', in Tony Mason (ed.), *Sport in Britain: a social history* (Cambridge, 1989), p. 259.
3   Tom Higgins, *The history of Irish Tennis* (Sligo, 2006), vol. 1, p. 7, pp. 235–285. I am indebted to Tom Higgins, Sligo, for providing me with details of the early history of Irish tennis clubs prior to the publication of his own forensic volumes on the history of Irish tennis.
4   John Arlott, *The Oxford Companion to Sports and Games* (St. Alban's, 1977), p. 534.
5   Gillmeister, *Tennis*, p. 177.
6   John Lawrence, *Handbook of cricket in Ireland, 1874–75* (Dublin, 1875), pp. 252–53.
7   Lawrence, *Handbook, 1873–74*, pp. 230–31; *Handbook, 1872–73*, p. 261. John Lawrence also advertised his lawn tennis sets in the *Irish Sportsman* and in January 1878, a lawn tennis set that included four rackets, six covered and six uncovered balls, full size nets, strong ash poles with brass mountings, ropes, pegs and a copy of the Marlyebone laws and a brush for marking the courts could be purchased for £5 5s. Cheaper sets were available from as little as £2 (*Irish Sportsman*, 5 January 1878)
8   Rouse, 'Sport', p. 14.
9   *Lilywhites' Gazette*, 1 August 1890, vol. viii, p. 8.
10   *WG*, 8 July 1887.
11   Ibid.
12   Ibid.
13   Ibid.
14   *WG*, 2 June 1893.
15   *WG*, 4 May 1894.
16   NLI, Fishing diary of George L. Adlercorn, book number 22, 6 September 1878 to 11 April 1880, Ms 3,800, diary entry for 4 June 1879.
17   The *Westmeath Independent* of 17 September 1898 reported that the club was in existence for over fourteen years.
18   *WG*, 13 April 1889.
19   *WI*, 2 April 1887.
20   *WG*, 23 July 1887.
21   *WG*, 13 April 1889.
22   *WI*, 15 June 1889.
23   *WI*, 27 April 1895.
24   *WG*, 8 September 1900.
25   *WI*, 14 April 1888; 16 June 1894.
26   *WI*, 26 June 1886.
27   *WI*, 13 April 1895.

28   *WG*, 18 April 1892.
29   *WG*, 6 May 1892. It was announced that play would commence by 1 June.
30   Ibid.
31   *WG*, 17, 24 June 1892; 5 August 1892.
32   *WG*, 28 April 1893.
33   *WG*, 13 July 1894.
34   *WN*, 7 March 1901.
35   *WI*, 4 March 1893; 30 March 1893.
36   *WI*, 30 March 1893.
37   *WI*, 21 October 1893.
38   *WI*, 20 May 1893.
39   Ibid.
40   *WE*, 17 June 1893.
41   *WI*, 18 May 1895; 5 October 1895.
42   *WI*, 5 October 1895. The camen [sic] was the camán or hurley, the basic piece of equipment used by hurling players.
43   *WI*, 13 July 1906.
44   Tennis club membership was compiled from lists of those attending annual meetings of the two clubs, attending functions and competing in club competitions. The Westmeath Club list consisted of the names of fifty-two of those involved between 1892 and 1901, of which the social status of forty-nine was established. The Garden Vale list of seventy members was compiled of those active between 1889 and 1902 and the social status of forty-four of these was established. Wives and daughters were assigned the same social category as their husbands or fathers.
45   Penny Bonsall, *The Irish RMs; the resident magistrates in the British administration in Ireland* (Dublin, n.d.), pp. 88–89.
46   Trevor E. Winckworth, *All Saints Church, Mullingar: notes concerning the history of the church since 1814* (Mullingar, 1989), p. 9.
47   *WG*, 1 June 1901.
48   *WG*, 1 April 1892.
49   *WN*, 7 March 1901.
50   *WG*, 22 October 1903.
51   *WI*, 21 October 1893.
52   Representative Church Body (RCB), Vestry minute book, 1787–1965, Kilcleagh parish, P.0412.05.1 minutes of Easter 1885; 7 April 1890; 15 April 1895; 13 April 1900; 24 April 1905.
53   *WG*, 10, 17 August 1888.
54   *WG*, 8 September 1888.
55   *WN*, 27 July 1893.
56   *WG*, 21 July 1893.
57   Ibid.
58   *WG*, 13 July 1894.
59   *WG*, 17 September 1898.
60   *WN*, 22 September 1898.
61   *WI*, 30 March 1901.
62   *WI*, 4 August 1888.
63   *WI*, 9 August 1890.
64   *WI*, 27 June, 1 August 1891.
65   *WG*, 30 June 1893.
66   Cartriona M. Parratt, 'Athletic "Womanhood": Exploring Sources for female sport in Victorian and Edwardian England', in *Journal of Sport History*, vol. 16, no. 2, 1989, p. 150.
67   Parratt, 'Athletic "Womanhood"', p. 151.
68   *WI*, 20 July 1901.
69   *MR*, 18 July 1901.

70   *WG*, 2 July 1898.
71   *WG*, 1 October 1898.
72   *WG*, 1 September 1900.
73   *MR*, 18 July 1901.
74   *MR*, 8 August 1901.
75   *WI*, 13 July 1901. Later in the month, the East Galway Club provided the opposition.
76   *WI*, 13 July 1901.
77   Ibid.
78   Diary of W. E. Wilson, entries for 18, 20, 23 August 1898. See also entries for 16, 27 August 1902; 5 October 1904.
79   William H. Gibson, *Early Irish golf* (Naas, 1988).
80   Menton, *The Golfing Union*, p. 1.
81   These calculations are based on detail contained in the publications of Menton and Gibson.
82   Menton, *Golfing Union*, p. 49.
83   Ibid., p. 7.
84   Gibson, *Early Irish golf*, pp. 59–60; Menton, *Golfing Union*, pp. 8–16.
85   Gibson, *Early Irish golf*, pp. 34–39.
86   *The Golf annual*, 1896.
87   *WG*, 23 November 1895.
88   David Walsh, *Mullingar Golf Club: the first 100 years* (Mullingar, 1994), p. 9. The story is remarkably similar to the folklore associated with the introduction of association football to Ireland in 1878 when J. A. McAlery, the manager of a gentleman's outfitters in Belfast, allegedly became interested in the game after seeing a match played while on honeymoon in Scotland.
89   *WG*, 5 April 1895.
90   Ibid.
91   *WI*, 14 February 1896.
92   Ibid.
93   *WI*, 22 October 1904.
94   *WG*, 25 March 1904. *MR* 31 March 1904.
95   *WG*, 29 April 1904.
96   *WG*, 3 January 1902.
97   *The Irish Golfer*, 23 January 1901.
98   Record of Garrison Golf Club (hereafter GGC), Athlone, minute of 2 September 1900.
99   Menton, *Golfing Union*, Appendix X, p. 336.
100   *The Irish Golfer*, 8 November 1899.
101   Tom Collins, *Athlone Golf Club 1892–1992:100 years of golf* (Athlone, 1992), p. 18.
102   GGC, minute of 5 May 1899.
103   GGC, minute of 20 May 1900.
104   GGC, minute of 30 March 1901, 2 July 1901.
105   Hunt, 'Mullingar sport', p. 17.
106   Lowerson, *Sport and the English Middle Classes*, p. 127.
107   *WG*, 5 April 1895.
108   Ibid.
109   Paul M. Kerrigan, 'The Batteries, Athlone', in the *Journal of the Old Athlone Society*, vol. 1, no. 4, 1974–75, pp. 264–271. The Batteries formed part of a series of defences along the line of the Shannon against a possible French invasion from the west, built between 1803 and 1806 and formed a large-scale bridgehead defence of the bridge of Athlone. The invasion never materialised.
110   Collins, *Athlone Golf Club*, p. 17.
111   *Golfing annual*, 1896.
112   GGC, cash accounts, 1900, 1901, 1902.
113   GGC, cash accounts, February 1901, p. 96.
114   Minute book of County Westmeath Golf Club (henceforth CWGC), 1904–1935, minute of 17 October 1904.

115 *WE*, 18 April 1896.
116 *WG*, 4 December 1896.
117 David Rubinstein, 'Cycling in the 1890s', in *Victorian Studies*, vol. 21, no. 1, Autumn, 1977, p. 51.
118 Padraig Griffin, *The politics of Irish athletics* (Ballinamore, County Leitrim, 1990).
119 *Irish Cyclist*, 18 March 1891; 27 May 1891; 8 November 1893.
120 Brian Griffin, 'The wheels of commerce? Cycling agents and manufacturers, and the Irish cycling craze of the late nineteenth century', unpublished paper delivered at 'The state of play – Sports history in Britain and Ireland, past, present and future' conference, hosted by the Academy for Irish Cultural Heritages at the University of Ulster, Belfast Campus, 21–23 November 2003.
121 *Census of Ireland, 1901*, p. 72.
122 The local newspapers in the 1890s carried considerable advertising for bicycle suppliers and agents; *WI*, 15 August 1898.
123 Bob Montgomery, *R. J. Mecredy; the father of Irish motoring*, (Garristown, County Meath), 2003, pp. 8–9.
124 Ibid., p. 9.
125 *WE*, 2 September 1892; 9 September 1892.
126 *WE*, 10 August 1901.
127 *WG*, 20 March 1891; *WE*, 26 March 1892.
128 *WE*, 25 March 1893.
129 *WG*, 15 March 1895.
130 *WE*, 4 November 1893; 23 May 1903.
131 *WE*, 7 May 1898.
132 *WE*, 27 June 1903.
133 *WG*, 24 March 1882.
134 *WG*, 29 April 1882.
135 David Rubinstein, 'Cycling', p. 59.
136 *WE*, 4 November 1893.
137 *WN*, 6 August 1896.
138 *WG*, 1 August 1890.
139 *WG*, 24 April 1891.
140 *WE*, 9 May 1891.
141 See Chapter 5.
142 Wheatley, *Nationalism and the Irish Party*, p. 43.
143 *WN*, 30 April 1891; 7 May 1891; 30 July 1891.
144 *WN*, 10 August 1893.
145 *WN*, 6 July 1893. The three were Philip Shaw, Dick Rogers and J. Hope, members of the commercial community.
146 *WE*, September 1893.
147 *WN*, 12 May 1894.
148 *WE*, 25 July 1896.
149 *WE*, 20 March 1897.
150 *WE*, 10 July 1897.
151 *WE*, 17 July 1897; *WN*, 22 July 1897.
152 *WN*, 7 August 1897.
153 *WI*, 16 April 1892.
154 *WI*, 8 April 1893.
155 *WI*, 24 March 1894.
156 *WI*, 2 June 1894.
157 *WI*, 9 June 1894.
158 *WN*, 14 May 1896.
159 *WI*, 18 April 1896.
160 *WI*, 20 June 1896.
161 *WI*, 24 March 1894.

162   *WI*, 28 July 1894.
163   *WI*, 1 September 1894.
164   *WI*, 18 April 1896.
165   *WN*, 12 June 1897.
166   *WE*, 16 March 1893; 1 April 1893.
167   *WE*, 28 July 1900.
168   *WI*, 16 March 1895.
169   *WI*, 4 March 1893.
170   *MR*, 20 July 1899.
171   *MR*, 9 May 1901.
172   *WE*, 16 May 1901.
173   *Irish Cyclist*, 24 May 1892.
174   *WI*, 16 July 1894.
175   *WI*, 6, 20 July 1895.
176   *WE*, 18 August 1894.
177   *WE*, 3 August 1893; *WN*, 20 August 1896; 18 August 1898.
178   *WI*, 19 August 1893; *WI*, 18 August 1894; 3 September 1896.
179   *WE*, 11 September 1897; 22 July 1899.
180   Hunt, 'Mullingar sport', pp. 18–20.
181   *WE*, 24 August 1901.
182   *WE*, 24 August 1901; 12 July 1902; 27 June 1903; 4 June 1904. The 1901 sports
       provided Kiely with an opportunity to showcase his extraordinary athletic talent
       as he was a winner in the hammer throw, the 56lb weight-throwing event, the long
       jump and the 120 yards hurdles open handicap race. He also finished in third place
       in the high jump.
183   Peter Lovesey, *The official centenary history of the Amateur Athletic Association*
       (Enfield, 1979), p. 48.
184   Hunt, 'Mullingar sport', pp. 18–19.
185   *WE*, 12 July 1902.
186   *WE*, 24 August 1902; 27 June 1903; 4 June 1904.
187   *WI*, 16 March 1894.
188   *WE*, 7 December 1901.
189   *WI*, 2 April 1887.
190   *WI*, 2 April 1887.
191   *WI*, 12 March 1887.
192   *WI*, 12 April 1888.
193   *WI*, 13 April 1889.
194   *WI*, 29 February 1896.
195   For a similar policy in cricket see Chapter 4.
196   *WI*, 13 April 1888.
197   *WI*, 30 March 1901.
198   *WG*, 3 May 1893.
199   *WG*, 29 April 1898.
200   *WG*, 20 July 1900.
201   *WI*, 28 August 1886.
202   *WI*, 31 July 1886.
203   *WI*, 31 July 1886.
204   *WI*, 28 August 1886.
205   GGC, 8 May, 17 July 1899, p. 54.
206   *WE*, 12 April 1904.
207   Ibid.
208   CWGC, minute of 17 October 1904.
209   *WI*, 1 December 1894.
210   GGC, minute of 10 October 1898, p. 132.
211   GGC, cash accounts, October 1898, p. 26.
212   *WI*, 5 November 1904.

213 *WG*, 30 January 1903.
214 *WI*, 27 February 1903.
215 CWGC, minute of 10 July 1905.
216 *Agricultural returns, 1901.* An agricultural labourer in 1901 in Mullingar was paid between 1s 6d and 2s daily, pp. 148–149.
217 CWGC, 1904–1935; CWGC account, 1904–1905.
218 CWGC, minute of 14 October 1905.
219 GGC, pp. 3–36.
220 GGC, minute of 2 September 1900, p. 147.
221 Ibid.
222 GGC, 3 March 1898, p. 12.
223 GGC, 30 December 1899, p. 62.
224 GGC, 31 October 1898, p. 26.
225 GGC, 8 November 20 December 1898, p. 30, p. 34.
226 *Irish Times*, 30 April 1900.
227 CWGC, minute of 17 October 1904.
228 Walsh, *Mullingar Golf Club*, p. 8.
229 Tranter, 'Chronology', p. 379.
230 Jennifer A. Hargreaves, '"Playing like gentlemen while behaving like ladies": contradictory features of the formative years of women's sport', in *The British Journal of Sports History*, vol. 2, no. 1, 1985, p. 43.
231 Ibid., p. 46.
232 Parratt, 'Athletic "Womnahood"', pp. 147–50.
233 See Chapter 1, pp. 18–20.
234 Maria Luddy, *Women and philanthropy in nineteenth century Ireland* (Cambridge, 1995), pp. 214–18.
235 *WI*, 17 June 1899.
236 *WI*, 1, 8, 22 February 1902.
237 *WI*, 8 March 1902.
238 *WG*, 9 May 1902.
239 *WI*, 27 April 1895.
240 *WI*, 31 July 1886; 7 August 1886.
241 *WI*, 28 April 1894.
242 *WI*, 12 May 1888.
243 *WI*, 2 April 1887.
244 CWGC, minute of AGM of 17 October 1904.
245 CWGC, minute of 2 December 1905.
246 CWGC, membership list written on front pages.
247 CWGC, membership list for 1909–10.
248 Neil Tranter, 'Organized sport and the middle-class woman in nineteenth century Scotland' in *International Journal of the History of Sport*, 1989, vol. 6, no. 1, p. 41.
249 *WI*, 20 April 1895.
250 *WI*, 16 March 1896.
251 *WI*, 7 March 1896.
252 *WN*, 14 May 1896.
253 *WI*, 14 May 1898.
254 Quoted in *Westmeath Independent*, 3 June 1899.
255 *WG*, 17 September 1898.
256 *WI*, 4 May 1901.
257 *WI*, 31 August 1901.
258 *WI*, 26 July 1902.
259 Nicky Smith, *Queen of Games: a history of croquet* (London, 1991), p. 46.
260 Ibid., p. 47.
261 Ibid.
262 *WI*, 23 May 1903.
263 Ibid.

264 *WI*, 19 July 1902.
265 *Census of Ireland, 1901*, Enumerators' returns.
266 *WI*, 20 September 1902.
267 Richard Holt, *Sport and the British: a modern history* (Oxford University Press, 1990), p. 126.
268 WGC, minute of AGM of 17 October 1904.
269 Neil Tranter, 'Women & sport in nineteenth century Scotland', in Grant Jarvie and Graham Walker (eds.), *Scottish sport in the making of the nation: ninety minute patriots?* (Leicester, 1994), p. 39.

4. CRICKET, 1850–1905

1 Gerard Siggins, *Green days: cricket in Ireland, 1792–2005* (Gloucestershire, 2005). Neal Garnham, 'The Roles of Cricket in Victorian and Edwardian Ireland', in *Sporting Traditions, Journal of the Australian society for sports history*, vol. 19, no. 2, 2003, pp. 27–48; Davis, 'Irish cricket and nationalism', in *Sporting Traditions*, vol. X, no. 2, 1994, pp. 77–96; Tom Hunt, 'Classless cricket? Westmeath, 1880–1905', in *History Ireland*, vol. 12, no. 2, 2004, pp. 26–30; Patrick Bracken, *'Foreign and fantastic field sports': cricket in County Tipperary* (Thurles, 2004); Michael O'Dwyer, *The history of cricket in County Kilkenny – the forgotten game* (Kilkenny, 2006).
2 Marcus de Burca, *The GAA: a history of the Gaelic Athletic Association* (Dublin, 1980), p. 25.
3 John Sugden and Alan Bairner, *Sport, sectarianism and society in a divided Ireland* (Leicester University Press, 1995), p. 50.
4 Garnham, 'Roles of cricket', pp. 28–29.
5 Ibid., p. 32.
6 Siggins, *Green days*, pp. 26–27.
7 West, *The bold collegians: the development of sport in Trinity College* (Dublin, 1991), p. 13.
8 Stanley Bergin and Derek Scott, 'Cricket in Ireland', in E. W. Swanton (ed.), *Barclay's world of cricket* (London, 1980), p. 508.
9 Lawrence, *Handbook*, 1880–81, p. 2.
10 Bracken, *Foreign and fantastic field sports*, p. 102, pp. 105–24.
11 James S. Donnelly jnr, *Landlord and tenant in nineteenth-century Ireland* (Dublin, 1973), pp. 69–71.
12 Andrew C. Murray, 'Nationality and local politics in late nineteenth-century Ireland: the case of County Westmeath', in *Irish Historical Studies*, vol. xxv, no. 98, 1986, p. 157.
13 Andrew C. Murray, 'The politics of nationality in Westmeath, 1868–1892', PhD thesis, Manchester University, 1986, pp. 287–294.
14 O'Dwyer, *Kilkenny cricket*, pp. 49–50. For land league activity in Tullaroan see Edward Kennedy, *The land movement in Tullaroan, County Kilkenny, 1879–1891* (Dublin, 2004). Meagher reputedly attended the meeting that established the GAA in Thurles and was the father of one of Kilkenny's most famous hurlers, Lory Meagher.
15 W.P. Hone, *Cricket in Ireland* (Tralee, 1956), pp. 6–15.
16 West, *Bold collegians*, p. 14.
17 N. D. McMillan, *One hundred and fifty years of cricket and sport in County Carlow: an illustrated history of conflict and sport, 1823–1981* (Dublin, 1981), p. 5.
18 T. M. Payal, *The Phoenix Club, 1830–1980, a history of the club* (Dublin, 1981), unpaginated.
19 West, *Bold collegians*, p. 14.
20 Garnham, 'The roles of cricket', p. 29.
21 *WI*, 23 September 1852; 14 October 1852.
22 *WI*, 16 September 1854.
23 *WG*, 23 August 1855; 6 September 1855; 18 September 1855.
24 *WG*, 15 January 1874.

25   Lawrence, *Handbook*, 1869–70, p. 147.
26   Lawrence, *Handbook*, 1873–4, p. 160.
27   *WG*, 17 October 1862.
28   Lawrence, *Handbook*, 1865–66, p. 63; Arthur Samuels, *Early cricket in Ireland*, (Dublin, 1888), p. 12.
29   Arthur Samuels, *Early cricket in Ireland; a paper read before the Kingstown Literary and Debating Society on 22 February 1888* (Dublin, 1888) pp. 18, 21–22.
30   *Slater's Directory*, 1870 (London,1870), pp. 10–13. The club included two Burgess brothers, members of one of Athlone's most important milliner families; J. Kilkelly from a linen and woollen draper family; J. Turkington from one of Athlone's principal bakeries; three Charlton brothers who were medical students; J. O'Connor, whose family manufactured billiard tables and were billiard room keepers and M. Hynds, who was a tax collector. Thomas Hogan, the treasurer, was the post-master and the proprietor of a fancy goods store.
31   *WG*, 17 August 1865.
32   *WG*, 21, 26 July 1864; 2 August 1866.
33   Lawrence, *Handbook*, 1865–66, p. 63.
34   Lawrence, *Handbook*, 1878, p. 22; Garnham, 'The roles of cricket', p. 33.
35   Michael Byrne, 'Tullabeg, Rahan, Tullamore, 1818–1991', in *Offaly Heritage: journal of the Offaly historical and archaeological society*, vol. 2, 2004, p. 93.
36   Lawrence, *Handbook*, 1867–68, pp. 75–6.
37   See Introduction.
38   *WE*, 30 August 1889.
39   Diary of William E. Wilson, diary entries of 7 August and 8 August 1901.
40   *WG*, 1 April 1881.
41   *WG*, 20 May 1881.
42   *WG*, 8 July 1887.
43   Lawrence, *Handbook*, 1880–81, p. 167.
44   *WG*, 22 April 1892.
45   *WG*, 20 May 1892.
46   Apart from the County Club, Muldowney played with the Mountain Parish, Clonhugh, D. Kiernan's XI, Mount Street and Coolamber selections. He was also a Mullingar Shamrock footballer.
47   *WG*, 20 May 1892.
48   *WG*, 26 July 1895.
49   *WE*, 20 September 1902.
50   See Chapter 6, pp. 173–177.
51   Shan F. Bullock, *After sixty years* (London, 1936), pp. 78–79.
52   Malcolm Brodie, *Linfield; 100 years* (Belfast, 1985), pp. 3–4. Two of Ireland's foremost association football clubs owed some of their initial success to company support. The Distillery club in Belfast was formed in 1879 from employees of Dunville's distillery. The Linfield club was originally formed in 1886 from workers at the Ulster Spinning Company's Linfield Mill.
53   Tom Hunt, *Portlaw, County Waterford, 1825–1876: portrait of an industrial village and its cotton industry* (Dublin, 2000), p. 45.
54   Siggins, *Green days*, p. 36.
55   See Chapter 6, p. 176.
56   *MR*, 1 September 1898.
57   Richard Holt, 'Working-class football and the city', in *The British Journal of Sports History*, vol. 3, no.1, 1986, pp. 7–8.
58   *WN*, 12, 19 May 1892.
59   *WE*, 5 March 1904.
60   Minute book of Carrick-on-Suir Athletic, Cricket and Football Club, established around 1879, minute of 27 May 1881 and 28 June 1881. This was the club of one of the founders of the GAA, Maurice Davin and his brother the noted athlete, Tom Davin. Minute book held privately.

61   *WI*, 31 July 1886.
62   *WI*, 13 May 1865. Ballymahon is located just outside the north-western border of Westmeath in County Longford.
63   *WG*, 15 November 1866.
64   Income and Expenditure of Carrick-on-Suir Amateur Athletic Cricket and Football Club from its formation in August 1879 up to its first general meeting, 23 February 1880. Minute book privately held.
65   These included the Marquis of Waterford, Lord Charles Beresford, Lord Arthur Butler and the Earl of Bessborough. Over £10 was received on subscription cards and entrance fees received for the athletic sports amounted to £1 8s 6d.
66   The club paid £24 annually in rent for its field and recouped some of this money by renting the grazing rights of the land. A minute of 27 May 1881 recorded the fact that the Michael Quirke offer of £1 for the grazing of the field for four days was accepted provided he paid a man at his own expense to keep cattle off the cricket crease and also to take away what dung might be dropped near the crease.
67   *WI*, 31 August 1867.
68   *WE*, 20 June 1903.
69   *WG*, 28 October 1893.
70   *MR*, 9 August 1900.
71   *WN*, 27 August 1891.
72   *WE*, 26 August 1899.
73   *WE*, 20 September 1902.
74   *MR*, 1 September 1898.
75   *WG*, 2 August 1889.
76   *WN*, 27 August 1891.
77   Mike Huggins, 'The spread of Association Football in North–East England, 1876–90: the pattern of diffusion' in *International Journal of the History of Sport*, vol. 6, 1989, pp. 299–318; Andrew Hignell, *Rain stops play* (London, 2002), pp. 37–54; Ian David Clarke, 'The development and social history of cricket in Cornwall 1815 to 1881', PhD thesis, De Montfort University, Leicester, May 2004.
78   Hignell, *Rain stops play*, pp. 37–8.
79   Ibid., p. 51.
80   Ibid., p. 17.
81   *WG*, 12 September 1861; 29 May 1862; 13 August 1863; 10 August 1865; 9 August 1866.
82   *WG*, 21 August 1862.
83   Lawrence, *Handbook*, 1866–67, p. 90.
84   Ibid., p. 73.
85   Ibid., p. 73.
86   *WG*, 14 August 1862.
87   Hignell, *Rain stops play*, p. 52.
88   *WE*, 15 September 1883.
89   *WG*, 30 August 1894; Slater, *Directory*, 1891, p. 192.
90   *WG*, 8 September 1894.
91   Lawrence, *Handbook*, 1866–67, pp. 88–90.
92   Lawrence, *Handbook*, 1867–68, pp. 100–101.
93   VO, Valuation lists: County Westmeath, district of Delvin, electoral division of Faughalstown, 1860–1930, valuation revision 1884–1898, 15. This land was valued at £155. Smith held a second farm of land of 40 acres, valued at £26 6s at Streamstown, p. 16.
94   *WN*, 14 May 1892.
95   *WE*, 5 August 1899.
96   *WE*, 26 August 1899.
97   O'Dwyer, *Kilkenny cricket*, pp. 27–28; Bracken, *Cricket in County Tipperary*, p. 6.
98   The figure refers to the number of games where the opposition was identified. In total, 1,003 games were reported for the period between 1880 and 1905.

99   *WG*, 14 June 1895; 16 August 1895.
100   Patricia Gibney, 'The Military in Mullingar', research project presented to the Department of History, NUI Maynooth, 1998, pp. 15–23.
101   Campbell, 'Sport and the army', pp. 47–48.
102   *WG*, 29 May 1862; 5 June 1862; 21 August 1862. Lawrence, *Handbook*, 1871–72, pp. 215–18; *WN*, 19 May, 1892; 26 May 1892; *WG*, 27 May 1892; 8 July 1892.
103   *WI*, 13 May 1893; 9 June 1894; *WE*, 9 May 1895.
104   *The Lilywhites' Gazette* (Journal of the 2nd Brigade East Lancashire Regiment), 1 August 1890, vol. viii, p. 8.
105   Joseph Robins, *Champagne and silver buckets, the Viceregal court and Dublin Castle, 1700–1922* (Dublin, 2001), pp. 133–35.
106   *WG*, 21 July 1864.
107   *WG*, 19 June 1862.
108   *WI*, 2 August 1862.
109   *WG*, 27 June 1890.
110   *WG*, 20 September 1901.
111   *WE*, 24 February 1900; *MR*, 5 January 1899; *WE*, 17 December 1896; 27 November 1902; *WG*, 28 October 1893; *WN*, 13 April 1899; 19 January 1893; 17 June 1897.
112   Ibid.
113   *WE*, 13 April 1899.
114   *WN*, 19 January 1893.
115   *MR*, 5 January 1899.
116   Lowerson, *Sport and the English Middle Classes*, p. 98.
117   *WE*, 24 February 1900.
118   In both the categories of single male and female, one thirteen-year-old student attended.
119   Myrtle Hill, *Women in Ireland: a century of change* (Belfast, 2003), p. 21.
120   *WE*, 29 July 1893.
121   *WG*, 8 June 1888.
122   *WE*, 16 August 1902.
123   *WG*, 9 October 1885.
124   *WG*, 5 November 1886.
125   *WG*, 16 September 1887; *WE*, 17 September 1887.
126   *WE*, 20 September 1894.
127   Tranter, 'Social and occupational structure', vol. 4, no. 3, 1987, p. 309.
128   *WI*, 18 May 1895; 13 June 1896; 22 August 1896.
129   *WI*, 16 June 1900.
130   *WI*, 27 July 1901.
131   *WI*, 16 July 1892; 30 July 1892.
132   *WI*, 6 August 1892.
133   Bracken, *Foreign and fantastic*, p. 117.
134   O'Dwyer, *Kilkenny cricket*, pp. 44–62.

5. The embryonic GAA in Westmeath, 1884–1895

1   In this chapter, the commonly used Irish terminology will be used to describe these games: Gaelic football will be referred to as football; association football will be referred to as soccer and rugby football will be simply referred to as rugby.
2   de Burca, *The GAA*, p. 9.
3   Ibid., p. 17.
4   Seamus Ó Riain, *Maurice Davin (1842–1927), first president of the GAA* (Dublin, nd), p. 26.
5   Ó Riain, *Maurice Davin*, pp. 17–19.
6   Lovesey, *Amateur Athletic Association*, p. 36. The Amateur Athletic Association was founded in 1880 and was the national governing body for British athletics. Its first championships, the oldest in the world, were held the same year. The AAA set out to govern athletics firmly and fairly and one of its declared objectives was to

deal repressively with any abuses of athletics sports. In 1887 it became the first official governing body anywhere in the world to ratify official records. From the start the AAA championships were open to the world and were effectively world championships in athletics. By 1900 athletes from five continents had won AAA titles.

7   Mandle, *Gaelic Athletic Association*, p. 5.
8   Ibid., p. 4.
9   de Burca, *The GAA*, p. 49.
10   NA, CBS, DICS, Midland Division, 1887–1894, Monthly report of work done by DI crimes branch special, July 1889, S21/10305.
11   NA, CBS, S21/159.
12   NA, CBS, S21/665.
13   *WE*, 31 January 1885.
14   *WE*, 14 Fegruary 1885.
15   Ibid.
16   Griffin, *Irish Athletics*, pp. 37–9.
17   *WI*, 1 May 1886.
18   R. V. Comerford, *Inventing the nation: Ireland* (London, 2003), p. 223.
19   NAI, CBS, S/2452.
20   NA, CBS, S/6216.
21   Based on an analysis of the local papers *Westmeath Examiner*, *Westmeath Nationalist*, *Westmeath Independent* and *Westmeath Guardian*.
22   Tony Collins, *Rugby's great split: class, culture and the origins of rugby league football* (London, 1998), p. 1.
23   WCL, Evidence collected by folklore commissioners, parish of Killucan, pp. 340–1.
24   *GAA Golden jubilee supplement* (Dublin, 1934), p. 80.
25   *WE*, 15 December 1887; 25 April, 29 September, 6 October, 12 November, 17 November, 24 November, 1 December, 1888.
26   *WE*, 2 February 1889.
27   *WE*, 26 October 1889.
28   Ibid.
29   *WI*, 4 January 1890. *Sport*, 28 August 1887. An Athlone club may have existed prior to this one as in August 1887 the Henry Grattan Club from Dublin travelled to town and played an Athlone team described as 'old association players'.
30   *WI*, 11 January 1890.
31   *WI*, 21 June 1890. Canon Kearney was the only Catholic priest who regularly hunted with the County Westmeath Hunt and was a strong advocate of temperance. He refused to allow any alcohol sales at the annual Moate races organised in the 1890s.
32   *WI*, 22 November 1890.
33   *WN*, 2 February 1893; 6 March 1893.
34   *WE*, 8 November 1890.
35   *WE*, 22 November 1890.
36   Murray, 'Nationality and local politics', p. 151.
37   Gabriel Flynn, 'Bishop Thomas Nulty and the Irish Land Question, parts II and III, 1879–1898', in *Ríocht na Midhe*, vol. vii, no. iv, p. 106.
38   A.C. Murray, 'Nationality and local politics', pp. 144–158; Wheatley, *Nationalism and the Irish Party*, p. 119.
39   *WN*, 3 December 1891.
40   *WN*, 10 February 1893.
41   *WN*, 2 March 1892. The affiliated clubs were Mullingar Football Club, Mullingar Shamrocks, Kinnegad Slashers, Thomastown Rangers, Cullion Celtics, Raharney Rovers, Wooddown Rackers, Corbetstown Home Rulers and the Athlone T. P. O'Connor's Club.
42   *WN*, 13 April 1893.
43   Ibid.

44   *WN*, 20 April 1893.
45   *WG*, 5 May 1893.
46   *WN*, 27 April 1893.
47   *WN*, 27 July 1893.
48   *WN*, 15 February 1894.
49   NA, Crime Branch Special: GAA reports from SW and Midlands Division on clubs etc. at the end of the year, 1890, 2452/S.
50   Alan Metcalf, 'Football in the mining communities of east Northumberland, 1882–1914', in *International Journal of the History of Sport*, vol. 5, no. 3, 1988, pp. 269–91.
51   Tranter, 'Chronology', pp. 188–203.
52   Melvin L. Adelman, *A sporting time: New York City and the rise of modern athletics, 1820–70* (Urbana and Chicago, 1990), p. 6.
53   *WN*, 24 November 1892.
54   These games were played in the period 1888–99.
55   *WE*, 26 September, 1891.
56   Comerford, *Inventing Ireland*, p. 221; Joe Lennon, *Towards a philosophy for legislation in Gaelic Games* (Gormanstown, County Meath, 2000), p. 17.
57   Neal Garnham, 'Accounting for the early success of the Gaelic Athletic Association', in *Irish Historical Studies*, vol. xxxiv, no. 133, May 2004, p. 75.
58   Ó Riain, *Maurice Davin*, p. 61.
59   Joe Lennon, *The playing rules of football and hurling 1884–1995* (Gormanstown, County Meath, 1997), pp. 32–33.
60   Lennon, *Rules*, p. 32.
61   *WG*, 4 April 1890.
62   *WN*, 17 September 1891.
63   *WN*, 5 November 1891.
64   *WN*, 4 February 1892.
65   *WN*, 26 November 1891.
66   Collins, *Rugby's great split*, pp. 10–16.
67   *WN*, 16 March 1893.
68   *WN*, 23 March 1893.
69   *WN*, 9 February 1893.
70   *FJ*, 19, 21 July 1892. *Sport*, 23 July 1892.
71   *WE*, 10 March 1893.
72   *Sport*, 28 January 1893.
73   *Sport*, 4 March 1893.
74   *WN*, 14 April 1892.
75   *WN*, 15 June 1893.
76   *WN*, 12 May 1892.
77   *WN*, 26 May 1892.
78   *WN*, 2 June 1892.
79   WI, 10 May 1890.
80   O'Dwyer, *Kilkenny cricket*, p. 46, p. 50, p. 53, p. 62, pp.106–121, p. 161. pp. 225–29. See Antóin Ó Dúill, *Famous Tullaroan 1884–1984* (Tullaroan, 1984), pp. 146–55 for details of Tullaroan's success in Kilkenny senior hurling championships when the club won eight titles between 1887 and 1904. James Grace was the first captain of the Tullaroan senior hurling team and Pierce Grace has the distinction of winning two All-Ireland senior football medals with Dublin (1906 and 1907) and three All-Ireland senior hurling medals with Kilkenny (1911, 1912 and 1913). For information on Matt Gargan's Kilkenny career see Tom Ryall, *Kilkenny, the GAA story, 1884–1984* (Kilkenny, 1984), pp.23–39. Gargan played in the 1905 All-Ireland senior hurling final with Kilkenny despite having also played for Waterford in the Munster senior hurling championship in the same year. Kilkenny were beaten in the final but objected to a member of the Cork hurling team. Gargan was the subject of a Cork counter-objection and as a result Central Council ordered a replay which was won by Kilkenny.

81   Neal Garnham, 'Introduction' in *The origins and development of football in Ireland being a reprint of R. M. Peter's Irish Football Annual of 1880* (Belfast, 1999), p. 11.

82   Garnham, 'Accounting for the early success of the GAA', pp. 72–3. In 1878 Sunday closing of public houses was introduced to Ireland with the exception of the five main cities in Ireland (Belfast, Dublin, Cork, Limerick and Waterford) where opening time was limited to the hours between 2 pm and 7 pm. An individual travelling more than three miles from his residence the previous day was entitled to be served at any pub or inn as a 'bona fide' traveller.

83   Lowerson, *Sport*, p. 95.

84   *WN*, 28 January 1892.

85   *WE*, 26 September 1891.

86   Ibid.

87   Ibid.

88   *WN*, 22 June 1893.

89   NLI, Account book of Kilruane Football Club, 1876, Ms. 9515.

90   *WI*, 15 February 1890.

91   *WE*, 4 February 1893.

92   *WN*, 2 February 1893.

93   *WN*, 24 November 1892.

94   Mike Cronin, 'Enshrined in blood; the naming of Gaelic Athletic Association grounds and clubs', in *The Sports Historian*, vol. 18, no. 1, 1998, p. 91.

95   Ibid., p. 95.

96   The names used included John Dillon, Tim Healy, Michael Davitt, the Leaguers or nationalist icons from the past such as Daniel O'Connell, Hugh Roe O'Donnell, John Mitchell, Henry Grattan, Edward Fitzgerald and the Volunteers.

97   NA CBS, 2452/S.

98   Cronin, *Enshrined in blood*, p. 96.

99   Ibid.

100   *WG*, 22, 29 September, 6 October 1893.

101   NA CBS, 1/22594; 6247/S.

102   The only mention of R. W. Moorwood in Mullingar is in connection with football but the *Westmeath Independent* of 21 September 1895 carried an advertisement from Roland Moorwood, 'the head agent for the Williams typewriter', described as 'the latest and most up to date machine in the market'. His premises were located at 5, Upper Ormond Quay, Dublin.

103   *WE*, 26 October 1889.

104   *WE*, 2 November 1889. Rugby was the alternative choice.

105   Tom Hunt, 'Mullingar sport', p. 23.

106   *WN*, 5 November 1891.

107   *WN*, 15 December 1892. Following the success of the club in the Westmeath championship of 1892 the *Westmeath Nationalist* published a series of profiles of the playing members and these form a useful source in compiling a socio–economic profile of the club's members. This information together with reports of testimonials presented to departing members has been the main source of data used in constructing the profile.

108   *WN*, 11 August 1892.

109   *WG*, 7 November1890.

110   *WN*, 12 January 1893.

111   *WN*, 2 February 1893.

112   JMJ, *Centenary record: Men's confraternity of the Holy Family, Mullingar 1867–1967* (Mullingar, 1967).

113   *WN*, 9 February 1893.

114   Wheatley, *Nationalism and the Irish Party*, pp. 124–125; *M.R.*, 30 July 1936. This newspaper's report on his death credited him with being 'prominently identified with every movement that had for its object the amelioration of popular griev-ances'. He was one of the first members of the Mullingar Sinn Féin Club in

Mullingar and was elected its first chairman. During the War of Independence he was interned in Ballykinlar and not surprisingly given his background, his final political resting place was in the Fianna Fáil party. See Chapter 7, p. 210 for Brett's involvement in the Shamrocks Hurling Club in Mullingar.

115 *WG*, 14 February 1890.
116 A townland formed the smallest territorial unit of civil administration used in Ireland.
117 *WE*, 13 December 1890, 3 October 1891.
118 *WE*, 28 January 1893.
119 *WN*, 19 January 1893.
120 Neil Tranter, 'The patronage of organised sport in central Scotland, 1820–1900', in *Journal of Sports History*, vol. 16, no. 3, 1989, p. 227.
121 Ibid., pp. 229–30.
122 See Chapters 2, p. 67.
123 *WE*, 22 November 1890.
124 *WG*, 12 December 1890.
125 *WN*, 5 May 1892.
126 *WN*, 20 October 1892.
127 *WN*, 23 December 1892.
128 *WI*, 4 January 1890; *Sport*, 28 August 1887. According to a report in *Sport* football had been played in Athlone prior to the establishment of the T. P. O' Connor Club. In August 1887 the employees of the GSWR of Inchicore travelled to Athlone for their annual excursion. The members of the Henry Grattan GFC travelled to Athlone on the occasion and played an Athlone team on the Fair Green as part of the day's entertainment. Reportedly the Athlone Gaels showed great skill 'being old association players'.
129 Jeremiah Sheehan, *Worthies of Westmeath* (Moate, 1987), pp. 95–6. For an aspect of T. P. O'Connor's career see Ian Sheehy, 'T. P. O'Connor and *The Star* 1886–90', in D. George Boyce and Alan O'Day (eds.) *Ireland in Transition, 1867–1921* (London, 2004), pp. 76–91.
130 NA, CBS 1893, Western Division–County Roscommon; returns showing the number of branches of the GAA in the above county on 31 December 1892, 6247/S.
131 *WI*, 18 January 1890.
132 *WI*, 10 May 1890.
133 *WI*, 30 August 1890.
134 Ibid.
135 *WN*, 4 January 1894.
136 The use of the 1901 census forms to establish detail on individuals active ten years earlier is problematic. However, occupational mobility was extremely limited at the time so the conclusions on occupations of the early footballers may be regarded as accurate. This was calculated by adjusting the age given in the 1901 forms to 1892. It would not be safe to make any statistical analysis of the conjugal status of this group in 1892 using the 1901 information.
137 It was possible to identify the occupational status of 120 players but it was only possible to establish the age of eighty–nine of these. The age of only seven Athlone players could be established with certainty as opposed to seventeen occupations.
138 *Census of Ireland, 1891, Part I: Area; houses and population: Also the ages, civil or conjugal conditions, occupations, birthplaces, religion, and education of the people. Vol. 1. Province of Leinster, No.10. county of Westmeath*, [c–615–ix.], p. 905.

6. The development of soccer and rugby, 1875–1905

1 Garnham, *Association football*; Mason, *Association football and English society*, (Brighton, 1980); Collins, *Rugby's great split*.
2 Malcolm Brodie, *100 years of Irish football* (Belfast, 1980), p. 2. See also Ian Nannestad 'The origin of association football in Ireland', in *Soccer History*, vol. 5, 2003, pp. 8–11. Garnham, *Association football*, pp. 2–41.

3   Garnham, *Origins and development of football*, pp. 162–8.
4   Ibid., p. 163.
5   Garnham, *Association football*, p. 5.
6   Ibid., pp. 5–6.
7   *Burke's Peerage, Baronetage and Knighthood* (London, 1911), pp. 637–8. He was the third son of Ireland's premier baronet, Rev. Sir Algernon Coote and although the family's ancestral seat was located at Ballyfin, Queen's county, the family resided at Wavertree, Tunbridge Wells in Kent.
8   Dooley, *Decline of the big house*, p. 77.
9   *WI*, 8 January 1887.
10   Ibid.
11   *WI*, 20 October 1894. Garnham incorrectly suggests that Coote succeeded in involving members of his father's tenantry and local shopkeepers in the clubs.
12   *WI*, 16 February 1887.
13   *WI*, 3 November 1888; *WI*, 16 February 1887. Both were listed on the Ranelagh School rugby football team that defeated Roscommon.
14   *WI*, 18 February 1887; 5 March 1887; 12 March 1887; 19 March 1887; 26 March 1887; 2 April 1887.
15   *WI*, 7 January 1888.
16   *Sport*, 7 January 1899.
17   *Ellis's Irish education directory and scholastic guide for 1887 (Sixth year of issue)* (Dublin, 1887), p. 153.
18   Ibid., pp. 273, 281.
19   *WI*, 1 July 1893.
20   *WI*, 27 December 1890.
21   Michael Quane, 'Ranelagh Endowed School, Athlone', in *Journal of the Old Athlone Society*, vol. 1, no. 1, 1969, p. 32.
22   Garnham, *Association football*, pp. 22–23.
23   *Slater's Directory*, 1892, p. 17; *WI*, 14 November 1903; 19 December 1903.
24   *WE*, 6 February 1904; 5 March 1904; 26 March 1904; 16 April 1904; 30 April 1904; 25 March 1905.
25   Garnham, 'Introduction', pp. 5–7. Edmund Van Esbeck, *The story of Irish Rugby* (London, 1986), pp. 12–37.
26   Both graduated at the level of MA.
27   *WG*, 28 February 1879.
28   Quane, 'Ranelagh', p. 32; according to his obituary Foster was a founder member of Bective Rugby Football Club and was also amateur lightweight boxing champion of Ireland in 1880-81, *WE*, 3 June 1939.
29   *WG*, 23 November 1883.
30   *WG*, 11 December 1885.
31   Bullock, *Sixty Years*, pp. 79–80. I am indebted to Neal Garnham for this reference. Bullock was a student in Farra School from 1878–79.
32   *WG*, 21 April 1898.
33   *WG*, 22 April 1892.
34   *WI*, 20 April 1889; 27 December 1890.
35   *WG*, 17 December 1880.
36   *WG*, 25 September 1885.
37   *WI*, 21 February 1897; 13 March 1897.
38   *WI*, 14 November 1891; 9 January 1892. On these occasions teams of the RIF played civilian selections.
39   *WI*, 10 September 1896.
40   *WI*, 7 November 1896; 5 December 1896; 23 January 1897.
41   *WI*, 3 April 1897.
42   *WI*, 8 May 1897. They were replaced by the Connaught Rangers.
43   *WI*, 15 February 1898. These men also played on the early Athlone soccer teams.
44   *WI*, 22 October 1898. Galway, Queen's College, Gort, Tuam, Castlebar, Westport,

Portumna and Ballinasloe clubs also entered the initial Connacht league.

45 *WI*, 18 November 1899. This meeting was held at the Ranelagh School with Robert Bailie in the chair.

46 *WG*, 25 June 1886.

47 *WG*, 22 June 1889; 12 July 1889. As stated earlier Newburn, on 16 July 1898, became the first athlete in history to long-jump over 24' when he jumped 24'½" in the international match against Scotland at Ballsbridge. See Chapter 3, p. 100.

48 Mason, *Association football*, p. 29.

49 Garnham, *Association football and English Society*, p. 47.

50 *WI*, 4 September 1886.

51 *WI*, 1 May 1886. The game in which 'no special rules seemed to be observed' ended scoreless.

52 *WI*, 16 July 1892.

53 Burke, 'Victorian Athlone', p. 285.

54 *WI*, 28 October 1899.

55 *WI*, 17, 24 March 1894.

56 Holt, *Sport and the British*, p. 154.

57 Frank Lynch, *The history of Athlone Town Football Club the first 101 years* (Athlone, 1991), pp. 13–15.

58 Ibid., pp. 13–22.

59 Ibid., pp. 22–26.

60 *WI*, 10 September 1892.

61 Bairner, 'Ireland, sport and empire', p. 63.

62 Garnahm, *Association football*, pp. 18–21.

63 Burke, 'Victorian Athlone', pp. 162–74; NA, County Inspectors report for the county of Westmeath, October 1899 (CBS, IGCI), 20411/S.

64 WCL, Burgess papers: Typescript of marriage registers 1845–1890 of St Mary's parish, Athlone. Typescript of marriage registers 1851–1870 of St Peter's church, Athlone. RCB, Register of marriages, St Mary's parish (Athlone), 1863–90, P.0392.03.2; Register of marriages, St Mary's parish (Athlone), 1891–1940, P.0392.03.3; Register of marriages, St Peter's parish (Athlone), 1870–1939, P.0400.03.3; Register of marriages of parish of Mullingar, 1880–1905, P. 0366.02.2. For marriage practices in the Curragh district see Con Costello, *A most delightful station* (Cork, 1999), pp 196–197. For relationships between civilians and soldiers see Burke, *Athlone in the Victorian Era*, pp. 155–169.

65 The Beverley Rovers were, presumably, a military team.

66 *WG*, 15 November 1878.

67 *WI*, 30 March 1891.

68 Based on newspaper reports carried in the *Westmeath Examiner*, *Westmeath Independent*, *Midland Reporter* and the *Westmeath Guardian* over the period.

69 Campbell, 'Sport and the army', p. 43.

70 Ibid., p. 45.

71 Ibid., p. 47.

72 *WI*, 31 October 1890.

73 *Athlone Times*, 11 February 1893.

74 *WN*, 20 April 1893.

75 *WI*, 26 March 1892; 23 April 1892; 7 May 1892.

76 *WI*, 17 December 1887; 31 December 1887. Also Lynch, *Athlone Town Football Club*, pp. 9–10. Lieutenant Bolton was described as an English international although his name does not appear on any compendium of English international players.

77 *WI*, 14 February 1891; 24 February 1894.

78 *WI*, 27 August 1892.

79 *WI*, 10 September 1892.

80 *WG*, 30 December 1904.

81 *WI*, 23 May 1891.

82 *WE*, 17 March 1883.

83   *WN*, 26 October 1893.

84   *WG*, 14 May 1896; *WE*, 2 December 1899.

85   Garnham, *Origins*, p. 171.

86   Rev. Daniel Callogly, *Cavan's football story* (Cavan, 1979), pp. 45–47.

87   This information was gleaned from comparing the manuscript census returns of 1901 with a list of names associated with the club.

88   *WE*, 14 March 1903; 4 April 1903; 9 May 1903; 3 October 1903; 24 October 1903; 31 October 1903; 5 December 1903.

89   *WI*, 10 December 1904.

90   *WG*, 31 March 1905; 28 April 1905; 12 May 1905. *WE*, 5 November 1905; 16 December 1905.

91   *WI*, 16 September 1905.

92   Joseph Garry was the vice-president of the young Ireland football club and was accidentally killed in a rail accident in October 1903. Of the thirteen members of the St Patrick's club present at the funeral, eight were on the Newbrook Wanderers team that won the tournament.

93   *WE*, 3 October 1903.

94   *WI*, 24 April 1897. The Lancashire Fusiliers were particularly successful in the Army Cup competition in the 1896–7 season eventually reaching the United Kingdom final where they were defeated by the Royal Artillery (Portsmouth), in a final watched by 15,000 to 20,000 people. In an earlier round (*WI*, 12 December 1896), they reportedly changed into a set of Sunderland gear at half–time in their match against Sherwood Foresters. The semi-final was played on the grounds of Everton Football Club.

95   For examples of these inter-rural district games see *WI*, 19 March 1898; 16 April 1898; 26 February 1999; 6 May 1899; 13 May 1899; 22 July 1899.

96   *WI*, 25 October 1902. The club had won nine games, drawn four and in the process scored thirty goals.

97   *WI*, 18 April 1903.

98   Lynch, *Athlone Town Football Club*, p. 33.

99   *WI*, 25 October 1902.

100 *WI*, 11 October 1902.

101 *WI*, 25 October 1902.

102 *WI*, November 1 1902; November 8 1902; 6 December 1902; 27 December 1902.

103 *WI*, 11 October 1902.

104 *WI*, 14 May 1904.

105 *MR*, 27 April 1905.

106 Tranter, 'Occupational structure', p. 303. Ian Nannestad, 'From Sabbath breakers to respectable sportsmen: the development of football in Lincolnshire, 1855 to 1881', MA thesis, De Montfort University, Leicester, 2003, p. 131.

107 Garnham, *Association football*, p. 92.

108 Ibid., pp. 96–7.

109 Tranter, 'Organized sport', p. 303; Nannestad, 'Sabbath breakers', p. 131.

110 Michael Mullen, 'The devolution of the Irish economy in the nineteenth century and the bifurcation of Irish sport', in *International Journal of the History of Sport*, vol. 13, no. 2, 1996, p. 43.

7. Cultural ferment and the re-emergence of the GAA, 1900–1905

1   Tom Garvin, *The evolution of Irish nationalist politics* (Dublin, 1972), pp. 91–2.

2   Patrick Maume, *The long gestation: Irish nationalist life, 1891–1918* (Dublin, 1999), p. 27.

3   Maume, *Long gestation*, p. 48.

4   John Hutchinson, *The dynamics of cultural nationalism: the Gaelic revival and the creation of the Irish nation state* (London, 1987), p. 168.

5   Maume, *Long gestation*, pp. 48–59.

6   Ibid., pp. 53–5.

7 Hutchinson, *Dynamics*, p. 173.
8 Ibid., p. 174.
9 Maume, *Long gestation*, p. 59.
10 Hutchinson, *Dynamics*, p. 178.
11 Tom Garvin, *Nationalist revolutionaries of Ireland, 1858–1928* (Oxford, 1987), p. 79.
12 Ibid., p. 85.
13 John Wylie, 'Laurence Ginnell, 1852–1923; Westmeath's radical agrarian', MA thesis, NUI, Maynooth, 1999,unpublished, pp. 23, 76.
14 *WE*, 2 March 1901.
15 *WE*, 4 April 1903.
16 *WE*, 18 April 1903.
17 Ibid.
18 Ibid.
19 *WE*, 25 April 1903.
20 *WE*, 2, 9, 16 May 1903.
21 *WI*, 24 October 1902.
22 *MR*, 17 December 1903; 7 January 1904.
23 Ibid.
24 *WE*, 4 July 1903.
25 *WE*, 8 July 1905.
26 *WE*, 3 November 1904; *MR*, 16 March 1905.
27 O'Dwyer, *Kilkenny cricket*, pp.14-15.
28 Neal Garnham, 'Football and national identity in pre-great war Ireland', in *Irish Economic and Social History*, vol. xxviii, 2001, p. 19.
29 *WI*, 28 March 1905.
30 *MR*, 24 July 1904.
31 Ibid.
32 *MR*, 15 June 1905.
33 *MR*, 25 March 1905.
34 *MR*, 16 February 1905.
35 *MR*, 15 September 1904.
36 *WI*, 13 February 1904.
37 de Burca, *GAA: A history*, p. 1.
38 Comerford, *Inventing*, p. 215.
39 Both the Statutes of Kilkenny (1367) and the Statutes of Galway (1537) made references to versions of hurling that were restrictive in intention. The Galway statutes for instance ordered that 'at no time to engage in the hurling of the little ball with hockey sticks or staves, or use the handball for playing outside the walls but only to play with the great football . . .'.
40 Kevin Whelan, 'The geography of hurling', in *History Ireland*, spring, 1993, p. 27.
41 Ibid., p. 28.
42 Patrick Fagan, *A Georgian Celebration: Irish poets of the eighteenth century* (Dublin, 1989), pp. 34–36.
43 *WI*, 16 August 1932.
44 *WE*, 8 October 1896.
45 *WE*, 8 March 1902; 22 March 1902.
46 *WI*, 20 June 1903.
47 *MR*, 20 October 1904.
48 *MR*, 3 December 1903; see also Paddy McCabe, *Hurling in Castlepollard: a history 1899–2005* (Castlepollard, Patrick McCabe: 2006,), pp. 19–40.
49 *MR*, 17 December 1903.
50 *MR*, 15 June 1905.
51 David Gorry, 'The Gaelic Athletic Association in Dublin, 1884–2000, M.Litt. thesis, University College Dublin, 2001, pp. 97–98.
52 Jimmy Wren, *Saint Laurence O'Toole GAC 1901–2001: a centenary history* (Dublin, 2001), p. 3.

53   Eoghan Corry, *Oakboys: Derry's football dream comes true* (Dublin, 1993), pp. 55–57.
54   *MR*, 3 March 1904.
55   *MR*, 16 March 1905.
56   *MR*, 9 February 1905; 12 May 1905; 15 June 1905.
57   *United Ireland*, 27 December 1884. This letter was written by Dr Croke, the Archbishop of Cashel, in acceptance of the invitation of Michael Cusack to become patron of the new association, the GAA.
58   *WE*, 28 October 1899.
59   *WE*, 6 December 1902.
60   *WE*, 17 January 1903.
61   The Young Ireland team affiliated to the national body and were ineligible for this competition.
62   *WE*, 4 July 1903.
63   Joseph Garry was the President of the Young Ireland football club and was accidentally killed in a rail accident in October 1903.
64   *WE*, 3 October 1903.
65   *WE*, 31 October 1903.
66   The area covered Westmeath, Galway, Roscommon, Cavan, Longford, Leitrim, part of King's county and Meath.
67   *WI*, 1 March 1902.
68   *WI*, 12 April 1902.
69   Ibid.
70   *WI*, 10 May 1902.
71   *WI*, 11 October 1902; 18 October 1902; 25 October 1902.
72   *WI*, 19 March 1904.
73   *WI*, 12 November 1904; 12 December 1904; 25 March, 8 April, 15 April, 22 April, 6 May 1905.
74   O'Growney was a Catholic priest and Gaelic League pioneer with Westmeath connections.
75   Cronin, 'Enshrined in blood', p. 96.
76   *WE*, 13 October 1905.
77   *WE*, 4 July 1903.
78   *WE*, 21 November 1903.
79   *WE*, 10 October 1903.
80   Garnham, 'Accounting for the early success of the GAA', p. 74.
81   Mandle, 'Sport as politics', p. 114.
82   Paul Rouse, 'The politics of culture and sport in Ireland: a history of the GAA ban on foreign games 1884–1971. Part One: 1884–1921', in *International Journal of the History of Sport*, vol. 10, no. 3, 1993, pp. 348–9.
83   Brendan MacLua, *The steadfast rule; a history of the GAA ban* (Dublin, 1967), pp. 39–41.
84   Helen Brennan, *The story of Irish dance* (Dingle, 1999), p. 31; also pp. 29–43 for a detailed account of this particular debate.
85   Ibid., p. 33. When these dances were included in a County Mayo dance competition a correspondent to the *Mayo People* newspaper was prompted to ask 'Is it possible that in Gaelic Mayo there are some who still hanker after the fleshpots of Egypt.'
86   R.V. Comerford, *Inventing the nation*, p. 220.
87   MacLua, *Steadfast rule*, pp. 43–8.
88   *WI*, 18 February 1905.
89   O'Dwyer, *Kilkenny cricket*, pp. 66–67. O'Dwyer also lists a re-awakening of nationalism, land agitation, and Kilkenny's first All-Ireland hurling title win in 1904 (played on 24 June 1906) as factors that contributed to cricket's reduced popularity.
90   Bracken, *Foreign and fantastic*, p. 120.
91   *MR*, 7 October, 1905.
92   *WE*, 5 March 1904. Seven clubs (Mullingar Hurling Club, Mullingar Young Irelands, Rochfortbridge, Newbrook Wanderers, Cullion Celtics, Athlone, Castlepollard

Hurling Club) attended this meeting and three more (Moate, Ballymore, Riverstown) sent letters of support.

93   Eoghan Corry, *An illustrated history of the GAA* (Dublin, 2005), p. 44.

94   De Burca, *GAA: A history*, pp.85–8.

95   Lennon, *Playing Rules*, pp. 10–65.

96   *WE*, 5 March 1904. Ironically the improved bureaucracy provided clubs with the opportunity to lodge numerous objections following defeats in championship matches. Early Westmeath championships (and the championships of other counties) are characterised by numerous objections that caused long delays in the organisation of championship games. The 1905 Westmeath football championship was beset by a series of objections that delayed the playing of the first semi-final between Cullion and Riverstown until January 1906. The objection that followed this match was the subject of five different hearings that eventually concluded with a decision to order a replay, which the Cullion Celtic club as the initial winners refused to accept. Athlone Volunteers refused to accept the championship winners medals and the administrative nightmare that was the 1905 Westmeath football championship ended without a final being played. However, the crucial difference from the 1890s was that clubs accepted the administrative structures and remained within the GAA fold.

97   *WI*, 25 March 1905.

98   *WI*, 9 April 1904.

99   Pierre Lanfanchi, Christiane Eisenberg, Tony Mason and Alfred Wahl, *100 years of football: the FIFA centennial book* (London, 2004), pp. 21–22.

100   Adelman, *A sporting time*, p. 6.

101   *WE*, 27 February 1904. The distance from Ballymore to Mullingar was approximately eighteen miles.

102   Ibid.

103   *WE*, 20 August 1904.

104   *WE*, 28 May 1904; 3 November 1904. This edition carried a report on the last game played by the club when they were heavily defeated by the Riverstown Emmett club. The latter club was to dominate the Westmeath football championship for the next decade.

105   *WE*, 12 September 1903; 19 September 1903; 6 October 1903.

106   *WE*, 24 December 1904.

107   *WE*, 18 June 1904.

108   *WE*, 8 June 1905.

109   *MR*, 6 July 1911.

110   *WI*, 29 April 1905.

111   *WG*, 6 July 1906.

112   *WI*, 24 February 1906.

113   *WI*, 25 March 1905.

114   *WI*, 27 January 1906.

115   *WI*, 15 April 1905; 7 April 1906.

116   *WI*, 19 May 1906.

117   Garvin, *Nationalist revolutionaries*, p. 85–90. Hutchinson, *Cultural nationalism*, p. 179.

118   *MR*, 12 February 1903.

119   Peter Hart, *The IRA at war 1916–1923* (Oxford, 2003), p. 132.

120   De Burca, *GAA: A history*, p. 87.

121   Wheatley, *Irish Nationalism*, pp. 25–30; Maume, *Long Gestation*, p. 229.

122   Mandle, *Gaelic Athletic Association*, p. 5.

123   Comerford, *Inventing the nation*, p. 219.

124   *WE*, 19 April 1924.

8. SPECTATOR SPORT, 1850–1905

1   S. C. and A. M. Hall, *Ireland: its scenery, character& c.* (London, 1841-43), vol. iii, p. 422.

2   Elizabeth Malcolm, 'Popular recreation in nineteenth-century Ireland', in Oliver MacDonagh, W. F. Mandle and Pauric Travers (eds.), *Irish Culture and Nationalism, 1750–1950* (London, 1983), p. 51.

3   Rev. Wallace Clare (ed.), *A young Irishman's diary (1836–1847) being extracts from the early journal of John Keegan of Moate* (No place of publication: 1928), pp. 104–05.

4   Stiofán Ó Cadhla, *The holy well tradition: the pattern of St Declan, Ardmore, County Waterford 1800–2000* (Dublin, 2002), p. 53.

5   Seamas Ó Maitiú, 'Changing images of Donnybrook fair', in Denis A. Cronin, Jim Gilligan & Karina Holton (eds.), *Irish Fairs and Markets: Studies in local history* (Dublin, 2001), pp. 165–6. A more detailed account of the Donnybrook Fair is found in Ó Maitiú's, *The humours of Donnybrook: Dublin's famous fair and its suppression* (Dublin, 1995).

6   Malcolm, 'Popular recreation', pp. 46–7.

7   W. H. Crawford, 'The patron, or festival of St Kevin at the seven churches, Glendalough, County Wicklow 1813', in *Ulster Folk Life*, vol. 32, 1986, p. 38.

8   Ibid., pp. 37–47. Cadhla, *The holy well tradition*, pp. 26–31.

9   S. J. Connolly, *Priests and people in pre-famine Ireland* (Dublin, 2001 edition), p. 151.

10 Connell, *Diocese of Meath*, pp. 239–43.

11 Ibid., p. 166.

12 Ibid., p. 151.

13 Ibid., p. 171.

14 Mason, *Association football*, pp. 155–7; Garnham, *Association football*, pp. 115–17; Neil Tranter, 'The Cappielow riot and the composition and behaviour of soccer crowds in late Victorian Scotland' in *International journal of the history of sport*, vol. 12, no. 3, 1995, pp. 125–40.

15 *WI*, 6 April 1889.

16 *WG*, 19 May 1893.

17 *WE*, 2 June 1894; 19 June 1899.

18 *WI*, 12 April 1893.

19 *WI*, 21 April 1894.

20 *WI*, 6 April 1889.

21 *WI*, 14 April 1894.

22 *WI*, 11 August 1906.

23 *WI*, 20 August 1887.

24 *WI*, 20 August 1887; 3 September 1887.

25 *WI*, 13 August 1887.

26 *WI*, 10 May 1890.

27 *WN*, 23 March 1893.

28 *WI*, 19 May 1906. In the hurling semi-final Galway played Kilkenny and in the football Mayo played Dublin. For a detailed analysis of attendance and crowd structure at soccer matches in particular see Garnham, *Association football*, pp. 99–131.

29 *WI*, 6 July 1889.

30 *WI*, 19 August 1893.

31 *WG*, 30 June 1899.

32 *WI*, 6 April 1861. Hunt, 'The Thomastown and Garrycastle Races 1857–1868', in *Journal of the old Athlone society*, vol. 11, no. 8, 2005, p. 297.

33 *WG*, 20 September 1895. See *Westmeath Guardian*, 22 July 1892 and 22 September 1893 for particularly comprehensive attendance lists, which include representatives of numerous landed families in the county and catchment area. For a detailed list of those attending a match at Castlepollard between the North Westmeath Polo Club and County Kildare see *Westmeath Examiner*, 15 August 1903 and *Midland Reporter*, 11 July 1901 for those in attendance when North Westmeath played County Antrim.

34 *WE*, 28 September 1901.

35 *WG*, 22 July 1892.

36 *WG*, 28 October 1852.

37   *WG*, 10 August 1883.
38   *WE*, 21 May 1892.
39   *WE*, 7 September 1901.
40   Ibid.
41   *WE*, 2 December 1901.
42   Huggins, *Flat racing*, p. 120.
43   *WI*, 17 June 1899.
44   *WI*, 11 June 1904.
45   *WG*, 31 July 1862; 16 July 1863.
46   *WE*, 19 May 1892.
47   *WE*, 22 August 1892.
48   *WE*, 20 March 1899, 7 February 1903.
49   *WI*, 4 May 1895.
50   *WE*, 12 May 1883.
51   *WG*, 27 June 1890.
52   *WE*, 3 May 1890.
53   *WG*, 21 April 1882.
54   *WG*, 13 June 1878.
55   *WI*, 27 July 1872.
56   *WI*, 11 August 1896; 15 August 1896.
57   *WI*, 11 August 1906.
58   *WE*, 8 March 1890; 11 June 1904.
59   *WI*, 4 March 1896.
60   *WI*, 10 May 1890.
61   *WE*, 26 January1895.
62   *WE*, 6 February 1904.
63   *WI*, 1, 15 April 1905; 10 June 1905.
64   *WI*, 9 April 1904.
65   *MR*, 4 May 1905.
66   Agricultural Statistics of Ireland, 1902, [Cd 1263], 661, pp. 148–9.
67   *Westmeath Herald and General Advertiser*, 31 March 1860.
68   *FJ*, 28 March 1860.
69   *FJ*, 16 May 1859; 26 March 1860.
70   *W.I.*, 6 April 1861.
71   *WI*, 30 April 1864.
72   *FJ*, 22 May 1866; see also *The Irish Times*, 9 May 1865 for advertisements for special trains organised for the races of 9 and 10 May 1865.
73   *WG*, 1 May 1851.
74   *WG*, 7 June 1860.
75   *WG*, 8 June 1865.
76   *WI*, 8 June 1868.
77   *MR*, 15 May 1902.
78   *WE*, 7 June 1902.
79   *WE*, 10 June 1905.
80   Ibid.
81   *WI*, 24 February 1906.
82   *WI*, 17 August 1901.
83   *WI*, 17 June 1899.
84   *WI*, 17 August 1901.
85   *WG*, 19 May 1905.
86   *WI*, 28 May 1904.
87   *WG*, 19 May 1905.
88   *WE*, 11 June 1904; *WI*, 11 June 1904.
89   *WE*, 2 June 1906.
90   *WI*, 6 April 1889.
91   *WI*, 17 June 1899.

92   *WI*, 11 May 1850; 13 May 1851.
93   *WI*, 6 July 1889. The Ranelagh sports were held on Friday and the AWM event on the following Saturday with the latter event held on the Ranelagh grounds.
94   *WI*, 19 August 1893.
95   *WI*, 21 April 1894.
96   *WG*, 6 April 1888.
97   *WI*, 1 April 1863.
98   *Irish Sportsman*, 17 July 1875.
99   *WI*, 3 August 1850.
100   *WG*, 28 June 1895.
101   Brailsford, *Sport, time and society*, p. 70.
102   *WG*, 4 April 1850.
103   *WI*, 25 April 1857.
104   *WI*, 24 September 1853.
105   *WI*, 17 June 1899.
106   *WI*, 31 May 1902.
107   *WI*, 11 May 1850; 3 May 1851. The landed gentry present included George Boyd, Henry Murray, Richard Connolly, J. de Blaquire, D. Reynell, C. Lyons etc.
108   *WI*, 14 September 1867.
109   *WI*, 6 April 1889.
110   *Irish Sportsman*, 22 September 1877. This was the first 'public' athletic event held in the region.
111   *WI*, 21 April 1894.
112   *WG*, 22 September 1893.
113   Wray Vamplew, *The Turf: a social and economic history of horse racing* (London, 1976), p. 132.
114   Ibid., p. 134.
115   *WI*, 29 April 1893.
116   *WN*, 22 April 1897.
117   *WI*, 16 April 1898.
118   *WI*, 17 June 1899.
119   *WI*, 10 May 1873.
120   *Sport,* 23 November 1898.
121   *Sport*, 7 September 1901.
122   *WE*, 19 March 1904.
123   Ibid.
124   *WI*, 17 June 1899.
125   *WI*, 4 May 1901.
126   Vamplew, *The Turf*, p. 131, Huggins, *Flat Racing*, p. 122.
127   *WG*, 4 November 1852.
128   Anthony McCan, 'The diary of a young lady, Mary Anne Power, 1868–1873', in *Decies: journal of the Waterford archaeological & historical society*, vol. 57, 2001, pp. 135–7.
129   *Leinster Express*, 10 April 1880, quoted in Dooley, *The Decline of the Big House*, p. 54.
130   *WE*, 2 May 1903.
131   *WI*, 4 May 1895.
132   *WE*, 25 August 1888.
133   *WI*, 11 June 1904.
134   *WI*, 6 April 1889.
135   Vamplew, *The Turf*, p. 137.
136   *WI*, 17 June 1899.
137   *WI*, 6 April 1889.
138   *WI*, 12 April 1890.
139   *WI*, 18 April 1891.
140   Ibid.
141   *WI*, 17 June 1899.

142 *Sport*, 10 June 1893.
143 *WI*, 11 May 1850; 15 September 1851.
144 *WG*, 1 May 1851.
145 *WI*, 20 August 1887.
146 *WG*, 26 June 1903
147 *WI*, 22 August 1893.
148 *WE*, 2 December 1901.
149 *WE*, 25 June 1904; 1 July 1905. *WG*, 24 June 1904.
150 Minute book, Carrick-on-Suir Athletic, Cricket and Football Club, established around 1879 (privately held).
151 Ibid., 11 March 1880; 15 March 1880.
152 Ibid., 28 June 1880, 14 October 1880, 29 September 1881, 4 April 1882, 4 August 1882.
153 *MR*, 21 September 1899.
154 *WI*, 17 June 1899.
155 *WI*, 30 August 1856.
156 *WI*, 30 August 1863.
157 *WI*, 10 August 1872.
158 William Bulfin, *Rambles in Eirinn* (Dublin, 1907), vol. 1, p. 64.
159 Jeremy Crump, '"The great carnival of the year": the Leicester Races in the nineteenth century', in *Transactions of the Leicestershire Historical and Archaeological Society*, vol. 58 (1982–3), p. 65.
160 *WI*, 5 August 1850; 13 September 1851.
161 *WI*, 13 May 1899.
162 Ibid.
163 Ibid.
164 Ó Cadhla, *The holy well tradition*, pp. 58–9.
165 *WG*, 8 April 1892.
166 *WI*, 27 July 1867; 1 June 1867; 9 May 1868; 16 May 1868.
167 *WG*, 21 April 1905.
168 *WG*, 16 June 1899.
169 *WI*, 14 June 1873.
170 *WG*, 5, 12 August 1881.
171 Ibid.
172 *WE*, 7 April 1888.
173 *WI*, 21 April 1894.
174 *WI*, 17 June 1889.
175 *MR*, 31 March 1900.
176 *WI*, 4 May 1901.
177 *WG*, 22, 29 September 1899.
178 *WE*, 30 September 1899.
179 *WE*, 2 July 1898.
180 *MR*, 18 July 1899.
181 Ibid. *WG*, 30 June 1899.
182 Vamplew, *The Turf*, pp. 138–9.
183 Wray Vamplew, 'Sports crowd disorder in Britain, 1870–1914: Causes and controls' in *Journal of Sport History*, vol. 7, no. 1 (Spring, 1980), p. 11.
184 *WG*, 15 May 1891.
185 *WG*, 29 July 1887.
186 *WI*, 22 September 1900.
187 *WI*, 22 August 1868.
188 *WI*, 1 November 1902.
189 *WI*, 12 April 1890.
190 Ibid.
191 Ibid.
192 *WI*, 14 April 1894.

193   *WG*, 26 March 1840.
194   *WI*, 6 June 1868.
195   *WI*, 17 June 1899.
196   *WG*, 30 May 1890.
197   *WG*, 5 September 1890.
198   *WG*, 6 June 1879.
199   *WI*, 3 June 1899.
200   *WE*, 13 June 1905.
201   *WI*, 31 May 1902.
202   *WG*, 19 September 1902. This was reportedly the first case of its kind in Ireland. In a sixteen foot square booth, the Gonouds were packing up 96 dozen empty and full bottles at the end of the day, when the police raid occurred.
203   *WG*, 9 January 1891.
204   *WE*, 11 September 1898, also 23 September 1899.
205   *WE*, 7 June 1902.
206   *WE*, 11 April 1903.
207   *WE*, 13 June 1903.
208   *WE*, 10 June 1905.
209   *WE*, 5 April 1905.
210   Peter Jupp and Eoin Magennis, 'Introduction: crowds in Ireland, c.1720–1920', in Peter Jupp and Eoin Magennis (eds.) *Crowds in Ireland, c.1720–1920* (Basingstoke, 2000) p. 30.

EPILOGUE

1   Huggins, *Victorians*, p. 19.
2   Tranter, *Sport, economy and society*, pp. 40–41; also Tranter, 'Social and occupational structure', pp. 308–11.
3   Timothy W. Guinnane, *The vanishing Irish: households, migration, and the rural economy in Ireland, 1850–1914* (Princeton, 1997), pp. 193–240.
4   *Census of Ireland, 1901*. Based on calculations from detail on conjugal status of different age groups, p. 54.
5   Garnham, *Association football*, p. 95.
6   The Dease, O'Reilly and Nugent families were Catholic as were several of the substantial farmers who joined in the 1890s.
7   At least 340 different sports clubs, of varying longevity, were identified in the period covered by this study. This number is far greater than other political and social organisations.
8   Tranter, 'Chronology', p. 379.
9   For Irish attitudes to women's participation in sport in the 1880s see Rouse, 'Sport and Ireland in 1891' in Bairner (ed), *Sport and the Irish*, pp. 18–20.
10   *WI*, 4 Sept 1886. The Athlone Woollen Mills athletic sports of 1886 included a girls' race in which eleven girls competed for prizes of 3s and 2s.
11   Anon, *British Hunts and Huntsmen*, pp. 415–416.
12   Lawrence, *Handbook*, 1867–68, p. 123. Lawrence credited Mrs Smyth of Gaybrook, near Mullingar, for the introduction of archery to Ireland. In the company of Mr Lambert of Beauparc and Mr Napier of Loughcrew they established the Meath Archers in 'about' 1833.
13   Parratt, 'Athletic womanhood', pp. 144–45.
14   Hargreaves, 'Playing like gentlemen', p. 43.
15   Collins, *Rugby's great split*, p. xiii.
16   Fingall, Elizabeth Countess of Fingal, *Seventy Years Young* (Dublin, The Lilliput Press, first published in 1937, 1995 edition), p. 98.
17   Maume, *Long gestation*, p. 53.
18   The diaries of Laeda Reynell (1862) and of Mary B. Sommerville (1860–1902) and of H. S. Tottenham of Tudenham in particular provide evidence of the mobility and the continuous socialisation that surrounded sports events for this particular class of

society. I am grateful to Marian Keaney for drawing my attention to these sources.

19 *WI*, 17 June 1899.

20 *WI*, 31 May 1902.

21 Huggins, *Victorians*, p. 112. For a detailed exploration of the economic impact of sport see Ibid., pp. 111–138. Also Tranter, *Sport, economy and society in Britain 1750–1914* (Cambridge, 1998), pp. 20–22. The most detailed economic history of Victorian sport is Vamplew's *Pay up and play the game.*

22 *WE*, 6 March 1897. This letter sought to encourage reluctant subscribers to increase their subscriptions beyond the minimum £10.

23 *WE*, 22 Nov. 1902.

24 *WG*, 24 June 1881, *WN*, 2 June 1892, *MR*, 2 June 1904, *WG*, 17 Aug. 1894, *WE*, 23 June 1895. For a detailed examination of Victorian angling in the Mullingar district see Tom Hunt, 'Angling in the Mulingar district in Victorian times: a class act?' in Seamus O'Brien (ed.), *A Town in Transition – Post Famine Mullingar* (Mullingar, 2007), pp. 102–133.

25 Daniel Gerard O'Sullivan, 'Sport, leisure and class in Cork, 1870–1939', M Litt thesis, NUI Galway, 2002. This thesis attempts an analysis of the development of sport in Cork but adopts a different approach to the one used in this study. It makes greater use of club minute books and tends to concentrate more on the elite involvement in sport. The study of cricket in Cork aimed to 'look at the growth and development of the sport in general during the later decades of the nineteenth century and earlier decades' but depended almost totally on the Cork County Cricket Club, and as a result the focus is on the development of elite cricket, pp. 616–80. The study is qualitative rather than quantitative in nature.

26 Speak, M. A., 'Social stratification and participation in sport in Mid–Victorian England, with particular reference to Lancaster, 1840–1870', in J. A. Mangan (ed.), *Pleasure, profit and proselytism: British culture and sport at home and abroad, 1700–1914* (London, 1988), p. 43.

Appendices

Appendix 1

Population change in County Westmeath, 1851–1901

Census period	Total population	Male	Female	Decrease	Percentage decrease
1851	111,407	56,095	55,312	29,893	21.15
1861	90,879	46,218	44,661	20,528	18.42
1871	78,432	39,804	38,628	12,447	13.69
1881	71,798	36,478	35,320	6,634	8.46
1891	65,109	33,927	31,182	6,689	9.32
1901	58,433	30,093	28,340	6,676	10.25

Source: *Census of population*, 1901

Appendix 2

Agricultural and recreational horses in nine selected counties in Ireland, 1901

County	Acreage	Number of agricultural horses	Number of recreational horses	Recreational horses as % of total horses
Meath	577,735	15,699	2,129	11.94
Dublin	226,784	22,202	2,931	11.66
Kildare	418,497	12,774	1,471	10.33
Westmeath	454,104	11,502	1,031	8.22
Limerick	662,973	16,003	1,072	6.28
Cork	1,838,921	55,539	2,962	5.06
Tipperary	1,050,172	29,950	1,641	5.19
Antrim	711,666	32,832	1,246	3.65
Down	312,113	33,152	1,285	3.73

Source: *Agricultural returns*, 1901

Appendix 3

Land farmed by 'bona fide' farmers who were members of Westmeath Hunt Club

Name	Land held	Valuation £	Number of units held
Ballesty, Michael	266	228	3
Brabazon, Alfred	789	715	3
Brabazon, Robert	270	188	5
Cleary, Patrick	179	136	1
Hope, Michael	531	318	3
McLoughlin, William	553	330	9
Mitchell, Frank	281	167	8
Murray, William	577	419	3
Ronaldson, G.V.	366	261	1
Salmon, Eugene	256	183	4
Taaffee, James	143	113	6
Taaffee, Christopher	118	95	1
Taylor, James	425	380	8

Appendix 4

Races ridden and win ratio of leading gentlemen jockeys in Ireland, 1871–77

Name	1871	1872	1873	1874	1875	1876	1877
T. Beasley	29/5	26/1	31/6	48/12	76/25	57/18	52/9
Capt. Bates	—/—	—/—	11/3	13/4	24/8	45/17	31/9
'St James'	—/—	23/5	55/12	47/22	30/14	70/19	43/15
G. Moore	36/9	58/18	68/16	60/17	44/12	29/8	51/16
D. Murphy	3/1	10/1	12/3	18/4	29/8	30/6	6/2
T. Widger	9/2	8/0	5/1	2/0	16/2	46/9	56/10

Dashes = No races ridden
Source: *The Irish Sportsman*, 24 November 1877

Appendix 5

Subscriptions to the Westmeath Hunt Club, 1890–1901

Season	Amount subscribed	Number of subscribers
1890–1	£829 17s	99
1891–2	£793 13s	101
1892–3	£826 4s	107
1893–4	£941 7s	116
1894–5	£873 15s	104
1895–6	£854 15s	103
1896–7	£820 14s	101
1897–8	£826 4s	108
1898–9	£774 17s	103
1899–00	£814 16s	103
1900–01	£988 13s	114

Source: Account material of Westmeath Hunt Club

Appendix 6

Frequency of participation in Athlone races, 1857–68

Frequency of participation	Westmeath residents	Outside the county residents	Unidentified residents
1	7	29	34
2	1	14	7
3	1	11	2
4	0	2	0
5	0	1	0
6	0	2	0
7	0	2	0
9	0	1	0
12	0	1	0
15	0	1	0
16	1	0	0
35	0	1	0

Source: *Westmeath Guardian*, 1857–68

Appendix 7

Races held, number of horses running and prize-money available in Ireland, 1860–70

Year	Races	Horses running	Prize-money (£)
1860	337	556	20,654
1861	352	640	20,915
1862	272	538	17,661
1863	265	550	15,693
1864	287	625	18,217
1865	346	717	19,321
1866	322	738	19,212
1867	333	660	20,979
1868	369	674	22,048
1869	419	770	25,385
1870	397	845	27,041

Source: *Racing Calendar* 1878, 541–2

Appendix 8

Identified shareholders and directors of Westmeath (Mullingar) Racing Company Limited

Name	Year	Occupation	Political/other positions	Other information
Bannon, J. C.	1890	China/Glass dealer		Shareholder
Berry, William	1890	Butcher	Pres. MCCC*	Shareholder
Branigan, James	1890	Unknown		Shareholder
Briscoe, E.T.F.	1891	Gentry		Shareholder
Burke, Mr	1890	Unknown		Shareholder
Cleary, Patrick	1905	Auctioneer		Director 1895
Daly, P.	1893	Grocer, spirit dealer (GSD)	Chairman Town Commissioners	Shareholder
Dillon-Kelly,	1894	Doctor		Shareholder
Doherty, George T.	1901	Butcher		Shareholder
Donohoe, James	1890	Auctioneer		Shareholder
Dowdall, Jos. P.	1890	Leather seller	County Council	Director
Downes, Christopher	1890	Baker/Confectioner		Director

Name	Year	Occupation	Political/other positions	Other information
Downes, N. J.	1890	Lawyer	Vice-Ch. Co. Co.	Shareholder
Downes, Robert	1890	Farmer	Ch. Co. Co.	Director
Doyne, James	1892	Milliner/Dress-maker	JP & TC	Shareholder
Fetherstonhaugh, Capt. C.	1890	Gentry		Director
Fetherstonhaugh, Thomas A.	1893	Gentry/Lawyer		Shareholder
Gordon, John W.	1890	Draper		Director
Greville, Lord	1890	Aristocrat	MFH (1886–93)	Director
Hayden, John P.	1896	Newspaper pro-prietor	MP	Shareholder
Henehan, Ml.	1893	GSD		Shareholder
Kellaghan, James	1892	Ironmonger	TC	Shareholder
Kerrigan, L.	1890	Doctor	Coroner	Shareholder
Locke, James H.	1892	Industrialist		Director 1892–4
Lucas, V.	1894	Bank manager		Shareholder
Maguire, Patrick	1896	Boot & shoe maker		Shareholder
Malone, Col. J.R.	1903	Gentry	Deputy Lieu-tenant	Director
McCormick, Michael	1890	GSD		Shareholder
McDonnell, Jos.	1895	GSD		Shareholder
Mullally, James	1895	Baker & confec-tioner		Shareholder
Newburn, Walter	1891	Land steward		Shareholder
Nooney, T. F.	1890	Hardware mer-chant		Director
Nugent, Sir Walter	1905	Aristocrat		Director
O'Reilly, P. P.	1891	Gentry/Land agent	Director MGWR	Shareholder
Purcell, B. J.	1893	GSD/Wine im-porter		Shareholder
Rogers, Hubert	1893	Boot maker		Shareholder
Salmon, Eugene	1890	Farmer		Director
Smyth, Capt. Ralph	1890	Gentry		Director
Sullivan, Owen	1890	GSD	PLG*	Director
Thomas, W. J.	1893	Insurance agent		Shareholder
Weymes, Maurice	1894	Wool merchant		Shareholder

* MCCC = Mullingar Catholic Commercial Club   PLG = Poor Law Guardian

Appendix 9

Place of residence of owners and their frequency of participation in the Mullingar June meet, 1890–1905

Frequency of participation	Westmeath	Outside the county
1	27	70
2	14	31
3	4	13
4	2	8
5	6	1
6	2	1
7	2	2
8	0	2
9	0	1
10	1	0
13	1	0
18	1	0
19	1	0

Appendix 10

Number of wins and average prize-money won by Westmeath owners in selected years

	Winning owners	Number of wins	Total prize-money (£)	Average win per race (£)
1892	9	36	1,284	36
1894	10	30	1,266	42
1895	21	42	2,009	48
1896	18	43	1,545	36
1897	23	44	2,773	63
1898	19	40	2,299	58
1899	16	44	1,451	33
1900	18	43	1,377	32
1901	19	39	1,304	33
1902	17	33	1,513	46
1903	21	55	3,938	72
1904	22	49	2,503	51

Source: *Westmeath Guardian; The Irish Field*

Appendix 11

Number of races run, available prize-money, number of horses running and average prize-money available per horse in Irish racing, 1890–1905

Year	Races	Horses running	Prize-money (£)	Prize-money per horse (£)
1890	638	1,105	39,524	36
1891	603	1,095	39,144	36
1892	596	1,081	40,185	37
1893	617	1,169	40,407	37
1894	669	1,448	41,313	29
1895	636	1,289	42,023	33
1896	636	1,277	42,370	33
1897	626	1,293	42,852	33
1898	629	1,282	43,746	34
1899	623	1,346	45,926	34
1900	622	1,239	46,678	38
1901	674	1,245	51,281	41
1902	720	1,328	61,324	46
1903	715	1,282	60,960	48
1904	708	1,315	57,524	44
1905	711	1,223	57,087	47

Source: *Racing Calendar*, 1897, p. 197; 1905, p. 185

Appendix 12

Matches played by Westmeath cricket combinations, 1880s

	1880	1881	1882	1883	1884	1885	1886	1887	1888	1889
Asylum XI								1		
Athlone Brass Band XI							1			
Athlone Comm. Club				3			9			
Àthlone Woollen Mills							3		2	
Ballinagall		2								
Ballinagall 2nd XI		1								
Ballyhealy					3			2		
Balrath					2		2	3		
Belvedere							1	1		
Bracklyn					1					
Bunbrosna			1							
Bunbrosna		2								
Carrick							1		2	
Castlepollard	6	2								
Castletown-Geoghegan									1	5
Cloughan							1			
Clonhugh									4	1
Clonickavant XI						3	3	6	3	1
Clonickavant 2nd XI								1		
Clonkill								1		
Clonlost							2		2	
Coolamber							2	4	6	4
Coolure						1				
Delvin					3	4			1	
Drumcree								1		
Farra School		3		1		1				
Gaybrook							1	1		
Graftonstown					1	3				
Hodgestown					1				3	
Kenny								1		
Kilbeggan		1			1				3	1
Kilbeggan Home Rule										1
Kilbeggan Home Rule Jr									2	1
Kilbeggan National										5
Kilbride								3	3	3
Killucan Juvenile						1				
Killula Castle								1	1	1

	1880	1881	1882	1883	1884	1885	1886	1887	1888	1889
Knockdrin		1						1		1
Larkfield							1	2	1	
Master Percy O'Reilly XI						2				
Moate					4	3	4	3	3	4
Moate Juvenile									1	1
Moortown							1			
Mountain							1			
Mr Corcoran's XI								1		1
Mr Dease's XI		2								
Mr Hannon's XI						1				
Mr Tottenham's XI										2
Mr Waters XI		1								
Mr Young's XI		1								
Mullingar Comm. Club*	2				6	1			1	
Mullingar			1							
Mullingar Juvenile						1				
Mullingar Shamrocks								2	7	5
Mullingar Wanderers								1		
Mullingar Wanderers Jnrs								2		
Ranelagh School			2			2			3	3
Rathcolman									1	
Rathowen						2	2	5		
Ringtown								2		
Riverstown		1						3	4	
Riverstown Mills	1									
Sonna		3	1	1						
Tudenham Park										2
Turbotstown				1			2	3		
Turin							1			
Turin 2nd XI								1		
Walshestown				1				1	2	
Wardenstown	1				2	3				
Westmeath		16	15	7	9	3	2	2	5	
Westmeath Polo XI								1		

*Comm. = Commercial

Appendix 13

Matches played by Westmeath cricket combinations, 1890s

	1890	1891	1892	1893	1894	1895	1896	1897	1898	1899
Ardnaglue										1
Athlone Comm. Club							1			
Athlone Cricket Club									1	
Àthlone Woollen Mills			2	5	2	2	2	1		
Ballinagall	1	3	6	2					3	
Ballinderry						1				1
Ballyhealy				2						
Balrath						1				
Bracklyn				1		1	7	2	2	1
Bracklyn 2nd XI							1			
Bunbrosna		1								
Capt. Daniel's XI				1						
Capt. Lewis's XI				1						
Carrick	2									
Castlepollard				1	3	3				4
Castlepollard 2nd XI										1
Cloughan			6	5	1	1			2	5
Clonhugh				3	5	4				
Clonickavant XI		1								
Clonlost				9	2		2		1	2
Clonlost Juvenile										2
Clonlost 2nd XI								1		1
Collinstown	1	1		4	2	3	1			
Coolamber	3	1	2	4	2	5	3	1		
Craddinstown										4
Crookedwood									4	1
Crookedwood Juvenile										1
Crowinstown			2	1						
Cullion		3								
Delvin						5	3			2
Donore			2							
Drumcree				3						
Fennor	1				1	7	5			1
Gaulmoylestown				1			2			
Gaulstown							1			

	1890	1891	1892	1893	1894	1895	1896	1897	1898	1899
Gilbertstown								1	1	
Gillardstown		2		1						
Graftonstown								3		
Griffinstown					1	1				
Hodgestown			1	2	2				4	2
Hodgestown 2nd XI								1		
Independent Wanderers			1							
Kilbeggan		5				6	3	7	8	7
Kilbeggan 2nd XI							1			1
Kilbeggan National	6	1					5	4		
Kilbride National 2nd XI							1			3
Kilbeggan Rovers		2	1							
Kilbeggan Willow									2	3
Kilbride					2			1		
Kilbride 2nd XI								2		
Killadoran					3					2
Killucan								2		5
Killucan Station									2	3
Killucan Workingmen's Club										1
Kilbride National				1	3	6	1			
Kilshrewley								2		
Kiltoom							1	2	3	3
Knockdrin	3					1	5			
Knockmant										3
Larkfield	4	4	4		3	2			5	5
Loughegar	1									
Moate	3		3	1	5	8	5	2	8	
Moate 2nd XI			2		1					
Mountain	1	14	6		2					3
Mount Street										6
Mr Bailie's XI			1							
Mr E. Dames-Long-worth XI			1							
Mr Kiernan's XI						1				
Mr Locke's XI		1				1				
Mr Lyon's XI						1				
Mr. P. P. O'Reilly's XI			2					1		
Mr Pilkington's XI						1				

	1890	1891	1892	1893	1894	1895	1896	1897	1898	1899
Mullingar Asylum XI	1		1							
Mullingar Comm. Club			4			1				
Mullingar				3	2					
Mullingar Wanderers			1							
Multyfarnham		5	2							
Newtown	2					1				
Raharney							3			
Ranelagh School	3	1	3		3		1	7		
Rev. H. St George									1	
Reynella						2		8		
RIC		1								
Ringtown	2		6	2	9	1	3	3	1	3
Riverstown										2
Riverstown Juvenile										3
Robinstown							2	1		
Rochfort		2			1					
Shaw's XI										2
Stonehall				3	4			1		
Stonehall										2
Stonehall Workingmen's Club										1
Stoneyford										1
Taughmon				3	4				2	
Thomastown										3
Tuberquill	1									
Tullaniskey			1							
Turbotstown					3	1				
Turin					1	2	3	3	7	2
Tyrrellspass					1					2
Tyrrelstown	2	1		3						
Tyrrelstown 2nd XI				1						
Wardenstown	1	4	2					3		5
Westmeath	6	8	3		8					

*Comm. = Commercial

Appendix 14

Matches played by Westmeath cricket combinations, 1900-05

	1900	1901	1902	1903	1904	1905
Addinstown				2	1	4
Ardnaglue	1	1				
Ballinea				1		
Belmont						1
Belvedere					1	
Boher		4				
Bracklyn		2	7	1		
Bracklyn Juvenile XI			1			
Carrick	2					
Carrick Juvenile		1				
Castlepollard	5	3	8	9		
Castlepollard Commercial	3	4				
Castlepollard Wolfe Tones	5	6				
Castlepollard Workingmen's Club	1					
Cloughan	4	10	8	9	3	5
Clonhugh		1	5	7	6	3
Clonhugh 2nd XI					2	
Clonhugh Juniors				2		
Clonlost			5	5		
Clonmore			1	1		
Cloonagh	1	3	2	2		3
Collegians (St Mary's Coll.)						2
Coolamber				2		
Craddinstown	4	4	1	2		
Crookedwood					4	
Crowinstown			2		1	1
Dalystown					4	2
Delvin	2		4			
Derryrow	1	2				
Donore						2
Fennor	2				4	
Fore	1					
Fr Mathew Hall XI						2
Gainstown						1
Gaulmoylestown	1		1			
Gibbonstown						1

	1900	1901	1902	1903	1904	1905
Gilbertstown					4	
Graftonstown	1					
Hodgestown	6					
Kilbeggan	13	5	2	3	1	7
Kilbeggan Willow	3					
Kilbride	3			2	1	7
Kilbride National	1					
Killadoran		3	2	2		
Killucan	1	1				
Killucan Workingmen's Club	1					
Kiltoom	3	2	2	1	3	
Larkfield	3	2	1			
Leney					1	
Leney 2nd XI					2	
Little Island				2	3	1
Lismacaffry				1		
Lord Longford's XI						1
Martinstown				6	3	
Moate	1	6	3	1		3
Mooretown		2				
Morningtown	1		1			
Mountain				4	3	
Mount Street	8	2	1			
Miss Levigne's XI			1			
Miss Montgomery's XI			1			
Mr Charter's XI		1				
Mr C. Clibborn's XI		1				
Mr Eastwood's XI				1		
Mr Ludlow				1		
Mr Montgomery's XI		1	1			
Mr Murray's XI		3				
Mr Russell's XI		1				
Mr Tottenham's XI					1	
Mrs Dease's XI				1		
Mrs O'Reilly's XI				1		
Multyfarnham				4		
Newtown	1					
Pakenham Hall	3	1	1	2	1	
Patterson's XI (C'pollard)			1			

	1900	1901	1902	1903	1904	1905
Raharney		2				
Ranelagh School					I	
Ringtown	2	3		I		
Simonstown				I		
Stonehall	5	2		4		
Taughmon			I	3		
Turbotstown			2	8	3	3
Turin	2	2	I			
Tyrrellspass	8	2		I	I	
Tyrrelstown		I				
United Banks XI					I	
Wardenstown	4		2			

Appendix 15

Number of GAA clubs and membership of GAA in Midlands division of RIC 1889–1892, as documented in police reports

	1889		1890		1892	
	Clubs	Members	Clubs	Members	Clubs	Members
Cavan	37	2,750	38	2,640	39	1,500
Kildare	38	1,900	38	1,980	19	480
King's	22	1,190	20	1,050	6	180
Leitrim	21	980	25	1,260	12	360
Longford	13	580	25	1,000	26	1,030
Meath	36	1,900	14	930	9	350
Sligo	25	1,660	18	1,300	15	500
Westmeath	9	460	5	290	12	503

Appendix 16

Matches played by Westmeath football combinations, 1890s

	1890	1891	1892	1893	1894	1895	1896	1897	1898	1899
Athlone T.P. O'Connor's	4	1	4	4						
Ballinahown	2	3		2			2			
Ballinalack Erin go Bragh			1							
Ballinalack Inny Rangers					1	3	3	1		1
Ballinalack Sally Pickers				1						
Ballinea			1							
Ballynacarrigy Abbey Rovers								1		
Bunbrosna			1							
Castletown-Geoghegan Volunteers								2		
Cloughan				2						
Cloneyheigue							2	1		
College Rovers								1		
Coralstown Campaigners							1			
Corbetstown Home Rulers		7	5							
Corbetstown Home Rulers II			1							
Cullion Celtics	1	5	5	4	2	3	2			
The Downs Pigeons					1					
Fox Covert Rangers		1								
Frewin										1
Gainstown Home Rulers									2	
Gaulstown Park Lovers of Erin				3	3	2	2			
Glasson	2									
Greville Street										2
Independent Sexton Club			1							
Independent Wanderers		1	4							
Kilbeggan Emeralds				3						
Kilbeggan Nationals	6	1								
Kilbeggan Nationals II	1	1								
Kilbeggan Wolfe Tones							3			
Kilbride					3		2			
Killucan	1									
Killucan Emmett's			5							
Killucan Emmett's II			1							
Kinnegad Slashers	9	3	2	4			1			

	1890	1891	1892	1893	1894	1895	1896	1897	1898	1899
Kinnegad Slashers II	4	2								
Lacken Golden Flags			1	1			1			
Larkfield										1
Lynn Mallards								1	1	
Milltown										1
Moate (The Gap)		1								
Moate (The Turnpike)	1									
Moate John Dillon's		2								
Moate Parnellites		1								
Moate Shamrocks		1								
Moate Stars of Erin			3				4		2	
Moate William O'Brien's	4	2								
Moate Young Emmetts									1	
Mount Street								1		2
Mullingar Commercials	2	5								
Mullingar Football Club		5	8	10	4	2	4			
Mullingar Football Club II		1	1	3						
Mullingar Shamrocks	5	7	3	5	1					
Mullingar Shamrocks II		3	1	3						
Multyfarnham Stars			4	4						
Newbrook Wanderers		1		2						
Portloman Rackers							1			
Raharney Rovers	4	7	5							
Raharney Rovers II		2								
Rathwire Leaguers					2					
Rathwire Sir Charles Russell's	4									
Rochfortbridge Erin's Hopes					4	1				
Robinstown							1			
Springfield Wanderers								1	1	
St Patrick's								4	1	
Tang									1	
Thomastown Rangers	5	19								
Thomastown Rangers II	3	1								
Tubberclair									1	
Tyrrelstown					2					
Walshestown				2	1		1			
Wooddown Rackers			3	10	3				1	
Wooddown Rackers II				2						
World Recorders								1		
Young Irelanders			4							

Appendix 17

Naming policies of Westmeath GAA hurling and football clubs, 1903–05

Name	Code	Political or local relevance
Athlone St Ciaran's	H	A locally celebrated saint
Athlone Volunteers	F	A part-time military force established in 1778–9
Ballymore Brian Borus	F	Leader at Battle of Clontarf, 1014
Brownstown Clan na Gael	F	Irish-American revolutionary organization formed to pursue Irish Independence after 1867
Castlepollard O'Growney's	H	Gaelic League activist with Westmeath connections
Castlepollard Sarsfields	F	Irish commander on the Jacobite side in Williamite War (1689–1691)
Clonlost Croppy Boys	F	1798 Rebellion
Coosan Fenians	F	Fenians: organised the 1867 rebellion
Cullion Celtics	F	
Delvin Hibernians	F	
Derrymore St Patricks	F	Celebrated national saint
Graftonstown Shamrocks	F	
Inny Gaels	F	
Inny Rangers	F	
Kilbixy Gaels	F	
Kiltoom Cruickilawee	H	Microtoponym
Kinnegad Slashers	F	
Lismacaffry St Fintan's	F	Locally celebrated saint
Moate Invincibles	F	Assassins of chief secretary in Phoenix Park, 1882
Mooretown Myles the Slashers	F	Local historical figure
Mullingar Shamrocks	H	
Mullingar Young Irelanders	F	1848 rebellion organisers
Ringtown Myles O'Reilly's	H	Local historical figure
Riverstown Robert Emmetts	F	Organiser of 1803 rebellion
Simonstown Michael O'Dwyers	H	Figure associated with 1798 rebellion
Stoneyford Confederates	F	Confederate War (1641–55) association
Stoneyford Fitzgeralds	F	Lord Edward Fitzgerald had 1798 involvement although he died before the rebellion
Thomastown Rangers	F	
Tubberclair O'Connells	F	Daniel O'Connell, democratic leader 1820s–1840s
Wooddown Pigeons	F	Microtopnym

Appendix 18

Matches played by Westmeath hurling clubs, 1903–1905

	1903	1904	1905
Athlone, St Ciaran's	0	2	12
Castlepollard O'Growney's	0	8	9
Delvin	0	1	6
Kiltoom Cruickilawees	0	0	3
Lismacaffry St Fintan's	0	0	3
Mullingar Shamrocks	12	6	12
Ringtown Myles O'Reilly's	0	7	6
Simonstown Michael Dwyer's	0	0	6
Westmeath county	0	2	1

Appendix 19

Matches played by Westmeath football clubs, 1900–1905

	1900	1901	1902	1903	1904	1905
Athlone			1			
Athlone Volunteers					2	12
Ballinalack Inny Rangers						9
Ballinalack Rebels	1					
Ballymore			2	2		
Ballymore Brian Borus					2	1
Ballynacarrigy						1
Brownstown Clan na Gael						6
Brownstown Cossacks					1	
Castlepollard Celtics				1		
Castlepollard O'Growneys						3
Castletown-Geoghegan		1				
Clonlost Croppy Boys						5
Clonmellon						2
Collinstown Celtics					3	6
Coosan					2	
Coralstown Campaigners					2	
Cullion Celtics				10	4	10
Dalystown				1		8
Delvin						1
Delvin Juveniles						1

	1900	1901	1902	1903	1904	1905
Derrymore St Patricks					2	
Erin's Hopes (Ballynacarrigy)	1					
Fore, St Feichin's					1	
Gibbonstown Prosperities						1
Glasson					1	
Glenidan Wanderers					1	
Graftonstown Fitzgeralds/Shamrocks					1	15
Graftonstown Juveniles						1
Inny Rovers						3
Kilbixy Gaels					1	7
Kilbride Volunteers						3
Kinnegad Slashers		2		1	1	4
Lynn Ramblers						2
Midland Rovers					2	
Milltown Hardly Ables						1
Moate Stars of Erin					2	
Moate Young Invincibles			3	1		
Moortown Slashers					6	7
Mount Street	1	2				
Mullingar Football Club						6
Mullingar Independent Wanderers				1		
Mullingar Shamrocks				2	3	
Mullingar Young Irelanders				11	4	
Mullingar Young Irelanders II				1	2	
Multyfarnham College Boys				1		
Multyfarnham Confederates					1	
Multyfarnham Donore Castles			1	4		
Multyfarnham Stars						2
Pakenham Rovers				1		
Raharney Stars				2		
Rathcolman			2	4		
Riverstown Emmetts					5	11
Rochfortbridge Warriors		4		6	7	2
Rochfortbridge Warriors II					2	
St Mary's Temperance Society	1					
Stoneyford Rovers						4
The Downs						1
The Pigeons						1
Thomastown Rangers					1	2
Tubberclair O'Connells					1	8

	1900	1901	1902	1903	1904	1905
Tyrrellspass					1	1
Westmeath					5	3
Wooddown Pigeons					1	5
Wooddown Rackers				2		

Appendix 20

Introduction of various sports in an institutionalised form in Westmeath

Sport	Club formed/ event organised
Angling	1885
Archery	1833
Athletics	1877
Badminton	1895
Coursing	1896
Cricket	1852
Croquet	1894
Cycling	1882
Football	1885
Golf	1892
Hockey	1892
Hunting	1854
Hurling	1902
Lawn Tennis	1884
Polo	1881
Racing	1731
Rowing	Pre-1850
Rugby	1879
Soccer	1887
Table Tennis	1901
Yachting	c.1770

Bibliography

Primary source material

Privately held

Income and Expenditure of Carrick-on-Suir Amateur Athletic Cricket and Football Club from its formation, August 1879, up to its first general meeting, 23 February 1880

Minute Book of County Westmeath Golf Club, 1904–35

Minute Book of Carrick-on-Suir Athletic, Cricket and Football Club, established around 1879

The diary of A. B. Sommerville, 1866–1902

The diary of William Edward Wilson of Daramona, January 1889–January 1908

Westmeath Hunt Club Financial Records from 1890–91 to 1900–01

Westmeath Hunt Club Minute Book, 30 April 1877 to 28 December 1899

Westmeath Hunt Club Minute Book, 25 November 1904 to 10 April 1920

Westmeath County Library

(A) ATHLONE BRANCH

Record of Garrison Golf Club, Athlone

(B) MULLINGAR BRANCH, HEAD OFFICE

Marriage registers 1845–1890 of St. Mary's parish, Athlone (Burgess Papers typescript)

Marriage registers 1851–1870 of St. Peter's parish, Athlone (Burgess Papers typescript)

Evidence collected by folklore commissioners, parish of Killucan, 340–1

Moore Papers:
Hunting register for the season, 1879–80
Hunting register for the season, 1880–81
The sportsman's game book, 1879–88
Rules and byelaws of the Westmeath Polo Club, 1905
Rules and byelaws of the Westmeath Polo Club, 1911

Freemasons' Library, Dublin

Ledger 1–199, (1760–1860) Membership of Mullingar Lodge 131

Ledger 95–188, (1860–1900) Membership of Mullingar Lodge 131; Membership of Lodge 123, Albert Edward Lodge, Mullingar; Membership of Lodge 124, Castlepollard; Membership of Lodge 101, Athlone

National Library of Ireland, Dublin

Account book of Kilruane Football Club, 1876. Ms. 9,515
Fishing diary of George L. Adlercorn, book number 22, 6 September 1878 to 11 April 1880, Ms 3,800
Minute book of Irish Polo Club Union, Ms 16,830
Reynell Papers: The Diary of Laeda Reynell, 1862, P.C. 601(II)

Representative Church Body, Dublin

Biographical succession list of the clergy of Meath diocese by Rev. Canon J. B. Leslie D. Lit., volumes 1 and 11 (typescript)
Church of Ireland Archives, P. 0238, records of parish of Killucan (Meath), county of Westmeath
    Register of vestrymen, 1891–1961, P. 0238.06.1
    Register of marriages, 1846–1948, P. 0238.03.1
Church of Ireland Archives, P. 0340, records of parish of Stonehall (Meath), county of Westmeath
    Combined register (Stonehall), register of baptisms, 1814–57; marriages, 1814–54; and burials, 1815–1979, P. 0340.01.1
    Register of baptisms (Stonehall), 1878–1914, P. 0340.02.1
    Register of marriage (Stonehall), 1850–1912, P. 0340.03.1
Church of Ireland Archives, P. 0419, records of parish of Castlepollard (Meath), county of Westmeath
    Register of vestrymen, 1870–1935, P. 0419.06.1
    Register of marriages, 1845–1903, P. 0419.06.1
Church of Ireland Archives, P. 0412, records of parish of Kilcleagh (Meath), county of Westmeath
    Register of vestrymen, 1888–1978, P. 0412.06.1
    Register of marriages, 1845–1922, P. 0412.03. 1
    Vestry minute book, 1787–1965, P. 0412.05.1
Church of Ireland Archives, P. 336, records of parish of Mullingar (Meath), county of Westmeath, 1843–1976
    Select vestry minute book, 1872–1906, P. 0336.4.2; P. 0336.05.1
    Register of marriages, P. 0336.02.2
Church of Ireland Archives, P. 0337, records of parish of Portnashangan (Meath), county of Westmeath
    Vestry minute book, 1822–1920, P. 0337.05.1
    Register of marriages, 1858–1923, P. 0337.03.2
Church of Ireland Archives, P. 0392, records of parish of Athlone (St Mary's), county of Westmeath, P. 0392.01.4
    Combined register, Athlone (St Mary's), 1849–1875, Register of baptisms,1849–1903; marriages, 1849–61 and burials, 1849–1892, P. 0392.01.4
    Register of baptisms, 1903–1999, P. 0392.03.1
    Register of marriage, 1863–1890, P. 0392.03.2
    Register of marriage, 1891–1940, P. 0392.03.3
    Vestry minute book, (4), 1881–1930, P. 0392.95.1
Records of parish of Athlone, St Peters (Elphin), county of Roscommon, 1845–1941, P. 0400
    Register of baptisms, 1813–1941, P. 0400.02.1
    Register of marriages, 1870–1939, P. 0400.03.3
    Register of vestrymen, 1870–1941, P. 0400.06.1

Valuation Office, Dublin

Valuation Lists, county of Westmeath, district of Athlone, No. 1, electoral division of Umma, 1855–1937, No. 15 (1897–1903 revision)

Valuation Lists, county of Westmeath, urban division of Athlone, No. 1, electoral division of Athlone eastern urban, 1893–1907, No. 16

Valuation Lists, county of Westmeath, district of Delvin, electoral division of Faughalstown, 1860–1930, No. 30 (1884–1898 revision)

Valuation lists; county of Westmeath, district of Delvin, electoral division of Killulagh, 1860–1936. Valuation list number 15, 1884–1898 revision, 15 (Gigginstown); 27 (Rickardstown).

Valuation Lists, county of Westmeath, district of Mullingar, electoral division of Dysart, 1860–1924, No. 15 (1897–1907 revision)

Valuation lists: county of Westmeath, district of Mullingar, electoral division of Mullingar rural, number 34, 1891–1904

Valuation Lists, county of Westmeath, district of Mullingar, electoral division of Stonehall, 1860–1932, No. 46

Valuation Lists, county of Westmeath, district of Mullingar, electoral division of Killucan, 1860–1924, No. 28 (1897–1906 revision)

Valuation Lists, county of Westmeath, district of Mullingar, electoral division of Portloman, 1860–1936, No. 40 (1893–1907 revision)

Valuation Lists, county of Westmeath, district of Mullingar, electoral division of Knockdrin 1860–1930, No. 30 (1892–1902 revision)

Valuation Lists, county of Westmeath, district of Mullingar, electoral division of Mullingar north urban, 1882–1912, No. 35 (1891–1897 revision)

Valuation Lists, county of Westmeath, district of Mullingar, electoral division of Multyfarnham, 1860–1940, No. 37 (1897–1907 revision)

Valuation Lists, county of Westmeath, district of Mullingar, electoral division of Taghmon, 1860–1937, No. 48 (1897–1907 revision)

Valuation Lists, county of Westmeath, district of Mullingar, electoral division of Churchtown, 1860–1932, No. 10 (1897–1907 revision)

Valuation Lists, county of Westmeath, district of Mullingar, electoral division of Carrick, 1860–1936, No. 6 (1897–1907 revision)

Valuation Lists, county of Westmeath, district of Mullingar, electoral division of Raharney, 1860–1936, No. 41 (1897–1908 revision)

Valuation Lists, county of Westmeath, district of Mullingar, electoral division of Ballynagore, 1860–1940, No. 4 (1882–1891 revision)

Valuation Lists, county of Westmeath, district of Mullingar, electoral division of Owel, 1860–1945, No. 39 (1882–1893 revision)

Valuation Lists, county of Westmeath, district of Mullingar, electoral division of Tulaghan, 1860–1932, No. 47 (1882–1891 revision)

Valuation Lists, county of Westmeath, district of Mullingar, electoral division of Rathconnell, 1860–1945, No. 42 (1897–1909 revision)

Valuation Lists, county of Westmeath, district of Mullingar, electoral division of Enniscoffey, 1860–1932, No. 17 (1897–1909 revision)

Parliamentary papers

Agricultural statistics of Ireland for the year 1871 [C.762], HC, 1873, lxix, 375

Agricultural statistics of Ireland, 1882, General abstracts showing the acreage under crops and the number and description of livestock in each county and province, 1881–1882 [C 3366], HC, lxxv, 93

Agricultural statistics of Ireland for the year 1891 [C.6777], HC,1892, lxxxviii, 285

Agricultural statistics of Ireland, 1891, General abstracts showing the acreage under crops and the number and description of livestock in each county and province, 1891–1892, [C 6762], HC, lxxxviii, 461

Agricultural statistics of Ireland, 1902, General abstracts showing the acreage under crops and the number and description of livestock in each county and province, 1901–1902 [Cd 1263], 661

A return showing according to provinces and counties the number of cases in which judicial rents have been fixed by all the methods provided by the Land Law Acts for a first and second statutory term, respectively, to 31 December 1902 with particulars as to acreage, former rents of holdings, and percentages of reductions in rents HC, 1903, lvii, 91

Census of Ireland, 1891. Part 1. Area, houses and population: also the ages, civil or conjugal condition, occupations, birthplaces, religion and education of the people. vol. 1. Province of Leinster, No. 10. County of Westmeath [C–6515–IX]

Census of Ireland, 1901. Part 1. Area, Houses and Population: also the Ages, Civil or Conjugal Condition, Occupations, Birthplaces, Religion and Education of the People. Volume 1. Province of Leinster, No. 10. County of Westmeath [Cd. 847.–IX]. *1901, vii*

Land Owners in Ireland. Return of owners of land of one acre and upwards, in the several counties, counties of cities, and counties of towns in Ireland, showing the names of such Owners arranged Alphabetically in each county; their addresses–as far as could be ascertained–the extent in Statute Acres, and the Valuation in each case; together with the number of Owners in each county of less than One Statute Acre in extent; and the total Area and Valuation of such properties: and the Grand Total pf Area and Valuation for all Owners of property in each county, County of a City, or County of a Town. [C 1492], *1876*

Return of payments made to landlords by the Irish Land Commissions pursuant to the first and sixteenth sections of the Arrears of Rent (Ireland) Act 1882, HC, 1884, lxiv

Return of untenanted lands in rural districts, distinguishing demesnes on which there is a mansion, showing: rural districts and electoral divisions; townland; area in statute acres; poor law valuation; names of occupiers as in valuation lists. HC, 1906, C.177

Royal Commission to inquire into horse breeding in Ireland, 1898 [C.8651, 8652], *xxxiii, 261, 295*

National Archives

MANUSCRIPT CENSUS RETURNS

Census 1901: Westmeath, 1–106.

1/DED Athlone east, 1–28; 2/DED Athlone town, 1–51; 3/DED Athlone town urban (w), 1–71; 5/DED Auburn, 1–31; 7/DED Glasson, 1–14; 8/DED Moydrum, 1–13; 15/DED Moate, 1–30c; 17/DED Umma, 1–11; 19/DED Ballymore, 1–20; 26/DED Collinstown 1–6; 27/DED Faughalstown, 1–8; 30/DED Kilpatrick,1–6; 32/DED Ballinlough, 1–6; 38/DED Ballyhealy, 1–7; 41/DED Delvin, 1–17c; 45/DED Coole,1–8; 46/DED Coolure, 1–15; 47/DED Glore, 1–14; 54/DED Rathaspic, 1–18; 56/DED Portloman,1–20; 65/DED Killare, 1–23; 67/DED Cloughan, 1–16; 68/DED Clonlost, 1–11; 69 DED Derrymore, 1–7; 70 DED Huntingdon, 1–12; 71/DED Killucan, 1–19c; 72/DED Kinnegad, 1–6; 73/DED Raharney, 1–13; 75/DED Gaybrook, 1–8; 76/DED Griffinstown,1–8; 77/DED Heathstown, 1–6; 79/DED Russelstown, 1–14; 80/DED Belvedere, 1–10; 81/DED Gainstown, 1–6; 83/DED

Hopestown, 1–10; 84/DED Knockdrin, 1–20; 85/DED Mullingar rural, 1–20; 86/DED Mullingar north urban, 1–24; 87/DED Mullingar urban, 1–25; 88/DED Owel, 1–8; 90/DED Ballinalack, 1–18; 91/DED Lacken, 1–3; 92 DED/Multyfarnham, 1–17; 93/DED Stonehall, 1–13; 94/DED Taghmon, 1–11; 95/DED Woodlands, 1–11; 97/DED Ballynagore, 1–17c; 98/DED Carrick, 1–16; 100/DED Clonfad, 1–12; 104/DED Kilbeggan, 1–23c

CSO PAPERS

Report of Captain Butler, December 1882, registered papers, 1888/20736.

POLICE REPORTS

Crime Branch Special: GAA reports from south–west and the midland divisions on clubs etc. at the end of the year 1890s 2452/S

DC's report on the state of the GAA in their divisions on 31 December 1891 compared with their state in 1889, 4467/S

Crime Branch Special: Box No. 6: Crime dept–special branch; approximate numbers, strength of secret societies and other associations, 31 October 1889, 501/10821

Crime Branch Special: Box No. 6: Crime dept–special branch; approximate numbers, strength of secret societies and other associations, 31 December 1890, 501/2357

Crime Branch Special: Box No. 6: Crime dept–special branch; approximate numbers, strength of secret societies and other associations, 11 June 1892, 501/8727

Crime Branch Special, 1893, annual report on crime special work for 1892–midland division, 1/22594

Crime Branch Special, 1893, Western Division–County Roscommon; return showing the number of branches of the GAA in the above county on 31 December 1892, 6247/S

Valentine McDonnell Papers: Fox–hunting diary, 1901–02, Business Records Roscommon, 11/3; Shooting diary, Business Records, Roscommon, 11/10; Horse–racing diary, 1912, Business Records, Roscommon, 11/12

Offaly Heritage Centre, Tullamore, County Offaly

Tudenham Diaries: Tottenham diary, I, Tudenham (Rochfort) Mullingar; Volume 2, Somerville, County Meath and Tudenham (Mullingar)

Newspapers and periodicals

High Ball: the official GAA monthly magazine
Leicester Weekly Post
Sport
The Freeman's Journal
The Irish Cyclist
The Irish Sportsman and Farmer, 1870–1894
The Irish Field and Gentlemans [sic] Gazette
The Irish Golfer
The Irish Times
The Lilywhites' Gazette
The Midland Reporter and Westmeath Nationalist
The Waterford Daily Mail

The Waterford News
The Westmeath Examiner
The Westmeath Guardian
The Westmeath Independent
United Ireland
Vanity Fair

Directories and works of reference

Arlott, John, *The Oxford companion to sports and games* (St Albans: Paladin, 1977)

Bateman, John, *The great landowners of Great Britain and Ireland* (London: Harrison and sons, 1879)

British Hunts and Huntsmen, in four volumes, England (North), Scotland, and Ireland (London: The Biographical Press, 1911)

Burke, Ashworth P. (ed.), *A genealogical history of the landed gentry of Ireland, by Sir Bernard Burke* (London: Harrison and sons, 1904)

Burke's Irish family records (London: Burke's Peerage Ltd, 1976)

Burke's Peerage, Baronetage and Knighthood (London: Harrison and sons, 1911)

Charles's Irish Church Directory and Yearbook for 1900 (Dublin: Church of Ireland printing and publishing company limited, 1900)

Connolly, S. J. (ed.), *The Oxford companion to Irish history* (Oxford University Press, 1998)

de Burgh, Hussey, U. H., *The landowners of Ireland: an alphabetical list of the owners of estates of 500 acres of £500 valuation and upwards in Ireland, with the acerage and valuation in each county* (Dublin: Hodges, Foster & Figgis, 1878)

Dod's Peerage, Baronetage, Knightage etc. of Great Britain and Ireland for 1917 (London: Dod's Peerage Limited, 1918)

Dublin, Leinster and Connaught trades' directory accompanied with a gazetteer of Ireland, 1912 (Edinburgh and Birmingham: Trades' Directories, Limited, 1912)

Ellis's Irish education directory and scholastic guide for 1887 (Sixth year of issue) (Dublin: E. Ponsoby Limited, 1887)

Farming since the Famine: Irish farm statistics 1847–1996 (Dublin: Stationery Office, 1997)

Land owners in Ireland. Return of owners of land of one acre and upwards, in the several counties, counties of cities, and counties of towns in Ireland (Baltimore: Genealogical Publications Company, 1988)

Lawrence, John, *Handbook of cricket in Ireland*, 1865–1880 (Dublin: John Lawrence)

Lewis, S., Topographical dictionary of Ireland, with historical and statistical descriptions (London: S. Lewis & Co., 1837), 2 vols.

Racing Calendar, 1850–1905

Slater's Directory, 1856, 1870, 1881, 1894 (London: Slater's directory company)

Thom's Irish almanac and official directory of the United Kingdom of Great Britain and Ireland, 1850–1905 (London: Slater's directory company)

Walford's county families of the United Kingdom, a royal manual of the titled and untitled aristocracy of England, Wales, Scotland and Ireland (London: Spottiswoode, 1915)

Contemporary publications

BOOKS

Aflalo, F.G. (ed.), *The cost of sport* (London: John Murray, 1899)

Anonymous, *Memoir of the Kilkenny Hunt* (Dublin: Hodges Figgis, 1897)

Becker, Bernard, H., *Disturbed Ireland, being the letters written during the winter of 1880–81* (London: Macmillan, 1881)

Clare, Rev. Wallace (ed.), *A young Irishman's diary (1836–1847) being extracts from the early journal of John Keegan of Moate* (No place of publication, Rev. William Clare, 1928)

Corballis, James Henry, *Forty–five years of sport*, edited by Arthur T. Fisher (London: R. Bentley, 1891)

Dease, Edmund F., *A complete history of the Westmeath Hunt from its foundation* (Dublin: Browne and Nolan, 1898)

Fitzpatrick, B. M., *Irish sport and sportsmen* (Dublin: M. H. Gill & son, 1878)

Hall, S. C. and A. M., *Ireland: its scenery, character & c.* (London: How and Parsons, 1841–43), vol. iii

Mahaffey, J. P., 'The Irish Landlords', in *Contemporary Review*, vol. xli, 1882

Mayo, Earl of and W. D. Boulton, *A history of the Kildare Hunt* (London: St Catherine Press, 1913)

McCullam, Rev. Randall, *Sketches of the highlands of Cavan and of Shirley Castle, in Farney, taken during the Irish Famine* (Belfast: J. Read, 1856)

McGrath, Terence, *Pictures from Ireland* (London: C. K. Paul & Co., 1880)

Moore, George, *A drama in muslin* (Paris: Vizetelly & Co., 1886)

Pellew, George, *In castle and cabin or talks in Ireland in 1887* (New York and London: The Knickerbocker Press, 1888)

Samuels, Arthur, *Early cricket in Ireland; a paper read before the Kingstown Literary and Debating Society on 22 February 1888* (Dublin: William McGee, 1888)

Sargent, H. R., *Thoughts upon sport* (London: Photo–Prismatic Publishing Company Limited, 1894)

Smith, Harry Worcester, *A sporting tour through Ireland, England, Wales and France, in the years 1912–1913; including a concise description of the packs of foxhounds, mode of hunting, types of horses and the crack riders. General observations on the history of the counties of Ireland, the castles and cabins: a view of the customs and manners of the Irish people; together with a story of fox hunting in England and France* (Columbia, S.C.: The State Company, 1925)

Secondary sources

Adelman, Melvin L., *A sporting time: New York City and the rise of modern athletics, 1820–70* (Urbana and Chicago: University of Illinois Press, 1990)

Armstrong, W.A., 'The use of information about occupations', in E. A. Wrigley (ed.), *Nineteenth-Century Society* (Cambridge University Press, 1992), pp. 191–310

Bairner, Alan, 'Ireland, sport and empire', in K. Jeffery (ed.), *An Irish Empire? aspects of Ireland and the British Empire* (Manchester University Press, 1996), pp. 55–76

Bary, Valentine M., 'The hunting diaries (1863–1872) of Sir John Fermor Godfrey of Kilcoleman Abbey, County Kerry', in *Irish Ancestor*, 1979, vol. xi, pp. 107–119

—, 'The hunting diaries (1873–1881) of Sir John Fermor Godfrey of Kilcoleman Abbey, County Kerry', in *Irish Ancestor*, 1980, vol. xii, pp. 13–25

Bence–Jones, Mark, *Twilight of the ascendancy* (London: Constable, 1987)

Bergin, Stanley, and Derek Scott, 'Cricket in Ireland', in E. W. Swanton (ed.), *Barclay's world of cricket* (London: 1980), pp. 508–509

Bielenberg, Andy, *Locke's distillery, a history* (Dublin: Lilliput Press, 1993)

Birley, Derek, *A social history of English cricket* (London: Aurum Press Limited, 2000)

Bonsall, Penny, *The Irish RMs: the resident magistrates in the British administration in Ireland* (Dublin: Four Courts Press, 1997)

Bowen, Muriel, Irish hunting (Tralee: Kerryman Ltd, [1951])

Brabazon, Aubrey, *Racing through my mind* (Ardmore, County Waterford: Vota Books, 1998)

Bracken, Patrick, *'Foreign and fantastic field sports': cricket in County Tipperary* (Thurles: Liskiveen Books, 2004)

Brailsford, Dennis, *A taste for diversions: sport in Georgian England* (Cambridge: The Lutterworth Press, 1999)

Brailsford, Dennis, *Sport, time and society: the British at play* (London: Routledge, 1991)

Brennan, Helen, *The story of Irish dance* (Dingle: Brandon Publishers Ltd, 1999)

Brodie, Malcolm, *Linfield, 100 years* (Belfast: Linfield Football and Athletic Club, 1985)

Brodie, Malcolm, *100 Years of Irish Football* (Belfast: Blackstaff Press, 1980)

Browne, Noel Phillips, *The horse in Ireland* (London: Pelham Books, 1967)

Buchanan, Ian, *British Olympians: a hundred years of gold medallists* (Enfield: Guinness Superlatives Ltd., 1994)

Bulfin, William, *Rambles in Éirinn* (Dublin: M. H. Gill & son, 1908)

Bullock, Shan F., *After sixty years* (London: Sampson, Low, Marston, 1936)

Burke, John, *Athlone in the Victorian era* (Athlone: The Old Athlone Society, 2007)

Burnett, John, *Riot, revelry and rout: sport in lowland Scotland before 1860* (East Lothian: Tuckwell Press, 2000)

Byrne, Michael, 'Tullabeg, Rahan, Tullamore, 1818–1991', in *Offaly Heritage: journal of the Offaly historical and archaeological society*, vol. 2, 2004, pp. 90–111

Campbell, J. D., '"Training for sport is training for war": sport and the transformation of the British Army, 1860–1914', in *International Journal of the History of Sport*, vol. 17, no. 4, 2000, pp. 21–58

Cannadine, David, *The decline and fall of the British aristocracy* (Yale University Press, 1990)

Carr, Raymond, *English fox hunting: a history* (London: Weidenfeld and Nicholson, 1976)

Carter, J. W. H., *The Land War and its leaders in Queen's county, 1879–82* (Portlaoise: Leinster Express, 1994)

Clarke, Samuel, and Donnelly, James jnr, *Irish peasants: violence and political unrest, 1750–1914* (Manchester University Press, 1983)

Coleman, Marie, *County Longford and the Irish revolution 1910–1923* (Dublin: Irish Academic Press, 2003)

Collins, Tom, *Athlone Golf Club 1892–1992:100 years of golf* (Athlone: The Club, 1992)

Collins, Tony, *Rugby's great split, class, culture and the origins of rugby league football* (London: Frank Cass, 1998)

—, and Wray Vamplew, *Mud, sweat and beers: a cultural history of sport and alcohol* (Oxford: Berg, 2002)

Comerford, R. V., *Inventing the nation: Ireland* (London: Arnold, 2003)

—, *The Fenians in context: Irish politics and society 1848–82* (Dublin: Wolfhound Press, 1998 edition)

—, 'Tipperary representatives at Westminster, 1801–1918', in William Nolan (ed.), *Tipperary: history and society, interdisciplinary essays on the history of an Irish county* (Dublin: Geography Publications, 1985), pp. 325–338

Connell, Paul, *The diocese of Meath under Bishop John Cantwell 1830–66* (Dublin: Four Courts Press, 2004)

Connolly, S. J., *Priests and people in pre–famine Ireland, 1750–1845* (Dublin: Four Courts Press, 2001)

Corry, Eoghan, *An illustrated history of the GAA* (Dublin: Gill and Macmillan, 2005)

—, *Oakboys: Derry's football dreams come true* (Dublin: Torc books, 1993)

Costello, Con, *A most delightful station: the British army on the Curragh of Kildare 1885–1922* (Cork: The Collins Press, 1999)

Crawford, W. H., 'The patron, or festival of St Kevin at the seven churches, Glendalough, County Wicklow 1813', in *Ulster Folk Life*, vol. 32, 1986, pp. 37–47

Cronin, Mike, 'Enshrined in blood: the naming of Gaelic Athletic Association grounds and clubs', in *The Sports Historian*, vol. 18, no. 1, 1998, pp. 90–104

—, 'Fighting for Ireland: playing for England? The nationalist history of the Gaelic Athletic Association and the English influence on Irish sport', in International Journal of the History of Sport, Vol. 15, No. 3, 1998, pp. 35–56. (Dublin: Four Courts Press, 1999)

—, *Sport and nationalism in Ireland: Gaelic games, soccer and Irish identity since 1884* (Dublin: Four Courts Press, 1999)

—, 'Writing the history of the GAA', in *High Ball: the official GAA monthly magazine*, vol. 6, no. 6, 2003, pp. 50–53

Crossman, Virginia, *Local government in nineteenth-century Ireland* (Belfast: The Institute of Irish Studies, 1994)

Cruise O'Brien, Conor, *The shaping of modern Ireland* (London: Routledge & Kegan Paul, 1960)

Crump, Jeremy, '"The great carnival of the year": the Leicester Races in the nineteenth century', in *Transactions of the Leicestershire Historical and Archaeological Society*, vol. 58 (1982–3)

Curling, Bill, *The Captain, a biography of Captain Sir Cecil Boyd–Rochfort, royal trainer* (London: Barrie and Jenkins, 1970)

Curtis, L. P. Jnr, 'Stopping the Hunt, 1881–2: An aspect of the Irish Land War', in C. H. E. Philipin (ed.), *Nationalism and popular protest in Ireland* (Cambridge University Press, 1987), pp. 349–401

D'Arcy, Fergus A., *Horses, Lords and racing men: the Turf Club, 1890–1990* (The Curragh: The Turf Club, 1991)

D'Arcy, Fergus A. and Con Power (eds.), *Leopardstown Racecourse, 1888–1988, a centenary commemoration* (Dublin: Leopardstown Club Ltd, 1988)

Davis, Richard, 'Irish cricket and nationalism', in *Sporting Traditions*, vol. x, no. 2, 1994, pp. 77–96

Dease, Edmund F., *A complete history of the Westmeath hunt from its foundation* (Dublin: 1898)

de Burca, Marcus, *Michael Cusack and the GAA* (Dublin: Anvil Books, 1989)

—, *The GAA: a history of the Gaelic Athletic Association* (Dublin: Cumann Luthchleas Gael, 1980)

Dolan, Hugh (ed.), 'County Carlow Polo Club', in *Carloviana, journal of the old Carlow society*, vol. 30, 1983, pp. 11–13

Donnelly James jnr, *Landlord and tenant in nineteenth-century Ireland*, (Dublin: Gill & Macmillan, 1973)

Dooley, Terence, *The decline of the Big House in Ireland: a study of Irish landed families, 1860–1960* (Dublin: Wolfhound Press, 2001)

—, '"A world turned upside down": a study of the changing social world of the landed nobility of County Meath, 1875–1945', in *Ríocht na Midhe, Records of Meath archaeological and historical society*, vol. xii, 2001, pp. 188–227

—, *Sources for the history of landed estates in Ireland* (Dublin and Portland, Oregon: Irish Academic Press, 2000)

Drum and its hinterland: its history and its people (Athlone: Drum heritage group, 1994)

Elizabeth, Countess of Fingall, *Seventy years young: memories of Elizabeth, Countess of Fingall as told to Pamela Hinkson* (Dublin: The Lilliput Press, 1991 edition)

Fagan, Patrick, *A Georgian celebration: Irish poets of the eighteenth century* (Dublin: Branar, 1989)

—, 'Thomas Dease, Bishop of Meath, 1622–1651: his life and times', in *Ríocht na Midhe, records of Meath archaeological and historical society*, vol. xvii, 2006, pp. 77–115

Farrell, Mary (ed.), *Mullingar: essays in the history of a midlands town in the 19th century* (Mullingar: Westmeath County Library, 2002)

Farry, Michael, *The aftermath of revolution: Sligo 1921–23* (Dublin: UCD Press, 2000)

Flynn, Gabriel, 'Bishop Thomas Nulty and the Irish Land Question, parts II and III, 1879–1898,' in *Ríocht na Midhe*, vol. vii, no. iv, pp. 93–111, 1996

Foster, R. F., *Paddy and Mr Punch: connections in Irish and English history* (London: Allen Lane, 1993)

GAA Golden jubilee supplement (Dublin: GAA, 1934)

Gallogly, Rev. Daniel, Cavan's football story, (Cavan: Cavan county committee of the Gaelic Athletic Association, 1979)

Garnham, Neal, 'Accounting for the early success of the Gaelic Athletic Association', in *Irish Historical Studies*, vol. xxxiv, no. 133, May 2004

—, *Association football and society in pre–partition Ireland* (Belfast: Ulster Historical Foundation, 2004)

—, 'Football and national identity in pre-great war Ireland', in *Irish Economic and Social History*, vol. xxviii, 2001, pp. 13–31

—, 'Introduction', in *The origins and development of football in Ireland being a reprint of R. M. Peter's Irish Football Annual of 1880* (Belfast: Ulster Historical Foundation, 1999)

—, 'The roles of cricket in Victorian and Edwardian Ireland', in *Sporting Traditions, Journal of the Australian society of sports history*, vol. 19, no. 2, 2003, pp. 27–48

Garvin, Tom, *Nationalist revolutionaries of Ireland, 1858–1928* (Oxford: Clarendon, 1987)

—, *The evolution of Irish nationalist politics* (Dublin: Gill and Macmillan, 1972)

Gibson, William H., *Early Irish golf* (Naas: Oak Leaf, 1988)

Gillmeister, Heiner, *Tennis: a cultural history* (New York University Press, 1998)

Glennon, Chris (ed.), compiled by Tom Wynne, *90 years of the Irish Hockey Union* (Naas: Leinster Leader Ltd., n.d.)

Godley, General Sir Alexander, *Life of an Irish soldier: reminiscences of General Sir Alexander Godley, G.C.B., K.C.M.G.* (London: John Murray, 1939)

Green, Reg, *A race apart: the history of the grand national* (London: Hodder & Stoughton, 1988)

Griffin, Padraig, *The politics of Irish athletics, 1850–1990* (Ballinamore, County Leitrim: Marathon Publications, 1990)

Guinnane, Timothy W., *The vanishing Irish: households, migration, and the rural economy in Ireland, 1850–1914* (Princeton University Press, 1997)

Hannigan, Dave, *The garrison game: the state of Irish football* (Edinburgh: Mainstream Publishing, 1998)

Hargreaves, Jennifer, '"Playing like gentlemen while behaving like ladies": contradictory features of the formative years of women's sport', in *The British Journal of Sports History*, vol. 2, no. 1, 1985, pp. 40–51

—, *Sporting females: critical issues in the history and sociology of women's sports* (London and New York: Routledge, 1994)

Hart, Peter, *The IRA at war 1916–1923* (Oxford: Oxford University Press, 2003)

—, *The IRA and its enemies: violence and community in Cork, 1916–1923* (Oxford: Clarendon Press, 1998)

Higgins, Tom, *The history of Irish tennis* (Sligo: Tom Higgins, The Sligo Tennis Club, 2006)

Hignell, Andrew, *Rain stops play* (London and Portland, Oregon: Frank Cass, 2002)

Hill, J. R. (ed.), *A new history of Ireland 1921–1984*, (Oxford University Press, 2004)

Hill, Myrtle, *Women in Ireland: a century of change* (Belfast: The Blackstaff Press, 2003)

Holt, Richard, *Sport and the British: a modern history* (Oxford University Press, 1990)

—, 'Working-class football and the city: the problem of continuity', in *The British Journal of Sports History*, vol. 3, no. 1, 1986, pp. 5–17

Hone, W. P., *Cricket in Ireland* (Tralee: The Kerryman, 1956)

Hoppen, T. K., *Elections, politics and society in Ireland, 1832–1885* (Oxford University Press, 1984)

Huggins, Mike, *Flat racing and British society, 1790–1914, a social and economic history* (London: Frank Cass, 2000)

—, 'Horse-Racing on Teeside in the nineteenth century: change and continuity', in *Northern History*, vol. 23, 1987, pp. 98–118

—, 'The spread of association football in north-east England, 1876–90: the pattern of diffusion', in *International Journal of the History of Sport*, vol. 6, 1989, pp. 299–318

—, *The Victorians and sport* (Hambledon and London: Hambledon Books, 2004)

Huggins, Mike and Tolson, John, 'The railways and sport in Victorian Britain: a critical reassessment', in *The Journal of Transport History*, vol. 22, no. 2, 2001, pp. 99–114

Hunt, Tom, 'Angling in the Mullingar district in Victorian times: a class act?' in Seamus O'Brien (ed.), *A Town in Transition – Post Famine Mullingar* (Mullingar, Tathlainne Press, 2007), pp. 102–133.

—, 'Classless cricket? Westmeath, 1880–1905', in *History Ireland*, vol. 12, no. 2, Summer 2004, pp. 26–30

—, 'Mullingar sport in the 1890s: communities at play', in Mary Farrell (ed.), *Mullingar: essays on the history of a Midlands Town in the nineteenth century* (Mullingar: Westmeath County Library, 2002), pp. 1–38

—, *Portlaw, County Waterford, 1825–1876: portrait of an industrial village and its cotton industry* (Dublin: Irish Academic Press, 2000)

—, 'The Thomastown and Garrycastle Races 1857–1868', in *Journal of the old Athlone Society*, vol. 11, no. 8, 2005, pp. 296–311

Hutchinson, John, *The dynamics of cultural nationalism: the Gaelic revival and the creation of the Irish nation state* (London: Allen & Unwin, 1987)

Illingworth, Ruth, 'Transport, 1806–1905', in Mary Farrell (ed.), *Mullingar: essays on the history of a Midlands Town in the nineteenth century* (Mullingar: Westmeath County Library, 2002) pp. 126–166

Itzkowitz, D. C., *Peculiar privilege: a social history of English fox hunting, 1753–1885* (London: Harvester Press, 1977)

Jeffrey, K. (ed.), *An Irish Empire? aspects of Ireland and the British Empire* (Manchester University Press, 1996)

—, 'The Irish military tradition and the British Empire', in K. Jeffrey (ed.), *An Irish Empire? Aspects of Ireland and the British Empire* (Manchester University Press, 1996), pp. 94–122

JMJ, *Centenary record: Men's confraternity of the Holy Family, Mullingar 1867–1967* (Mullingar: The Westmeath Examiner Ltd, 1967)

Jones, David Seth, *Graziers, land reform and political conflict in Ireland* (Washington DC: The Catholic University of America Press, 1995)

—, 'The cleavage between graziers and peasants in the land struggle, 1890–1910', in Samuel Clark and J. S. Donnelly jr (ed.), *Irish peasants, violence and political unrest, 1780–1914* (Manchester University Press, 1983)

Jupp, Peter and Eoin, Magennis, 'Introduction: crowds in Ireland, c. 1720–1920', in Peter Jupp and Eoin Magennis (eds.), *Crowds in Ireland, c. 1720–1920* (Basingstoke: Macmillan Press, 2000)

Keogh, Dermot, *Twentieth-Century Ireland: nation and state* (Dublin: Gill and Macmillan, 1994)

Kennedy, Edward, *The land movement in Tullaroan, County Kilkenny, 1879–1891* (Dublin: Four Courts Press, 2004)

Kerrigan, Paul M., 'The Batteries, Athlone', in *Journal of the Old Athlone Society*, vol. 1, no. 4, 1974–75, pp. 264–271

Korr, Charles P., 'West Ham United Football Club and the beginnings of professional football in east London, 1895–1914', in *Journal of Contemporary History*, vol. 13, 1978, pp. 211–32

Lanfanchi, Pierre, Eisenberg, Christian, Mason, Tony and Wahl, Alfred, *100 Years of Football: the FIFA Centennial Book* (London: Weidenfeld & Nicolson, 2004)

Lee, J. J., *Ireland, 1912–1985, politics and society* (Cambridge University Press, 1989)

Lenehan, Jim, *Politics and society in Athlone, 1830–1885: a rotten borough* (Dublin: Irish Academic Press, 1999)

Lennon, Joe, *The playing rules of football and hurling 1884–1995* (Gormanstown, County Meath: The Northern Recreation Consultants, 1997)

—, *Towards a philosophy for legislation in Gaelic games* (Gormanstown, County Meath: The Northern Recreation Consultants, 2000)

Leonard, Jack, 'Polo in Ireland', in Noel Phillips Browne (ed.), *The Horse in Ireland* (London: Pelham Books, 1967), pp. 179–184

Lovesey, Peter, *The official centenary history of the Amateur Athletic Association* (Enfield: Guinness Superlatives Limited, 1979)

Lowerson, John, *Sport and the English middle classes, 1850–1914* (Manchester University Press, 1993)

Luddy, Maria, *Women and philanthropy in nineteenth century Ireland* (Cambridge University Press, 1995)

Lynch, Frank, *The history of Athlone Town Football Club the first 101 years* (Athlone: Frank Lynch, 1991)

MacDonagh, Oliver, W. F. Mandle and Pauric Travers (eds.), *Irish culture and nationalism, 1750–1950* (London: Macmillan in association with the Humanities Research Centre and the Australian National University, 1983)

MacLua, Brendan, *The steadfast rule: a history of the GAA ban* (Dublin: Press Cuchulainn, 1967)

Mahony, Edmund, *The Galway Blazers* (Galway: Kenny's Bookshops and Art Galleries, 1979)

Malcolm, Elizabeth, 'Popular recreation in nineteenth–century Ireland', in Oliver MacDonagh, W. F. Mandle and Pauric Travers (eds.), *Irish Culture and Nationalism, 1750–1950* (London: Macmillan in association with the Humanities Research Centre and the Australian National University, 1983)

Malcolmson, A.P.W., *The pursuit of the heiress, aristocratic marriage in Ireland 1740–1840* (Belfast: Ulster Historical Foundation, 2006)

Mallon, Bill and Ian Buchanan, *The 1908 Olympic Games; results for all competitors in all events with commentary* (Jefferson, NC: McFarland & Company Inc., 2000)

Mandle, W. F., 'Sport as politics: the Gaelic Athletic Association 1884–1916', in R. Cashman and M. McKernan (eds.), *Sport in History* (St. Lucia, Queensland: University of Queensland Press, 1979), pp. 99–123

—, *The Gaelic Athletic Association & Irish nationalist politics 1884–1924* (Dublin: Gill and Macmillan, 1987)

—, 'The GAA and popular culture, 1884–1924', in Oliver MacDonagh, W. F. Mandle and Pauric Travers (eds.), *Irish Culture and Irish Nationalism* (London: Macmillan in association with the Humanities Research Centre and the Australian National University, 1993), pp. 104–121

—, 'The IRB and the beginning of the Gaelic Athletic Association', in *Irish Historical Studies*, vol. xx, no. 80,1977, pp. 418–438

Mangan, J. A. (ed.), *Pleasure, profit and proselytism; British culture and sport at home and abroad, 1700–1914* (London: Frank Cass, 1988)

Mason, Tony, *Association football and English society 1863–1915* (Brighton: Harvester Press, 1980)

—, (ed.), *Sport in Britain: a social history* (Cambridge: Cambridge University Press, 1989)

Maume, Patrick, *The long gestation, Irish nationalist life, 1891–1918* (Dublin: Gill and Macmillan, 1999)

McCabe, Paddy, *Hurling in Castlepollard, a history 1899–2005* (Castlepollard: Castlepollard Hurling Club, 2006)

McCan, Anthony, 'The diary of a young lady, Mary Anne Power, 1868–1873', in *Decies: journal of the Waterford archaeological & historical society*, vol. 57, 2001, pp. 131–142

McCormack, Stan, *Against the odds, Kilbeggan races, 1840–1994* (Kilbeggan: Stan McCormack, 1995)

McMillan, N. D., *One hundred and fifty years of cricket and sport in County Carlow: an illustrated social history of conflict and sport, 1823–1981* (Dublin: Carlton, 1981)

Menton, William A., *The Golfing Union of Ireland, 1891–1991* (Dublin: Gill and Macmillan, 1991)

Metcalf, Alan, 'Football in the mining communities of east Northumberland, 1882–1914', in *International Journal of the History of Sport*, vol. 5, no. 3, 1988, pp. 269–91

Middleton, Iris M., 'The origins of English fox hunting and the myth of Hugo Meynell and the Quorn', in *Sport in History*, vol. 25, no. 1, April 2005, pp. 1–16

Montgomery, Bob, *R. J. Mecredy: the father of Irish motoring* (Garristown, County Meath: Dreoilín Specialist Publications Limited, 2003)

Moyvoughley historical committee, *Moyvoughley and its hinterland* (n.p.: [1999])

Mullen, Michael, 'The devolution of the Irish economy in the nineteenth century and the bifurcation of Irish sport', in *International Journal of the History of Sport*, vol. 13, no. 2, 1996, pp. 42–60

Mulligan, Fergus, *One hundred and fifty years of Irish railways* (Dublin: 1990)

Munting, R., *Hedges and hurdles: a social and economic history of national hunt racing* (London: J. A. Allen, 1987)

Murray, Andrew C., 'Nationality and local politics in late nineteenth-century Ireland: the case of County Westmeath', in *Irish Historical Studies*, vol. xxv, no. 98, 1986

Murtagh, Harman, 'Horse–racing in Georgian Athlone', in *Journal of the Old Athlone Society*, vol. ii, no. 6, 1985, pp. 85–87

Nannestad, Ian, 'The origin of association football in Ireland', in *Soccer History*, vol. 5, 2003, pp. 8–11

Nolan, William (ed.), *Tipperary: history and society, interdisciplinary essays on the history of an Irish county* (Dublin: Geography Publications, 1985)

Ó Cadhla, Stiofán, *The holy well tradition: the pattern of St Declan, Ardmore, County Waterford, 1800–2000* (Dublin: Four Courts Press, 2002)

Ó Cearbhaill, Diarmuid, 'The Colohans – a remarkable Galway family', in *Journal of the Galway archaeological and historical association*, vol. 54, 2002, pp. 121–126

O'Connor, Kevin, *Ironing the land: the coming of the railways to Ireland* (Dublin: Gill and Macmillan, 1999)

O'Duill, Antoin, (accent O, o, u), *Famous Tullaroan 1884–1984* (Tullaroan: Tullaroan GAA Club, 1984)

O'Dwyer, Michael, *The history of cricket in Kilkenny-the forgotten game* (Kilkenny: O'Dwyer Books, 2006)

O'Farrell, Fergus, 'Glimpses of County Longford's Hunting and Racing past', in Eugene McGee (ed.), *A century of Longford life: Longford Leader, 1897–1997* (Longford: Longford Leader, 1997), p. 175

Ó Maitiu, Seamas, 'Changing images of Donnybrook fair', in Denis A. Cronin, Jim Gilligan & Karina Holton (eds.), *Irish Fairs and Markets: Studies in local history* (Dublin: Four Courts Press, 2001), pp. 164–179

—, *The humours of Donnybrook: Dublin's famous fair and its suppression* (Dublin: Irish Academic Press, 1995)

Ó'Riain, Seamus, *Maurice Davin (1842–1927), first president of the GAA* (Dublin: Geography Publications, n.d.)

Pašeta, Senia, *Before the revolution: nationalism, social change, and Ireland's Catholic elite, 1879–1922* (Cork University Press, 1999)

Quane, Michael, 'Ranelagh Endowed School, Athlone', in *Journal of the Old Athlone Society*, vol. 1, no. 1, 1969, pp. 23–34

Parratt, Cartriona M., 'Athletic "Womanhood": exploring sources for female sport in Victorian and Edwardian England', in *Journal of Sport History*, vol. 16, no. 2, 1989, pp. 140–157

Pyal, T. M., *The Phoenix Club, 1830–1980, a history of the club* (Dublin: The Phoenix Cricket Club, 1980)

Refausse, Raymond, *Church of Ireland records* (Dublin: Irish Academic Press, 2000)

Robins, Joseph, *Champagne and silver buckets, the Viceregal court and Dublin Castle, 1700–1922* (Dublin: Lilliput Press, 2001)

Rouse, Paul, 'The politics of culture and sport in Ireland: a history of the GAA ban of foreign games 1884–1971. Part one: 1884–1921', in *International Journal of the History of Sport*, vol. 10, no. 3, 1993, pp. 333–360

—, '*Sport* and Ireland in 1881', in Alan Bairner (ed.), *Sport and the Irish: histories, identities, issues* (Dublin: UCD Press, 2005)

—, 'Why historians have ignored Irish sport: a note', *The History Review*, vol. xiv, 2003, pp. 67–73

Royle, Stephen, A., 'Small towns in Ireland, 1841–1851', in Howard B. Clarke, Jacinta Prunty and Mark Hennessy (eds.), *Multidisciplinary essays in honour of Angret Simms* (Dublin: Geography Publications, 2004), pp. 535–563

Rubinstein, David, 'Cycling in the 1890s', in *Victorian Studies*, 21, Autumn, 1997, pp. 47–71

Ryall, Tom, *Kilkenny, the GAA story 1884–1984* (Kilkenny: Kilkenny County GAA board, 1984)

Sheehan, Jeremiah, *South Westmeath, farm and folk* (Dublin: The Blackwater Press, 1978)

—, *Worthies of Westmeath* (Moate: Wellbrook Press and author, 1987)

Sheehy, Ian, 'T. P. O'Connor and *The Star* 1886–90', in D. George Boyce and Alan O'Day (eds.), *Ireland in Transition, 1867–1921* (London: Routledge, 2004), pp. 76–91

Shepherd, Ernest, W., *The Midland Great Western Railway of Ireland: an illustrated history by Ernest Shepherd* (Earl Shilton: Midland Publishing Limited, c.1994)

Siggins, Gerard, *Green days: cricket in Ireland 1792–2005* (Gloucestershire: Nonsuch Publishing Limited, 2005)

Smith, Brian, *The horse in Ireland* (Dublin: The Wolfhound Press, 1991)

Smith, Nicky, *Queen of games: a history of croquet* (London: Weidenfeld and Nicholson, 1991)

Speak, M. A., 'Social stratification and participation in sport in Mid–Victorian England, with particular reference to Lancaster, 1840–1870', in J. A. Mangan (ed.), *Pleasure, profit and proselytism: British culture and sport at home and abroad, 1700–1914* (London: Frank Cass, 1988), pp. 42–66

Sugden, John and Alan Bairner, *Sport, sectarianism and society in a divided Ireland* (Leicester University Press, 1995)

Tranter, Neil, 'Organised sport and the middle-class woman in nineteenth-century Scotland', in *International Journal of the History of Sport*, vol. 6, no. 1, 1989, pp. 31–48

—, *Sport, economy and society in Britain 1750–1914* (Cambridge University Press, 1998)

—, 'The Cappielow riot and the composition and behaviour of soccer crowds in late Victorian Scotland', in *International Journal of the History of Sport*, vol. 12, no. 3, 1995, pp. 125–40

—, 'The chronology of organised sport in nineteenth-century Scotland: a regional study. II. Causes ', in *International Journal of the History of Sport*, vol. 7, no. 3, 1990, pp. 365–87

—, 'The chronology of organised sport in nineteenth-century Scotland: a regional study. Patterns', in *International Journal of the History of Sport*, vol. 7, no. 2, 1990, pp. 188–203

—, 'The patronage of organised sport in central Scotland, 1820–1900', in *Journal of Sport History*, vol. 16, no. 3, 1989, pp. 227–47

—, 'The social and occupational structure of organised sport in central Scotland during the nineteenth century', in *International Journal of the History of Sport*, vol. 4, no. 3, 1987, pp. 301–314

—, 'Women and sport in nineteenth-century Scotland', in Grant Jarvie and Graham Walker (eds.), *Scottish sport in the making of the nation: ninety minute patriots?* (Leicester University Press, 1994), pp. 27–42

Vamplew, Wray, 'Horse–Racing', in Tony Mason (ed.), *Sport in Britain: a social history* (Cambridge University Press, 1989), pp. 215–37

—, *Pay up and play the game: professional sport in Britain* (Cambridge University Press, 1988)

—, 'The economics of a sports industry: Scottish gate–money football, 1890–1914', in *Economic History Review*, vol. 35, no. 4, 1982, pp. 549–67

—, *The Turf: a social and economic history of horse racing* (London: Allen Lane, 1976)

Van Esbeck, Edmund, *The story of Irish rugby* (London: Stanley Paul, 1986)

Vaughan, W. E. and Fitzpatrick, A. J. (eds.), *Irish historical statistics: population 1821–1971* (Dublin: Royal Irish Academy, 1978)

Walker, Helen, 'Lawn Tennis', in Tony Mason (ed.), *Sport in Britain: a social history* (Cambridge University Press, 1989), pp. 245–275

Walsh, David, *Mullingar golf club: the first 100 years* (Mullingar: The Golf Club, 1994)

Walvin, James, *Leisure and society, 1830–1950* (London: Allen Lane, 1978)

—, *The people's game* (London: Allen Lane, 1975)

Watson, Colonel S. J., MBE, MA, *Between the flags, a history of Irish steeplechasing* (Dublin: Allen Figgis, 1969)

Welcome, John, *Irish Horse-Racing, an illustrated history* (Dublin: Gill and Macmillan, 1982)

West, Trevor, *The Bold Collegians: the development of sport in Trinity College, Dublin* (Dublin: The Lilliput Press Limited, 1991)

Wheatley, Michael, *Nationalism and the Irish Party, provincial Ireland 1910–1916* (Oxford University Press, 2005)

Whelan, Kevin, 'The geography of hurling', in *History Ireland*, spring, 1993, 27–31

Williams, Guy St John and Francis P. M. Hyland, *Jameson Irish Grand National, a history of Ireland's premier steeplechase* (Dublin: The Organisation, 1995)

—, *The Irish Derby, 1866–1979* (London: J. A. Allen & Co., 1980)

Winckworth, Trevor E., *All Saints Church, Mullingar: notes concerning the history of the church since 1814* (Mullingar: All Saints Church, 1989)

Wren, Jimmy, *Saint Laurence O'Toole GAC 1901–2001: a centenary history* (Dublin, No publisher [The Club], 2001)

Unpublished theses and papers

Burke, John, 'Victorian Athlone: the struggle to modernise an Irish provincial town', MA thesis, Galway-Mayo Institute of Technology, Galway, 2004

Clarke, Ian David, 'The development and social history of cricket in Cornwall 1815 to 1881', PhD thesis, De Montfort University, Leicester, 2004

Gibney, Patricia, 'The Military in Mullingar', research project presented to the Department of History, NUI, Maynooth, 1998

Gorry, David, 'The Gaelic Athletic Association in Dublin, 1884–2000', M.Litt. thesis, University College Dublin, 2001

Griffin, Brian, 'The wheels of commerce? Cycling agents and manufacturers, and the Irish cycling craze of the late nineteenth century', paper delivered at 'The state of play – Sports history in Britain and Ireland, past, present and future' conference hosted by the Academy for Irish Cultural Heritages at the University of Ulster, Belfast Campus, 21–23 November 2003

Hunt, Thomas, 'The development of sport in Westmeath, 1850–1905', Ph.D thesis, De Montfort University, Leicester, 2005.

Middleton, Iris Maud, 'The developing pattern of horse racing in Yorkshire, 1700–1749: an analysis of the people and places', PhD thesis, De Montfort University, Leicester, 2000

Nannestad, Ian, 'From Sabbath breakers to Respectable Sportsmen: the development of football in Lincolnshire, 1855 to 1881', MA theses, De Montfort University, Leicester, 2003

O'Sullivan, Daniel Gerard, 'Sport, leisure and class in Cork, 1870–1939', M.Litt. thesis, NUI Galway, 2002

Tolson, John, 'The railways and racing', PhD thesis, De Montfort University, Leicester, 1999

Wylie, John, 'Laurence Ginnell, 1852–1923: Westmeath's radical agrarian', MA thesis, NUI, Maynooth, 1999

Index

A

Abbey Theatre, 199
Achill Island, 9
Adamson, C.G., 210
Adamson, Mr (SWHC), 10, 176
Adamson, Richard, 176
Adderley family, 81
Addington, Colonel, 16
Adelman, Melvin, 151, 208
Adlercorn, George L., 79
aeridheachta, 193, 196
agricultural economy, 7–8, 114–15, 224
alcohol consumption, 32, 134, 165, 217
   horseracing, 236–7
   restrictions, 243–5
   violent behaviour, 238–40
All-England Croquet Association, 75, 85
All-Ireland Polo Club, 33, 34, 37
All Saints' Church, Mullingar, 181
Anderson, E.S., 128
Antrim, county, 171
archery, 251
Ardcarne Golf Club, 87
Ardee, County Louth, 49, 50, 51
Ardmore, County Waterford, 217
Ardnaglue, County Westmeath, 27, 72
Argentina, 67, 68, 71, 165
Armagh, county, 48
Armstrong (soldier), 183
Arrears of Rent Act 1882, 24
Athboy, County Meath, 67
Athenry, County Galway, 49, 143
Athleague, County Roscommon, 203
athletics, 135, 141, 143, 205, 218, 230, 251
   schools, 176–7
   spectator sport, 220, 228
Athlone, County Westmeath, 5–7, 15, 20,
     93, 111, 123, 197, 227, 228
   cricket, 116, 118
   fairs, 217
   football, 142, 158, 161, 203–4, 220
   Freemasons, 25
   GAA, 142–3, 144, 148, 149, 152
   Gaelic League, 192

   golf, 87–8
   horseracing (*see* Garrycastle racecourse)
   hurling, 204
   military garrisons, 14, 36, 40, 77, 89,
     130–1, 180–1, 235–6, 252
   railway centre, 9, 224–5, 226
   regattas, 218, 219, 223, 226, 228, 235,
     237
     violence, 238
   rugby, 175–6
   soccer, 171–3, 180, 182, 185–6, 187, 203
   tennis, 79–80
Athlone and District Harriers, 14
Athlone Association Football Club, 166,
   172–3, 178–80, 182
Athlone Bicycle Club, 97–8, 100, 109, 220,
   228
   finances, 101
   membership, 98–9
   sports meeting, 223
Athlone Brass Band XI, 124
Athlone Commercial Club, 178
Athlone Football Club, 211, 223–4, 226–7,
   243
Athlone Garden Vale Hockey Club, 176
Athlone Garden Vale Tennis and Croquet
   Club, 75
Athlone Garrison Golf Club, 88, 89, 91–2,
   103
   finances, 104–5
   women in, 108, 109, 110
Athlone Golf Club, 89–92, 104, 112
Athlone Hurling Club, 206
Athlone Junior Football Club, 185–6
Athlone Lawn Tennis and Cricket Club,
   80, 102, 108, 103, 126, 129
   finances, 102
   women administrators, 108
Athlone National Band, 159
Athlone Ranelagh Hockey Club, 176
Athlone Saw Mills, 7, 228
Athlone Senior Football Club, 186
Athlone Shamrocks Football Team, 185
Athlone Soccer Club, 176, 223

Athlone T.P. O'Connors Club, 149–51, 160, 169, 178, 180, 182, 183, 188
  history of, 165–7
  matches, 155
  social activities, 159
Athlone Volunteers Football Club, 203–4, 213
Athlone William O'Briens, 144–5, 160
Athlone Woollen Mills, 7, 124, 131, 177, 228
Athlone YMCA, 98
Auburn, County Westmeath, 184
Auchterlonie, Mr, 104
Austria, Elizabeth Empress of, 13, 17–18
Avondale, County Wicklow, 115
Avonmore, Viscount, 230

B
Bacon, Sergeant, 100
badminton, 76–7, 80, 251
Bailie, Robert, 173–5, 185, 189
Bairner, Alan, 113
Baldoyle racecourse, 54, 226
Ballina, County Mayo, 9
Ballinahown, County Westmeath, 145, 156, 238
Ballinahown Court, 98, 165
Ballinasloe, County Galway, 49, 60, 85, 98, 154, 225, 226
  cricket, 115, 138
  football, 158, 159
  GAA, 152
  rugby, 182
Ballinderry, County Westmeath, 122, 135, 143
Ballinlough Castle, Delvin, 29
Ballinrobe, County Mayo, 60
Ballyglass, County Westmeath, 144, 161
Ballymahon, County Westmeath, 226
Ballymahon Cricket Club, 126, 128
Ballymahon Football Club (Leo O'Casey), 160
Ballymore, County Westmeath, 40, 49, 197, 209
Ballynacarrigy, County Westmeath, 54, 68
Ballynagall, County Westmeath, 12
Baltrasna, County Westmeath, 116
Banagher, County Offaly, 84, 85, 98, 110, 119, 226
Banbridge Academy football club, 171
bands, 134, 221, 235–6, 253
  GAA, 204–5
Bank of Ireland, Mullingar, 80, 88
Barnes, M.F., 80, 83, 88, 122
Barrett (soldier), 183

Barry, Captain, 245
Barry, Fr P., 245
Barton, Captain, 137
Barton, Mrs, 108
Barton, Robert, 137
Batten, Mrs, 18, 251
Batteries golf course, 91–2
Bayley, Captain, 34
Bealnamullia, County Westmeath, 184
Bective, Earl of, 229
Belfast, 93, 111, 218
  soccer, 170–1, 177, 179, 187–8
Belfast Celtic football club, 53
Bell, Mr, 48
Belmont, Mullingar, 35, 37, 42
Belmont Cricket Club, King's county, 127, 128
Belturbet Red Stars, 183
Belturbet United Gaelic and Soccer Club, 183
Belvedere, Lord, 58
Belvedere Cricket Club, 138
Bennett, James, 147, 148
Bergin, J.J., 159–60
Bergin, Stanley, 114
Berkshire Regiment, 103
Berry, J.W. Middleton, 12
Beverley Rovers, 181
Bielenberg, Andy, 72
Birr, County Offaly, 72, 85, 98, 175
Bishopstown, Streamstown, 66
Blackburn Rovers, 182
Blackrock College, Dublin, 137, 175
Blary, County Westmeath, 184
Blary McBride Football Club, 185
Boer War, 185, 190
Bohemians, 166, 173, 179, 180, 203, 223
Boher Cricket Club, 137
Bolton, Lieutenant W.N., 172, 182
Bond family, 122
bookmakers, 240–1
Boyan, G.J., 127
boycotts, 115, 192, 215
Boyd, G.A., 232
Boyd-Rochfort, Alice, 70–1
Boyd-Rochfort, Arthur, 19, 70
Boyd-Rochfort, Major Hamilton, 27, 70
Boyd-Rochfort, Mr, 37, 221
Boyd-Rochfort, Mrs, 70–1
Boyd-Rochfort family, 66
Boyde, G.A., 10
Boyle, County Roscommon, 84
Brabazon, James, 66–7
Brabazon, William Thomas, 66
Bracken, Patrick, 114, 139, 206

Bracklyn, County Westmeath, 40
Brailsford, Denis, 61
Brawney, Athlone, 240
Bray, County Wicklow, 86
Brett, Patrick, 162, 163, 212
Brian Boru club, Ballymore, 209
Brierley, Lieutenant E.C., 176
Briscoe, E.T.F., 55
Briscoe, H.L., 236
Briscoe, John Fetherstonhaugh, 12
Britannia Football Club, 179
British Hunts and Huntsmen, 14, 18, 33, 67
Brock, Laurence, 164
Buffs Regiment, 236
Bulfin, William, 237
Bunbrosna, County Westmeath, 32
Burgess, Messrs, 98
Burke, John, 180
Burnett, Royal, 15–16
Butler, Captain, 8
Byrne, Frank, 69

C
Cahir, County Tipperary, 48, 130
Caledonians, 170
Calverstone demesne, 118
Campbell, J.D., 14–15, 182
Campbell, Jim, 178
Cannadine, David, 14
Cantwell, John, bishop of Meath, 217
cardsharps, 233–4, 235, 240
Carlisle, Earl of, 131
Carlow County Cricket Club, 115
Carlow town, 115
Carpendale, Lieutenant-Colonel, 103
Carrick demesne, 118
Carrick-on-Shannon, County Leitrim, 162
Carrick-on-Suir, County Tipperary, 10–11,
    48, 130, 141, 232
Carrick-on-Suir Athletic, Cricket and
    Football Club, 125–6, 236
Carrickmacross, County Monaghan, 49, 72
Carter, J.H., 10
Casey, John, 193
Casey, P., 72
Cashel, County Tipperary, 48
Castlebar, County Mayo, 9
Castlemaine, Lord, 36, 42, 85, 118, 138, 230,
    231
Castlepollard, County Westmeath, 25, 81
    cricket, 118, 126
    cycling, 98
    Gaelic League, 192–3
    horseracing, 233
        death, 243

hurling, 198–9
polo, 33–4, 36–7, 139
Castlepollard Catholic Commercial cricket
    club, 124
Castlepollard Commercial Club, 123, 137
Castlepollard Commercial Cricket Club,
    129
Castlepollard Cricket Club, 129, 134, 199,
    201
Castlepollard Football Club, 204
Castlepollard Hurling Club, 199, 210
Castlepollard Sarsfields club, 211
Castlepollard Workingmen's Club, 124,
    129
Castlerea, County Roscommon, 9, 171, 225
Castletown-Geoghegan, County West-
    meath, 66, 227
Catholic National Young Men's Club, 158
Catholic Young Men's Society, 98
Catholicism, 2, 250
    alcohol consumption, 198, 244–35
    cricket, 135–6
    cultural nationalism, 190–1, 193
    entertainments, 162, 217–18
    fundraising, 236
    GAA, 142, 147, 193, 204, 251
    hunting, 26–7
    school sports, 174
    soccer, 188
    tennis, 82
cattle driving, 215
Caulfield, J.C., 122
Cavan, county, 8, 9, 31–2, 54, 225, 226, 227
    cricket, 118
    GAA, 143, 210
    horses, 11
    soccer, 183
Cavan Grammar School, 175
Chapman, Sir B., 22
Chapman, Sir Montague Richard, 25–6
Chapman, Thomas, 79
Chapman family, 21
Charlton brothers, 119
Cheltenham school, 174
Cheshire, James, 66, 255
Cheshire hunt, 14
Chichester, 111
Christian Brothers School, Mullingar, 174
Church of Ireland, 120, 188, 213, 250
    cricket, 135–6
    and military, 180–1
    tennis, 82–3
Churchill, Lord Randolph, 13
Cigas Bazaar, Dublin, 108
Civil Service Cricket Club, 118

C.J. Kickham's club, 158
Clancarty, Earl and Countess of, 230
Clara, County Offaly, 9, 143, 225, 226, 227
Clara Hurling Club, 205
Claremont College, Dublin, 100
Claremorris, County Mayo, 9, 60
Clarke, Ian, 127
Clarke, Private, 131
Cleary, James, 127
Cleary, Michael, 67
Cleary, R.G., 72
Cleary, W.D., 143, 144, 161
Clibborn, C., 120
Clibborn, W.C., 81, 138
Clifden, County Galway, 9
Clifford, tennis player, 84
Cliftonville football club, 53, 170, 171
Clinton, Patrick, 164
Cloghan, King's county, 156
Clonard, County Meath, 193
Clonbrock, Lord, 115
Clondaliever, County Westmeath, 231–2
Clonhugh, County Westmeath, 18, 54, 123
Clonhugh Cricket Club, 126, 132
Clonmacnoise Cricket Club, 119, 126
Clonmel, County Tipperary, 130
Clonmel, Earl of, 229
Clonmellon Saint Patrick club, 144
Clonmore, County Westmeath, 56, 162
Clonown, County Westmeath, 211
Clonyn, County Westmeath, 17
Cloughan Cricket Club, 127, 132, 133, 137,
    195, 222
clubs, 1, 4
cock fighting, 31–2
Cole, James, 68, 70, 73–4
Cole, Mary, 70
Coleman, J., 148
Collins, Tony, 154, 251
Colohan, Denis, 49
Comerford, R.V., 38, 197, 215
Coney Island, 185
Connacht Hockey Union, 176
Connacht Rugby Cup, 176
Connaught Rangers, 35, 91, 92, 105, 181,
    183, 192, 231
Connaught Wanderers Football Club, 184
Conneff, Tom, 135
Connell, Patrick, 148
Conniffee, A., 207
Connor, Michael, 242
Coogan, Lar, 157
Cookstown Swifts Club, 183
Coolamber, County Westmeath, 27, 70, 131
    cricket, 120, 122, 123

Coolatore, County Westmeath, 89
Coole, County Westmeath, 26
Cooper, Colonel, 83
Cooper, E.J., 118
Coosan, County Westmeath, 184, 185
Coote, Algernon, 171
Coote, Captain Charles, 31–2
Coote, G., 47
Coote, Nina, 110, 111
Coote, Orlando, 79, 84, 110, 171–2, 176,
    178, 183
Cootehill, County Cavan, 32
Corcoran, Patrick, 199
Cork, county, 54, 64, 68
Cork city, 111, 176, 197
Cornaher, County Westmeath, 116
Cornwall, 127
Corry, Eoghan, 207
Costello, Patrick, 61–2
Cottesmore hunt, 14
County Carlow Polo Club, 35
County Limerick Lawn Tennis Club, 76
Crawford, N., 138
cricket, 3, 22, 79–80, 113–40, 186, 190, 197,
    198, 250
    attacked, 194–5
    casual, 208
    civilian combinations, 120, 122, 128–9
    'decline,' 113–14, 120
    finances, 125–6
    and football, 156–7, 201, 209, 215, 252,
        253
    GAA ban, 113, 206–7
    hierarchical diffusion, 127–9
    and hurling, 199, 201
    limited companies, 53
    marching bands, 134
    military garrisons, 129–32
    patronage, 126–7
    players, 5, 10, 32–3, 117–25, 135–9, 211,
        213, 249
    schools, 119
    social occasions, 131–5
    spectator sport, 222
    women in, 251
Crofton, Lord, 230
Crofts, Mrs, 110
Crofts, Surgeon Major, 110
Croke, Dr, 201
Cronin, Mike, 3, 160
Crookedwood sports, 94, 139, 220, 228,
    235–6
    murder, 241–2
croquet, 75, 76, 80–1, 85–6, 108, 251
    women in, 110–11

Crotty, Rev. A.E., 83
Crowenstown Cricket Club, 222
Cuchulainn, 197
Culleen, County Westmeath, 31, 67
Cullen, Cardinal Paul, 27
Cullion Celtics, 148, 154, 164–5, 166, 202, 205, 206, 211
Curley, Mr, 102
Curragh, County Kildare, 52, 67, 71–2, 86
Curraghmore, Mullingar, 240
Curtis, L.P., 10, 26
Cusack, Michael, 141, 142, 205, 215
cycling, 5, 75, 92–101, 111, 227, 249, 251, 254
   management structures, 101–6
   Westmeath, 93–101
   women in, 109

D
Dagg, H., 100
Daily Telegraph, 165
Dames-Longworth, Edward, 26, 230
Dames-Longworth, F.T., 79, 138
dancing, 205–6
Danesfort, County Kilkenny, 157
Daramona estate, Street, 23, 122
D'Arcy, Fergus A., 39, 42, 52, 53, 61, 63
Davin, Maurice, 141–2, 152, 168, 215, 236
Davin, Pat, 141
Davin, Tom, 10–11
de Burca, Marcus, 113, 142, 207, 214
De Freyne, Lord, 49
Dease, Captain, MFH, 17
Dease, Captain Richard, 26
Dease, Edmund F., 12, 14, 26, 27
Dease, Mrs E.F., 81
Dease, Gerard, 12
Dease, James Arthur, 116
Dease, Mr, 127
Dease, Sir Walter, 26
Dease family, 26, 122
Declan, St, pattern of, 217
Delamere, Thomas, 88, 242
Delvin, County Westmeath, 98, 118, 224
Delvin, Lord, 26
Delvin Athletic and Cycling sports, 94
Delvin Cricket Club, 135
Delvin Emmet Football Club, 144
Delvin Hurling Club, 199, 201, 211, 212
Derby, 50
Derravaragh Lake regatta, 237
Derry, county, 171, 199
Derrymore, County Westmeath, 204
Dibbs, Thomas, 66
Dignam, Captain, 85

Dillon-Kelly, Dr, 82
Dinegan, James, 240
Directors' Plate, 59, 60
Distillery Football Club, 177
Doherty, Michael, 148, 156, 163
Donlon, Miss, 55
Donnybrook fair, 217
Donnybrook hockey club, 176
Dooley, Dr, 67
Dopping, Dr A., Bishop of Meath, 11
Doran, Frank, 138, 157
Dowdall, Joseph P., 54
Down, county, 171
Downes, Christopher, 54
Doyle, E.J., 165
Doyle, Peter, 240
Doyne, James, 57–8, 162
Drennan, Michael, 157
Drogheda, Marquis of, 48, 51–2
Drought, Rev. A., 81
Drumcree, County Westmeath, 12, 19
Drumraney, County Westmeath, 184, 238
Dublin, 29, 30, 97, 107, 108, 111, 184, 219, 227, 239
   clubs, 25, 37
   cricket, 115, 116, 118, 131
   cycling, 93
   football, 158–9, 166
   GAA, 143, 152, 154–5, 204
   hockey, 176
   hurling, 199
   railways, 8, 9, 62, 224, 225, 226
   RIC band, 101
   soccer, 172, 173, 179, 182
Dublin, county, 11, 20
Dublin Association Football Club, 172
Dublin Croquet Club, 85
Dublin Horse Show, 37
Dublin Metropolitan Police, 246
Dublin University Football Club, 173
Dublin University Lawn Tennis Club, 76
Duhallow, County Cork, 14
Dundalk, County Louth, 175
Dungarvan, County Waterford, 48
Dunleary Independent club, 155
Dunlo, Lord, 115
Dunlop, John Boyd, 95
Dunne, Jack, 210
Dunville, Sir Charles, 46
Dunville's distillery, Belfast, 177
Dwyer, Dr Jameson, 222

E
Earl, Daniel, 183
earth-stoppers, 31

East Galway hunt, 14
East Kent Regiment, 182
East Kent Regiment Band XI, 131
East Lancashire Regiment, 16, 77, 80, 84,
    131, 182, 222
Edenderry, King's county, 118, 127, 232
Edgeworth, Mr and Mrs T.N., 83
Edwards, Mary, 27
8th Hussars, 231
85th Regiment, 235
Elmville Cricket Club, 157
Elphin, County Roscommon, 49
Elvery's, 77
emigration, 210
Ennis, J.J., 118
Ennis, John, 29
Enniscorthy, County Wexford, 60
Enniscrone, County Westmeath, 68
Enniskillen, County Fermanagh, 72, 175
entertainment, 216–18, 228–9, 233–7, 254
    cricket, 132
    football, 159
    hunt balls, 16, 17, 29–31, 253

F
faction fighting, 50–1, 238, 240
fairground attractions, 233–4
fairs, 217
Fairyhouse racecourse, 49, 68
farmers
    cricket, 125, 136, 138
    football, 167, 213–14
    horseracing, 44, 66–7, 71, 72–3
    hunt subscribers, 28–9
    soccer, 186–7
Farra School, Bunbrosna, 118, 122, 129, 189
    athletics, 176–7
    cricket, 124
    rugby, 173–5
Father Mathew Club, Athlone, 177–8, 244
Father Mathew Hall XI, 124
Fermanagh, county, 6
Ferrie, George, 104, 105
Fetherstonhaugh, Captain Cecil, 54, 67
Fetherstonhaugh, Cecil, 19, 40
Fetherstonhaugh, Miss, 107–8
Fetherstonhaugh, Mr, 118, 127, 128
Fetherstonhaugh, Theobald, 14, 27
Fetherstonhaugh family, 21, 55
Ffrench, Mrs and Miss, 19
15th Regiment, 181
5th Northumberland Fusiliers, 183
Fingall, Earl of, 26
Fingall, Lady, 10, 18, 253
Finnegan, Dr, 222

fireworks, 219
fishing, 251, 255
Fitzgerald, Mrs, 231
Fitzgerald, P.N., 59, 62
Fitzpatrick, B.M., 13
Fitzpatrick, E.C., 89, 122
Fitzsimons, A., 148
Fitzsimons, Fr, 159
Fitzwilliam Lawn Tennis Club, 76, 110
Flanagan, P., 211
Fleming, P.S., 173
Flynn, J., 148
Fontenoys club, 154–5
football, 96, 125, 148–55, 186, 196, 210–11,
    214–15, 218, 249, 250. see also soccer
    combinations, 150–2
    and cricket, 113, 114, 156–7, 252
    crowd control, 243
    decline, 125, 170
    indiscipline, 154
    limited companies, 53
    Mullingar county committee, 166–7
    number of games, 208–9
    players, 167–8, 213–14
    revival, 190
    revival of, 190, 201–4
    rules, 142, 152–5, 166–7, 168–9, 251
    seasonal, 155–7, 209
    and soccer, 180, 183, 188, 203
    social activities, 158–61, 253
    spectator sport, 219–20
    Sunday games, 157
Foster, T.C., 122, 129, 174–5, 189
14th Regiment, 131
Foy, Edward, 165, 178
Foy, Michael H., 93, 98
Fraher, Dan, 205
Franciscan College, Multyfarnham, 174
Freeman's Journal, 155, 225
Freemasons, 25
French and Co., Messrs, 75
Frenchpark, County Roscommon, 49
Fry, tennis champion, 84
Fulham, Hugh, 157
fund-raising, 103–4, 252

G
Gaelic Athletic Association (GAA), 1, 2–3,
    96, 177, 185, 186, 195, 199, 251. see
    also football; hurling
    administration, 166, 207
    admission charges, 223–4
    and Catholic Church, 142, 147, 193, 204,
    251
    club names, 204

county basis, 145–6
and cultural nationalism, 142, 160, 180, 214–15, 251–3
demarcation lines, 183
exclusion rule, 203, 205–7, 208
Griffith on, 191
hurling, 197–8
marching bands, 134, 236
re-emergence, 1900-05, 4, 190–215, 251–2
rules, 166–9
social activities, 158–61, 205, 253
social class, 215, 249
spectator sport, 219–20
summer football, 156
tournaments, 204–5
in Westmeath, 1884-95, 5, 141–69
Westmeath county committee, 145, 147–8, 152, 162, 206, 207–8
Gaelic football. *see* football
Gaelic League, 191–2, 198, 205, 252
and GAA, 207, 212–13
hurling, 197, 199, 201
Gaffney, John, 241–2
Gainstown GAA club, 210
Galway, county, 9, 47, 49, 62, 84, 118, 197, 225
Galway Blazers, 14, 31
Galway Grammar School, 175
Galway town, 110, 165, 176, 225, 227
gaming, illegal, 233–5
Gannon, Eugene, 127
Garden Vale Tennis and Croquet Club, Athlone, 79, 80, 81–2, 85–6
finances, 102–3
tournaments, 83–4
women in, 108, 109, 110
Gargan, Matt, 157
Garland, John, 240–1
Garnham, Neal, 53, 113–16, 115–16, 157, 170, 180, 205, 218
Garry, Joseph, 162, 203, 210
Garrycastle Handicap, 44–9
Garrycastle racecourse, Athlone, 45, 46, 64, 68
horseracing, 39, 42–52, 58, 63, 219, 220, 221–2, 224–5, 226, 229, 231, 233, 235–7, 243
alcohol, 245
end of, 50–1
faction fighting, 238
grandstand, 230
interference, 243
participation, 47–50
prize-money, 45–7

public disorder, 240
riot, 239
meets end, 50–1
Garvin, Tom, 190
Gaulstown Cricket Club, 157
Gaulstown Park, Lovers of Erin, 145
Gaussen, Major, 88
Gavan, John, 239
Gaybrook, Mullingar, 54, 83
Gaynor, John, 245
Geasehill, King's county, 222, 225
Geoghegan, J.J., 162–3
Geoghegan, M., 172
Geoghegan family, 172
Gibbon, Dr, 89
Gibney's, Castlepollard, 199
Gibson, Bill, 86
Gibson, Jeremiah, 139
Ginnell, Laurence, 215
Gladstone, Miss, 109
Gladstone, W.E., 26
Glasson, County Westmeath, 13, 98, 184, 186, 238
Glasson Young Ireland Football Club, 185, 209, 224
Glendalough, County Wicklow, 217
Glenmore Football Club, 184
Glentoran Football Club, 53, 179
Glynwood Hounds, 44, 45
Glynwood Hunt Challenge Cup, 44–7, 49, 243
Godley, Lieutenant Alexander, 16, 18
golf, 75, 82, 86–92, 87–92, 249, 250, 251, 252
clubs, 1, 5
management structures, 101–6
professionals, 104
women in, 108–9, 110
Golf Annual, The, 88
Golfing Annual, 92
Golfing Union of Ireland (GUI), 87, 89, 104, 105
Goodwin, G.H., 203
Goodwin Cup, 210
Goodwyn, Colonel, 80
Gordon, John W., 54, 57–8
Gormanstown Strand, 33
Gounod, John and Margaret, 245
Gourlay, A., 104
GPO Football Club, 179
Grace, James, 157
Grace, Pierce, 157
Granard, Earl of, 22, 25
Grand Juries, 25
Great Exhibition, Dublin, 1865, 50
Great Famine, 4, 6, 39, 216, 217

Great Northern and Western Railway Company (GNWR), 9
Great Southern and Western Railway Company (GSWR), 9, 225
Green Road Football Club, Mullingar, 183
Grenadier Guards, 182
Greville, Colonel, 22
Greville, Lord, 230
   cricket, 123, 126, 132
   golf, 88, 90, 91
   hunting, 16, 24, 26, 28, 32, 36, 72
   racecourse, 54, 57
Greville Arms Hotel, 33
Greville Cup, 60
Greville-Nugent, Hon P., 118
Griffith, Arthur, 190–1
Griffith's Valuation, 14, 115
Grouse Lodge, 108
Grove Street Stores, Mullingar, 95
Grubb, Sir Howard, 23
Guinness, Messrs, 28
Guinness & Mahon, 92

H
Hall, Miss, 18, 19
Hall, Mr and Mrs S.C., 216
Halpin, Stoppford, 81
Ham, J.J., 72
Hamlin, Lieutenant, 88
Handcock, R.A., 42
Hannan, Cornelius, 67
Hargreaves, 107, 251
Harrington, Colonel, 34
Harrison, Major, 88
Harvey, James, 26
Haslam, Miss, 108
Hayden, John P., 147, 163
Hearn, William, 236
Heinekey, Messrs, 30
Henehan, J., 97
Hennessy's grocery store, Castlepollard, 199
Herdman family, 124
Hibernian Bank, Mullingar, 27, 59, 80, 128
Hickson, E.F., 129
High Ball, 3
Hignell, 127
Hill-of-Down, 226, 227
hockey, 176, 197, 206, 251
Hodgins, J.G., 93
Hodson, J., 172, 176
Hodson, Miss, 110, 111
Hodson, William, 122
Hodson family, 84
Hogan, Thomas, 165, 178

Holdwright, Ned, 127
Hollyville Pupils, 119
Holt, Richard, 112, 178
Holy Family Confraternity, 149, 163
Home Rule, 25–6, 196
   1893 Bill, 28
Hoppen, T.K., 21, 25
Horgan, Denis, 101
Hornridge, Mr, 118, 127
Horse Show, Mullingar, 56, 100–1, 254
   grounds, 202, 210–11
horseracing, 5, 39–74, 218, 222
   admission charges, 223
   ancillary activities, 233–7, 254
   bookmakers, 240–1
   categories of races, 31, 40–1, 42, 44–51
   costs, 73–4
   crowd control, 242–7
   enclosure, 246–7
   grandstands, 229–30
   horse ownership, 64–74
   interference, 243
   limited companies, 53–60
   ordinaries, 229
   participation, 47–50
   polo clubs, 220–1
   prize-money, 45–7, 73–4
   regulation, 41–2
   role of railways, 61–4, 224–6
   spectators, 218–19, 222, 227–8
   sponsorship, 47, 63–4
   training, 71–2
   types of meets, 42–3
   violence, 50
Horsleap, County Westmeath, 227
Howth and Baldoyle Great Municipal Steeplechase, 49
Hudson, Rowland, 118, 127
Hudson, Mrs Rowland, 19
Hudson, Rowland, 35
Huggins, M., 74, 221, 254
   and Tolson, J., 63
Hughes, James, 157
Hughes, John, 157
hunt balls, 16, 17, 29–31, 253
Hunter, R.J., 52
hunting, 3, 5, 10–38, 39, 82, 90, 112, 250, 251, 252, 253
   amount of sport, 12–13
   costs of, 23–4, 254–5
   diaries, 13–14
   history of, 11–12
   military garrisons, 14–17
   opposition to, 38
   social activities, 29–32, 253

social structure, 14–15, 19–22
subscriptions, 22–3
women in, 107
hurling, 143, 190, 193, 196, 197–201, 214–
    15, 249, 250
    Athlone, 141, 204
    and cricket, 157, 186, 195, 252
    number of games, 208–9
    players, 211–13
    rules, 142, 251
    venues, 210–11
Hurlingham Club, 34
Hutchinson, Hon W., 229

I
Illustrated London News, 221
Incorporated Society for Promoting Eng-
    lish Protestant Schools in Ireland,
    173
Independent Wanderers, 157, 202
Inglis, Captain, 172, 182
Inniskilling Dragoons, 16
Inniskilling Fusiliers, 133
Intermediate Education Act 1878, 119
Irish Amateur Athletic Association, 143
Irish Athletic and Cycling News, 93
Irish Champion Athletic Club, 141
Irish Christian Brothers, 124
Irish County Polo Club Union, 34
Irish Cricket Union, 122
Irish Cycling Association (ICA), 160
Irish Cyclist, 92–3, 99–100
Irish Field, 35, 37
Irish Football Association (IFA), 1, 171,
    183
Irish Golfer, 89
Irish Grand National, 68
Irish Hockey Union, 1, 176
Irish language, 192–3
Irish National Foresters Fife and Drum
    Band, 205
Irish National Hunt Steeplechase Com-
    mittee (INHSC), 41, 42, 51, 52–3,
    223, 243
Irish National League, 115, 190
Irish Parliamentary Party, 190, 191
Irish Provident Assurance Company, 203
Irish Republican Brotherhood (IRB), 2,
    142, 143, 145, 150, 160, 205, 251
Irish Rugby Football Union (IRFU), 1, 174
Irish Sportsman, 228
Irish Times, 51
Irish Turf Club, 52–3, 243
Irish Unionist Alliance, 26
Irish Wheelman, 93

Isles of the Sea, 166
Itkowitz, D.C., 23

J
Jackson, Driver, 182
Jackson, Mrs, 19
jarveys, 226
Jeffers, R., 178
Jeffers, W., 172
Jockey Club, 61
jockeys, 64
Johnson, Fr, 127
Johnston House, Mullingar, 66
Johnstone, R., 165
Jones, William, 219
Joy, Mr, 88
Joyce, A.E., 122
Junior United Services Club, 25

K
Kearney, Canon, 14, 145, 165, 244
Keegan, John, 216
Keeper of the Match Book, 52
'Keils,' 238
Kelleghan, Peter, 162
Kells Cycling Club, 98
Kells GAA, 157
Kelly, T., 145
Kelly, William, 128
Kelly's Hotel, Mullingar, 98
Kelsh, Fr, 127, 133
Kerry, county, 6, 183, 193
Kevin, St, pattern of, 217
Kiely, Tom, 101
Kiernan, Jane, 243
Kilbeggan, County Westmeath, 7, 26, 27,
    72, 99, 120, 195
    cricket, 116, 118, 222
    football, 145
    horseracing, 39, 42, 221, 226, 227, 231, 233
    race meets, 58
    and railway, 225
Kilbeggan Border Union Cricket Club, 127
Kilbeggan Cricket Club, 131–2, 137
Kilbeggan Willow Club, 127
Kilbride National Cricket Club, 127, 195
Kilcock, County Kildare, 49
Kildare, county, 143, 225, 226, 227, 232–3
    horses, 11, 64
    hunt, 14, 17
Kildare Hunt Steeplechase, 49
Kildare Street Club, 25
Kilkelly, Michael, 197
Kilkenny, county, 68, 207
    cricket, 139, 157, 194, 206

Kilkenny People, 194
Kilkenny town, 115
Killian, Mr, 105, 210
Killucan, County Westmeath, 11, 54, 67, 97, 100, 142, 224
  cricket, 129
  football, 144, 145, 157, 158
Killucan Cricket Club, 132
Killucan Fife and Drum Band, 134
Killucan Football Club, 220
Killucan (Railway) Station Cricket Club, 124, 127, 132–3
Killucan Ramblers, 98
Killucan Steeplechases, 223
Killucan Workingmen's Club, 124
Killula Castle, 123
Killynon, County Westmeath, 32
Kilmaine, Lord, 36
Kilroy, James, 92, 105
Kilruane Football Club, 159
Kiltoom, County Westmeath, 242
Kiltoom Cricket Club, 129, 137, 138–9
Kiltoom Cruickilawee Rovers Hurling Club, 199, 201
Kiltoom Football Club, 185
Kinahan, Pat, 157
King, James, 127
King-Harman family, 126
King's county (Offaly), 8, 9, 11, 14, 119, 128
King's Own Yorkshire Light Infantry, 16, 88–9
Kingstown racecourse, 49
Kinnegad, County Westmeath, 94, 144, 151, 158, 193
Kinnegad Catholic Commercial Club, 159–60
Kinnegad Commercial Football Club, 160
Kinnegad Slashers club, 144, 147, 148, 150, 154, 159
Kinrinckle, County Galway, 49
Kirwan, Joseph, 101
Knock football club, 171
Knockdrin Castle, 30, 132
Korr, Charles, 53

L
Lacken Lodge, 210
Lancashire Fusiliers, 131, 138, 176, 184, 223
Land Act 1881, 8, 24
land agitation, 3, 10, 113–15, 190, 215
Land League, 3, 10–11, 24, 113, 114–15
landed gentry, 20–1, 24, 248–9
  cricket, 114, 119, 120–1, 123, 126, 127–8, 136–7
  golf, 88, 90–1

and horse ownership, 65–7
  mobility, 253–4
  spectators, 229–31
  tennis clubs, 82, 112
Lane, Lord, 26
Langstaff, T., 172
Lanigan, John, 48
Lansdowne Lawn Tennis Club, 76, 84
Laune Rangers Football Club, 183
Lawn Tennis and Croquet, 110
Lawrence, Charles, 118
Lawrence, John, 36, 76
Lawrence's cricket handbooks, 113, 114, 116, 117, 128
Leader, The, 190, 191
Ledeston, County Westmeath, 34, 35, 37, 42, 72, 220–1, 230
Ledwith, Dr, 129
Leech brothers, 213
Leinster Council, GAA, 179, 206, 207
Leinster Cricket Club, 115
Leinster Express, 232–3
Leinster Football Association, 171, 184
Leinster Junior Cup, 179, 182, 184, 186
Leinster Nomads, 173
Leinster Senior Cup, 179, 184
Leinster Senior Schools Cup, 175
Leitrim, county, 87
Lenzie Football Club, 170
Leopardstown Club, 54, 68
Leopardstown racecourse, 54, 56, 67, 226
Levigne, Miss, 132
Levinge, Mrs C.E., 71
Levinge, Sir Richard, 11, 22, 30, 36, 227
Levinge, T.C., 83
Levinge, T.F., 255
Levinge family, Knockdrin, 16
Levington Park, 30
Lewis, Captain, 71, 160
Lewis, Mrs Loftus, 79, 160
Liddel, Mr, 31
Limerick Hunt Club, 21–2
limited companies, 53–60
Lincolnshire, 187, 188
Linfield Football Club, 177
Lipsett, Sergeant, 161
Lismacaffry, County Westmeath, 204
Lissanode, County Westmeath, 107
Liverpool, 125, 165
Lloyd, H.W., 80, 83
Lloyd, Major, 92
Locke, Flo, 18, 251
Locke, Mrs Jem, 18, 251
Locke, J.H., 27, 36, 37, 71, 73, 120, 221, 231
Locke, John, 72

Locke, John Edward, 27
Locke, Mr, 138
Locke family, 26–7
Locke's distillery, Kilbeggan, 7, 26, 36, 120
London, 25, 37
Londonderry, county, 64
Long, J.H., 89
Longford, Countess of, 123, 210
Longford, county, 8, 9, 20–1, 54, 162, 225,
    226, 227
  cricket, 118, 138
  cycling, 98
  football, 223–4
  horses, 11
  tennis, 83
Longford, Earl of, 19, 20–1, 23, 229, 242
  cricket, 123, 126, 137, 201
  hunting, 19, 24, 26
  polo, 33, 36
'Longford Slashers,' 32
Longford town, 117, 175
  military garrison, 15, 36, 40
Longworth, John, 20, 45, 46, 47, 48, 50–1
Longworth-Danes, F.T., 42
Longworth Hall, Athlone, 107, 108, 203
Lough Derravaragh, 242
Lough Ennell, 255
Lough Ennell Plate, 56
Lough Owel, 255
Lough Ree, 219, 226, 255
Lough Ree Rowing Club, 229
Loughegar races, 245
Loughrea, County Galway, 162
Louth, county, 14
Lowe, N., 98
Lowe, S., 98
Lowerson, John, 158, 253
Loyal North Lancashire Regiment, 16, 79,
    130, 160
Lucas, Mr, 88
Lucas, V., 82
Lyndon, Mr, 88
Lynn race meetings, 61–2
Lyons, John C., 34, 35

M
McAlery, J.A., 170
Macbeth, R., 80, 83
McBride, Major John, 185
McBride-Mitchell's Club, 204
McCann, William, 138
McCue, John, 98
McCullough, W.C., 89
McDonnell, Valentine, 14
McFarlan, Mr, 95

McGinley, Rev., 137
McGrane, Dr, 127
McGreevey, Martin, 147, 148, 149, 150, 154,
    162, 166
Macken, P., 92
McKeown, Daniel, 241–2
McLoughlin, William, 139
Macnaghten, Captain, 31
Magill, Mrs, 18–19
magistrates, 245
Mahaffey, J.P., 10
Maher, Mary, 29
Maher, Thomas, 27, 29, 138
Maher family, 81
Malcolm, E., 217
Malcomson family, 124
Mallow, County Cork, 229–30
Malone, Colonel J.R., 54
Malone, John, 39–40, 46, 49, 243
Malone, Mrs, 19
management structures, 1, 5, 101–6, 250
  women in, 108
Mandle, W.F., 2, 205
Marble City Cricket Club, 157
Marist Brothers, 174
Market House, Mullingar, 132
Marlay, Charles B., 123, 138
marriage, 19, 168, 249–50
Marylebone Cricket Club, 75
Mason, T., 170
Mason, Tony, 53, 170, 177, 218
Master of the Fox Hounds, role of, 24
Mathew, Fr Theobald, 177
Matthews, Will, 15, 23, 255
Maume, Patrick, 253
Maunsell, Adjutant, 15
Maxwell, A.D., 128
May Brothers, 160
Mayfield Cricket Club, 124
Mayo, county, 64
Meagher, Henry D., 115
Meagher, Henry J., 157
Meath, county, 7, 14, 160, 227, 253
  cricket, 116, 118
  horses, 11, 64
  hunting, 17, 18, 33, 67
  polo, 33, 34
Meath diocese, 217
Mecredy, R.J., 93, 99–100
Metcalf, Alan, 150
Middleton, Iris Maud, 39
Middleton Park, Castletown-Geoghegan, 66
Midland Great Western Railway, 9, 30, 55,
    224–6
  and racecourses, 59, 62

sponsorship, 47
Midland Herald, 195
Midland Reporter, 186, 193, 194–5, 199, 210,
    240–1
Midleton, Dr W., 128
military garrisons, 5, 6–7, 176, 252–3
    cricket, 114, 116, 118, 119–20, 122, 129–
        32
    cycling, 95
    entertainment, 16–17, 78–9
    fraternisation, 194
    GAA ban, 206
    golf, 87–8, 90
    horseracing, 40, 231
    hunting, 14–17
    marriage, 180–1
    polo, 35–6
    and public disorder, 239–40
    soccer, 180–4
    tennis, 84
Milligan, H., 172
Milligan family, 172
Milltown Gaelic League branch, 193
Milltown Pass Fife and Drum Band, 205
Mitchell, F.W., 68, 70, 71, 72, 73, 243
Moate, County Westmeath, 12, 13, 14, 27,
    29, 99, 142, 216, 226–7
    charity events, 107–8
    cricket, 120
    croquet, 85
    cycling, 98
    football, 165, 166, 211
    GAA, 144–5, 153
    golf club, 89
    horseracing, 39, 42, 218, 219, 233, 234–5
        alcohol ban, 244
        grandstand, 230
    polo, 139
    tennis, 81, 82, 83
Moate Cricket Club, 135, 137–8, 157
Moate Gaelic Football Club, 157, 206, 214,
    223, 243
Moate Lawn Tennis Club, 103, 104
Moate Shamrocks, 145
Moate William O'Briens, 144-45, 160
Monaghan, county, 31–2
Monahan, Jim, 165, 166, 178
Monkstown Lawn Tennis Club, 76
Monmouthshire, 127
Montgomery, Miss, 132
Moore, Colonel, 192
Moore, J.M., 13–14
Moore, Major, 117, 118, 126, 127
Moorehead, Dr H., 81
Moorwood, Roland W., 144, 161

Moran, D.P., 190–1
Mornington Cricket Club, 125
Morris, John, 157
Mosstown, 108, 137
motorcars, 227
Mount Murray, Mullingar, 83, 120
Mount Prospect golf course, 92, 105
Mount Street Cricket Club, Mullingar, 132,
    133, 137, 201
Mount Street Football Club, Mullingar,
    201, 202
Mount Temple, County Westmeath, 29
Moydrum, County Westmeath, 184
Moynihan, Maurice, 205
Moyola football club, 171
Moytura, County Galway, 197
Moyvannon Stakes, 46
Moyvoughley, Moate, 29
Muldowney, Percy, 122, 128, 157
Mullen, Michael, 188
Mullingar, County Westmeath, 6–7, 8, 99,
    111, 123, 209, 224, 228
    cricket, 116, 118, 122, 128, 195
    cycling, 58, 94, 95
    football, 142, 145, 156, 202–3
    Freemasons, 25
    GAA, 144
    Gaelic League, 191–2
    golf, 88–9
    horse show, 56
    horseracing (*see* Newbrook racecourse)
    hunting, 13
    hurling, 198
    military garrison, 14, 15–16, 30, 31, 36,
        40, 77, 130–1, 181, 235–6, 240
    polo, 35, 139
    railway, 9, 224, 225
    rugby, 175–6
    soccer, 182, 183, 187, 188
    tennis, 78–9, 80–1
Mullingar Brass and Reed Band, 101, 192,
    198, 202, 226, 236
    tournament, 204–5
Mullingar Catholic Commercial Club, 97,
    124, 128, 160, 162–3
Mullingar Catholic National Young Men's
    Society, 163
Mullingar Commercial Club, 128, 222
Mullingar Commercial Cricket Club, 135,
    156
Mullingar Commercial Football Club, 145,
    147, 160–1, 162, 163, 164
    established, 161
Mullingar Cricket Club, 97, 125, 135, 163
Mullingar Cycling Club, 96–7, 98–9, 100

Mullingar Football Club, 96, 97, 125, 148–51, 156, 160, 168, 183, 210
  attendance, 220
  established, 162–3
  matches, 151, 152, 154–5, 158, 164, 166, 223–4
  playing field, 165
  social events, 158
Mullingar Golf club, 112
Mullingar Lunatic Asylum, 222
Mullingar Mental Asylum XI, 124
Mullingar National Federation, 163
Mullingar National Workingmen's Club, 149
Mullingar Parochial Club, 82
Mullingar Shamrocks Cricket Club, 128, 156–7, 163
Mullingar Shamrocks Football Club, 147, 148–9, 149, 156–7, 162, 202
  attendance, 220
  established, 163–4
  matches, 153, 154
Mullingar Shamrocks Hurling Club, 198, 205, 207, 210, 211, 212, 213
Mullingar St Patrick's Football Club, 183–4
Mullingar Temperance Club, 98
Mullingar Wanderers, 128
Mullingar Workingmen's Club, 124
Mullingar Young Ireland Club, 202, 203, 207, 210
Mullingar Young Men's Parochial Club, 82
Multyfarnham, County Westmeath, 13, 42, 62, 174, 195, 242
Multyfarnham Harriers, 13
Mulvey, James, 96, 148, 149, 157, 162, 163
Munster Football Association, 171
Murphy, Ingram, 30
Murphy, P., 210, 224
Murray, Henry, 19
Murray, James, 147, 148
Murray, Mr, 120
Murray, Mrs, 103
Murray, W., 122
Murray family, 122
Murtagh, Miss, 19
Murtagh, P.V.C., 178
Murtagh, Thomas, 165
musical entertainment, 235–6
Musselburgh Golf Club, 86
Myles O'Reilly Hurling Club, Ringtown, 199, 211

N
Naghten, J.M., 48–9
Naghten, Thomas, 44, 50

Nally, P.W., 180, 182
Nannestad, Ian, 187
National Bank, 8
National Cycling Club, Dublin, 98
National Hunt, 28, 52
National Workingmen's Club, 143, 244–5
nationalism, 4, 5, 147
  brass and reed bands, 236
  club names, 185, 204
  and GAA, 142, 160, 180, 214–15, 251–3
  re-emergence of GAA, 190–215
Navan, County Meath, 142
Nea, Peter, 192, 199, 213
Nenagh, County Tipperary, 110, 130
New York, 84
Newbridge, County Kildare, 48
Newbrook Harriers, 222
Newbrook racecourse, 39, 40, 43, 232, 245
  cycling track, 97
  golf course, 90, 92
  limited company, 53–60
  participation, 64–74
  and railway, 61–4
Newbrook racecourse, Mullingar, 4, 39, 42, 43, 218, 221–2, 227, 231, 233, 235–6
  alcohol, 244, 245
  attendance, 227–8
  gate meet, 59
  limited company, 53–60, 61, 246
  riots, 239–40
  sponsorship, 63–4
Newbrook Wanderers, 162, 184, 202–3
Newburn, J., 128
Newburn, Walter, 100, 101, 177
Newcastle-on-Tyne, 84
newspapers, 1–2, 254
  horseracing, 218, 221
  hunting, 13, 17
  nationalism, 190–1
  soccer, 181
  spectators, 227–33
  violence, 238
Newtown Cricket Club, 137
97th Regiment, 31, 131
98th Regiment, 118
9th Lancers, 33
9th Regiment, 235
Nomads Football Club, 179
Nooney, P.J., 88, 106
North Lancashire Regiment, 16
North of Ireland Lawn Tennis Club, 84
North Westmeath Polo Club, 33–4, 34
Northumberland, 150
Norton, Maurice, 178
Nowlan, Jim, 207

Nugent, Captain, 118, 127
Nugent, Mrs Greville, 18
Nugent, Captain Hon Greville, 231
Nugent, Lieutenant-Colonel John James, 25
Nugent, Sir Percy, 22, 116
Nugent, Sir Walter, 36, 55
Nugent family, 21, 63, 123
Nulty, Dr, Bishop of Meath, 142, 147

O
Ó Cadhla, Stiofán, 217, 238
Ó Riain, Seamus, 152
O'Brien, Conor Cruise, 3
O'Brien, Major, 88
O'Brien, M.P., 127, 232
O'Brien, William, 144–5
O'Casey, Leo, 160
O'Connell, Daniel, 185, 220
O'Connell, J.J., 82
O'Connell, John, 149
O'Connor, T.P., 165
O'Donoghue, Charles, 89, 98, 165, 230
O'Donoghue, The, 79, 82
O'Dwyer, M., 139, 206
O'Flynn, J., 165
O'Flynn, Michael, 165, 178
O'Flynn (soccer), 182
O'Growney, 204
O'Hara, Dolly, 18
Old Berkshire hunt, 14
Old Muskerry, 14
Olympic Games
    1904, 101
    1908, 34, 101
103rd Royal Bombay Fusiliers, 15
100th Regiment, 16
105th Regiment, 239
Ordnance Survey, 216
O'Reilly, Anthony, 116
O'Reilly, Fr Edward, 147, 163, 192
O'Reilly, P.P., 27, 34, 55, 70, 82, 120, 131
O'Reilly family, 27, 63, 120, 122, 123
O'Ryan, Mr, 48, 49
Osbourne, Surgeon-Major, 88
O'Sullivan, Mr, 161
O'Sullivan, Owen, 54, 144
O'Sullivan, T.F., 205
O'Sullivan's Hotel, Athlone, 159
O'Toole, Luke, 207
Oxford Military College, 66

P
Pakenham, Hon Edward, 24, 36
Pakenham family, 13, 21, 24, 210

Pakenham Hall, 12, 122, 123, 210
    Cricket Club, 129, 137, 138
Palmerston hockey club, 176
Parnell, Charles Stewart, 118, 143, 147, 180, 190
Parnell, John, 115
Parratt, Cartriona M., 107
Pass of Kilbride, County Westmeath, 70
patronage, 22
    cricket, 126–7
    football, 164–5
    GAA, 210–11
    horseracing, 46–7
patterns, 217
penny-farthing bicycle, 95
Periott, tennis player, 84
Perry, James, 128
philanthropic societies, 107
Phoenix Cricket Club, 115, 118
Phoenix Park, Dublin, 33, 67, 99, 115
Pickeman, W.C., 90
pickpockets, 239, 240
Piercefield, County Westmeath, 70
Pilkington, A.J., 66, 71, 72, 255
Pilkington, H.L., 127
Plan of Campaign, 24
Pollard-Urquhart, Major, 24
polo, 10, 16, 32–7, 38, 72, 132, 139–40, 219, 249, 252
    costs of, 32–3
    military garrisons, 35–6
    social life, 253
Portarlington, County Offaly, 175, 225
Portlaw, County Waterford, 124
Portmarnock Golf Club, 90
Portora Royal School, Enniskillen, 175
Portumna, County Galway, 226
Power, Mary Anne, 232
Power, Sir John, 10
Presbyterians, 136, 174
Preston, Captain, 88, 110, 245
Preston, Mrs Edith, 85, 110–11
Preston, John, 111
Prince of Wales Hotel, Athlone, 172
Prospect Cricket Club, 157
prostitution, 239
provincial councils, GAA, 207
Punchestown, County Kildare, 49, 50, 232–3
Purdon, B.R., 79

Q
Queen's Meadow, Athlone, 183, 223, 243
Queen's county (Laois), 3, 10
Queen's Park, 170
Quinn, Tom, 118

R
racing. *see* horseracing
Racing Calendar, Irish, 41, 45, 51, 52
Radden, J., 178
Raftery, Thomas, 162
Raharney, County Westmeath, 94, 100, 145
Raharney Rovers, 148, 150, 153, 157, 164, 220, 222
Railway Hotel, Lough Ree, 229
Railway Plate, 44, 47
Railway Stars Football Club, 202
railways, 2, 8–9, 13, 72
    and horseracing, 48, 61–4
    and spectators, 224–6
    sponsorship, 63–4
Rainey, John, 239
Ranelagh School, Athlone, 80, 118, 189
    athletics, 176–7
    cricket, 124
    rugby, 173–5
    soccer, 172, 178, 182, 183, 185
    sports day, 220, 228
Rathconrath, Mullingar, 66, 195
Rathganny House, Multyfarnham, 13
Rathowen, County Westmeath, 69, 99, 145
    horseracing, 221, 223, 236
Rathowen Leaguers, 160
Rathwire, County Westmeath, 132–3, 193
Rebel Football Club, 184
Reddington, chief constable, 149
Reddy, Mina, 71
Reddy, T.M., 27, 67, 71, 164–5, 211
regattas, 218, 219, 223, 226, 228, 230, 235, 252
    alcohol consumption, 237
    balls, 229
    Mullingar, 58
    violence, 238
Reid, G.V., 66, 72
Reid, William, 137
Reynell, Sam, 10
Reynell family, 19, 32
Reynolds, James, 184, 203
RIC Challenge Cup, 99
Rifle Brigade, 160
Ringtown Cricket Club, 129, 132, 133, 134
Ringtown Hurling Club, 199, 201, 206
Ringtown Myles O'Reilly's, 199, 211
Rising, 1798, centenary, 190
Ritchie, David, 86
river transport, 226
Riverstown Emmet Football Club, 213
Robins, Joe, 207
Robinstown Levinge, 149
Robson, Mrs, 108

Rochfort, Alice, 27
Rochfort, George, 66
Rochfort demesne, 123, 138
Rochfort family, 63
Rochfortbridge Erin's Hopes, 145, 154
Rochfortbridge Warriors, 202, 205
Rockingham Harriers, 14
Roebuck Cricket Club, Dublin, 116
Rory O'More football club, 183
Roscommon, County, 8, 9, 54, 171, 203, 226, 227
    cricket, 118
    football, 166
    horses, 11, 47
    hunting, 14, 67
    racecourse, 49
    railway, 225
Roscommon Harriers, 14
Roscommon Staghounds, 14
Roscrea, County Tipperary, 48, 84, 110
Rosmead, County Westmeath, 12
Ross, Lord, 98
Rotherham, A.M., 34
Rouse, Paul, 4, 205
Royal Artillery, 172, 181, 182–3, 185–6
Royal Belfast Golf Club, 86
Royal Berkshire Regiment, 172
Royal Canal, 213
Royal City Hospital Bazaar, Dublin, 107
Royal Dublin Fusiliers, 16, 135
Royal Hibernian Academy, 199
Royal Highland Artillery, 231
Royal Hotel, Belfast, 87
Royal Irish Constabulary (RIC), 36, 40, 79, 161, 235
    bands, 236
    cycling, 94, 95, 99, 100, 101, 111
    and GAA, 143, 149, 206
    golf, 88
    and public order, 238, 239–40, 246
    tennis clubs, 81, 82
Royal Irish Rifles, 15, 83, 122, 132, 222, 240
Royal School, Banagher, 119
Royal School, Cavan, 175
rugby, 1, 5, 159, 170, 173–6, 189, 206, 251
Rugby school, 174
Russell, F.W., 42, 81, 120, 137, 138
Russell, Mrs, 107, 108
Russell family, 81

S
Sackville Street Club, 25
St Andrew's Golf Club, 104
St Ciaran's Club, Athlone, 204, 211
St Fintan Club, Lismacaffry, 204

St George, Rev. H., 120
St Helen's Football Club, 179
Saint Laurence O'Toole branch, Gaelic League, 199
St Lawrence, Lord, 229
St Mary's Church, Athlone, 181
St Mary's College, Mullingar, 124
St Mary's Intermediate School, Athlone, 174
St Mary's Temperance Club, 198
St Michael's Cycling Club, 98
St Patrick's Association Football Club, 203
St Patrick's Church, Moate, 27
St Patrick's Club, Derrymore, 204
St Peter's Church, Athlone, 181
St Stanislaus College, Rahan, 119, 171
St Vincent de Paul Society, 101
Salmon, Eugene, 54
Sandymount school, 119
Sargent, Harry, 64, 73
Sarsfield Hurling Club, Castlepollard, 199, 211, 213
Savage, Florence, 27
Savage, Mr, 63
Scally, John, 127
schools
   athletics, 176–7
   cricket, 118, 123–4
   GAA, 204
   rugby, 173–5, 189
Scotland, 100, 106, 109, 112, 249
   golf, 88
   soccer, 150, 170, 187, 188
Scott, Derek, 114
Scott, G.W., 55
Scott, R., 139
Seagrave, T.A., 122
2nd Loyal North Lancashire Regiment, 79, 84
2nd Queens Regiment, 126
Seven Houses cricket club, 157
71st Highland Light Infantry, 235
Seymour, Rev. Dr, 83
'Shanbeens,' 238
Shannon, river, 219, 226, 255
Shannon Development Company, 226, 231
Shannonbridge, 226
Shaw, Eddie, 27–8, 67, 72
Shaw, Lieutenant, 88
Shaw, W.T., 89
Shaw family, 27, 128, 198
Shaw's, Messrs, 162
Shaw's XI, 124
Sheffield family, 108
Shinglass Stakes, 46

Shinrone, County Tipperary, 84
shinty, 197
shooting, 117, 251
Showgrounds, Mullingar, 186
Siggins, Gerard, 114
Simonstown Gaels Hurling Club, 199, 201, 211
Singer Machine Company, 163
Sion Mills Cricket Club, 124
Sisters of Mercy, Kilbeggan, 27
6th Battalion Rifle Brigade, 235–6
Skerries, County Dublin, 49
Sligo, county, 9, 16, 49
Smith, Denis, 129
Smith, Captain Ralph, 54
Smith, Sam, 104
Smith, Miss S.J., 108
Smith, Thomas J., 25
Smith family, 124, 177
Smyth, Colonel, 88
Smyth, Denis, 201
Smyth, Robert, 83
Smyth, Sam, 90
Smyth, Captain W.M., 19
Smyth family, Gaybrook, 16, 21
soccer, 5, 79, 166, 169, 170–3, 194, 203, 218, 220, 249
   admission charges, 223
   clubs, 150–1
   and football, 183, 188, 203, 253
   and GAA, 196, 206–7
   military garrisons, 180–4, 252
   players, 177–8, 186–8
social class. see also farmers; landed gentry
   cricket, 5, 10, 32–3, 117–25, 138–9, 249
   football, 167–8, 213–14
   hunting, 14–15, 19–22
   hurling, 211–13
   polo, 36
   soccer, 177–8, 186–8
   tennis, 79–82, 112
social work, 107
Sonna, County Westmeath, 68
South African war, 130
South Lancashire Regiment, 182
South Westmeath Hounds, 18–19
South Westmeath Hunt Club, 10, 39, 40
South Westmeath Polo Club, 34
Sparkes, Colour-Sergeant, 160
spectator sport, 78–9, 218–47, 227, 254
   admission charges, 223
   ancillary activities, 233–7
   class structure, 227–33
   crowd control, 242–7
   social exclusion, 229–31

transport, 224–7
violent behaviour, 237–42
women and children, 221–2
Sphairsitke, 75
sport
   and class structure, 248–50
   economic impact, 254–5
   employment in, 255
   lack of study on, 3–4
   and national identity, 193–6
   role of clubs, 250
   Victorian developments, 1–2
Sport, 56, 60, 73, 154, 155, 156, 235
Sportsman, 73
Springfield playing field, Mullingar, 165
Stanley Stakes, Liverpool, 66
Starley, John, 95
steamers, 226
steeplechasing, 39, 40, 43–4, 52
   categories of races, 44–5
   code of rules, 51–3
   regulation, 41–2
Stenson, H., 184, 203
Stokes, Misses, 108
Stonehall Cricket Club, 134, 139
Stoneyford, County Westmeath, 99, 195
Stoneyhurst College, 119
Streamstown, County Westmeath, 66, 216
Street, County Westmeath, 23, 93
Sugden, John, 113
Sullivan, P.D., 242
Summerhill house, County Meath, 17, 118
Sunday games, 157
sweepstakes, 44, 46

T
Taaffee, Christopher, 68, 69
table tennis, 107, 110, 251
Tailteann games, 197
Taylor, Mr, 231
Telford, G.V., 98
temperance movement, 107, 145, 177, 198
Temple Mungret, County Limerick, 232
Templemore, County Tipperary, 48, 130
tennis, 5, 10, 16, 33, 75–86, 101, 132, 140,
   249, 251–2
   bands, 235
   Church of Ireland, 250
   denominational, 82–3
   management structures, 101–6
   players, 79–83, 112
   regulation, 75–6
   social life, 253
   tournaments, 83–4
   women in, 109–10

10th Hussars, 33
thimble-riggers, 233–4
13th Hussars, 37
Thomastown Park demesne, 44, 46, 47, 48–
   9, 229
Thomastown Rangers club, 144, 148, 150,
   164, 220
Thorpe, Lieutenant, 110
Thurles, County Tipperary, 60
Tighe, Miss, 108
Tipperary, County, 114, 159
   cricket, 130, 139, 206
Tipperary town, 130
Tolson, John, 39, 61, 63
Tottenham, C.L., 89
Tottenham family, 16, 122, 123
Town Plate, 57, 60
trade unions, 190
trainers, 64
Tralee, County Kerry, 93
Tranter, Neil, 61, 106, 107, 112, 150, 164,
   187, 218, 249
Treacy, P.B., 172, 178
Trim, County Meath, 72
Trimble, William, 95
Trinity College Cricket Club, 115
Trinity College Dublin, 172, 174, 175, 176,
   189
Trinity Hall, Cambridge, 84
Triscott, A.E., 88
Trotter, Dr D., 118
Tuam, County Galway, 227
Tubberclair, County Westmeath, 184, 185
Tubberclair Football Club, 210
Tudenham Park, 89, 123
Tuite family, 22
Tullamore, County Offaly, 9, 225, 226,
   227
   cricket, 138
   golf, 111
   horseracing, 49, 72
   soccer, 171
Tullamore Golf Club, 92
Tullamore Harriers, 72
Tullamore Lawn Tennis Club, 84
Tullamore Ramblers Cycling Club, 98
Tullaroan, County Westmeath, 115, 157
Turbotstown, Coole, 26, 116, 127
Turin Cricket Club, 132, 133
Turrock, County Westmeath, 49
23rd Fusiliers, 231
23rd Welsh Fusiliers, 239
Tyrone, county, 64, 124
Tyrrellspass, County Westmeath, 66, 118,
   127, 137

U
UHC, Cork, 14
Ulster Bank, Mullingar, 88, 128
Ulster Cricket Club, 53, 170
Ulster Spinning Company, 177
unionism, 25–6, 196
United Banks XI, 124
United Irish League (UIL), 163, 190, 191
United Irishman, 190–1
University College Football Team, 186
Upton, H.A.S., 88, 89
Urquhart, William Pollard, 22
Ussher, Christopher, 49, 243

V
Vamplew, Wray, 50, 53, 61, 73, 230–1, 242–3
Vandaleur, Mrs, 127
Vaughan, H., 98
Vaughan, J., 92
Vaughan, J.S., 98
Vaux of Harrowden, Lord, 12, 22
Victoria Barracks, Athlone, 6, 181
Victors Football Club, Mullingar, 183
Vignoles estate, 116
violence
    GAA, 148–9
    murder, 241–2
    race meetings, 50–1
    spectators, 237–42
voluntary associations, 124

W
Wakefield, E., 42
Wakefield family, 81
Wallis's drapery store, 58
Walsh, David, 88
Walsh, J.J., 203, 212–13
Walvin, James, 53
War Office, 183
Ward Union Staghounds, 14, 17, 67
Wardenstown Cricket Club, 127, 132, 133, 137, 138
Wardenstown Cycle Club, 93–4, 98, 100
Waterford, county, 6, 64
Waterford, Lord, 10
Watson, John, 33
Watson-Murray, Mrs, 132
Wesleyans, 136, 174
West, Trevor, 114, 115
West Britonism, 193–5, 203, 204, 252
West Hampstead football club, 53
Westmeath, county. *see also* individual sports
    description of, 6–9
    horseracing, 39–74

range of sports, 4
Westmeath Bicycle Club, 94
Westmeath County Cricket Club, 116, 117, 122, 123, 127, 128, 129, 131, 135, 138, 222
    matches, 132
    membership, 117–18
    schools cricket, 119
    women in, 108–9
Westmeath County Golf Club, 88, 89–92
    finances, 104, 105–6
    professional, 104
Westmeath County Hunt Club, 223, 248
Westmeath County Lawn Tennis Club, 102–3
Westmeath County Polo Club, 33, 34, 35, 36
    horseraces, 220–1
Westmeath Examiner, 42
    admission charges, 224
    cricket, 128
    cultural nationalism, 163, 192, 194
    cycling, 95, 96, 97, 99
    GAA, 143, 147, 201–2
    horseracing, 66, 218–19, 228, 246–7
    Mullingar races, 54, 58, 60
    Parnellite, 147
    soccer, 183
Westmeath Golf Club, 103–4, 210
Westmeath Guardian, 9, 19, 50, 225
    alcohol consumption, 236–7
    cycling, 94, 96
    football, 164
    golf, 89
    horseracing, 72
    lawn tennis, 77–8
    soccer, 181
    tennis, 80
Westmeath Hunt Club, 11, 14, 49, 66, 117, 139, 250, 255
    balls, 29–31
    finances, 23–4, 102
    and horseracing, 65, 228, 231–2, 238–9
    membership profile, 16, 19–22, 25–9, 72
    race meets, 39, 40
    steeplechases, 62
    subscriptions, 22–3
    women in, 18
Westmeath Hunt Cup, 60
Westmeath Independent, 20, 50, 197, 240
    alcohol consumption, 237
    cricket, 126, 134
    croquet, 85–6
    cultural nationalism, 193–4, 195–6
    football, 166, 211

GAA, 144, 186, 219
golf, 88
horseracing, 222, 225, 227, 229
illegal gaming, 235
soccer, 171
tennis, 81
Westmeath Lawn Tennis Club, 80–1, 81–3, 108
croquet, 85
tournaments, 83–4
Westmeath (Mullingar) Racing Company Limited, 8, 53–60, 88, 100–1, 225–6
Westmeath Nationalist, 84, 148
cycling, 95, 97
GAA, 151, 153, 156, 220
Westmeath Polo Club, 66, 72
horseracing, 41–2, 230, 240–1
Westmeath RIC Cycling and Athletic Club, 100–1, 236
Westmeath Rifles, 117
Westport, County Mayo, 9
Wexford, county, 197
Wheatley, Michael, 97
Whelehan's Temperance Bar, Ballinasloe, 158
White, Dr Hill Wilson, 83
Whitestone, J.R., 129
Whitney family, 86
Whitworth, Harry, 31, 36, 231–2
Whyte, Laurence, 197
Wicklow, county, 6, 118, 207
William O'Brien club, Athlone, 144–5, 160
Williams, Charles, 157
Wilson, H.P., 122

Wilson, Laurence, 7
Wilson, S., 171
Wilson, William Edward, 23, 86, 122
Wilson family, 122
Wilson's Hospital school, 118
Wiltshire Regiment, 182
Wimbledon, 75, 76, 110
Winchester, J., 236
Winder, C.H., 81
Wingfield, Major Walter, 75
Wisthoff, Fr, 119
Wolfe Tone, Theobald, 185
women
cricket, 132
horserace ownership, 70–1
hunting, 14, 17–19
participation, 5, 75, 106–11, 112, 250–1
as spectators, 221–2
tennis, 77–8, 81
Wooddown, County Westmeath, 145
Wooddown Rackers, 149, 154, 202, 220
Woodlands, Mullingar, 66
Woods, Corporal, 131
Worcestershire hunt, 14

Y
York Hotel, Mullingar, 229
York Regiment, 231
Yorkshire Light Infantry, 16
Young Ireland, 185
Young Men's Christian Association (YMCA), 80
Young Women's Christian Movement, 80
Yourell, James, 68–72, 74